FLORIDA

Travel Planner & Guide

FLORIDA

Travel Planner & Guide

Paul Strathern

Duncan Petersen

This first edition published 1996 by
Duncan Petersen Publishing Ltd
31 Ceylon Road,
London W14 OYP

Sales representation in the U.K. and Ireland by
World Leisure Marketing
9 Downing Road
West Meadows Industrial Estate
Derby DE21 6HA

Distributed by
Grantham Book Services
Tel: 01476 67421

Conceived, edited, designed and produced by
Duncan Petersen Publishing Ltd from a concept by Emma Stanford

Typeset by Duncan Petersen Publishing Ltd
Film output by Reprocolour International, Milan
Originated by Reprocolour International, Milan
Printed by GraphyCems, Navarra

A CIP catalogue record for this book is available from the British Library

ISBN 1 872576 56 7

Editorial director Andrew Duncan
Assistant editor Nicola Davies, Sarah Barlow
Art director Mel Petersen
Maps by Chris Foley and Beverley Stewart and Julian Baker
Illustrations by Beverley Stewart

Paul Strathern was born in 1940 and took a degree in philosophy at Trinity College, Dublin. He has written five novels and worked for more than 20 years as a travel writer, visiting four continents in the course of his work. He first visited Florida nearly 20 years ago, and has returned many times since in the course of his work and on vacation.

He has survived drinking mean cocktails with Captain Tony in Key West, and been instructed in the secrets of alligator wrestling by a native American named Fred. His most frightening experience in Florida was finding himself playing pool with a mafia don in Palm Beach. After being instructed by the attendant large men in suits to lose at all costs, he eventually succeeded, and thus only lost $100.

Photographic credits
All photographs by Jeroen Snijders

except photos reproduced courtesy of:
Alachu County Visitors and Convention Bureau: 221, 223; Alachua County Visitors and Convention Bureau/ University of Florida Athletic Association Inc: 216, 217, 219; The Amelia Island Tourist Development Council: 118, 119, 129; The Bok Tower Gardens: 171, 172; Lans Christensen: 209; Daytona Beach Convention and Visitors Bureau: 107; Florida Department of Commerce, Division of Tourism: 32, 48, 54, 62, 69, 73, 107, 111, 127, 187, 227; Florida Keys and Key West Department of Tourism: 74, 75, 82, 93; Florida Southern College: 169, 170; Florida's Space Coast Office of Tourism: 13, 13, 46, 48; Lee County Visitors & Convention Bureau: 206; Metro-Dade County and the Greater Miami Convention and Visitors Bureau: 67, 70, 163; Monroe County TDC: 78, 79, 83, 86, 87, 88, 89, 94, 97, 98; Sarasota Convention and Visitors Bureau: 242, 243, 245, 246, 247; St Petersburg / Clearwater Area Convention & Visitors Bureau: 234; Tampa Convention & Visitors Association / The Eliot Group: 234, 236, 237, 238; Universal Studios, Florida: 30,31 36, 37.

Master contents list

This contents list is for when you need to use the guide in the conventional way: to find out about where you are going, or where you happen to be. The index, pages 252-256, may be just as helpful.

Conventions used in this guide	12
Something for everyone	13
Florida: an introduction	14
Before you go	16
Getting there / Getting around	20
Essential practical information	22
A brief history of Florida	25
Central Florida	**30, 46, 166, 174, 190**
Southern Florida *and the Keys*	**62, 74, 86, 198, 206**
Northern Florida	**106, 118, 130, 216, 224**
Western Florida	**230, 242**
Miami	**142**
Index	252

HOWEVER
There is much more to this guide than the region by region approach suggested by the contents list on this page. Turn to page 8 and also pages 10-11.

BAREFOOT BOB'S
A.C. INSIDE
HAPPY HOUR
4-7
1.00 BUD
BUD LT
2.00 WELL
3.00 CALL

Contents

Florida Overall
- *master map*

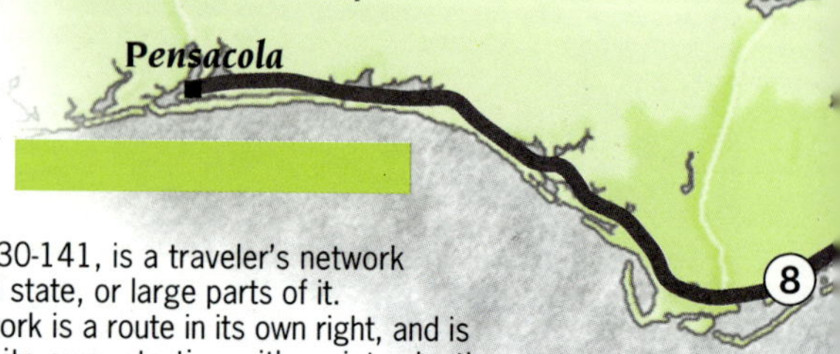

Florida Overall, pages 30-141, is a traveler's network for taking in the whole state, or large parts of it.

Each "leg" of the network is a route in its own right, and is covered in a section of its own, starting with an introduction and a simplified map. The sections are numbered – see below – and the numbers are used in cross-references throughout the guide.

The routes are not merely lines on a map. Each features a whole region, and describes many places both on and off the marked trail. Think of the overall routes not only as itineraries, but as interesting ways of describing and connecting the main centers of Florida, and of making travel sense of the state as a whole.

The overall route network is designed to be used in these different ways:

1 *Ignore the marked route entirely:* simply use the alphabetically arranged Sights and Places of Interest, and the map at the start of each section, as a guide to what to see and do in the region, not forgetting the hotel and restaurant recommendations.

2 Treat the route as an itinerary, following it by car or by public transportation. You can do sections of a route, or all of it; and you can follow it in any direction. Link the routes to travel the length and breadth of Florida. The introduction to each route summarizes what you can expect, and gives an idea of how long it will take.

1 *Between Orlando and Tampa*

The Heart of Florida 30

2 *Between West Palm Beach and Cape Canaveral*

The Space and Treasure Coasts 46

3 *Between Miami and Flamingo*

Miami South to the Everglades 62

4 *Between Florida Mainland/Miami and Marathon*

The Upper Keys 74

5 *Between No Name Key and Fort Jefferson*

The Lower Keys 86

6 *Between Cape Canaveral and Jacksonville*

The North-Eastern Coast 106

7 *Between Jacksonville and Tallahassee*

Jacksonville and the North 118

8 *Between Tallahassee and Pensacola*

The Panhandle Coast 130

The Florida Overall section is ideal for:

■ Planning and undertaking tours of the whole state, or parts of it.

■ Making the journey to or from your eventual destination as interesting and as rewarding as possible.

■ Linking the in-depth explorations of local sights provided by the Local Explorations section, pages 166-251.

Miami has a section of its own, pages 142-165

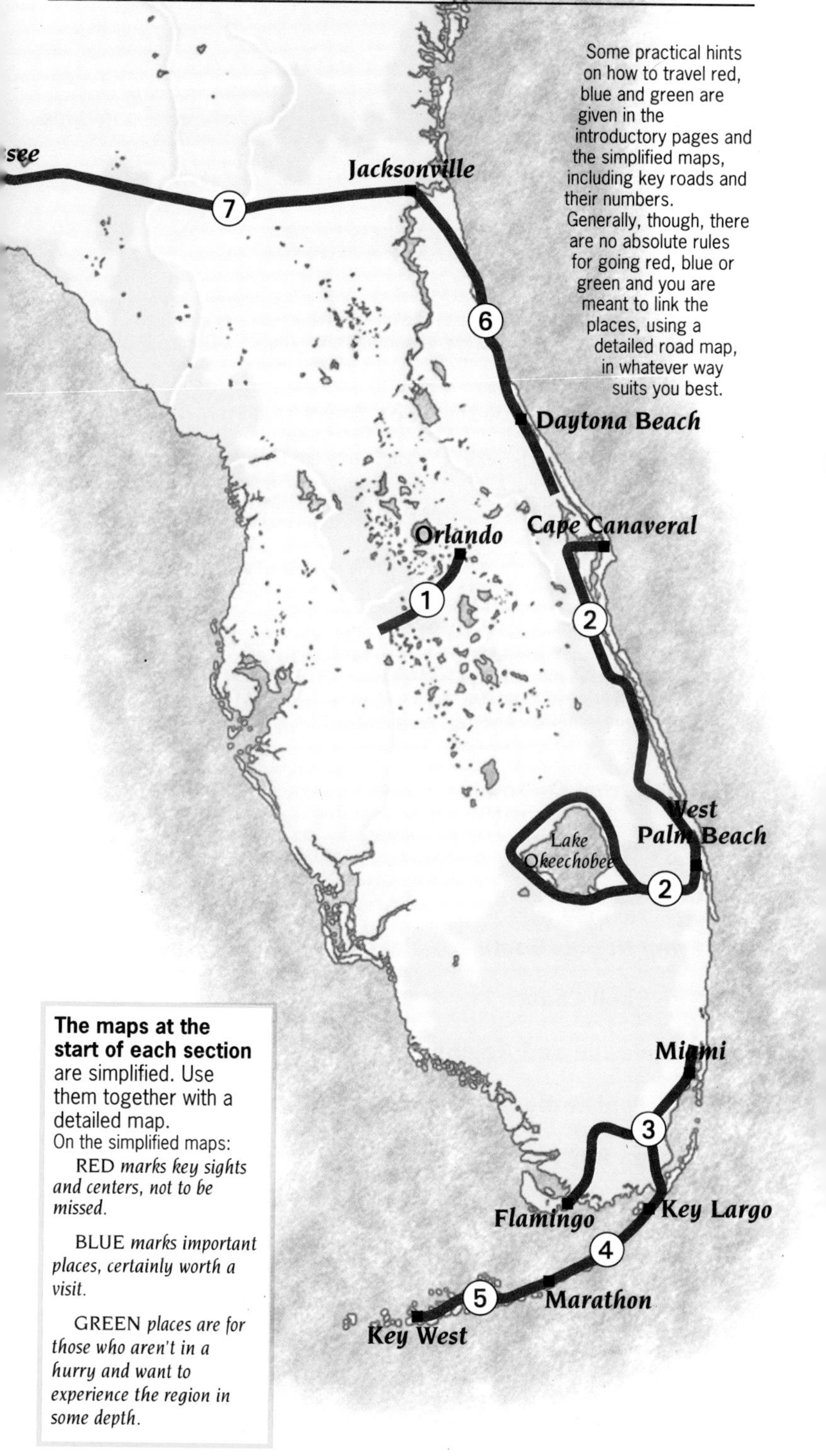

Some practical hints on how to travel red, blue and green are given in the introductory pages and the simplified maps, including key roads and their numbers. Generally, though, there are no absolute rules for going red, blue or green and you are meant to link the places, using a detailed road map, in whatever way suits you best.

The maps at the start of each section are simplified. Use them together with a detailed map.

On the simplified maps:

RED *marks key sights and centers, not to be missed.*

BLUE *marks important places, certainly worth a visit.*

GREEN *places are for those who aren't in a hurry and want to experience the region in some depth.*

Contents

The Local Explorations
- *master map*

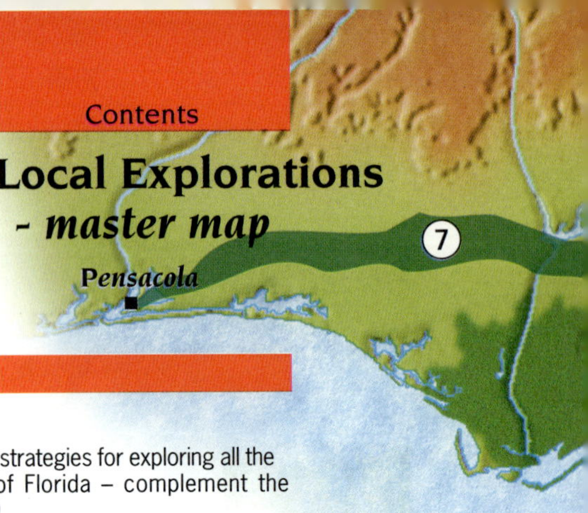

The Local Explorations – strategies for exploring all the interesting localities of Florida – complement the regional routes, pages 8-9.

They are designed to be used in these different ways:

1 *Ignore the marked route entirely*: simply use the alphabetically arranged Sights & Places of Interest, and the map at the start of each Local Exploration, as a guide to what to see and do in the area, not forgetting the hotel and restaurant recommendations.

2 Use the marked route to make a tour by public transportation (see the transport box), ferry, or by car. You can do sections of the route, or all of it. (In the introduction it tells you how long you might take to cover everything the quickest way, by car.)

If you are driving, you can generally follow the tour in any direction; usually, the route as marked is an attractive and convenient way to link the places of interest; you may well find other ways to drive it. Always use our map in conjunction with a detailed road map (suggestions are given on each introductory page).

1	**South from Orlando**	**166**
2	**The Gold Coast**	**174**
3	**Ocala and Region**	**190**
4	**From Naples South**	**198**
5	**The Shell Coast**	**206**
6	**Gainesville and Region**	**216**
7	**The Panhandle Inland**	**224**
8	**Tampa Bay Region**	**230**
9	**South of Tampa**	**242**

The Local Explorations are ideal for:

■ **Planning single-center vacations:** each Local Exploration covers an area that would make a great vacation spot. The introduction to each exploration sums up its appeal.

■ **Working out what to see and do**: Most of the sights and places of interest listed make interesting day trips, or part-day trips.

■ **Planning multi-center vacations:** the map on this page shows at a glance all the interesting local sights of Florida. Combine them to experience different aspects of the state, or mix them with the overall routes, pages 30-141.

Miami has a section of its own, pages 142-165

The Local Explorations, pages 166-251, generally follow each other in a north-south/west-east sequence.

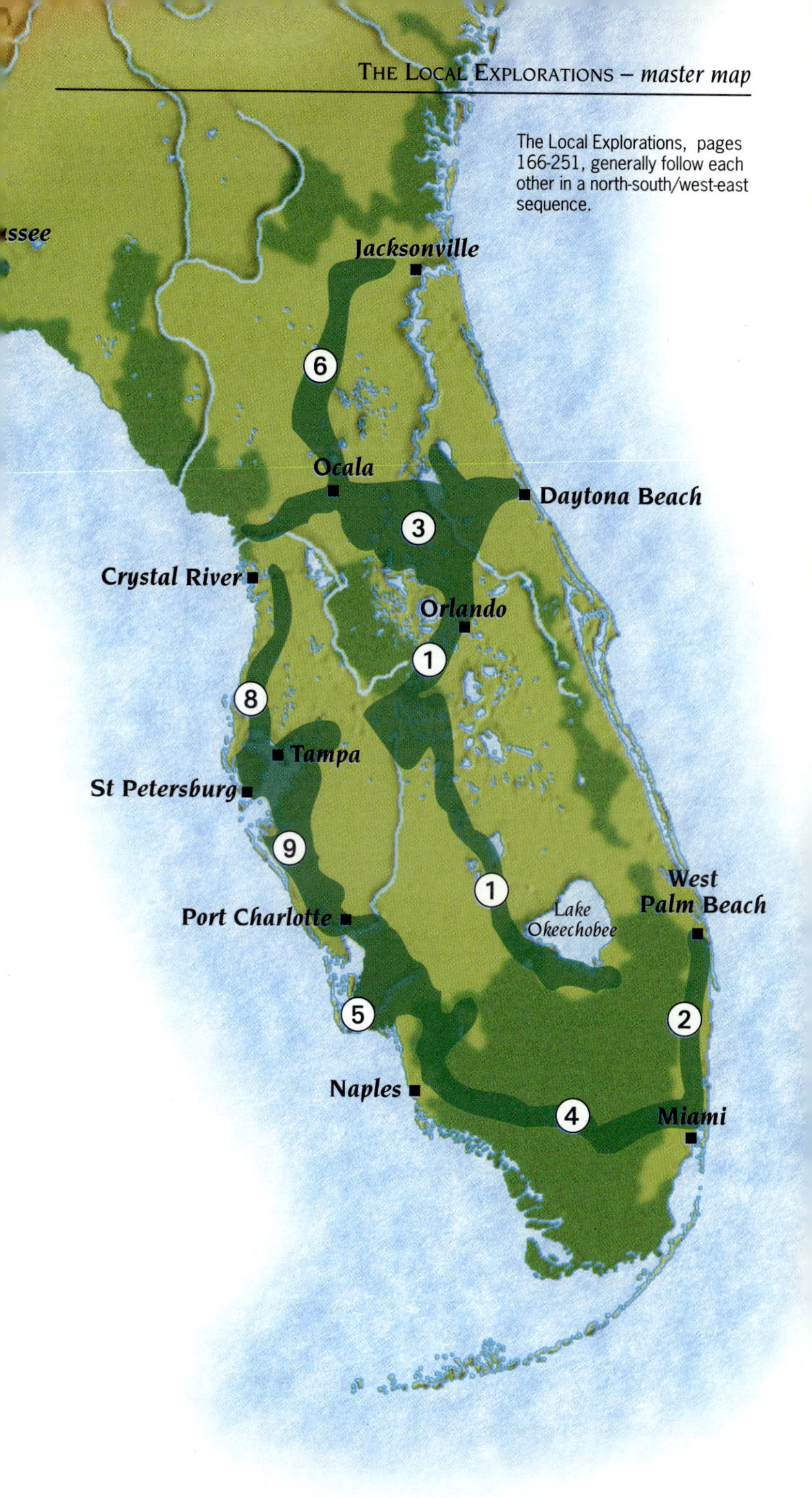

Conventions used in this guide

One dollar sign – **$** – or several dollar signs, such as **$$$**, in a hotel or restaurant entry, denotes a price range. Its object is to give an indication of what you can expect to pay.

Bear in mind that accommodations or food offered at any one place may span more than one price range.

Hotels
For an average-quality double room for one night in mid-season:

$	less than $50
$$	$40-$80
$$$	more than $80

Single occupancy will often cost the same as double, or only marginally less. For an extra bed in the same room, there is usually a standard additional charge of anything up to a third of the room price. (This doesn't just apply to children's beds – though not all hotels allow extra adult beds in the same room.)

Off-season weekday prices may dip lower, and it's also possible to negotiate lower room prices at this time of year. During the high season, prices are likely to rise 20 to 50 percent, or more.

Restaurants
For a two-course meal for one with a drink:

$	less than $20
$$	$15-$50
$$$	more than $50

Hotels and restaurants in this guide are a selection of personal recommendations – not exhaustive lists. They have been chosen to represent interest and quality, or to satisfy specific needs, at every price level.

Credit cards
These are widely accepted in restaurants and hotels throughout Florida, and all our hotel and restaurant entries indicate which cards are taken. Where "all major cards" is indicated, this means a minimum of American Express, Diners Club, MasterCard and Visa.

Opening times of restaurants
Most inexpensive restaurants mentioned in this guide are open all day. Expect minimum hours of 9 am to 9pm. More expensive restaurants tend to open for lunch and dinner. Expect minimum hours of 11.30 am to 2.30 pm, and 6 pm to 10 pm. Unless otherwise stated, restaurants are open seven days a week. Out of season, restaurants sometimes close early, or close on certain days of the week, or sometimes close altogether. This will often depend upon how business is going: in other words, it's unpredictable.

Map legend
↗ after a place on a map means that the sight or place of interest is covered in detail in another part of the book. To find out exactly where, look up the place in the **Sights & Places of Interest** gazetteer which follows the map: a cross-reference is given in every case.

On Florida Overall maps, a **red, blue or green square** by a place name means that sight or place of interest has an entry in the Sights & Places of Interest section. Red means it's a major attraction; blue means it's certainly worth a visit; green means see it if you aren't in a hurry.

On Florida Overall maps a black square by a place name (and no arrow following) means that the place is not described in the text and is on the map for orientation only.

On Local Explorations maps, place names in boxes are on the map for orientation only. All other places named are described in the text.

🛏 after a heading in **Sights & Places of Interest** means that there is an accommodations suggestion for that place in **Recommended Hotels**.

Ⓢ after a heading in **Sights & Places of Interest** means that there is a suggestion for that place in **Recommended Restaurants.**

Opening times – museums and tourist attractions
See Essential practical information, page 23.

Mileages for routes and tours are approximate. In the Florida Overall section they represent the shortest distance you could expect to travel, just taking in major sights and places of interest (marked with red squares on the maps).

In the case of Local Explorations, they also represent the shortest distance you could expect to cover, excluding detours.

Because the routes and tours are designed to be traveled in whole, in part, or indeed not at all, the mileages given are as much for passing interest as for practical value.

On maps and in text, *all* roads are referred to as Routes (abbreviation Rt), whether they are 'Interstate', Highways or Routes. This simplification is used commonly in Florida.

Something for everyone

Getting the most from your guide
Here is a small selection of ideas for enjoying Florida. The list is just a start: the guide offers many, many more ideas for what really matters – suiting yourself.

Family fun
Florida Overall: 1, The Heart of Florida, especially Orlando.

Paradise islands
Florida Overall: 5, The Lower Keys.

Cape Canaveral and U.S. space exploration
Florida Overall: 2, The Space Coast.

Stylish resorts
Local Explorations: 2, The Gold Coast.

Old and new Florida
Florida Overall: 6, St Augustine and Daytona Beach.

A taste of the Deep South
Local Explorations: 7, The Panhandle Inland.

Sport fishing, coral reefs and submarine life
Florida Overall: 4, The Upper Keys.

America's most laid-back, one-off resort
Florida Overall: 5, Key West in The Lower Keys; the author's favorite spot in Florida.

The Old South
Florida Overall: 8, The Panhandle Coast (Tallahassee and Pensacola).

FLORIDA:
an introduction

One upon a time, Florida was an unspoiled paradise. Above the miles of pristine beaches, palm-fringed islands, lush tropical flowers and virgin wilderness, the hot, humid air was filled with the whine of mosquitoes. Now there are fewer mosquitoes, there's air conditioning and iced drinks – and they say it's been spoiled.

There's no denying that parts of Florida have been developed to the point of lunacy. Yet it also contains the Everglades, a swamp wilderness as big as Corsica that, unlike most such few remaining spots on the globe, is easily accessible. Here you can follow canoe trails for hundreds of miles past literally thousands of islands.

Up in the Panhandle you're in the Deep South, and down on the Keys you're in Caribbean island territory. The skyscrapers and high-rise blocks of downtown Miami look like a sci-fi dream, and in the Kennedy Space Center you're at the gateway to the Solar System. Daytona Beach is wild, Palm Beach super-sophisticated, and St Augustine is the oldest continuously inhabited city in the United States. And plumb in the heart of Florida there's something that combines all these elements – Walt Disney World.

Florida is a new state. Much of it was built yesterday, and less than one tenth of its population was born here. Its inhabitants, old and new, are a varied bunch. The laid-back concho selling beads in Key West, the Southern gentleman in his antebellum mansion in Pensacola, the racehorse stud farmer outside Ocala, the Bahamian fisherman, the space technocrat, the computer executive, the person in the Mickey Mouse outfit at Walt Disney World, the hot-rod kid on Daytona Beach, the Cuban waiter in Miami, the bored socialite in her Palm Beach chateau, the black factory worker in Jacksonville, the native American striving to maintain his traditional way of life on the reservation, the Haitian counter hand in Fort Lauderdale – they're all citizens of the state of Florida, the most popular vacation destination in the world.

I first reluctantly visited Florida almost 20 years ago. I'd been sent there for the weekend, on a rush assignment. It was just as I'd imagined it would be – and yet completely different. This was the bait, and I was hooked. I didn't have time to see much, and nobody has time to see everything. There's always a good reason for going back to Florida.

FOR OVERSEAS VISITORS

Climate: when and where to go
Florida is famous for sunshine and blue skies, and rightly so. Those travel posters of sunny palm-fringed beaches are no lie.

All year round it feels warm in Florida, but in fact the state is divided into two climatic zones. South of Orlando the climate is subtropical, with a distinct Caribbean feel to it. North of Orlando has a warm, temperate climate, much the same as the rest of the southeastern United States.

So, in winter, from November to April, it's pleasantly warm south of Orlando. This is the peak season for southern Florida: Miami, Palm Beach, Naples and Key West all become Meccas for those fleeing the cold northern winters. And the prices go up accordingly. Out of season, the prices drop, the temperatures rise, and the crowds melt away.

In fact, it is not unbearably hot during the southern Florida summer, though it can become very muggy, with the high humidity. This is alleviated by frequent afternoon thunderstorms and coastal breezes. Inland, it is so hot that you just dissolve unless you are inside an air-conditioned building.

North of Orlando it's pleasantly warm in the summer, and this is when the crowds arrive at St Augustine, Panama City and Daytona Beach. In winter, things cool down and quiet down, and the prices drop accordingly. Even so, it's seldom actually cold. Frosts are rare, and when snow fell in the Panhandle a few years ago, it made nationwide news.

Tropical storms and hurricanes tend to arrive between July and November. Hurricane Andrew, the last whopper that tore through southern Miami, arrived in August 1992. But don't worry, if a hurricane is on the way, you'll be given ample warning and evacuated to a safe place – where you can plan exactly how you're going to tell the tale of your heroic survival to the folks back home.

What to wear
The most important thing to wear in Florida is suntan oil – though even on the most deserted beaches, you'll be well advised to wear something else too. Remember, most of Florida is subtropical. It's on the same latitude as Saudi Arabia – Miami is closer to the equator than Cairo. Make sure that you pack a powerful sunscreen lotion, and

Average Florida Temperatures

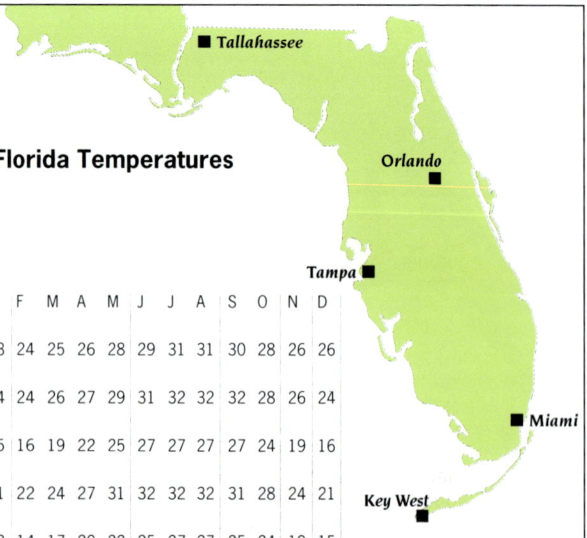

	J	F	M	A	M	J	J	A	S	O	N	D
MIAMI	23	24	25	26	28	29	31	31	30	28	26	26
KEY WEST	24	24	26	27	29	31	32	32	32	28	26	24
TAMPA	15	16	19	22	25	27	27	27	27	24	19	16
ORLANDO	21	22	24	27	31	32	32	32	31	28	24	21
TALLAHASSEE	12	14	17	20	22	25	27	27	25	24	19	15

The figures are the average maximum temperature in degrees centigrade for each month.

use it liberally at all times.

Your next most important item is a hat – to prevent brainfry, hallucinations, and the world's turning into a spinning saucer. Heatstroke is no joke. You haven't come all the way to Florida to spend your days in a darkened motel room doing even worse things to your brain – watching daytime TV. But if you follow a few simple rules, the sun can be as much fun as a mudbath for a hippo. Just take it easy for the first few days and get acclimated. Avoid exposing yourself to the sun for long periods and try to avoid walking around outside between 11 am and 2.30 pm. Also, drink plenty. This is your chance to sample such local delights as Gatorade, Cherry Coke, Vanilla Pepsi, and that poisonous green liquid the kids at the next table are drinking.

Remember: alcohol dehydrates you, and makes matters worse. Drinks "around the pool" should end with a long belt of the soft stuff – unless you want to wake up next morning in the Sahara Desert.

You'll find that not everyone wearing sunglasses in Florida belongs to the Mafia. You, too, can (and should) look like the Godfather. Most people dress casually. Beachwear is usually acceptable in all but formal restaurants. This is your chance to don that blindingly brilliant beach shirt and garish sky-blue shorts. You'll find they're all the rage. But make sure that you haven't expanded during those long nights at home as a couch potato. It's essential for your comfort – and the well-being of those in your immediate proximity – that your clothes are loose fitting.

Off-season, it can become cooler in the evening, so it's worth bringing some of your normal leisure wear. You'll also find this useful when you visit museums, where the air-conditioning can cool things down. Sandals are also useful. Flip-flops are OK for the beach, but not so practical for nature trails. Running shoes will make your feet too hot.

Documentation

Check that your passport is still valid *before* you buy your tickets. A temporary visitor's passport is no good for entry into the U.S. For citizens of the U.K. and of most EC countries, there is no need for a visa, provided that the visa waiver form, issued on the plane, is completed; that you do not intend to stay for more than 90 days; and that you possess a valid passport and a return ticket.

If you have an Irish, Australian or New Zealand passport, you'll have to get a non-immigrant visitor's visa from your local U.S. embassy or consulate. Communists are not welcome in the U.S., nor are members of private militias or of other extremist organizations, nor of course anyone intending to deal in drugs.

You'll also be asked to provide evidence that you have sufficient funds to support yourself during your stay.

Medical and travel insurance

There is no reciprocal agreement between the United States and the EC for medical care. Should you require medical attention, this can be horrendously expensive. You are *strongly advised* to provide for private medical insurance for the length of your stay.

This insurance can be obtained at almost all travel agents, as well as at airports. The policy invariably covers medical bills, travel costs arising from illness or accident, loss of property and car accidents and personal injury. Some credit cards offer insurance plans if you use them to buy your tickets.

You won't be able to make a claim against your insurance company unless you have irrefutable documentary evidence to support your claim. Also, in case of accident or theft, a local police report on the incident is usually essential.

Money

Before arriving in the U.S., convert most of your spending money into U.S. dollar travelers' checks – the safest way to carry large sums of money. Travelers' checks can be used as currency in most places of business: restaurants, hotels, shops, and so on. For this reason, it makes sense to order some of your travelers' checks in $20 denominations.

Once inside the U.S., trying to convert foreign currency to dollars is almost impossible outside the major international airports and a few banks in major cities. It can also be difficult to convert travelers' checks to cash in a

U.S. bank. If you try to do this, you'll need to show ID and may have to pay a fee. Be sure to check that your particular travelers' checks can be replaced in Florida in case of loss.

Credit cards are an essential part of the American way of life. You won't be able to rent a car without one, and some hotels may want to see a card in order to establish your credit worthiness. The most widely accepted cards are American Express, Diners Club, Visa and MasterCard (which is the same as Access). At present, foreigners cannot use their cards to get money out of an automatic teller machine (ATM). Don't try; the machine will only steal your card. Ask your bank whether your particular card enables you to withdraw cash from an American bank which displays your sign.

Notes and coins: American dollar bills come in denominations of $1, $5, $10, $20, $50, $100. There are even higher denominations, but these are rare and looked upon with suspicion. Just to make life difficult, all denominations of U.S. dollar bills are greenbacks. That is, they are the same size and color regardless of value. Always check the number before parting with a note.

A dollar is worth 100 cents. There are coins worth 1 cent (called pennies), 5 cents (nickels), 10 cents (dimes) and 25 cents (quarters). It's essential to carry a handful of change on you at all times, as you'll need coins for telephones, automatic toll booths and vending machines.

Import and export

On entry to the U.S., you'll be required to fill out a customs declaration. Items you're *not* allowed to bring in include fresh food and agricultural products (this includes cookies and any of the kids' orange juice left over from the flight). Also, don't let on that you've been on a farm recently, or you risk having your dress and shoes sprayed with an abrasive disinfectant, which may ruin their finish. Alternatively, your shoes may simply be removed for incineration.

Other items that you will not be permitted to bring in include products originating from Cuba, Kampuchea, North Korea and Vietnam; obscene publications; liquor; chocolates; pre-Columban art; and lottery tickets.

Don't even think about trying to import drugs, even the most minute amount for strictly personal use. Conditions in a Florida State penitentiary may compare favorably with student lodgings, but you'll face far worse company than the average landlady. Also, your name will go on The List, which means you won't be able to enter America again.

You're allowed to bring in as much cash as you can muster, in any currency. But if this comes to more than the equivalent of U.S. $5,000, you have to declare it.

As for duty-free goods: anyone over 18 is allowed to bring in up to 200 cigarettes and 100 cigars (forget the Havanas), and if you're over 21 you can bring in up to a liter of the alcohol of your choice.

Local customs: what to expect, how to behave

If all Americans behaved the way they do in the movies, no one would go anywhere near the place. Of course, there's no denying the fact that they do have their Dirty Harrys, Jack Nicholsons and Hannibal Lecters – but, for the most part, the people you'll encounter will be refreshingly sane.

Americans tend to be more open and immediately friendly than Europeans. If they ask you to drop by their home, they usually mean it – and you'll be made welcome when you get there. But just because they speak English, this doesn't mean they're just the same as the British. Many basic European assumptions are not shared. The U.S. is a harsh, tough country, and they like it that way. Remember, this is a nation of immigrants. The American Dream is no myth – it's an integral part of the American psyche. As is the belief in the American Way. Patriotism is alive and kicking in America, in a straightforward enthusiastic way that hasn't been general in Europe since before the First World War.

There's also a tremendous diversity. The U.S. is more like a continent than a country. (Some claim it's more a state of mind than either.) Meet an American in a bar, and within five minutes he's likely to have told you how American he is, but on the other hand he'll also have told you how Polish (or Italian, or Irish) he is. And besides being endearingly open, Americans tend to be more polite than most Europeans. Also, they tend to be honest. Cheating and overcharging on bills is a rarity.

So much for the generalizations – all of which you'll probably find contradicted within your first couple of days. To avoid such contradictions turning into a nightmare, it's worth taking a few precautions. Mugging, murder and rape do happen. But there's absolutely no need for them to happen to you. If you behave sensibly, you'll be as safe as you are back home. (Out of almost a million Britons who visited Florida last year, three were murdered. During the same period, four times as many people in the state were struck by lightning.) For free advice on how to protect yourself, you can phone the Miami Police at 1 800 342 7768.

A few dos and don'ts: If you arrive at the airport at night, don't pick up your rental car unless you know *precisely* where you are going. Take a taxi, and get your car in the morning from the rental office in town.

Always store your valuables in the hotel safe; never leave them in your room, even if it is locked. Don't open your hotel room door to strangers. (It will probably be room service, but you can always phone reception to be sure.)

The principal tourist areas in all main cities are safe and well-policed during the day. The main areas where you'll find tourist nightlife are usually well lit and also maintain a reassuring police presence. Most cities in Florida have their trouble spots, which should be avoided day and night. These include districts such as Liberty City and Overtown in Miami. When you reach a new city, ask at your hotel about which spots to avoid.

Don't walk though areas you don't know, even in daytime. At night, take a cab home if you haven't got a car.

If you do find yourself becoming a crime statistic, do as your mugger says. Hand over your charitable contribution as amicably and readily as you can. This considerably lessens your chances of suffering a more serious crime.

Never sleep in your car, and always leave it fully locked (all doors, sunroof and trunk checked). Keep the doors locked when you're traveling. Follow the road signs to your destination: don't work out your own clever shortcut from the map. Never stop for a stranger by the roadside, and don't lower your window if someone comes up to ask you directions. Stow all cameras and valuables in your car out of sight. If your car is "bumped" (rammed from behind), continue driving until you get to a gas station or safely populated spot. Dial 911 for a free call which gets straight through to the police.

However, your most likely encounter with the police may well come as something of a surprise. Unlike many European pedestrians, the Americans take traffic lights seriously. "Don't Walk" means what it says, even if there's no one for miles around. Disobey at your peril. When you've got to the other side of the deserted street, a police officer will miraculously materialize and present you with a $20 ticket.

Another activity which is illegal in Florida is topless sunbathing. And as for nude sunbathing, this is unthinkable. Such activity is considered an official outrage and can get you into a surprising amount of trouble.

However, we're all human – of one sex or another. And willingness to exhibit this is *very slowly* becoming acceptable in certain spots. On some beaches in Miami, for instance, you'll notice topless sunbathers nowadays. And the habit is said to be spreading to other less metropolitan spots. Just be careful, and observe what the locals are doing. "When in Rome..." also applies to Venice and Naples (Florida). On the other hand, when in the Panhandle – forget it. The influences of the Deep South, the Bible Belt and so on are still strong in this region. To expose certain parts of the body here evokes a similar reception to declaring you're a communist.

GETTING THERE

If you're an overseas visitor, you're almost certain to arrive in Florida by air. The good news is that price wars are frequent. Prices are often low, especially during the off-season, which as far as the transatlantic carriers are concerned is between November and April. Peak season, when the prices are highest, is from late June until early September. Prices are also high during the Christmas break. Shop around at any time of year, and you're still likely to come up with a bargain.

Two British carriers (British Airways and Virgin) run daily non-stop flights from London to Miami and Orlando. Half a dozen American airlines also run regular non-stop flights from London to Miami and Orlando. These flights take eight hours. Usually they leave around noon, and arrive at mid-afternoon local time. (Florida, apart from a section of the Panhandle, runs five hours behind Britain and six hours behind mainland European time.) This gives you time to look around, before a reasonably early night, if you want to avoid jet lag. On the way back you usually fly overnight, which enables you to discover first-hand what a red-eye special is all about.

Several American airlines run one-stop flights to Tampa, Jacksonville and Fort Lauderdale. Northwest flies from Glasgow to Miami and Orlando via Boston. Britannia flies weekly non-stop from Birmingham to Orlando. A number of charter companies run seasonal non-stop flights from London, Birmingham and Glasgow to Orlando and Miami.

Many people prefer to buy a package deal. These usually include the price of a flight plus accommodation in some mid-range hotel. There are package deals to many of the popular coastal resorts, as well as Orlando.

Another alternative is a fly-drive deal. This includes the price of your air ticket and a week's car rental. But remember to read the small print. The price quoted is usually with four people in the car. If there's only two of you, then you'll have to pay a surcharge.

If you're going to Florida via another part of America, it's still best to fly. There are regular connections from cities all over America to most major Florida airports. It is also possible to travel there by train. This takes a long time, but you get to see America on the way. There are daily trains from New York and Los Angeles. Train fares vary with the seasons, but are usually a little more expensive than air fares. Cheapest of all is to travel by Greyhound bus. There are connections to all over the States, but long trips can be grueling. It's not worth traveling to Florida by rented car. Rental rates shoot up if you're planning to cross a state line.

GETTING AROUND

Car

Car rental is cheaper in Florida than anywhere else in the States. You'll need a valid driving license from your country of origin, and this should have been valid for at least a year. The actual minimum age limit for car rental is 21, but in effect it's 25 as the extra insurance premiums are often prohibitive. There are car rental offices all over the state. Hertz, Avis, Alamo and Budget also have offices in Europe. For Europeans, arranging car rental at home can be cheaper than doing it in Florida.

But exactly how much does it cost? The very lowest rates run from $100 per week. Make sure you get an unlimited mileage deal. Then come the extras. The most irritating of these is the Collision Damage Waiver (CDW), which will cost you $10–15 per day. This covers you for any damage you inflict on your rental vehicle. Without it, you're liable to pay for that almost invisible dent and scratch, which, as we all know, costs an arm and a leg to fix. Damage to other cars is, at any rate, already covered by the insurance included in your initial price. Then comes the irritating sting called the Florida Surcharge, which bumps the price up by another $2 per day. All this will probably double your initial expense. Be prepared for it, and it won't increase your blood pressure. Even $200 a week is not that expensive.

Driving and rules of the road

The good news is that gas is cheap in the U.S. Almost all cars (and all rental cars) are automatic. In America they drive on the right, and they obey the posted speed limit. Most highways have both minimum and maximum speed limits. There are several toll roads. You'll need change if you want to get quickly through the automatic booths. The same applies to the many toll bridges that connect the mainland to the barrier islands. In Florida you're allowed to turn right on a red light unless there's a sign forbidding this.

Only park at meters or designated parking spots. Otherwise you'll almost certainly get a ticket – or, worse still, wheel-clamped or towed away. Always try to park your car in the shade, or you may make your next journey in a mobile sauna.

If you are stopped by the police, stay in your car and keep your hands on the wheel. Jokes are not appreciated. The police have guns (which they are used to using). Even attempting to reach for the glove compartment or putting your hands above your head may be misinterpreted as going for your gun. (Drivers of pick-up trucks often keep their rifles racked to the inside roof.) All this may sound extreme, and for the most part you won't enter such situations. But in case you do...

A few other basic rules: seat belts are compulsory for all front-seat passengers; it's illegal to make a U-turn on a road with a continuous line down the middle; if you're carrying alcohol in your car, it must be in the trunk, and it cannot be opened; drunk driving is taken seriously and if you fail the breathalizer, you're put in jail.

Taxis
A typical 5-mile journey in town will cost you around $15. The standard tip is 15 percent. You can pick up a taxi easily at an airport; otherwise call from your hotel, bar or restaurant. Never accept a lift from anything except a registered taxi.

Domestic air travel
Florida is less than 500 miles from tip to tail, but it has regular internal air services connecting all major cities. These are quicker than any other method of travel, and sometimes surprisingly inexpensive if you travel off-peak. The one-way flight from Miami to Orlando can cost less than $70, but the normal fare can be double this.

There are major airports at Miami,

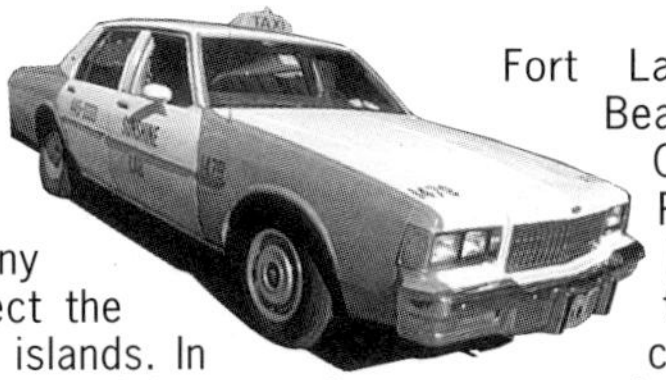

Fort Lauderdale, Palm Beach, Jacksonville, Orlando, Tampa, St Petersburg and Key West. All these have interconnecting flights of one sort or another.

Buses
By far the cheapest way to get around Florida is by Greyhound bus. There are regular services between all main towns, which link up with most of the smaller towns. A one-way ticket between Miami and Orlando will cost around $40. Remember, these services connect population centers – they often leave you some way from the sights or the beaches.

There are also local buses, especially between the resorts on the southeastern coast. These are very cheap, but also very local – only good for short distances.

Rail
Rail travel is not recommended. The service is not comprehensive, takes time, and is not particularly cheap. A one-way ticket from Miami to Orlando will cost you more than $50. Call Amtrak at 1 800 USA RAIL for free details of services.

On the other hand, the new TriRail system which runs along the east coast between Miami and West Palm Beach is a much better bet. This has a dozen or so stops at the main urban centers, and an unbelievably low flat fare of $2.50 for single journeys. But there is a snag. This service is mainly intended for commuters, so it mostly runs during the morning and evening rush hours. Services at other times are few and far between. Call TriRail at 1 800 TRI RAIL for free details of services.

Hitching
Don't.

Cycling
Long-distance cycling along main roads, as in Europe, is not recommended. It's too hot, and can be dangerous. This said, biking in Florida is becoming increasingly popular. But it is mainly limited to parks and beach resorts areas. See details of bike rental under individual sights.

• *Typical style of a Miami Beach hotel.*

Accommodations

Florida abounds in that great American institution, the **motel**. These are usually inexpensive, and even the cheapest motel usually has a pool of some sort. Occasionally they're small, but most are big enough for that obligatory 20 laps before breakfast.

Accommodations are for the most part standard: a large double bed, a TV with a screen only slightly smaller, bath or shower, and air-conditioning. The latter, in some of the cheapest spots, will produce sounds like an avant-garde orchestra, but with less wind. In order to protect your sanity, many motels subscribe to some sort of cable TV. This usually means endless movies. But the alternative has to be seen to be believed. And indeed it should be seen, as part of your American experience. But be warned: overexposure to this combination of wrestling, quiz shows and commercials could do serious damage to your mental health.

Hotels are the next step up. They usually have pools, and often have a range of other facilities such as tennis courts, barbecues and the like. The much-used word "efficiencies" means there's a kitchen and a fridge in your room. This usually costs $15 or so extra.

Bed-and-breakfast is becoming increasingly popular in Florida, but such places can be pricey. They are usually small (fewer than a dozen rooms), family-run, and genuinely friendly. Misanthropes who don't enjoy shooting the breeze on the veranda with their hosts and fellow guests, or can only bear breakfast in silence, should try the motel down the road. But a word of warning here: bed-and-breakfast places sometimes don't have TV in the rooms. It's a sort of upmarket affectation, which goes with the antique furniture.

Resorts are often just dressed-up motels or hotels with a range of facilities, a bar, and a private beach. On the other hand, a first-class resort will have everything a tycoon could require. But you're in for a shock when you see the bill.

For price ranges and seasonal variations, see Conventions used in this guide, page 12.

Banks and currency exchange

Banks in Florida are open from 9 am to 3 pm Monday to Thursday, and from 9 am to 5 pm on Friday. The exchange rate at press time is around $1.55 to the pound. There is a currency exchange desk at Orlando airport, and the BankAmerica office at Miami Airport (Concourse E) is open 24 hours for foreign currency exchange. For further details of exchange and the best way to bring your money into the country, see above under Before you go, page 17, under Money.

Breakdowns

All rental cars have an emergency number on the dashboard. If your car breaks down on the highway, wait for a passing police or Highway Patrol vehicle. (There will usually be one within ten minutes.) Raising the hood of your car is the generally understood way of indicating that you have broken down.

Wait *inside* your car, and don't lower the window to anybody but the police. Women travelers may feel safer with a mobile phone. Most rental companies offer these at minimal extra cost – though this shoots up if you start using the phone regularly. Dial 911 for a free call which puts you in immediate contact with the police.

For further important information, see Local customs, page 21.

Credit cards

See Before you go, page 18, under Money.

Crime

See Local customs, page 19.

Electricity

U.S. electricity runs at 110 volts AC. All plugs are two-prong and surprisingly flimsy. Almost all non-American appliances will need an adaptor. These are on sale at many hardware stores. Big tourist hotels often give out adaptors at the reception desk.

Embassies and consulates

There is no **Australian** consulate in Florida. The Australian Embassy in the U.S. is at 1601 Massachusetts Avenue, NW, Washington, DC 20036; tel. 202 797 3000.

Austrian Consulate Suite 200, Republic Building, 1454 Northwest 17th Avenue, Miami, 33125; tel. 305 325 1561.

British Consulate Suite 2110, South Bayshore Drive, Coconut Grove, Miami, 33131; tel. 305 374 1522.

Canadian Consulate Suite 1600, 200 South Biscayne Boulevard, Miami, 3131; tel. 305 579 1600.

German Consulate 100 North Biscayne Avenue, Miami, 33132; tel. 305 358 0290.

There is no **Irish** consulate in Florida. The Irish Embassy in the U.S. is at 2234 Massachusetts Avenue, NW, Washington, DC 20008; tel. 202 462 3939.

Netherlands Consulate Suite 918 A/B, 801 Brickell Avenue, Miami, 33131; tel. 305 789 6646.

There is no **New Zealand** consulate in Florida. The New Zealand Embassy in the U.S. is at 37 Observatory Circle, NW, Washington, DC 20008; tel. 202 328 4800.

Emergencies

Dial 911 for a free call which puts you immediately in contact with the police. Most visitors will have plane tickets linked with some travel operator or organization. Its local representative will be named on the folder accompanying your ticket. If you find yourself in trouble, this is the best person to contact. Be sure to report any accident to the police, and obtain an offical document stating you have done this, otherwise you won't be able to make a claim against your insurance.

Lost property

Contact your tour representative, or the police – and see Emergencies, above.

Measurements

America does not in general use the metric system. Pounds and ounces, miles and yards, pints and gallons are the order of the day here.

1 kilometer = 0.62 miles.

To convert kilometers to miles, multiply by 5 and divide by 8.

Liquid measurements:

1 U.S. gallon = 1.2 Imperial gallons.
1 U.S. pint = 0.47 liter.
1 U.S. quart (2 pints) = 0.94 liter.
1 U.S. gallon = 3.79 liters.

To convert degrees Fahrenheit to degrees Centigrade: subtract 32, then multiply by 5, and divide by 9.

1 pound = 0.45 kilogram.
1 square mile = 2.6 sq km.

Medical matters

No innoculations are required for your visit. Lists of doctors can be found in the yellow pages under "Physicians" or "clinics". A basic consultation costs around $65, which you must pay beforehand. To call an ambulance, dial 911. Remember to keep all receipts and bills for your insurance claim. (See under Medical and travel insurance, page 17). You'll find drugstores in every town. Many brand names for pills and other medications are different in the U.S. from the rest of the world. If in doubt, ask at the pharmacy counter in the drugstore.

All public buildings must have wheelchair access by law.

Opening hours
Most shops are open from 10 am to 6 pm, Monday to Saturday. Some close on Saturday afternoons. Supermarkets tend to open earlier (around 8 am) and close later (around 9 pm). Drugstores usually open at 9 am and stay open until at least 9 pm.

Banks are open from 9 am to 3 pm Monday to Thursday, and 9 am to 5 pm on Friday.

Museums are *usually* open from around 10 am until 5 pm Monday to Saturday, opening on afternoons only on Sunday, but there are many variations. See individual entries for exact times.

Post and telephone
Post offices are mostly open 9 am to 5 pm from Monday to Friday, and from 9 am to midday on Saturday. Postcards to Europe cost 40¢ and usually take about a week to arrive. Mailboxes are blue, sited on street corners. Letters to anywhere in the U.S. must have the zip code.

You're never far from a telephone. They're on street corners, in bars, restaurants, hotel and motel lobbies. Public phones take 5¢, 10¢ and 25¢ coins. Many phones now accept credit cards. It's more convenient, but more expensive to make a phone call from your hotel room. It costs even more if you don't dial direct and use the operator instead. You can dial the international operator service free at 1 800 874 4000. But be sure to have a bundle of change ready if you want to be connected. The cheapest time to phone abroad is between 6 pm and 7 am. A five-minute call to Europe costs around $7.

To make a direct international call from the United States, dial 011. A selection of international dialing codes:

Australia	61
Austria	43
Germany	49
Ireland	353
Netherlands	31
New Zealand	64
UK	44

Remember, always strike off the initial 0 on your home number when dialing from the U.S.

To send a telegram, go to Western Union (see yellow pages for nearest office).

Public holidays
January 1, New Year's Day; January 15, Martin Luther King's Birthday; third Monday in February, President's Day; Good Friday (half day); Easter Monday; last Monday in May, Memorial Day; July 4, Independence Day; first Monday in September, Labor Day; second Monday in October, Columbus Day; November 11, Veterans' Day; fourth Thursday in November, Thanksgiving; December 25, Christmas Day.

On these days all shops, banks and offices are closed.

Public washrooms
For some reason, these are extremely rare. But the good news is that every bar, restaurant, hamburger joint and many gas stations usually have one. You're meant to be a customer. Either buy a cheap soft drink, or risk the wrath of the owner.

Safety
For important advice on basic precautions, see Local customs, page 19.

Tax
There is a 6 percent sales tax, which is added on to almost everything you buy. This won't be included on the displayed price, but will bump up your final bill. In addition to this, most urban districts have a special tax of their own which will be added to your hotel and restaurant bills.

Allow for at least 10 percent on top of stated prices *beforehand*, to avoid constant aggravation.

Time
Florida operates on Eastern Standard Time, apart from a small section of the Panhandle which runs one hour later on Central Standard Time. Eastern Standard Time is five hours behind Greenwich Mean Time. This means that Florida is five hours behind Britain, and six hours behind continental European time.

Tipping
In restaurants you should tip 15 percent and round your bill up to the nearest 50 cents. (Most waiters and waitresses depend on tips to make the job worthwhile.) Taxis expect 15 percent. Hotel porters expect $1 per item.

• *Lightner Museum, St Augustine.*

FLAGLER – THE MAN WHO MADE FLORIDA

Henry M. Flagler was born in New York State in 1830, the son of an impecunious Presbyterian minister. He left home when he was 14 to seek his fortune. This he made and lost several times during the next 20 years. Then, at the age of 37, he joined forces with a young man starting out in the oil business. This was John D. Rockefeller, and three years later they started Standard Oil together.

In 1883 Flagler visited St Augustine on his honeymoon. He realized at once that Florida was a huge opportunity waiting to happen. Within three years Flagler had bought some local railway lines and combined them into the Florida East Coast Railroad. His idea was to turn the east coast of Florida into the American Riviera. As he extended his line down the coast, he built grand hotels at each new resort that the railway created. By 1893 this had reached Palm Beach, which Flagler's Royal Poinciana Hotel established as a high society resort.

Flagler's railways also carried on a lucrative trade transporting the citrus crops north. When the citrus crops were destroyed by a disastrous frost which reached south of Palm Beach, Flagler was persuaded to extend his railway line further south to the sleepy settlement of Miami. This was the inauguration of Miami as America's foremost tourist city. Flagler also dredged the harbor, and established regular steamship services to Key West and the Bahamas.

Later Flagler was to extend his railway all the way to Key West. This involved bridging the Keys, the most ambitious engineering project of the era. The railway finally reached Key West in 1912, with Flagler arriving on the inaugural ride. A year later, he died.

Flagler's railway company went bust in the Depression, and the railway line to Key West was destroyed by a hurricane in 1935. But there was no undoing what Flagler had done for Florida. He had laid the foundation that established the state as the major tourist destination in the U.S.

See also under Palm Beach, page 184; Miami, page 148 and Florida Overall: 1, The Lower Keys.

this, there were now more blacks with the vote than whites. All this brought about increasing conflict with white landowners and small farmers. In 1866 the Ku Klux Klan was founded in Tennessee, and its advocacy of racial segregation (often backed by lynchings) soon found widespread support in Florida. The politics of the state descended into corruption and vote-rigging, and the political machine was soon in the hands of all-white Southern Democrats. The situation for many blacks remained little better than before the Civil War.

But the population was changing. White settlers were now arriving in increasing numbers from the north. Political power began to shift from the Panhandle (which remained very much a part of the Old South) to the pioneer farms and northern investors who aimed to cash in on Florida's climate. The state was soon being touted as a tourist center, and well-off northerners began taking winter vacations along the St Johns River, which even had paddle steamers.

Henry Flagler, who had made his fortune in oil, began opening up resorts along the northeast coast. Within a few years he was induced to extend his Florida East Coast Railroad down the coast to Miami. Meanwhile, rival railroad magnate Henry B. Plant extended his railway down the west coast to Tampa. This linked up with Plant's Cuban shipping interests, and what had been a sleepy fishing village was transformed into a booming center of the cigar manufacturing industry. The central Florida citrus estates and cattle ranches now thrived, with the railways carrying their products to markets all over America.

The early 20thC: boom and bust

In 1905, Napoleon Bonaparte Broward was elected state governor. He at once launched a program to ensure the benefits of Florida's prosperity would be enjoyed by all – not just the tycoons and railway magnates. (The latter's exploitation of black labor for laying their railways had been a national disgrace.) Broward was also the first to bring in conservation laws aimed at protecting the state's fragile environment. Ironically, his drainage systems – intended to produce more land for the poor – were to wreak havoc on the Everglades' ecosystem.

When Prohibition was introduced after the First World War, it sparked a boom of a different kind. Florida's coastline proved ideal for smuggling in liquor from the Bahamas and Cuba. With the booze came gangland culture, and the usual sleaze.

At the classier end of the social scale, things began to take off in Palm Beach and then Boca Raton, which were now established as millionaires' playgrounds. At the same time, George Merrick built Coral Gables, a huge Mediterranean-style resort, on the outskirts of Miami. In no time, Florida was experiencing a land boom.

A couple of hurricanes, scores of investors overreaching themselves, several bankruptcies (including a few banks) – and the bubble burst. The Florida land boom was already over by the time the Wall Street Crash came in 1929. During the ensuing Depression, even the Flagler railroad went bust.

The forties, fifties and sixties

Despite the efforts of Roosevelt's New Deal, Florida never really recovered from the Depression until America entered the Second World War in 1941. Miami Beach and stretches of the east coast were turned into a gigantic boot camp, with thousands of GIs housed in the empty hotels and drilling on the beaches.

This proved as good as free advertising, and after the war many of the GIs returned as tourists. By 1950 over 4.5 million visitors were coming every year to Florida – more than the entire permanent population. But the state administration remained as corrupt as ever. In the same year, even the state governor, Fuller Warren, was found to be on the payroll of the syndicate formerly run by Al Capone.

During the 1950s the boom continued. Over this period more hotel rooms were built in Florida than in the entire U.S., and in 1959 the first jet airliner link in the country was opened between New York and Miami. The 1950s also saw the advent of another kind of air travel in Florida, with the first rockets launched from Cape Canaveral.

During the early 1960s, the Civil Rights movement gathered momentum in Florida. Reform was long overdue. Blacks were banned from Miami Beach

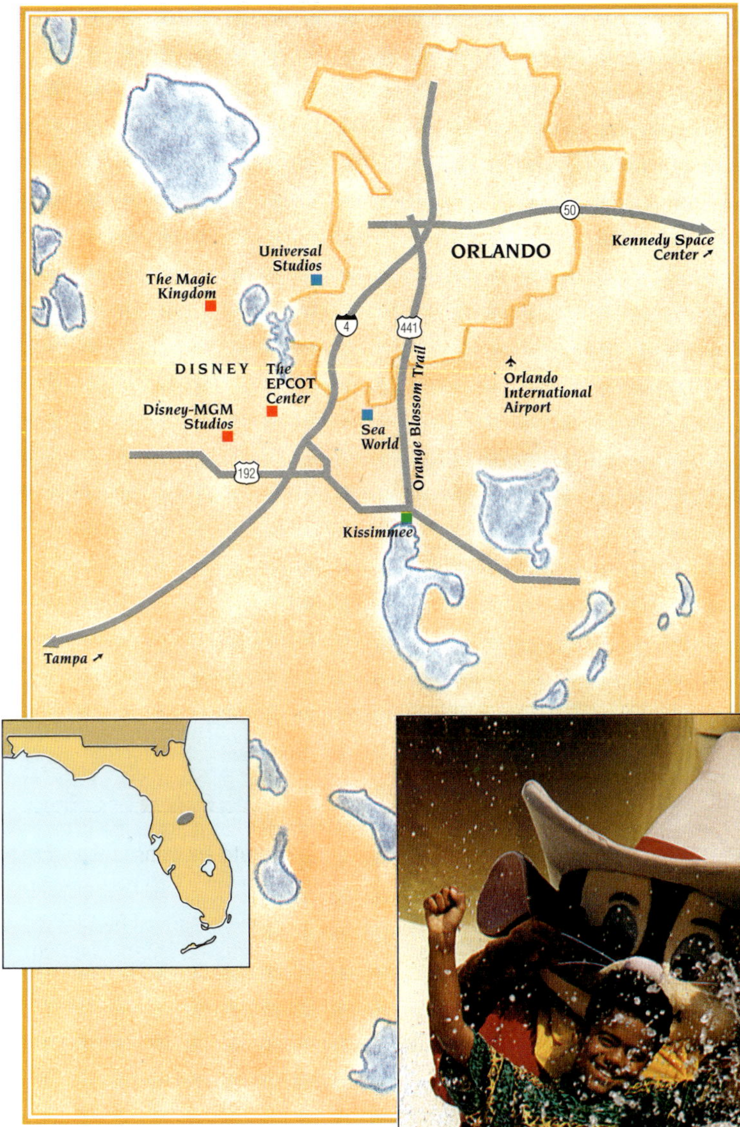

© Universal Studios 1996

TRANSPORTATION
Most hotels have transportation links of some kind with Walt Disney World and the other main sights, so a car isn't strictly necessary. But if you want to explore further afield, you'll need one. Orlando has air links to the main cities in Florida, bus links to all over Florida, and train links to both the east and west coasts.

• *Cowboys in Kissimmee.*

SIGHTS & PLACES OF INTEREST

KENNEDY SPACE CENTER

see Florida Overall: 2, *page* 52.

KISSIMMEE 🛏 ✕

13 *miles* SE *of* Orlando *on* Rt 4. For years in danger of being swallowed up by nearby Orlando, Kissimmee (stress on the second *i*) has so far managed to retain an identity of its own. It is still very much a cow town, and the main event each week is the cattle auction held on Wednesdays in the **Cattle Market** at 805 East Donegan Avenue. This is when the cowboys hit town. The main events in their year are the **Kissimmee Valley Livestock Show** in February, and the seasonal **Silver Spurs Rodeos**, held in February and July.

The modern Kissimmee cowboys are still a tough breed, but none of them lives up to local legend "Bone" Mizell. This mean critter operated around the turn of the 20thC, and was renowned for branding cattle with his teeth. As one local dryly informed me: "Bone liked his steak raw."

It sure doesn't fit the cowboy image, but there's no getting away from the fact that Kissimmee is also the home of Tupperware. You can visit the **Tupperware World Headquarters** on Rt 441, where they'll take you on a conducted tour. Avid surrealists who have taken this tour can also visit the **Museum of Dishes.**

The major tourist sight in Kissimmee is the **Gatorland Zoo** at 14501 *South Orange Blossom Trail* (Rt 441). *Open 8 am - 6 pm (8 in summer); entry* $11. This attraction dates from the preDisney era, opening up way back in 1949. Here you can learn all you wish to know (and perhaps a bit more) about Florida's ugliest resident. Like many aesthetically disadvantaged folks, the gator is deeply misunderstood. All he really wants to do is doze and dream all day in a swamp. This is amply borne out by the behavior of the 5,000 alligators at Gatorland. Unfortunately, they also get hungry every now and again. This is when things really start to liven up. **Feeding time** here is every two hours, beginning with breakfast at 10 am. Then you can see what the gator lies there dreaming about all day in his swamp.

Other ugly customers on display include reptiles and rattlesnakes. The **Snake Pit** is something else, and not for the queasy. There are free rides around the park on the Gatorland Express, and also various shows in which the gators more or less willingly take part, such as gator jumping, gator wrestling and so forth. But the gators are not allowed to do what they'd really like, such as enter the turtle enclosure or join the children in line for ice cream.

Head down to **Lake Front Park**, and you can see the **Monument of States**. This cultural oddity consists of 21 concrete slabs piled one on top of the other, rising to 50 feet. The decorated and painted blocks contain more than 1,500 stones gathered from every state in the United States and also from dozens of foreign countries. It is a monument devoid of any real significance or aesthetic grace, but is of more interest than many which claim to have both these qualities.

You enter town by way of the aptly christened **Tourist Trap Trail**, which links Kissimmee to the interstate highway (Rt 4). Here there's everything from a "home of the future" to an **Elvis Presley Museum**. The latter is no Graceland, but remains a must for Presley

•Dolphin acrobatics, right, and whale display, below, Sea World.

rine. Your mission is to explore the notorious Bermuda Triangle, the 400,000-square-mile triangular tract of the Atlantic where dozens of ships and aircraft have mysteriously vanished. In mid-dive, *your* dive, your craft too suddenly finds itself in danger of vanishing.

Other attractions include acrobatic dolphins, cowboy waterskiers, and hundreds of penguins all impeccably dressed for dinner.

The vast Coral Reef Aquarium contains literally hundreds of vibrant fish. And for those who can't keep their hands out of the water, there's even a Sting-Ray Lagoon filled with stingless members of the species, which you can touch.

TAMPA

See Local Explorations: 8, page 235.

UNIVERSAL STUDIOS

SW of downtown Orlando, at 1000 Universal Studios Plaza; open 9-7 (later during summer vacation); admission $35. This is a working film studio, spread over 444 acres, making it the largest studio outside Hollywood. It's also a movie theme park – working in direct competition with Disney-MGM down the road. Here you can see more than 40 movie sets, and there are even more special attractions.

The star feature is undoubtedly the **Back to the Future ride**. Many rank this as the greatest experience in Orlando. Enter Doc Brown's Laboratory of Future Technology and join the mission to rescue the DeLorean time machine from the clutches of Biff. This takes you on a mind-blowing trip through the space-time continuum from pre-history to the 21stC . It may only last five minutes, but you emerge having been eaten by a dinosaur, hurtled through lava fields and Ice Age glaciers, and... well, see for yourself.

Another shattering experience is to be had at Earthquake, The Big One. This starts as an ordinary ride on the San Francisco subway – until The Big One strikes, at 8.3 on the Richter Scale. Fire, flood and cataclysm ensue, with you in the hot seat.

For a big city thrill of a different kind, try Kongfrontation. This time, it's the Big Ape in the Big Apple. He's over 30 feet tall, weighs 13,000 pounds and looms so close you can even smell his breath (fortunately he only had bananas for dinner). Nearby, you're in a different kind of mess with Ghostbusters. Here you enter a haunted house, and volunteers get smeared with slime.

At Jaws, you're in danger of being turned into something even less appetizing – until the tables turn and Jaws himself fries before your eyes (and nose).

Things take a turn for the better at the FUNtastic World of Hanna-Barbera, where you get to meet your old pals the Flintstones, and Yogi Bear. You even have a chance to add your own oops-splat-kaplonk soundtrack to a cartoon.

• *Universal Studios, this page and opposite.*

WALT DISNEY WORLD

10 miles SW of Orlando, off Rt 4; open 9 am-9 pm daily (11 pm Feb-Aug). A one-day ticket for just one of the three parks is $40 *(children* $30*). A five-day World Hopper pass costs* $208 *(children* $166*).*

- *Disney fans.*

To visit only once is a crime, and gives you no idea of all there is to see. After about the fourth day, addiction can begin to set in (or you're being led away by the men in white coats).

The Walt Disney World Vacation Kingdom (to give the place its full title) consists of three separate parks: the **Magic Kingdom,** the **Epcot**, and **Disney-MGM Studios.** We cover them here under separate headings.

Magic Kingdom

The Magic Kingdom is what everyone *imagines* Disney World to be. It has Cinderella's Castle at its center, and Mickey Mouse walking down Main Street U.S.A.

The Magic Kingdom extends over 100 acres and has almost 50 attractions. These are divided into seven distinct "lands".

Main Street U.S.A.

This is the first "land" you encounter. It's laid out like a typical American main street at the beginning of the century, with Cinderella's Castle rising at the far end. (This fairy-tale castle in fact contains the electronic wizardry which keeps the Magic Kingdom whizzing, hurtling, rising, splodging, hootling and tootling.) The best thing here is the Main Street Cinema, which shows old black-and-white Disney cartoons, including Mickey's first talking appearance, in *Steamboat Willie*. (This dates from 1928, which means that by now our black-eared friend is spry for his age.)

Adventureland

Home of the Swiss family Robinson, who live in a tree house in the sprawling jungle. Jump aboard for the Jungle Cruise, which takes you in ten minutes down the Congo, the Nile, the Amazon and the Mekong. Even better is the Pirates of the Caribbean ride, where an entire settlement goes up in flames.

Frontierland

You enter the frontier era, with real-life cowboys and pioneers strumming their banjos in synthetic, log cabins.

One of the high points is a hair-raising ride on the Big Thunder Mountain Railroad. Here your runaway train eludes a volcanic eruption, an avalanche, and an earthquake. Afterwards you can relax during a 40-minute show in a Wild West saloon. (This is called the Diamond Horseshoe Jamboree, and only takes place five times a day, so be sure to book in advance on

Main Street, U.S.A.)

Those who prefer bears playing banjos, rather than Mae West-style wisecracking, should check out the Country Bear Jamboree. But best of all is the Frontierland Shootin' Arcade, where you can partake in a surprisingly authentic carnage using a 54-caliber buffalo rifle.

Liberty Square

Here you're in colonial times, amidst the neat gardens and cobbled streets of Williamsburg. Don't miss The Hall of Presidents, where all 42 presidents from George Washington on are represented by audio-animatronic robots. Bill Clinton even recorded his own voice for his lifelike robot.

Afterwards, you can take a ride on an old riverboat, which gives you a chance to rest your feet for 15 minutes. Then it's time to be scared out of your wits in the Haunted Mansion. A word of warning: although this is presented in a comical fashion, which most kids enjoy, the luminous creepie-crawlies, haunted graveyard and ghostly xylophone player can be too much for some.

Fantasyland

We all have our own version of this, and spend many happy hours in it. This is the Disney version. In fact, it's surprisingly close to our own daydreams. What child has not imagined himself (or herself) at a Mad Hatter's Tea Party, flying like the ever-youthful Peter Pan, in the company of Cinderella or Snow White, or hogging the road like Toad of Toad Hall?

Mickey's Toontown Fair

In a festive fairground setting, this is *the* place to meet and greet all your favorite Disney characters. You can visit Minnie Mouse's house and explore Mickey's bungalow next door. For young riders there is Goofy's barnstorming roller coaster.

New Tomorrowland

This used to contain the Disney version of the future. But it soon became apparent that we're all now living in this Disney future – so they've come up with a new idea. We now visit "the future that never was." This is the future envisioned by all those prophetic sci-fi writers, the one we knew could only happen on TV, and to people who believe in UFOs. Aided by a Transportarium, an AstroOrbiter and the Tomorrowland Transit Authority you can whizz through distant galaxies and time-travel back and forth through the centuries. Or in the ExtraTERRORestrial Alien Encounter you can participate in a teleportation experiment that goes shockingly wrong.

Now that you've completed your tour of Walt Disney World, it's time to move on to Epcot.

Epcot

Epcot stands for Experimental Prototype Community of Tomorrow. It opened in 1982, and soon the public began flocking in to see this fantastic theme park.

Epcot covers more than 250 acres, and is divided into two main sections: Future World, and World Showcase.

Future World

Here you are brought face to face with scientific achievements and tomorrow's technologies. It is divided into ten pavilions, most of which are individually sponsored by large U.S. corporations. The best of these are Spaceship Earth, The Wonders of Life, and Journey into the Imagination.

World Showcase

An open door to cultures around the globe, celebrating sights, sounds and cuisines from eleven nations.

SPACESHIP EARTH

This is the major WOW of Epcot: a 180-foot high anodized aluminium geosphere. (A geosphere is two halves of a geodesic dome brought together to form a geodesic sphere, but with such force that the name contracts.) The Geosphere has a volume of 2 million cubic feet, and inside is the Spaceship Earth Ride, the most popular feature of Epcot. This is a trip down the time superhighway, as imagined by sci-fi writer Ray Bradbury, narrated by Walker Kronkite. Your journey starts in pre-history with an Audio-Animatronic Cro-Magnon shaman. You then pass through Ancient Egypt, Ancient Rome and the Renaissance, learning how human ideas and human achievement gradually evolved to create the modern era. Next, steam and electricity give way to the age of modern technology, until you journey into space for a new perspective on "Spaceship Earth." The accompanying visual effects are suitably dazzling.

THE WONDERS OF LIFE
Beyond the 75-foot high model of a DNA molecule, you enter a huge geodesic dome (sponsored by Metropolitan Life). Inside there are various shows, which succeed in being exciting, amusing and educational at the same time. Try Body Wars, which takes you on a ride through the circulatory system of the human body. Or Cranium Command, where a whacky "brain-pilot" shows you how he tries to control the brain of a 12-year-old during the rigors of a normal day. Parents who have been shirking The Serious Talk will be pleased to introduce the kids to The Making of Me, a suitably instructive 15-minute film, whose finer biological details will probably come as a surprise only to adults. There's also a fitness fairground where you can take part in activities designed to demonstrate precisely how unfit you are. There's also a film in which Goofy abandons his slobby existence and adopts a more fitting lifestyle.

JOURNEY INTO THE IMAGINATION
Here Kodak explains to your naturally creative child how he can stimulate his imagination to the heights of Disney. You can go on a Journey into the Imagination Ride, accompanied by the red-bearded Dreamfinder (the Dr Freud of Phantazy) and his pal Figment; enter Image Works, a land of interactive electronic wizardry; or be reduced to the size of a thimble in the high-tech 3-D misadventure "Honey, I Shrunk the Audience". The kids love it – and so will you.

Other pavilions not to be missed include **The Living Seas, The Land, Horizons**, and the spectacular **Universe of Energy**.

World Showcase
This is the other section of Epcot and consists of 11 territories around a lake, each representing a different international country – the Disney version, of course.

Canada features *O Canada!*, a "scenic rhapsody" in 360-degree Circle-Vision. The United Kingdom includes a pub, thatched cottages, and a chance for the kids to take part in one of Shakespeare's plays without getting stabbed, poisoned, or confused by all the fancy verbiage. France is, of course, Paris, with the Eiffel Tower and Bohemians in berets and striped sailor vests. Then comes magical Morocco, complete with belly-dancers in the restaurant. As with all countries, you get a chance to sample the national fare. Make prior reservations at Earth Station, beneath Spaceship Earth. Japan has a pagoda, a superb Japanese garden and sells everything from bonsai plants to samurai swords. America is represented by the American Adventure, which takes you on a lightning tour through American history with the aid of dozens of audio-animatronic robots. Also on display here is The Magical World of Barbie. Italy, Germany, China, Norway and Mexico are also represented. This is intended as an hors d'oeuvre of our international world, before we one day travel there for the less palatable main course. And as such it succeeds spectacularly.

DISNEY-MGM STUDIOS
Walt Disney World's third magical kingdom opened in 1990, as a rival to nearby Universal Studios in Orlando (see page 36). Here you can meet Robert Redford and Burt Reynolds wandering down Hollywood Boulevard with their intellectual cronies, the Muppets. Best of the supporting features is The Great Movie Ride, where audio-animatronic robots enact classic scenes ("Round up all the usual suspects"; "Frankly my dear, I don't give a damn", and so on.)

Other favorites include the Backstage Studio Tour (where you get to ride through an earthquake in Catastrophe Canyon), The Twilight Zone Tower of Terror (where the elevator cable snaps and plunges you down 13 stories), The Magic of Disney Animation (heartbreak when you learn that Bambi isn't real after all), and the Indiana Jones Epic Stunt Spectacular (where our hero cheats death, and you get to see how the cheating is done).

Your Walt Disney 5 Day World Hopper Pass also gives you entry to Blizzard Beach, Discovery Island, River Country, Pleasure Island and Typhoon Lagoon, which are intended to provide pleasant relief after the non-stop WOW of the magical worlds themselves.

River Country

By the shore of Bay Lake, across from Discovery Island. Open 10 am-5 pm daily, longer hours in summer; day ticket $13.25. This small theme park is modeled on Tom Sawyer's swimming hole. The hole itself is large enough for all the gang. (It contains almost a third of a million gallons.) At Whoop 'n' Holler Hollow there are a couple of corkscrew slides which induce panic and vertigo (or squeals of delight) before spewing you out into the water with a splash.

Only a little less exciting (but great for the younger ones) is a descent on an inner tube down the White Water Rapids. On the lake shore you come to Bay Cove, a cordoned-off section of the lake, complete with a beach, ropes which swing out over the water and a nature trail through the woods.

Typhoon Lagoon

East of Epcot, off Buena Vista Drive. Open 10 am-5 pm; entry $20.50. Bigger and better water theme park than River Country, but it gets much more crowded. The shore of the huge lagoon has been landscaped like a tropical island after a typhoon has passed through. Amongst the wreckage is a fishing boat left stranded on top of 100-foot Mount Mayday. Every now and again a huge plume of water shoots up into the sky out of its funnel, which sets the tone of things. Other attractions include artificial waves which crash onto the beach (great for surfing); Storm Slides which pass assorted nautical flotsam before reaching a pool at the bottom of the mountain; three different rafting adventures; and the Humunga Kowabunga. These are a couple of 200-foot slides which plunge down the mountainside and through a cave, breaking all speed limits, and your resolve, (but too late) before hurtling you into the lagoon. Castaway Creek and Ketchakiddee Creek cater for the fainter-hearted. There's also a large coral reef tank called Shark Reef, where you can snorkel among thousands of colorful tropical fish and explore a wreck. But be warned: Shark Reef lives up to its name – though the resident sharks are not in fact man- (or child-) eaters. Even so, the unexpected looming presence

Disney-wise

Walt Disney World attracts 100,000 visitors a day, *on average*. The reality is that the numbers are highest during the summer, at Easter, and at Christmas. The snag is, of course, that these are the times when the kids are out of school, so you can't really avoid visiting at the peak periods. In summer, things quiet down somewhat towards late afternoon and evening. Otherwise, there can be long lines, especially for food and drinks. The Disney people are well aware of this, and they go out of their way to entertain you while you're waiting. Even on the most popular days, life in Walt Disney World is seldom a drag. But the sheer volume of the crowds can wear you out quicker than you might expect. For the kids it's a different matter. Many never want to leave. (And this includes some of those who entered as adults.) Others, especially young children, can tire quickly – so don't plan anything too ambitious on your first visit.

October, and March to May (except for Easter) are the best times to visit. Because of the way the touring companies run their schedules, it's usually busier during the beginning of the week at the Magic Kingdom and Epcot, and during the end of the week at the Disney-MGM Studios. No need to ask what happens on the weekends.

A friend who recently returned from taking his family to Walt Disney World offers three tips:

- Always queue on the left, for some unknown reason the left-hand part of a stream of people seems to move quicker than the right.
- Saturdays are said to be least crowded — it's changeover day – visitors arriving and leaving the area.
- The Magic Kingdom appears to be by far the most popular and crowded attraction within the park.

© Disney Enterprises, Inc.

of Jaws can certainly induce a sudden record-breaking sprint.

Blizzard Beach

SW of Disney MGM Studios, off Buena Vista Drive. Open 9 am-6 pm (until 8 pm at peak times); entry $ 25.39.

A zany place that combines the atmosphere of a ski resort with a water park. Ski slalom courses, bobsled and sledding runs become downhill water-rides. At a breathtaking 55 mph Summit Plummet plunges you straight down to a splash landing at the base of Mt. Gushmore; Slush Gusher drops through a snow-banked mountain gully. White-water raft rides, "tobaggan" racers and a chair lift complete the scene. Below

• *Main Street,* U.S.A. *and Cinderella Castle.*

Mt. Gushmore is a beach area with pools and water-slides.

Pleasure Island

Buena Vista Drive. Open 7 pm-2 am; entry $18

For those people with any remaining energy, and a hunkering after some night-life, Pleasure Island offers 7 night-clubs, entertainment, cinemas and restaurants galore. The **House of Blues** music hall will appeal to blues, rhythm and blues, jazz, and country fans, while **Lario's** nightclub features Latin American music.

• *Walt Disney at the original theme park in California: Disneyland.*

WALT DISNEY – THE MAN WHO CREATED A WORLD

Walt Disney was born the son of a carpenter in Chicago in 1901. His parents soon moved to Marceline, Missouri, where they stayed long enough for Walt to look upon this typical midwestern town as a childhood paradise. (Years later, it was the inspiration for Main Street U.S.A. in Disneyland.)

The family then moved to Kansas City, where Walt helped his father run a paper route and took a correspondence course in drawing cartoons. Next the family moved back to Chicago. During the First World War, Disney served as an ambulance driver in the American Red Cross in Europe. (An experience which paralleled that of fellow Chicagoan Ernest Hemingway.)

Back in Kansas City in 1919, Walt Disney teamed up with artist Ub Iwerks, and together they started a film studio. They produced a number of short cartoons, until a fraudulent New York distributor left them bust.

In despair, Walt went to stay with his brother Roy in Hollywood. Here Iwerks joined them, and they began producing more cartoons, with Roy as their business manager.

In 1927, Walt Disney and Ub Iwerks created Mickey Mouse. The emergence of Mickey coincided with the first talkies, and Mickey was adapted to sound with huge success in *Steamboat Willie*, which came out in 1928. Disney's world of cartoon characters soon expanded – with, Pluto (1930), Goofy (1932) and Donald Duck (1934). This was just what audiences needed to see them through the hard years of the Depression, and Disney's characters became part of the American psyche. Mickey, Donald and company became as American as hamburgers and Coca Cola.

Meanwhile, Disney expanded into full-length features with *Snow White* and *Pinocchio*. Disney seldom stood still, and soon began plans for a vast amusement park, featuring many of his favorite creations. Disneyland opened in California in 1955. When TV came along, Disney Studios was quick to exploit the new possibilities. The Disney fortune continued to grow, and so did Walt's ambitions. By the time Walt Disney died in 1966, the colossal project of Walt Disney World in Florida was only just starting.

The world of Disney became archetypically American; but it was also criticized for its low-brow commercialism. Disneyland was called "an amusement supermarket." Yet Disney remained unrepentant. He knew what he was doing. "I'm not an artist, I'm a showman," he insisted. And Walt Disney World was his legacy – where the entire world as we know it is put on as a show.

RECOMMENDED HOTELS

KISSIMMEE

Larson's Lodge Kissimmee, $-$$; *2009 West Vine Street (Rt 192), Kissimmee 34741; tel. 407 846 2713; all major cards.*

As close to Walt Disney World as many of the hotels in Orlando, yet the prices are a little lower. The big bonus is that the kids stay free (as long as they're in your room). All you need for the family, including a great pool (and wading pool), children's playground and handy restaurant.

Slightly more upscale is:

Holiday Inn Maingate East, $$-$$$; *5678 Irlo Bronson Highway, Kissimmee 34746; tel. 407 396 4488; all major cards.*

Large (600-plus rooms), and set amid 20 acres, with all the facilities you expect of a Holiday Inn. Special attention is paid to the kids, with huge swimming pools, video arcades and customized facilities for the under-12s (including Gingerbread House restaurant complete with cartoons). Adults will go for the superb seafood in the Vineyard Cafe – one of more than a dozen eateries.

ORLANDO

In a town replete with over-the-top hotels at over-the-top prices, one luxury hotel with real class is:

Marriott's Orlando World Center, $$$; *8701 World Center Drive, Orlando 32821; tel. 407 239 4200; all major cards.*

Almost a small (and luxurious) town set amid 230 acres of landscaped grounds. The latter includes duck-filled lagoons with waterfalls, an 18-hole championship golf course (designed by champion Joe Lee), four swimming pools, a dozen floodlit tennis courts, and a 2-mile jogging course.

The hotel itself has a 27-storey tower and over 1,500 rooms. Name your cocktail at any hour, and room service will provide. Surprisingly, it needn't be all that expensive. Off-season, a room for five sinks well below $200.

At the other end of the market is:

Red Roof Inn, $-$$; *9922 Hawaiian Court, Orlando 32819; tel. 407 352 1507; no cards.*

About as good a bargain as you'll get in Orlando. It's on the way to the main attractions, and has that essential pool.

If you want to stay downtown, your best bet is:

Harley Hotel, $$-$$$; *151 East Washington Street, Orlando 32801; tel. 407 352 0008; no cards.*

Sophisticated spot, rooms with views over Lake Eola, and a great swimming pool. Tony, at reception, is typically helpful and a fund of esoteric local lore. According to him, this hotel was once in the *Guinness Book of Records* for having 'The World's Shortest Lift', but they lost out to a hotel in Tokyo.

Besides these hotels in Orlando, there are also some hotels which are actually in Walt Disney World. These are invariably pricey, but it makes sense to stay at one if you've only come to visit your friend Goofy and his pals. One of the least expensive of these is:

Howard Johnson Resort at Walt Disney World Village, $$; *1805 Hotel Plaza Boulevard, Lake Buena Vista 32830; tel. 407 828 8888; all major cards.*

Tall, 300-room hotel with the standard rooms you can rely on from this ubiquitous chain. The pool here is heated and stays open all year.

RECOMMENDED RESTAURANTS

KISSIMMEE

Little Darlins Rock and Roll Palace, $-$$; *5770 Orlo Bronson Highway (Rt 192), Kissimmee; tel.* 407 396 6499; *cards* MC, V.

This is what Europeans come all the way to America to experience. Step in through the two-storey high juke box to a world that never noticed Elvis was gone. During the day it's a great diner, with burgers, shakes and beers. At night you can jive to The Shirelles and reminisce about what it was really like in the 1960s.

ORLANDO

At the Epcot World Showcase, you can sample the cuisine of 11 nations (for booking see under World Showcase entry). Not surprisingly, the best of these is **Les Chefs de France, $$-$$$** in the French section. The menu here was conceived by three of France's greatest chefs (including the celebrated Paul Bocuse) with the aim of showing off their nation's cuisine in classic style. They succeeded.

If you want something different, but not too exotic, try the **Restaurant Akershus, $$,** in the Norwegian section. Here they serve a typical Norwegian version of smorgasbord (called *koldtboard*). This features some superb fish and salads.

For that table-thumping Teutonic experience, complete with Bavarian band playing oompa-pa and vunderful *wurst*, head for the **German Biergarten, $-$$**. The British pub, **The Rose and Crown, $-$$**, is said to be the favorite of Disney workers.

However, by far the best restaurant in Walt Disney World serves American cuisine. This *isn't* at the Epcot, but is across at the Magic Kingdom:

Victoria & Albert's, $$$; *Grand Floridian Beach Resort,* 4401 *Grand Floridian Way, Walt Disney World, Lake Buena Vista; tel.* 407 824 2383; *cards* AE, MC, V.

Here you get the full Disney treatment (sophisticated style). Instead of waiters, you're attended by a maid (called Victoria) and a butler (Albert). Unlike her namesake, Victoria is always amused – and you will be too. The $80 seven-course fixed price menu changes daily, but maintains a high standard of American cuisine (regional and new). Dinner only: sittings at 6 pm and 9 pm.

Outside Walt Disney World, try:

Hard Rock Cafe, $-$$; *Universal Studios,* 5800 *Kirkman Road, Orlando; tel.* 407 351 7625; *cards* AE, MC, V.

"World's Greatest Hard Rock Cafe." Built in the shape of a guitar. Burgers in the shape of burgers, and they live up to the "World's Greatest" claim.

Coq au Vin, $$; 4800 *South Orange Avenue, Orlando; tel.* 407 851 6980; *all major cards.*

It's difficult not to rave about this one. The French provincial cuisine is authentic and comes at very reasonable prices.

Florida Overall: 2

Central Florida

Between West Palm Beach and Cape Canaveral

The Space and Treasure Coasts

150 miles; map Hallwag Florida

Once, the Treasure Coast was littered with treasure from wrecked Spanish galleons; now, it's littered with bodies, baking in the sun. However, it's not as crowded as the Gold Coast, further south. Here, the condos lining the coast begin to thin out somewhat, allowing room for the loggerhead turtles to come ashore and lay their eggs.

Take a detour inland and you can visit Lake Okeechobee, whose over-spill creates the vast swamps of the Everglades, which cover so much of southern Florida. This region is not as picturesque as the coast, but it's great for fishing, and also gives you a picture of what Florida was really like in the old days.

Further north you come to the Space Coast, home of the Kennedy Space Center. There's no place like this anywhere else on earth, and if you come during a space shuttle launch you'll be able to see for yourself what it's all about.

By far the best way to see this stretch of the coast is to stick to Rt A1A, which travels along the narrow barrier islands, separated from the coast by Indian River. Even following this slower route, you can easily cover the ground in a day. But if you want to take in the beaches and a few of the sights, and visit the Kennedy Space Center (which will take you a day), you should allow three or four days.

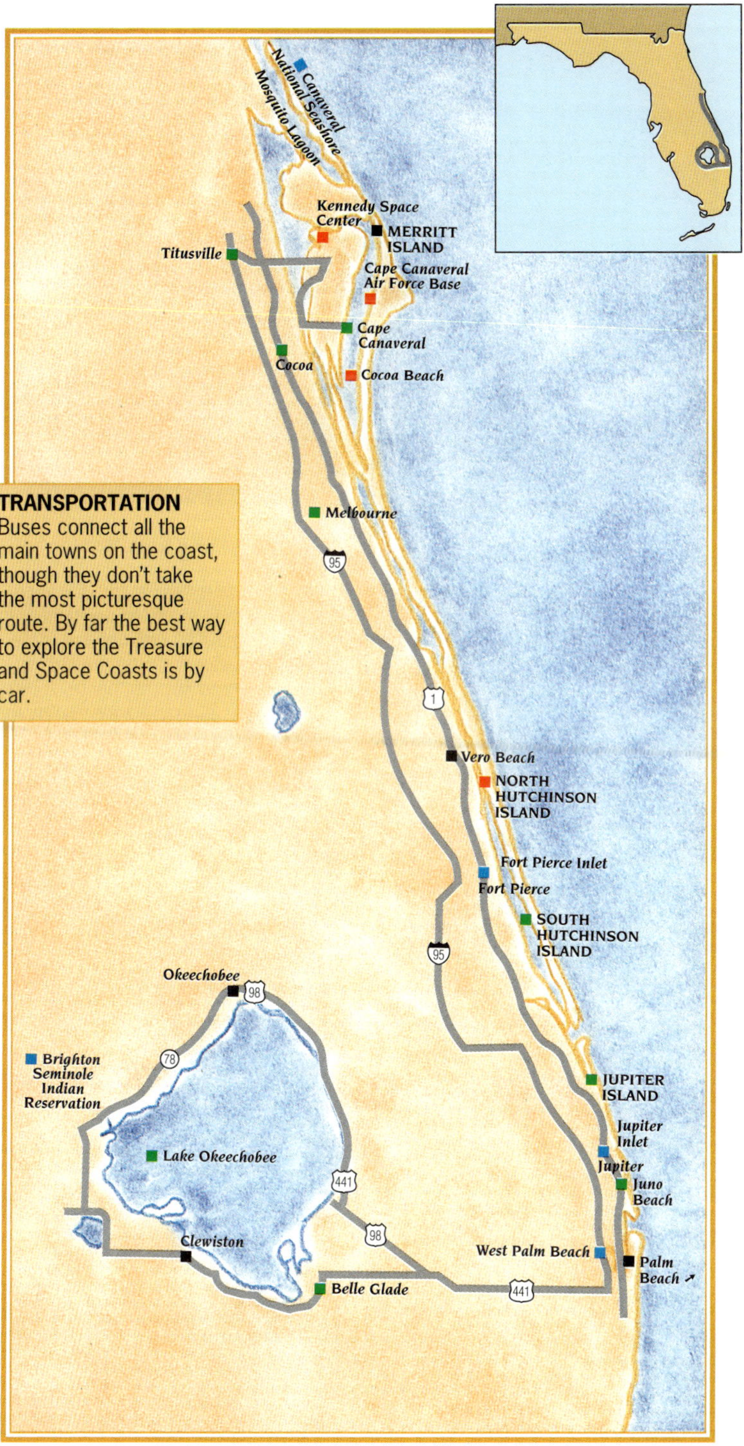

TRANSPORTATION
Buses connect all the main towns on the coast, though they don't take the most picturesque route. By far the best way to explore the Treasure and Space Coasts is by car.

• *Ron Jon Surf Shop, Cocoa Beach.*

SIGHTS & PLACES OF INTEREST

BELLE GLADE
See Lake Okeechobee, page 57.

BRIGHTON SEMINOLE INDIAN RESERVATION
See Lake Okeechobee, page 57.

CANAVERAL NATIONAL SEASHORE
See Merritt Island, page 56.

CAPE CANAVERAL AIR FORCE BASE
See Kennedy Space Centre, page 55.

COCOA
10 miles NW of Melbourne on Rt 1. The name of this spot may conjure up visions of coconut palms fringing a sandy beach, but the reality is rather different. Cocoa began life in 1882, when it was called Indian River. The locals must have been a difficult bunch, because the postal authorities eventually decided they wouldn't deliver any more letters here. Reason: the name of the town was "too long." (One wonders what they made of Apalachicola and Tallahassee.) A meeting was called at the local store. Could anyone suggest a new and shorter name? Everyone coughed and kicked their heels for a while, until someone noticed that postal workers had just brought in a consignment of cocoa (labeled to this effect). If they couldn't manage Indian River, it sure looked as if they could manage Cocoa. Everyone agreed, and the name stuck.

There's not much to see here – and most visitors head on to the delights of **Cocoa Beach**, 6 miles west of town on the barrier island (see below). But if you do find yourself in Cocoa, try a stroll along the pleasant flower-lined streets of **Cocoa Village**, which has a thriving artistic community and a friendly atmosphere.

COCOA BEACH 🛏 ✕
Some 15 miles N of Melbourne on Rt A1A. A pleasant seaside spot on the barrier island just south of the Kennedy Space Center. This is your best base for visiting the Space Center and the Merritt Island Wildlife Refuge. It also has some of the best **surfing** in Florida. The main focus of interest is the Ron Jon Surf Shop at 4151 Atlantic Avenue, which caters to surfers 24 hours a day. A visit here is a major experience for all aspiring beach bums. Even the unconverted

• *Fort Pierce store sign, advertising local citrus fruit.*

can rent a surfboard here for $8 a day.

If after this you still remain unconverted, you can always try fishing from Canaveral Pier, which juts out over 800 feet into the ocean. According to a fisherman I once met here, the largest grouper ever caught in Florida was landed at this pier. So there.

FORT PIERCE 🛏 ✕

On the coast 55 miles N of Palm Beach. When you pick up a grapefruit labeled Indian River at your local supermarket, this is where it comes from. The Intracoastal Waterway is called Indian River at this point, and inland is one of Florida's main citrus exporting regions.

Fort Pierce began as a military settlement in 1883. A few years later some soldiers from the fort set out west into the swamps to hack out the first trail across Florida. After swinging their machetes through the mangroves and providing hearty dinners for millions of mosquitoes, they finally emerged on the west coast at Tampa Bay, having created the Capron Trail.

The main town of Fort Pierce, which is on the mainland, is largely commercial. (Recently, it's also become a big player in the crime leagues, though steps are being taken to remedy this.) However, there are a few points of interest.

Down on Indian River Drive (overlooking the Intracoastal Waterway north of downtown), you can see some fine old **wooden houses** put up by early settlers around a century ago.

Four miles north of downtown at 5600 Old Dixie Highway (Rt A1A) is the **Harbor Branch Oceanography Institution**, *open 10 am-4 pm Mon-Fri; entry*

THE WALKING CATFISH

A local curiosity which can sometimes be spotted along this part of the coast.

There are more than 2,500 different species of catfish, all of which have the distinctive cats' whiskers trailing from their mouths. Notable members of the breed include the upside down catfish, the electric catfish (capable of delivering 450 volts, when angry), the banjo catfish (appearance, rather than sound) and the beguilingly invisible glass catfish. But none of these compare with the celebrated walking catfish (*Clarias batrachus*), which originates in the Mekong River in Southeast Asia.

A quarter of a century ago, a number of these fish managed to escape from a fish tank where they were being kept in Boca Raton, just down the coast. Eluding the attention of the state troopers, the illegal immigrants headed north in the direction of Rt 1. They then laid low for a while, with little else to do but breed. After this they spread out across the coast, and started integrating into the community.

The walking catfish has gills which enable it to breathe out of water. It propels itself along the ground with its pectoral fins, and is said to be particularly keen on well-watered motel lawns, but not so keen on the chlorine-filled pools beside them. When in shallow water, it sometimes stands and raises its head above the surface, giving the appeance of a small, slightly fishy walrus. The walking catfish is a scavenger, eating animal as well as vegetable matter. Despite this indiscriminate diet, it is much favored by local pelicans, who continue to achieve a measure of success where immigration control failed.

• *Harbor Branch Oceanographic Institution, Fort Pierce.*

$3; *tel.* 407 465 2400 *for details of guided tours.* This is one of the world's finest deep-sea research centers, with displays featuring all kinds of specimens from the silent depths, as well as some fascinating videos taken from the underwater pressure chambers. The tour takes you aboard one of their vessels, as well as explaining the life lived by the creatures that crawl the ocean floor. Pay attention; for as your guide will tell you, these unlovely creatures may well be the ultimate goal of evolution – all that survives after we've fouled up the planet.

Out on the two barrier islands you'll find a pleasant resort atmosphere. This area hasn't suffered so much from Florida's mania for overdevelopment, and it retains a pleasant, laid-back ambience. **North Hutchinson Island** is divided from **South Hutchinson Island** by the Fort Pierce Inlet. On the northern shores of the inlet, you'll find the **Fort Pierce Inlet State Recreation Area,** *open 8 am-sunset; entry* $3.25 *per car.* This is a favorite spot with local surfers – while those who work for a living tend to take over on the weekends with picnics.

A mile or so north is the 600-acre **Jack Island Wildlife Refuge**, which is reached by a footbridge. The main features here are **The Marsh Rabbit Trail**, a mile-long boardwalk through the mangrove swamp, and a 30-foot observation tower. Apart from the usual greedy pelicans, you'll see some rare and statuesque herons who demonstrate how fishing can be done with decorum.

Also at the southern end of North Hutchinson Island is the **Elliott Museum**. This is at 825 North East Ocean Boulevard, Stuart; *open* 11 *am*-4 *pm daily; entry* $3.50. The museum was built in 1961 to commemorate the inventor Sterling Elliott, the man who gave us the four-wheel bicycle. The varied collection here includes a superb display of vintage bicycles, a number of great old motorcycles and some classic cars.

Also on North Hutchinson Island is

• *Below and opposite: vehicles in Elliot Museum, Fort Pierce.*

the famous **UDT-SEAL Museum**, at Pepper Park on Rt A1A, *open 10 am-4 pm Tues-Sat, Sun afternoon only; entry* $2. This museum is dedicated to the U.S. Navy's Underwater Demolition Teams (UDT) and their modern successors the Sea Air Land units (SEAL). During the Second World War, the navy trained its UDTs here on the shores of Hutchinson Island, and you can see exhibits which explain many of their subsequent daring exploits on the Normandy Beaches and in the Korean War. They were on hand to ensure the safety of the first returning spacecraft on their splashdowns, and also apparently to make sure they weren't nabbed by any passing Russian submarine. The museum was vastly expanded in 1993, allegedly in response to demands about the precise nature of the clandestine operations on which SEALs had spent their vastly expanded budget. The new exhibits account for further heroic undercover operations from the past, though what exactly the *present* budget is being spent on is anybody's guess.

HUTCHINSON ISLAND, NORTH AND SOUTH

See Fort Pierce, page 50.

JUNO BEACH

Some 15 miles N of West Palm Beach on Rt A1A. Nowadays, Miami sprawls over most of Dade County, but a hundred years ago it was different. In those days Dade County stretched all the way from the tip of Florida to over half way up the east coast. When Dade County was in its prime, Juno Beach was the county administrative center, and no one (except the tax department) had even heard of Miami.

Today, Juno Beach has just a couple of thousand permanent residents, many of whom are retired and spend all day hitting golf balls. Even the actual beach here looks something like a large, long bunker. Walk down one of the paths leading from Rt A1A, and you'll often find the beach pleasantly deserted, even in season.

JUPITER

About 15 miles N of Palm Beach. Flagler's railway skirted around this part of the coast, which meant that it remained untouched for many years – and was then developed unobtrusively, in part by millionaires who found Palm Beach "too damn noisy." A local judge once pronounced: "The town doesn't have what many others have, but many others would be better off if they had more of what this town has and wants to keep – seclusion, solitude and tranquility."

The town's most famous resident is Burt Reynolds. At the height of his fame, a couple of decades ago, he founded the local **Jupiter Theater**, which is now one of the best in the state. Reynolds often appears here himself. Burt's father was once sheriff, and last I heard was still running the **Burt Reynolds Ranch Tack and Feed Store** at Jupiter Farms Road. Burt also owns the **Backstage** Restaurant on Indiantown Road, where he can occasionally be seen living it up with his stellar pals.

On the north side of Jupiter Inlet, there's an old **red lighthouse**, which rises to over 100 feet. In 1870, the keeper of this lighthouse was the only white man living on this entire stretch of coast.

The only other sight of interest here is:

Loxahatchee Historical Museum, *Burt Reynolds Park, off Rt 1.* It's a genuinely local museum, with a wide range of exhibits covering such items as Flagler's railway, shipwrecks and early Seminole Indian life. Further displays range from the sublime (old photos) to Burt Reynolds' boots.

JUPITER ISLAND

Facing the ocean, N of Jupiter. From here on north, the endless line of high-rise condos and hotels lining the beach begins to thin out. The sea views from Rt 707 as it runs along the island are particularly stunning. Early in the morning on the beach you can see the pelicans skimming the waves, and further offshore you can often see dolphins swimming in the Gulf Stream.

On the way up Rt 707, you pass **Blowing Rocks Preserve**. If you're here at high tide, you can see the explosions of spray bursting through the blowholes in the limestone – otherwise, it's just a disappointing gurgle.

KENNEDY SPACE CENTER

About 20 miles N of Melbourne. Reached via Rt 405 from Titusville, or via Rt 3, which branches north off Rt A1A *between* Cocoa *and* Cocoa Beach/Cape Canaveral.

When human beings end up living in space, this will be the most important site on the Solar System Tourist Trail. At present, it's only the 20thC's most advanced historic site.

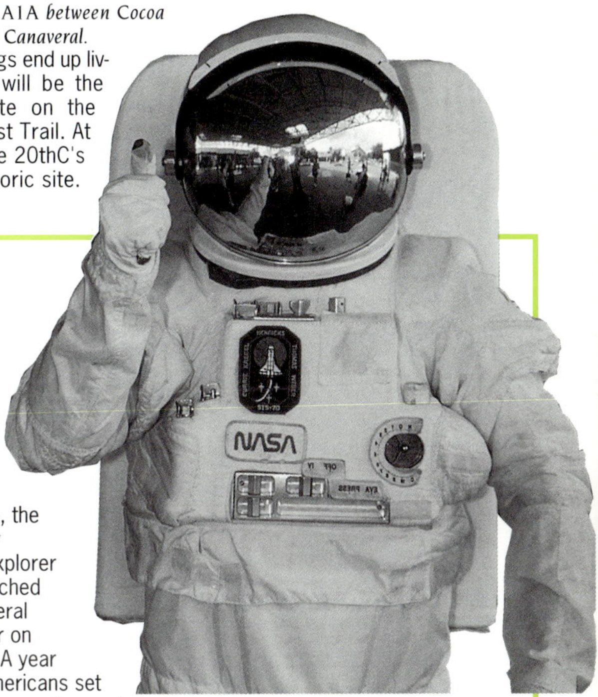

SPACE EXPLORATION

The first satellite launched into space was Sputnik 1, put up by the Russians on October 4, 1957. Stung by this surprise coup, the Americans quickly responded with Explorer 1, which was launched from Cape Canaveral three months later on January 1, 1958. A year afterwards the Americans set up the National Aeronautics and Space Administration (NASA). But this didn't stop the Russians from achieving another great triumph when they put the first person into space (Yuri Gagarin) on April 12, 1961. A month later President Kennedy announced America's intention to "achieve the goal, before the decade is out, of landing a man on the moon and returning him safely to earth." The Space Race was on – in earnest.

The first manned moon landing occurred on July 20, 1969, when Neil Armstrong made his "giant leap for mankind." The arrival of the 1970s saw a giant leap in the cost of space exploration, and many began to question the benefit of the entire exercise. (Billions of dollars for moon rocks, a new kind of shiny insulating foil, and photos of the earth.)

NASA's budget was slashed, and from now on it had to abandon all hope of penetrating the economic stratosphere. The end result was the first reusable spaceship: the Space Shuttle. It was soon carrying out missions delivering satellites, and even carrying out a few on-site repairs. All went well until January 1986 when the Challenger Space Shuttle blew up on take-off, killing its entire crew. This spectacular disaster – the rocket unfurling into plumes of fire and smoke against the blue sky – brought home to millions, on TV screens throughout the world, the sheer heroism of space exploration. But the lesson was learnt: NASA's safety control needed work. The Space Shuttle program was put on hold.

Although the Space Shuttle program has since continued, and achieved such successes as the Hubble Deep Space Probe, more ambitious plans for manned space flight remain in question. A quarter of a century later, those early moon landings are now seen from a more sober perspective, and opinion remains divided regarding the ultimate value of these expensive and dangerous missions.

• ***Opposite: Space shuttle launch pad.***

Unless you believe in ghosts, this is the only place where human beings have departed from our world to another and returned to tell the tale. Yes, there's plenty of hype about the Kennedy Space Center but if your imagination is fired by sci-fact, you won't be disappointed.

You arrive at **Spaceport U.S.A (Visitor Center),** *open 9 am-sunset; entry free.* Get here as early as possible to avoid the crowds – over 1.5 million visitors come to the Space Center every year. You should allow at least a day to see everything.

First stop is the **museum**, which is out of this world in several senses. Here you can see a bit of the moon, enter the flight deck of a space shuttle, and see models of many historic spacecraft (including the Viking which went to Mars). Outside, there's a **Rocket Garden** which contains eight of America's modern totem poles.

At the nearby **Galaxy Theater** they have two separate cinemas showing IMAX films on giant screens over five stories high. One shows the astronauts training, then lifting off into space, flying on missions, and returning to earth. The other features Spaceship Earth the way visiting Martians might view it. Here you can also enter a mock-up of the space station which will be orbiting the earth by the end of the century.

Now it's time to take the tour. The two-hour **Red Tour** is the best one to start with. This takes you to the simulated launch control, where the crews learn such vital details as which way to point the rocket, which buttons *not* to push, and so forth. You also visit the launch pads, get a chance to see an actual Apollo moon rocket, a monster Saturn V rocket, and visit the **Vehicle Assembly Building** – which is over 50 stories high and encloses one of the world's largest confined spaces.

If all this isn't enough, you can then try the **Blue Tour**. This also lasts two hours, and takes you to the **Cape Canaveral Air Force Base**. This is where America's first satellites were launched, where the first astronauts blasted off into space, and the site of the first Mission Control.

The films at the Galaxy Theater cost $4 each, and the tours cost $7 each. If your visit coincides with an actual launch, you can reserve free tickets by calling 407 452 2121. For details of future launches, phone 1 800 SHUTTLE.

MELBOURNE

Some 45 miles N of Fort Pierce, on Rt 1. A largish town of little tourist interest, Melbourne is occupied mainly by workers from the Kennedy Space Center. However, if you're here around the full moon during the height of summer, head for the beaches south of the city, where you can witness the eerie sight of huge **loggerhead turtles** coming ashore under cover of darkness to lay their eggs. They dig a hole in the sand and bury hundreds of tiny eggs, just as they've been doing at this spot since pre-historic times. Some of the turtles weigh over 500 pounds, and this is the only time they come ashore. Two months later the young hatch, no bigger than your palm, and begin their first crawling steps towards the sea. A large number never make it into the ocean depths. Seagulls and waiting fish pick them off – but they're now protected from human predators by federal law.

Another curious natural sight which you can observe in Melbourne is **manatees**. These pleasant, slothful creatures can sometimes be seen drifting through the water from the boardwalk at Crane Creek. According to historians, these were the creatures sailors originally mistook for mermaids.

AN UNSOLVED MYSTERY

At the Sebastian Inlet, near the McLarty Treasure Museum, there is an ancient Indian mound. This was once part of a settlement inhabited by the Ais, a tribe which is now extinct. Documents recently discovered in the Spanish national archives record that in the 16thC a French ship picked up two Spanish sailors on this stretch of coast. The sailors said they had been living in Florida amongst the Indians for many years. They claimed to be the last survivors of a crew which was shipwrecked on the coast in 1562. Many historians dismiss this story as a myth. (If it were true, this would mean that there were Europeans living on this stretch of coast three years before the founding of St Augustine.)

However, archaeologists are not so sure. They believe that the Indian mound at Sebastian Inlet may contain the skeletons of some of these early European arrivals who never survived to tell the tale. In support of their belief they point to the hitherto unexplained existence of a cross made out of conch shells, which was found on the grave of an early Ais chief. The archaeologists speculate that the chief may well have learned about Christianity from his shipwrecked Spanish guests.

MERRITT ISLAND

E across Indian River from Titusville on Rt 406. Merritt Island is that land of contrasts no real travel guide should be without.

On **Merritt Island National Wildlife Refuge** the natural world coexists with the aseptic technology of the Kennedy Space Center (see separate entry, page 52. The 200-square-mile wildlife refuge occupies the northern end of Merritt Island (open 8 am to 4.30 pm daily, closed Sundays April to October; entry free). Nature reigns supreme – and on the whole it's not half as beautiful as a space rocket on a launch pad. **Mosquito Lagoon** means what it says.

Other parts of the refuge contain uninviting swamp, salt marshes, slimy estuaries and clumps of flatwood and hardwood. However, its inhabitants are far more varied and colorful than any space technocrats. Bald eagles glide through the air, armadillos scuttle into the undergrowth, and manatees sway slowly through the sea. Without the example of the birds, there would have been no Space Center – and it's fitting that this wildlife refuge plays host to literally hundreds of different species. Some migrate to this spot from as far away as the Arctic and Latin America. Be sure to bring your binoculars (as well as your mosquito repellent).

There are some interesting walking trails into the refuge. For details, see the map that you can pick up at the visitor center. This is in mid-island, at the southern boundary of the park.

Across the other side of Mosquito Lagoon, and facing the ocean, is the **Canaveral National Seashore**, which has mile upon mile of sandy beach. This is great beachcombing territory, though be careful about swimming when the surf is up, as the offshore tides can be strong.

MOSQUITO LAGOON
See Merritt Island, page 56.

PALM BEACH
See Local Explorations: 2, page 184.

TITUSVILLE
About 33 miles N of Melbourne on Rt 1. Has views across the Indian River to the Space Center, but there's no other reason to stop here.

DETOUR – **LAKE OKEECHOBEE**
Drive west from West Palm Beach on Rt 98. After 20 miles of monotonous, straight road through the flat swamp, keep northwest on Rt 98 for another 17 miles and you come to the lake.

Okeechobee is the second largest freshwater lake in the United States (after Michigan). It covers over 750 square miles, but for most of this it's not much more than 10 feet deep. This is the water that drains out south through the swamps of the Everglades after the summer rainy season. However, the millennia-old natural process is at present under threat because too much water is being diverted from the lake for irrigation. The environmentalists and the local farmers are at loggerheads. Which should have priority – the booming citrus business upon which Florida depends, or the vast natural wilderness of the Everglades which attracts the tourists, upon which Florida also depends?

The long drive to Okeechobee takes you through mile upon mile of flat wilderness swamp covered in high grass. And your arrival at the lakeside is hardly promising. The lake may be almost 30 miles across at this point (you can't see the far shore), but the near shore is usually little more than a mud flat. Roads in either direction follow the shores of the lake.

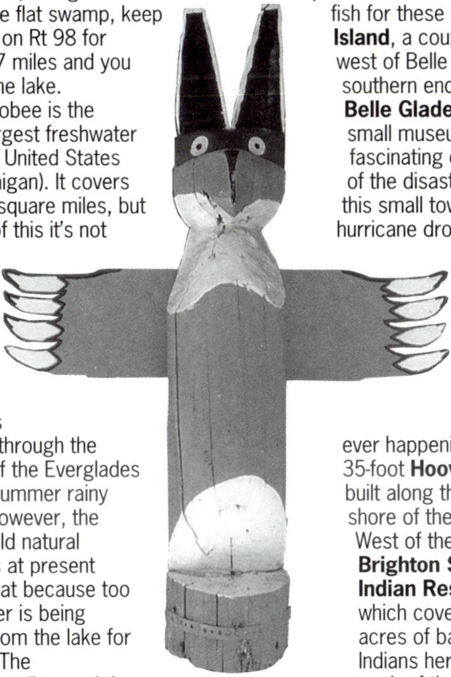

The lake itself is a well known fishing center, the best catches being large-mouth bass and speckled perch. One of the best places to fish for these is **Torrey Island**, a couple of miles west of Belle Glade, at the southern end of the lake.

Belle Glade is home to a small museum, containing fascinating documentation of the disaster which struck this small town in 1928. A hurricane drove the waters of the lake ashore with such force that 2,000 people lost their lives.

To prevent this ever happening again, the 35-foot **Hoover Dike** was built along the southern shore of the lake.

West of the lake is the **Brighton Seminole Indian Reservation**, which covers over 35,000 acres of bare prairie. The Indians here have given up much of their traditional way of life, but you can buy examples of genuine native American handicraft on sale at the roadside.

The southern shores of the lake – between Belle Glade, Clewiston and Moore Haven – are covered with sugar plantations. Over half the sugar produced in America is grown here, turning in huge profits for the U.S. Sugar Corporation. Sugar cane harvesting is a tough and difficult business. During the harvest season (April to November) thousands of Jamaicans are imported to do the work.

For Palmdale, home of the famous Gatorama, see Local Explorations: 1, page 172.

• *Driftwood Inn, Vero Beach.*

VERO BEACH

On the coast 16 miles N of Fort Pierce; open 10 am-4 pm daily; entry $1. Vero Beach has just 35,000 year-round inhabitants, and the majority of these are well-heeled retirees. This makes for a peaceful, civilized atmosphere. Many of the roads are tree-lined, and the beaches are great – but don't come here looking for a wild time.

There are a couple of local sights worth seeing. The **McLarty Treasure Museum** at *13180 North Rt A1A, 10 miles north at Sebastian*, owes its existence to a violent hurricane which took place in 1715. The hurricane drove a fleet of Spanish treasure ships into shallow water off the sands, where all of them were wrecked. For some reason, the salvage experts who arrived on the scene decided against placing their finds in a museum. So instead, we are forced to make do with counterfeits. Even so, the exhibits are fascinating. This is what treasure was all about, in the days when treasure *was* treasure.

No trip to Vero Beach would be complete without a visit to its famous **Driftwood Inn** at *3150 Ocean Drive*. This unusual structure was put up in the 1930s by globe-trotter Waldo Sexton. It was constructed of driftwood, local cypress logs and all kinds of exotic material Sexton picked up on his travels. He intended the place as his home, but people kept arriving on the doorstep and asking if it was possible to rent a room – so he turned it into a hotel. It's now been expanded into a resort. See Recommended Hotels, page 59.

WEST PALM BEACH ×

On the mainland, opposite Palm Beach. West Palm Beach was originally the servants' quarters for the staff of Flagler's vast luxury hotels on Palm Beach. It still retains a certain humble quality, despite recent efforts to gentrify the place. So what's in it for you? Less expensive accommodation, for a start – also restaurants where you can afford to eat. And there have been some spin-offs from its chic neighbor, which means that West Palm Beach has a few more interesting sights than you might expect.

Norton Art Gallery

1451 South Olive Avenue; open 10 am-5 pm Tues to Sat, Sun afternoons only; expected donation, $5. Here you'll find a respectable collection of modern European Masters, ranging from the Impressionists to the mid-20thC, when this species became extinct. Apart from lapses of taste in the form of Renoir and Dufy, there are some excellent works by Gauguin, Picasso, Matisse *et al*. There's also a *really* interesting modern American collection, ranging from Winslow Homer, through Pollock and Tobey, to the present.

RECOMMENDED HOTELS

COCOA BEACH

Cocoa Beach has three seasons: height of summer, a brief winter season (February), and another during every space shuttle launch. At other times prices shrink considerably. For a real bargain, try:

Econo Lodge, $-$$; *5500 North Atlantic Avenue, Cocoa Beach 32931; tel. 1 800 446 6900; no cards.*

Perfect for surfers. It's basic, friendly and near the beach.

Those who aspire to a higher level of culture should try:

Royal Mansions Resort, $$-$$$; *8600 Ridgewood Avenue, Cape Canaveral 32920; tel. 407 784 8484; most major cards.*

This is, in fact, a couple of miles north of Cocoa Beach, nearer to the air force base and Space Center. It has a superb stretch of shorefront as well as a heated pool. Accommodation in villas with patios.

FORT PIERCE

Harbor Light Inn, $$-$$$; *1160 Seaway Drive, Hutchinson Island 34949; tel. 407 468 3555; all major cards.*

Great waterway spot with swimming pool and sun deck. Many rooms have fine views out over Indian River.

Also on Hutchinson Island and close to the water is:

Dockside Inn, $-$$; *1152 Seaway Drive; tel. 407 461 4824; no cards.*

Friendly spot with basic accommodations. If it's full, there are several others in the same price range further along Seaway Drive.

OKEECHOBEE

The best place to stay is at one of the fishing camps on Torrey Island, a couple of miles west of Belle Glade.

J-Mark Fish Camp, $; *Rt 717, Torrey Island; tel. 407 996 6322; no cards.*

Camping site, which also has a number of motel-type rooms. Book ahead for weekends.

VERO BEACH

Driftwood Resort, $$-$$$; *3150 Ocean Drive, Vero Beach 32963; tel. 407 231 0550; cards AE, MC V.*

A local landmark. The original hotel was built out of driftwood and bric-a-brac in the 1930s by traveler Waldo Sexton. Now it's been considerably expanded and has more than 100 rooms. Despite this, much of the original ambience has been retained, with most of the rooms having their own distinctive individual decoration.

WEST PALM BEACH

Although accommodation is nowhere near as expensive as across the water in Palm Beach, hotels still tend to be pricier than you'd expect. By far the best reasonably priced overnight stop is:

Hibiscus House, $$; *501 30th Street, West Palm Beach 33407; tel. (407) 863 5633; cards AE, MC, V.*

New England-type bed-and-breakfast, with fairly standard accommodations. Just eight rooms (so be sure to book ahead), each named after its color scheme. After a day's traveling, my partner surrendered to the soothing properties of the Peach Room.
Great outside breakfasts in the gazebo.

Otherwise, try the more conveniently situated:

Parkview Motor Lodge, $$; *4710 South Dixie Highway (Rt 1), West Palm Beach 33407; tel. 1 800 545 1520; no cards.*

Friendly welcome, and the usual range of amenities.

This was once the collection of Chicago industrialist Ralph H. Norton. (And even now there are said to be houses across the water in Palm Beach which have private collections almost as good as this.)

No trip to the Palm Beach area would be complete without a visit to:

Palm Beach Polo and Country Club
13198 *Forest Hills Boulevard; tickets from* $6; *for a schedule of events, tel.* 407 793 1440. Games are played here every Sunday during the winter season (December to April).

The big event of the year is the $100,000 World Cup. Polo is an exciting game to watch, but you'll have just as much fun watching the spectators. Prince Charles has played here, although nowadays you're more likely to see Dustin Hoffman or Silvester Stallone. Bring your binoculars and a champagne picnic.

More exotic species can be seen at:

Dreher Park Zoo
1301 *Summit Boulevard; open* 9 *am*-5 *pm daily; entry* $10. The zoo stretches over 22 acres of parkland, and contains more than a hundred different kinds of animals. There's also a petting zoo for the very young.

If you prefer to see animals in a more natural setting, head for:

Lion Safari Country
About 18 *miles* W *of* West Palm Beach *on* Rt 98 *for* Lake Okeechobee; *open* 9.30 *am*-4.30 *pm; entry* $12. This 500-acre park contains elephants, giraffes, zebras, ostriches, lions and you (in your car, with the windows shut tight). The chimps are often particularly interested in this species which has wheels instead of legs. Be sure to bring your camera.

Palm Beach County is renowned for its **golf courses**. There are now no fewer

RECOMMENDED RESTAURANTS

COCOA BEACH
The place in Cocoa Beach is:

Herbie K's Diner, $-$$; 2080 *North Atlantic Avenue, Cocoa Beach; tel.* 407 783 6740; *all major cards.*

The 1950s are alive and kicking at Herbie K's. This rock 'n' roll diner serves it like it really was. "Jen-you-wine" burgers and ice-cream desserts like cartoon dreamscapes. Open all day for hot cats, and all night for cool ones. Four am is the time for the best over-the-top sundae in the world (with a cherry on top) after your head-clearing dip in the ocean. If you think you know all about Buddy Holly, you'll change your mind after you've spoken to your waitress.

Those who wish to remain on planet earth should try:

The Pier House, $-$$; *The Pier, Cocoa Beach; tel.* 407 783 7549; *no cards.*

At this spot tomorrow's menu is alive and swimming just a few feet beneath your table. The setting is romantic, the seafood superb, and the service extremely knowledgeable.

FORT PIERCE
The best place for an inexpensive bite in the town of Fort Pierce is:

Captain's Galley, $-$$; 827 *North Indian River Drive, Fort Pierce; tel.* 407 466 8495; *cards* MC, V.

Great breakfasts, bountiful burgers and scintillating seafood suppers – all at prices to whet the appetite. A friendly spot, popular with the locals.

Over on Hutchinson Island, try:

Cafe Coconuts, $-$$; 4304 *North East Ocean Boulevard, Hutchinson Island; tel.* 407 225 6006; *cards* MC, V.

Large, popular restaurant, justly renowned for its steaks, seafood and salads. Pastel-toned decoration and wide-ranging menu with something to suit all tastes.

For something special, try:

Mangrove Mattie's, $$; 1640 *Seaway Drive, Fort Pierce; tel.* 407 466 1044; *all major cards.*

This one is right on the Fort Pierce Inlet, with great views out over the water. Not surprisingly, their seafood is excellent, but they also do good steaks. Come early, and you can try

than 150 in the area, and many of them are superb. Unfortunately, most of them are strictly members only. However, several hotels in the area have formed a **Golf-A-Round** scheme. This enables guests to play at a number of courses free of charge out of season (ie from late April to the end of November). For details phone 407 471 3995.

South Florida Science Museum
4801 Dreher Trail North; open 10 am-5 pm daily; entry $5. User-friendly modern museum, with all kinds of hands-on displays. Learn about sub-atomic particles, the universe and all that, without even noticing that you're being educated. The kids love it. There's also a great laser show, planetarium and observatory.

For the island of Palm Beach itself, see Local Explorations: 2, page 184.

• *Lion Safari Country, West Palm Beach.*

their tapas-style bites and a glass of wine from 4.30 to 6 pm – a great way to end the day, and prepare yourself for the rigors of the night.

JUPITER

Backstage, $$$; *1061 Indiantown Road, Jupiter; tel.* 407 747 9533; *no cards.*

This is the spot where Burt Reynolds entertains his big name pals. He doesn't like to disappoint them, so he owns the place. From this it seems that Burt likes his grub sophisticated, American-Continental and expensive. Pictures of the big man all over the walls, in case you miss him.

Those who want a real meal at realistic prices should try:

Log Cabin Restaurant, $-$$; 631 *North* Rt A1A, *Jupiter; tel.* 407 746 6877; *all major cards.*

After a hard day on the beach, you and your starving family can look upon this one as a challenge. The all-American grub comes in portions that might even defeat the Mongol hordes you've brought with you (doggy bags are supplied). Any true competitor will be sure to have a go at the all-you-can-eat special. Others will enjoy gazing at the bikes and old clocks hanging from the ceiling.

WEST PALM BEACH

Narcissus, $-$$; 200 *Clematis Street, West Palm Beach; tel.* 407 659 1888; *cards* AE, MC, V.

Great for a lunchtime snack outside under one of the umbrellas (try the falafel). At night it becomes the best jazz cafe in town. If you're on a budget, try dining between 5 and 7 pm, which covers the last two hours of the happy hour (everything half price) and the first two hours of jazz.

For lower decibel dining, try:

Cafe Prospect, $$; 3111 *South Dixie Highway, West Palm Beach; tel.* 407 832 5952; *cards* MC, V.

A real find, serving great European and American cuisine in a relaxed and friendly atmosphere. The day's menu is chalked up on the board bistro-style, and usually features at least one imaginative fish dish and a number of well-cooked classics. Good for a midday sandwich, or something more substantial with wine in the evening.

Southern Florida

Between Miami and Flamingo
Miami South to the Everglades

70 miles; map Hallwag Florida

This region contains one of America's greatest sights – the Everglades. It also has a host of smaller sights that appeal to everyone – from gardeners to animal lovers, from railway buffs to architecture enthusiasts.

The Everglades are one of nature's wonders. This vast unspoiled wilderness covers an area almost as large as Corsica. In its swampy terrain you can see alligators, the remains of old Indian settlements, and a vast array of birds, wildlife and subtropical vegetation. There are boat trips through the mangrove swamps, nature trails and some superb canoe trails through uncharted back country. You can easily drive to the Everglades from Miami in a day, but you should allow at least a couple of days to explore. Experienced canoeists may even want to spend a week canoeing the celebrated Wilderness Waterway, which covers more than a hundred miles from Flamingo up to Everglades City, passing through some of the finest scenery you'll find anywhere.

The other sights can all be reached on day trips from Miami. And indeed, this is your best base if you wish to explore this region. Don't miss the architectural delights of Coral Gables – the "Miami Riviera" built by George Merrick in a variety of Mediterranean styles. Romantics should head for the Coral Castle – the dream home built by a jilted lover. For animal lovers, there's the Monkey Jungle, the Parrot Jungle and the Metrozoo. And gardeners won't want to miss the Fairchild Tropical Garden or the Fruit and Spice Park.

BRIEF HISTORY OF FLORIDA

KEY DATES

First native Americans start settling in Florida	around 8000 BC
John Cabot sails along Florida coast	1498
Ponce de Léon lands in Florida	1513
Spain begins occupation of Florida	1562
Spain hands over Florida to Britain	1763
Florida returned to Spain	1783
First Seminole War	1817-18
Florida taken over by U.S.	1819
Second Seminole War	1829-1842
Florida becomes a state	1845
Outbreak of American Civil War	1861
Flagler extends his railway down east coast	late 1880s
Plant extends this railway down west coast	late 1880s
Broward becomes state governor, introducing reforms	1905
Flagler's railway reaches Key West	1912
Florida land boom collapses	1928
Railroad to Key West destroyed by hurricane	1935
Tourism tops 4.5 million visitors in a year	1950
Liberty City riots	1968
First manned launch from Cape Canaveral	1969
Walt Disney World opens in Orlando	1971
Hurricane Andrew devastates southern Florida	1992

Pre-history

The first American immigrants came from Asia. They are thought to have crossed the land bridge which joined Siberia to Alaska some 20,000 years ago. It took them another 10,000 years to get to Florida. These Paleo-Indians were hunter-gatherers, but around 5000 BC they settled down and began farming the land. A diet of high cholesterol bison steak was abandoned in favor of shellfish and seafood. This transformation may have been induced by the arrival of migrants from the south – modern experts have detected influences of South and Central American tribal culture. Around 2000 BC these Paleo-Indians began developing pottery skills, and 1,000 years later they were constructing primitive irrigation systems.

The Florida region was occupied by several distinct tribes. Among these were the Apalachee who occupied the Panhandle, the Timucuans who occupied central Florida, and the war-like Calusas who hunted up and down the southwestern coast. By the end of the 15thC it's estimated there were around 10,000 native Americans living in the Florida peninsula.

First European settlers

The first European to set eyes on Florida was almost certainly the Italian sailor John Cabot, who had been dispatched west by King Henry VII of England in 1498. Cabot never put ashore, but he put Florida on the map.

In 1513 the Spanish explorer Ponce de León arrived off the Florida Keys in search of the Fountain of Youth, which was said to be on an island called Bimini. He eventually put ashore near Cape Canaveral during the Spanish Festival of Flowers, Pascua Florida, and named his landfall Florida – "Land of Flowers". Eight years later, Ponce de León returned with 200 men to establish a colony, but was soon forced to leave by hostile native Americans. Further landings by the Spanish proved little more successful. In 1539, an expedition of 1,000 Spanish adventurers led by Hernando de Soto landed at Tampa Bay, and set off in search of gold. They found no gold, and de Soto lost his life on the expedition. But before they returned three years later the Spanish had covered thousands of miles; de Soto and his men reached as far north as the Smokey Mountains of North Carolina, and they were the first Europeans to cross the Mississippi.

After the Spanish had given up on Florida, a group of French Huguenots established a colony at Fort Caroline near the mouth of the St Johns River in 1562. Stung into action, the Spanish at once destroyed Fort Caroline, and founded a nearby settlement of their own – St Augustine, which was to become the earliest continuously inhabited European settlement in America.

St Augustine marked the beginning of the Spanish occupation of Florida. Various Franciscan missions were then established, with the aim of converting the native Americans. In 1586 Sir Francis Drake bombarded St Augustine, flattening the settlement – the start of English interest in the region. From then on, English ships frequently raided the coast for slaves, and English pirate ships preyed on the Spanish treasure galleons making their way up the coast from South America.

The 18th and early 19thC

The Spanish eventually handed over Florida to the British in 1763 in exchange for Havana. When the British were thrown out of America twenty years later after the War of Independence, Florida was returned to the Spanish. No one was particularly interested in the place. By now most of the aboriginal inhabitants had been wiped out by diseases from which they had no immunity, such as measles and the common cold.

The few remaining aboriginal inhabitants of Florida were now augmented by the arrival of native Americans, who had been dispossessed from their lands by American pioneer expansion to the north. These ragged fugitives were known collectively by the Spanish as Cimarrones (which means unruly runaways). This word was later corrupted into Seminoles.

Meanwhile, few Spanish were interested in settling this inhospitable territory, and large tracts of it were sold to American settlers. Relations between the Americans and the Seminoles quickly deteriorated, particularly in the border region. Whereupon the U.S. general Andrew Jackson took the law into his own hands, invaded Florida, and launched the First Seminole War (1817-18). Jackson issued an ultimatum to the Spanish: either they control the Indians, or hand over Florida to the United States. In 1819 the United States took over, and Jackson was sworn in as the first American governor of Florida.

The situation continued to deteriorate, and within a couple of years the Second Seminole War had broken out. In 1829 Jackson became president of the U.S. He soon began introducing legislation to dispossess the Indians of their lands throughout the eastern U.S. and to resettle them on reservations in the Midwest.

The beginnings of tourism

In Florida, Jackson's new laws only added fuel to the fire. The Seminoles took to guerrilla tactics, so the authorities invited their leader, Osceola, to peace talks in St Augustine – where he was immediately thrown into jail (where he later died).

The Americans then drove the Indians from the agricultural lands of the north into the southern swamps, often using bloodhounds to hunt them out. By 1842 the native Americans had been confined to the Everglades, and the Second Seminole War was over.

In 1845 the ravaged, impoverished territory of Florida became a state.

There followed a period of recuperation, with the railway arriving in the Panhandle and the population doubling to 60,000. But this prosperity was to a large extent achieved with slave labor, imported from the Deep South to work on the plantations. When the American Civil War broke out in 1861, Florida joined the southern Confederate states. Florida saw comparatively little fighting, but its coast was blockaded by the Union navy, ruining trade.

After the Yankee victory, the slaves were emancipated. But many of them had nowhere to go and were left simply roaming the countryside. On top of

after dark, and weren't allowed to swim anywhere near such spots as Palm Beach. Eventually, legal discrimination was abolished in the state, yet conditions for African Americans remained so bad that there were widespread urban riots in the late 1960s. The worst of these was in Liberty City (a district of Miami) during August 1968, an event which made headlines throughout the world.

By now the African Americans were not the only minority group. Since Castro had taken over Cuba in 1959, almost a third of a million Cubans had fled to the U.S. Many of these ended up in the greater Miami area, where Cubans continue to make up a large percentage of the population.

The Space Race had now begun in earnest, with NASA established at Cape Canaveral and supporting an entire space industry. All the investment and work came to fruition when Apollo XI landed the first person on the moon in 1969.

The arrival of Disney

Two years later it was the turn of creatures from another planet to arrive in Florida. The new arrivals set up shop in central Florida near a rural backwater called Orlando. The arrival of Walt Disney World from planet California transformed central Florida, making this region one of the world's top tourist destinations.

In the following decade a second region of Florida was transformed by the space business. Drug importing from South America became a major industry. Miami was soon sprouting spectacular high-rise buildings. South American dictators and mafia bosses voted Miami the best laundry in the business, and drug money flowed into the banks. Florida had not lost its flair where corruption was concerned.

But the biggest business of all in Florida is undeniably tourism. An astounding 25 percent of Florida's almost 12 million inhabitants now depend upon visitors to the state for their paychecks. Few states in the U.S. are so reliant on tourism.

This success story is not without its contradictions. Development may bring in more people, but it destroys what they come to Florida for in the first place. More marinas means less marine life. Meanwhile, the condos go up, and the water level in the Everglades continues to go down. Yet at the same time the gators thrive as never before, and the wildlife reserves grow larger and larger. As someone recently suggested, perhaps the only answer is to turn the entire state over to Walt Disney World.

• A *'tidy' sculpture sets visitors an example.*

TERMINOLOGY

The original inhabitants of the North American continent were called "Indians" by the first European arrivals. This was because these early European explorers thought they had arrived in China. Understandably, the so-called Indians take a dim view of this European logic. They prefer to be known as native Americans.

Purely for the purposes of avoiding confusion, these native Americans have sometimes been called Indians in the course of this book. Also, the word has been retained where it is in current usage, for example, as in Indian mounds, Mikosukee Indian Village, Paleo-Indians, Indian River, and so on. This is in no way intended to condone European lexical practices.

Central Florida

Between Orlando and Tampa
The Heart of Florida

20 miles; map Hallwag Florida

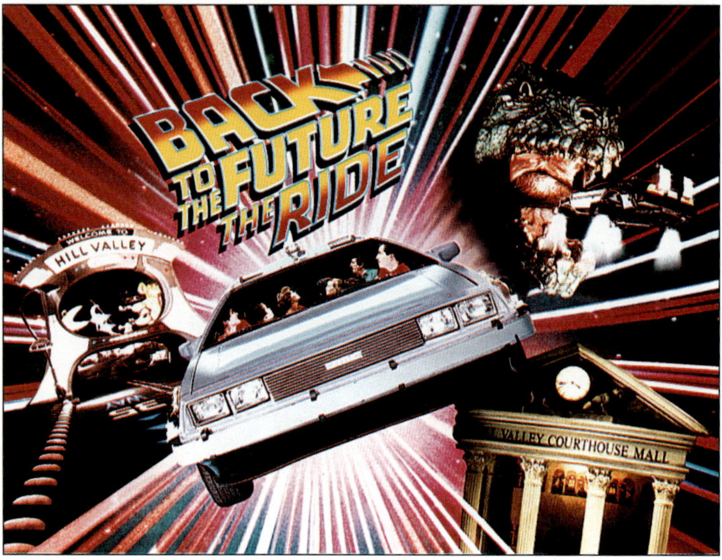

© Universal Studios 1996

This section is devoted to Orlando and its immediate environs. The major attraction is, of course, Walt Disney World, which may well be the main reason you've come to Florida in the first place. Walt Disney World is divided into three separate (and stupendous) theme parks: the Magic Kingdom (Mickey Mouse Disney), the Epcot (Disney Scienceland), and the Disney-MGM Studios (Disney Movieland). Each of these will take you at least a day to see, and in between you'll probably feel like letting off steam for the day at Disney's Typhoon Lagoon or Blizzard Beach. There are also water parks at Sea World and Wet'n'Wild.

Just down the road from Orlando is Kissimmee, which is still cowboy country. This provides a pleasant break from Disneymania, and also makes a (comparatively) inexpensive base.

If you've come on vacation with the kids to see Walt Disney World, and find yourself with time to explore further afield, try a visit to the Kennedy Space Center (see Florida Overall: 2), which is just 50 miles east of Orlando on the coast.

If you want to do justice to Orlando and all its many sights, you should allow at least a week. More than two weeks here could well do serious damage to your sanity, though the kids probably won't see it that way.

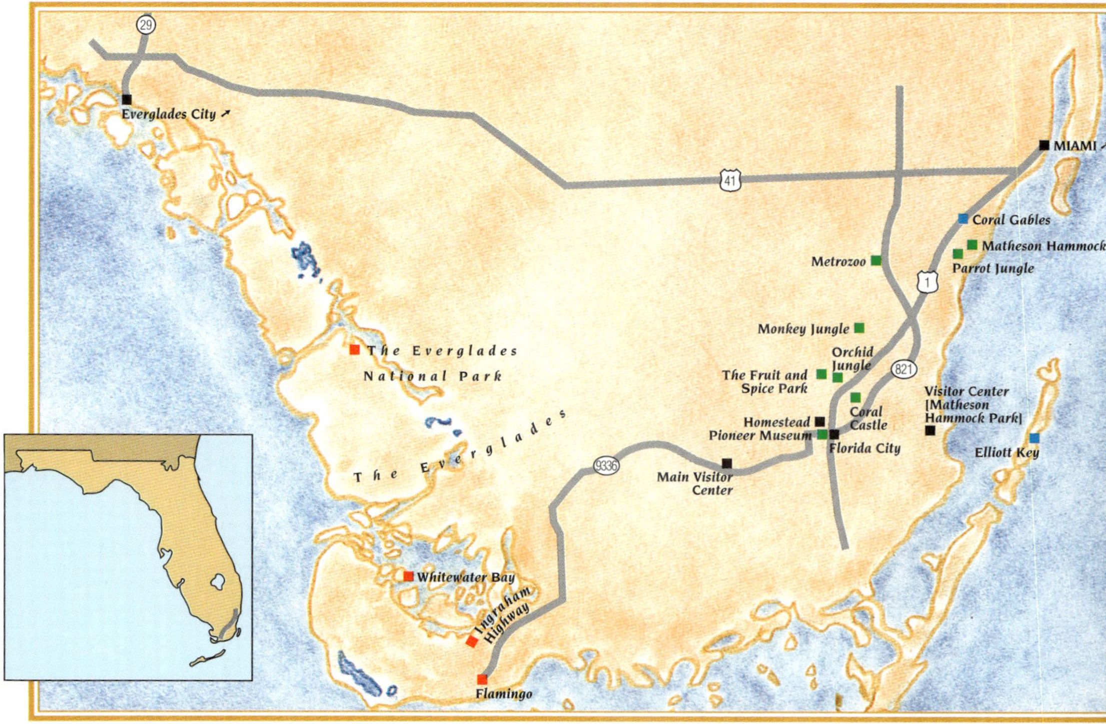

TRANSPORTATION
The only way to see this region is by car. There is no public transportation to the Everglades, though there are day trips from Miami which can be booked at any travel agent.

• *Coral Gables House.*

SIGHTS & PLACES OF INTEREST

BISCAYNE NATIONAL PARK

Head S on Florida's Turnpike Extension and at Homestead turn off for Canal Drive (328th Street). Drive as far as you can go, E, to the sea.

An underwater park where you can see the wonders of the coral reef – which include all kinds of exotic tropical creatures. There are glass-bottom boat tours, or you can rent snorkeling or scuba-diving equipment. But best of all is the **boat tour** which leaves from Convoy Point for **Elliott Key**, which is 6 miles out in the ocean. This long, narrow, remote key has a trail leading for miles through the woods, and a number of isolated beaches.

Before setting out for Biscayne National Park, be sure to phone the Visitor Center at 247 7275, for details of times and availability.

CORAL CASTLE

On Dixie Highway (Rt 1) 5 miles NE of Homestead at junction with 286th Street; open 9 am-5 pm daily; entry $8. A small monolithic castle, with a slightly Aztec appearance, whose romance is the equal of any in Europe.

In 1913, a 16-year-old Latvian called Edward Leedskalnin was jilted by his girlfriend. He left his Baltic home and began working his way around Europe, before taking ship across the Atlantic. After working his way around Canada and the U.S., he ended up buying an acre of land in Florida. But Edward still remained obsessed by the thought of the girl he had left behind in his native Latvia. On his acre of land he set to work building a dream castle for his distant beloved, using massive blocks of coral. He was entirely self-taught, and used homemade tools to carve the rocks into chairs and tables. Edward Leedskalnin was to spend 15 years – between 1925 and 1940 – on this task, and the result is an odd combination of the cumbersome and the delicate. Amongst the stone chairs (where Ed often sat reading) there are coral designs of the zodiac, and a 20-foot telescope. The castle even has a 9-ton gate, which is so well balanced that it can be opened and closed by hand. Ed always worked in secret, so no one knows quite how he managed to move the huge stones into place or carve his curious sculptures. He died here in 1951. According to a recent report, his beloved lived on in Latvia until she was well over 80, quite unaware of the dream castle which her jilted lover had spent half his life building for her.

CORAL GABLES 🛏 ✕

Strictly speaking, this is part of Miami, but it's several miles from downtown and has a distinct atmosphere of its own. Coral Gables is often called the "Miami Riviera," on account of its Mediterranean architecture. This is entirely due to one man – George Merrick.

The Merrick family moved to Florida at the turn of the century when George was 12. His father bought a 150-acre fruit farm at the site now occupied by Coral Gables. The farm prospered, and the Merricks built a grand mansion.

When George inherited his father's estate, he decided to cash in on the

Florida land boom. But this was to be no ordinary get-rich-quick scheme. George had big ideas, and he also had taste. He set about building a classy Mediterranean resort, even going so far as to pick the street names from maps of Europe and a Spanish dictionary. Grandiose gateways marked the entrance to the estate, and the drainage ditches were turned into a network of Venetian canals, complete with gondolas. He even created several distinct "villages," each with its own style. These included such Mediterranean spots as Chinese Village and Dutch South African Village.

The project was a huge success, and within five years he had sold nearly half the villas and mansions he had built. In doing so, he made almost $150 million. He then used $50 million of this to run an advertising campaign for his "City Beautiful." (Until recently this was the biggest advertising campaign ever launched; you can see some of the posters in Coral Gables City Hall.) Then the Florida property boom collapsed, and Merrick went bust. He left town and opened a fishing centre in the Keys. This, too, went bust after it was wiped off the map by a hurricane. But the indefatigable Merrick bounced back. He returned to Miami and ended up as the city postmaster, before dying in the early 1940s.

Merrick's legacy remains, in the form of modern Coral Gables. You can still see the entrances to the old Merrick estate. The most grandiose of these is the **Douglas Entrance**, complete with offices and artists' studios, at the junction of SW 8th Street and Douglas Road. It is said to have cost no less than a million dollars. Further inland at Granada Boulevard is the **Granada Entrance**, modeled on the gates of Granada in Spain. At 907 Coral Way, you can visit **Coral Gables House**, the mansion where George grew up, *open 1 am-4 pm Sun and Wed only; entry* $2. It is built of coral rock, and has gabled windows – the two features which gave the district its name.

Another Merrick legacy is the **Venetian Pool** at *2701 De Soto Boulevard, open 10 am-4.30 pm daily, longer in summer; entry* $4. This was once the quarry where Merrick excavated the stone for his houses, but he transformed what

HURRICANE ANDREW
The region south of Miami (South Dade County) was badly hit by Hurricane Andrew in August 1992. This devastated the agricultural area known as the "winter vegetable basket," which provides the entire U.S. with much of its winter strawberries, tomatoes, limes and avocados. Replanting will, in some cases, take years. Hurricane Andrew also struck Florida City and Homestead, where damage is still being repaired.

• *Venetian Pool, Coral Gables.*

• *Biltmore Hotel, Coral Gables.*

was an eyesore into a superb swimming pool, complete with grottoes, Venetian bridges and a sandy beach.

Merrick's grandest project (and for a while his grandest failure) was the **Biltmore Hotel** at the southern end of De Soto Boulevard. This was advertised as "the last word in the evolution of civilization." The architecture was suitably stupendous, with huge walls covered in murals, Italian marble staircases and that unmistakable atmosphere of millionaire megalomania. For the grand opening in 1926, the stars and society swells were shipped in on a specially hired train. Everyone, but everyone, stayed here. Johnny Weissmuller (the Olympic gold medalist and orginal Tarzan) was hired as the instructor for the olympic-sized swimming pool, and one guest used to have his ice flown in from the Rockies. It's *that* sort of place.

Inevitably, the hotel went into decline. But in 1983 it was bought out and a colossal $50 million remodeling project began. Not surprisingly, this bankrupted the firm involved. But in 1993 the Biltmore finally reopened, and over-the-top living once again became the order of the day. You can now take a "historical tour" of the building on Sundays. (From the lobby: 1.30 pm. 2.30 pm, 3.30 pm.) For further details, see Recommended Hotels.

ELLIOTT KEY

See Biscayne National Park, page 64.

THE EVERGLADES

The eastern entrance and Main Visitors Center is 12 miles W of Homestead on Rt 9336. Important: for information on the access to The Everglades via Rt 41 from the west, and parts of the area not described here such as Ten Thousand Islands and Big Cypress Swamp National Preserve, see Local Explorations: 3. The Everglades National Park was created in 1947 and covers almost 1 million acres at the southern tip of the Florida peninsula. That's larger than the state of Delaware.

The Everglades is mostly swamp and grasslands, fed by a river delta of sluggish waters filtering down from Lake Okeechobee in central Florida. The Indians called this river Pa-Hay-Okee, which means "the grassy waters." An early English explorer called it the River Glades, but someone copied it down wrong on the map as Ever Glades – and the name seemed so appropriate that it stuck.

The average depth of the water over the entire Everglades is little more than six inches, and its flow is barely discernable. For the most part it looks like an endless sea of sawgrass, with occasional "hammocks" (small islands with trees). Its estuarial coastline is rimmed with a forbidding barrier of mangrove trees, which act as a protection against sea storms.

It may not look like much at first sight, but this is one of the most exciting nature reserves in the world. Here, living in their natural state, you'll find

more than just the famous alligators (though there are quite enough of them). The coastal prairies, which dry out in the summer, are home to cacti, yucca and marsh rabbits. The channels abound with fish, and support otters, tree frogs, and herons. Indeed, the birds provide the most spectacular wild life. But be warned: in the summer (from May to October) there's a species

• *The waters of the Everglades, home to many species.*

even more numerous than the birds, and almost as frightening as the alligators – mosquitoes. Be sure to bring a large supply of mosquito repellent, or buy some at the shop in the visitors center.

The Everglades took more than five

million years to evolve, and the first human inhabitants probably arrived just over 2,000 years ago (about the same time Helen absconded from Ancient Greece to Troy). These early inhabitants of the Everglades were Calusa Indians, but their settlements were few and far between. The summer mosquitoes and the alligators made the area particularly inhospitable.

The first European to live in the Everglades was almost certainly a shipwrecked Spaniard named Hernando Escalante de Fontaneda. He stayed amongst the Indians, traveling from tribe to tribe, for 15 years or more. Finally he made it back to the civilization he had grown up in, where he dictated a brief and rather hazy account of his travels. This gives intriguing glimpses of life amongst the Calusa, Mayaimi and Tequesta Indians, a way of life which had continued for over a thousand years. Yet it was to last only a few more decades as the Europeans made increasingly aggressive inroads into Indian society.

• A *resident of the* Everglades.

Seminole Indians, retreating south, began settling in the Everglades at the end of the 18thC. Fifty years or so later, European fugitives from the law, outcasts and solitaries began establishing themselves on the shoreline, forming settlements at Everglades City and Flamingo.

It wasn't until the end of the 19thC that the first efforts were made to drain the Everglades, which until then had been looked upon as impenetrable swamp. In 1884 the governor of Florida, Napoleon Bonaparte Broward, started dredging the Miami Canal, which runs between Lake Okeechobee and Miami. This was the first of a network of canals. Even so, the manoeuvre failed to prevent severe flooding after the 1928 hurricane, which caused Lake Okeechobee to spill out over most of southern Florida. As a result, the lake was surrounded by the Hoover Dike in 1930, and a massive drainage scheme was started. Ironically, when a hurricane hit in 1947 accompanied by large-scale floods, this system of dikes and canals was thought to have been at least partly responsible.

Nowadays, the ever-increasing menace of pollution has begun to affect the Everglades. This, combined with the artificial canals and water control systems of southern Florida, has started to pose a dire threat. The delicate balance of water and nature is easily upset in such a region, and one conservationist I spoke to was convinced that the Everglades won't last long into the 21stC unless something is done at once. Apparently, it's not so much a matter of drastic measures, more just of making sure that the water levels are returned to their previous seasonal ebb and flow. This will allow the natural cycle of flora and fauna to re-establish itself over the whole area. The present area of the Everglades may look large enough on the map, but only a few centuries ago it occupied the whole of southern Florida (and much of northern Florida too).

Exploring the Everglades

At the eastern side you enter the Everglades on Rt 9336. From the **Main Visitor Center**, the **Ingraham Highway** leads 38 miles all the way down to Flamingo on the southwestern tip of the Florida peninsula. This is the only road leading through the national park. It has various attractions *en route*, and passes through eight different ecosystems – including sawgrass, mangrove thickets and a dwarf cypress forest. There are also several trails which lead off into the Everglades.

Two of the best trails start from the **Royal Palm Visitor Center**, which is just two miles inside the park. The **Anhinga Trail** leads you on a boardwalk along waters where you'll see alligators lying submerged (with only their

protruding eyes breaking the surface).

The **Gumbo Limbo Trail** leads through a hammock of Gumbo Limbo (hardwood trees) and typical subtropical terrain. These are both very short, and easy for anyone to walk, even when it's very hot. (Combined distance less than a mile.)

Further down the Ingraham Highway (the main road) you come to **Long Pine Key**, which has a 7-mile nature trail through pinelands. From the road you can also reach several ponds. **Mrazek** and **Coot Bay Ponds** are particularly interesting for migrant and wading birds, as is **Paurotis Pond**, which is fringed by rare paurotis palms that rise up to 30 feet. The **Mahogany Hammock Trail** takes you past some of the largest mahogany trees in North America. Look out for the colored snails which cling to their trunks, and the webs of the golden orb spiders. The **Noble Hammock Canoe Trail** leads you for miles through the mangroves. It is named after a legendary bootlegger who plied his trade in the Everglades. Other canoe trails, such as the **Hell's Bay Trail**, lead you on arduous journeys miles into virtually uncharted backcountry.

At the end of the Ingraham Highway, you come to Flamingo.

EVERGLADES CITY

See Local Explorations: 4, page 200.

• *Exploring Flamingo Bay.*

FLAMINGO 🛏 ✕

Not so long ago, this was a remote fishing settlement, accessible only by sea. The locals were an independent lot, many of whom had good reason to take up residence in a location far from the reach of the law. They supported themselves by hunting, fishing and shooting (occasionally at each other). The latter pastime was encouraged by hefty consumption of the main local product: moonshine whiskey. Finally a post office was established here, and the locals found themselves faced with a problem. Until then they hadn't got around to giving the place a name. They wanted to call their home town The End of the World, but this proved unacceptable to the postal authorities. So eventually they were persuaded to call the place Flamingo, after the local flocks of pink birds. Unfortunately, these weren't actually flamingoes; they were spoonbills, but by then it was too late. (Everyone still called them flamingoes anyway, so what the hell.)

The highway finally made it through the Everglades to Flamingo in 1922. This was the beginning of opportunity for Flamingo. Everyone expected a big rush to this remote spot. And there *was* a big rush – of locals packing their bags and heading up the road, now that they could at last get out.

• *Everglades tour.*

Flamingo collapsed in more ways than one. All the old buildings fell down. The ones you see now are all disappointingly contemporary. Nothing remains of the old off-the-map bootleggers' no-namesville. Today Flamingo caters purely for the tourists: there are now facilities for 200-plus motor campers, nearly a hundred tent sites, and over a hunded rooms at the Flamingo Inn (see Recommended Hotels). In the high season (October to May) reservations are essential. But all this tourist activity doesn't destroy that feeling of being at the end of the road. Flamingo remains a remote spot – but there's plenty to do here.

You can take all sorts of guided boat trips from the marina. Many of these lead you through the fabled **Backwater** region, and into **Whitewater Bay** with its myriad of mangrove-covered islands. There are several walking trails (though the best are the ones already mentioned, which lead off the Ingraham Highway). And there are a number of canoe trails. You can rent a canoe for around $30 a day, and choose a trail which suits you. Don't be too ambitious, first time out, or you'll get backache and blisters which will ensure it's your last time out, for this vacation at least. (If you don't want all the bother, you can always rent a motorized skiff for around $50 a half day.)

On the other hand, if you *are* an experienced canoeist, you should try the **Wilderness Waterway**. This is one of the finest canoe trails in the world, and leads for over 100 miles through the Everglades up to Everglades City, north along the coast. You start from the Flamingo marina and head up the **Buttonwood Canal** into Whitewater Bay. At the other end of the bay you come to the mouth of **Shark River**, which is renowned for its huge variety of fish. (According to one local fisherman's yarn, you can catch over four dozen different types of fish here.) At **Canepatch** you'll find wild sugar cane and banana trees, as well as remnants of Seminole and Calusa Indian camps which lasted here until 1928. Further on you pass such romantically named spots as **Big Lostman's Bay, Alligator Bay** and **Chokoloskee Island**, before arriving at Everglades City.

There are camping grounds along the way in the heart of the backcountry, where you will meet up with similarly intrepid boaters. Allow at least a week for this trip. Things being what they are, it is now possible to cheat and do the whole thing in a day, by hiring a motorboat. Or, if you want the best of both worlds, it's also possible to hire a houseboat and cruise at a more leisurely pace with all the modern conveniences.

See Local Explorations: 4, from Naples South, for details of Everglades City and the northwestern region of the Everglades.

famously used by President Truman during his election campaign of 1948, when he covered over 21,000 miles of the U.S., winning votes with dozens of whistle-stop speeches a day. This caused the election upset of the century when he defeated Dewey.

FLAMINGO

And other places within The Everglades National Park, *see* The Everglades, *page* 66 *to* 70.

FLORIDA CITY

See Recommended Restaurants, *page* 73.

FRUIT AND SPICE PARK

Some 6 miles N of Homestead, on 187th Avenue; open 10 am-5 pm daily ; entry $1. A must for gardeners. This 20-acre park was opened more than 50 years ago, and displays a huge variety of exotic fruits and spices. These include such wonders as the Panama Candle Tree, dozens of varieties of citrus and bananas, and a number of spooky poisonous plants. You're allowed to eat any fruit that has fallen to the ground, but only the tour guides know for sure which ones are poisonous. So if you have a yen for exotic tastes, you're well advised to take the tour (which only costs $1).

The park was badly hit by Hurricane Andrew, but has now been almost completely renovated. There's also an excellent shop, where you can buy all kinds of exotic jams, teas and seeds – which make original presents for the folks back home.

GOLD COAST RAILWAY MUSEUM

Right next door to the Metrozoo, on SW 152nd Street; open 10 am-3 pm daily; entry $6. Contains some fascinating classics from the great old days of American railways. My favorite is the *Silver Crescent* domed car (so archetypically 1950s you almost expect to see Doris Day singing at the window). But the much-vaunted star exhibit is the *Ferdinand Magellan* Pullman car, which was made in 1928 for President Coolidge (who never used it). Presidents who did use it include Roosevelt, Truman, Eisenhower and Reagan. It was most

HOMESTEAD 🛏 ✕

See Recommended Hotels *and* Restaurants, *pages* 72 *and* 73.

MATHESON HAMMOCK PARK

91 Old Cutler Road, Coral Gables; open 6 am to sunset daily; entry free - but parking will cost you $2. This former coconut plantation was transformed into the largest park in the South Miami region in the 1930s and has remained immensely popular ever since. On summer weekends the shores of the huge lagoon are packed with sunbathers, but there are trails through the trees where you can get away from it all. This is the sort of place where you can meet the real Miamians, who are a friendly, welcoming lot.

Nearby is the **Fairchild Tropical Garden**, which covers over 80 acres and claims to be the largest tropical garden in America. Here you can see a huge variety of exotic blooms set in a landscaped terrain with artificial lakes. There's a regular tram ride ($1) but, unless you want to see everything, by far the best way is to wander off and explore for yourself.

METROZOO

W off Florida's Turnpike Extension (Route 821) to 12400 SW 152nd Street; open 9.30 am-5.30 pm daily; entry $9). Three hundred acres of cageless habitats for the usual cross-section of animals. The zoo was badly hit by Hurricane Andrew a few years back. (Their showpiece 1-acre aviary was badly damaged, and one of their rare macaws was said to have been picked up limping on the beach at Boca Raton over 50 miles north.) The monorail was also destroyed, but is due to reopen soon. Children will love the Paws section, where they can lay their hands on all kinds of furry friends.

MIAMI

See pages 142-165.

MONKEY JUNGLE

About 10 *miles* NE *of Homestead at* 14805 SW 216 *Street; open* 9:30 *am*-6:30 *pm; entry* $12. For over 50 years this 30-acre site has been home to nearly 500 different types of monkeys, some of which are endangered species. Their dangerous visitors are kept in suitably caged walkways through the steamy tropical jungle. This enables the hosts to swing happily through the branches and examine closely the peculiar habits and plumages adopted by their primate cousins. The Indonesian orangutans find this a cause for much profound pondering, while the Brazilian tamarins seem to consider it hilarious. There are animal shows every hour.

ORCHID JUNGLE

About 6 *miles* NE *of Homestead, at the junction of* 157*th Avenue and* SW 264*th Street; open* 8.30 *am*-5.50 *pm daily; entry* $5. A horticulturalist's paradise of orchids and a number of other subtropical species. There are also some fine ferns and palms, and a shop where you can buy many of the plants on display.

PARROT JUNGLE

S *of Coral Gables at* 11000 SW 57*th Avenue; open* 9.30 *am*-6 *pm daily; entry* $12. The parrots are only the stars of

RECOMMENDED HOTELS

Much of this region is within easy reach of Miami, and it's best to use Miami as your base for exploring it. See the recommended hotels in Miami, page 162 to 163.

CORAL GABLES

Biltmore Hotel, $$$; 1200 *Anastasia Avenue, Coral Gables,* 33134; *tel.* 305 445 1926; *all major cards.*

Legendary 1920s hotel, the showpiece of George Merrick, the man who built Coral Gables. Garland, Gable, Garbo – they all stayed here. Recently refurbished in Hollywood Moorish style at a cost of $50 million. Facilities for the stars include a championship golf course, olympic-sized pool, and service to suit your every whim. Its telephone number includes the year it opened, and it even has historical tours – which are open to non-guests. (See also Sights & Places of Interest, Coral Gables, page 66.)

Hotel Place St Michel, $$$; 16 *Alcazar Avenue, Coral Gables* 33134; *tel.* 305 444 1666; *all major cards.*

Sophisticated European ambience and decoration: wood paneling, parquet floors and ceiling fans. Just 30 rooms, so be sure to reserve. A romantic hideaway popular with well-heeled intellectuals who like European style.

FLAMINGO

There is only one hotel in Flamingo, which means that it is *essential* to book well in advance, especially during the winter and spring season (October to May).

Flamingo Lodge Marina and Outpost Resort, $$; 1 *Flamingo Lodge Highway, Flamingo* 33034; *tel.* 305 253 2241; *all major cards.*

This is the only motel in the entire Everglades National Park. Basic rooms look out over Florida Bay, and there are cottages in the woods. There's a freshwater swimming pool (covered by an aviary-style net to keep out the mosquitoes), and the friendly staff are extremely helpful with advice about local excursions, boat trips, canoe trails and so on. At night you can see racoons in the garden and hear the nearby alligators making their raucous love cries (which sounded to me more like hunting calls for dinner). You'll probably be pleased to know they also have a laundry.

HOMESTEAD

Super 8, $-$$; 1202 *North Krome Avenue, Homestead; tel.* 1 800 800 8000; *cards* MC, V.

Standard chain motel, such as you'll find anywhere in America. Such places are an American institution; if you are from outside the U.S.A., your visit to the States will not be complete without a night in one.

• *Parrot Jungle, south of Coral Gables.*

the show here. You can also see macaws, toucans, cockatoos and flamingoes. Visit the Parrot Bowl Theater – where the parrots skate, cheat at cards, throw tantrums and shamelessly play to the crowd.

PIONEER MUSEUM

826 *Krome Avenue, Florida City, where* Rt 821 *meets* Rt 1 *on its way* S *from* Miami; *open* 1 *pm*-5 *pm daily* Nov-April; *entry* $1.50.

At the turn of the 19thC, Florida City and the Homestead area were on the very edge of civilization – pioneer territory. Then Flagler (see page 27) began building the railway down to the Florida Keys, and the place underwent a boom. This museum is housed in the former residence of Flagler's railway agent, and contains a range of fascinating exhibits and mementoes dating from this exciting period. At the back, there's a 1926 caboose. This managed to survive the recent hurricane, though unfortunately the old East Coast Railway Station here did not. Best by far are the old photos.

WEEKS AIR MUSEUM

At *Tamiami Airport,* 20 *miles* SW *of downtown Miami; open* 10 *am*-5 *pm daily; entry* $5. Their collection contains many classic planes, including the famous B-17 Flying Fortress of Second World War fame. Unfortunately, all of their First World War planes were smashed by the 1992 hurricane, but they still have nearly three dozen later models.

RECOMMENDED RESTAURANTS

CORAL GABLES

New Hickory Barbecue Restaurant, $-$$; 3170 *Coral Way, Coral Gables; tel.* 305 443 0842; *no cards.*

A local institution, great for inexpensive steaks and spare ribs. Plain decor.

FLAMINGO

Flamingo Restaurant, $$;
Flamingo Visitor Center, Flamingo 33034; *tel.* 305 253 2241; *cards* AE, MC, V.

Multi-level restaurant upstairs in the Visitor Center. Tables with views out over Florida Bay, where the wildlife wings in onto the local sandbar. You can also see vultures, who used to dine at this spot long before there was a restaurant here.

They do a fair range of meat and vegetarian dishes, but the fresh fish is the thing to go for. This lifts the cuisine to a suprisingly high standard. If you've been fishing, you can even bring along your own catch for them to cook. (Just make sure you have it gutted and cleaned down at the marina beforehand.)

During the summer off-season, the main restaurant closes down, but meals are still served on the patio downstairs.

FLORIDA CITY

Richard Accursio's Capri Restaurant, $-$$; 935 *North Krome Avenue,Florida City; tel.* 305 247 1544; *all major cards.*

Typical Italian family-run restaurant with great pasta and pizzas. Good fish dishes.

HOMESTEAD

El Toro Taco, $; 1 *South Krome Avenue, Homestead; tel.* 305 245 5576; *no cards.*

By far the best inexpensive eatery for miles around. Here the Mexican cuisine is utterly authentic. They have your usual range of favorite Mexican dishes, and a few unusual ones. For a real treat, try their *fajitas.*

Florida Overall: 4

Southern Florida

Between Florida Mainland/Miami and Marathon

The Upper Keys

60 miles; map Hallwag Florida

Route 1 through the Florida Keys is one of the greatest drives in the world. The road hops from island to island, often traveling for miles across the ocean itself. Some of the islands are miles long, some are just a dot of sand with a sprouting sprig of greenery.

That said, there's no denying that the start of Rt 1 is a disappointment. On weekends it's often clogged with traffic from Miami, and even when it isn't, the Key Largo strip of billboards, hamburger joints, souvenir shops and fishing tackle stores is of little interest to any but the most avid aficionado of Americana. (The Keys have a kitsch which is very much their own.)

But even at Key Largo there's the John Pennekamp Coral Reef State Park, said to have been the first underwater park in the world and one of the wonders of the Keys.

Further down the road you come to Islamorada, which claims to be the world's number one fishing capital. This is the place to hook your first marlin, and then pose for your Hemingway photo.

From now on you'll find the Keys becoming much more unspoiled. Although the next town of any consequence – Marathon – is hardly renowned for its beauty, there are beaches, nature reserves and historic islands within easy reach.

From the Florida mainland to Marathon is just over 50 miles, which means you can easily cover this stretch in a day. If you want to do justice to the sights, allow at least a couple of days.

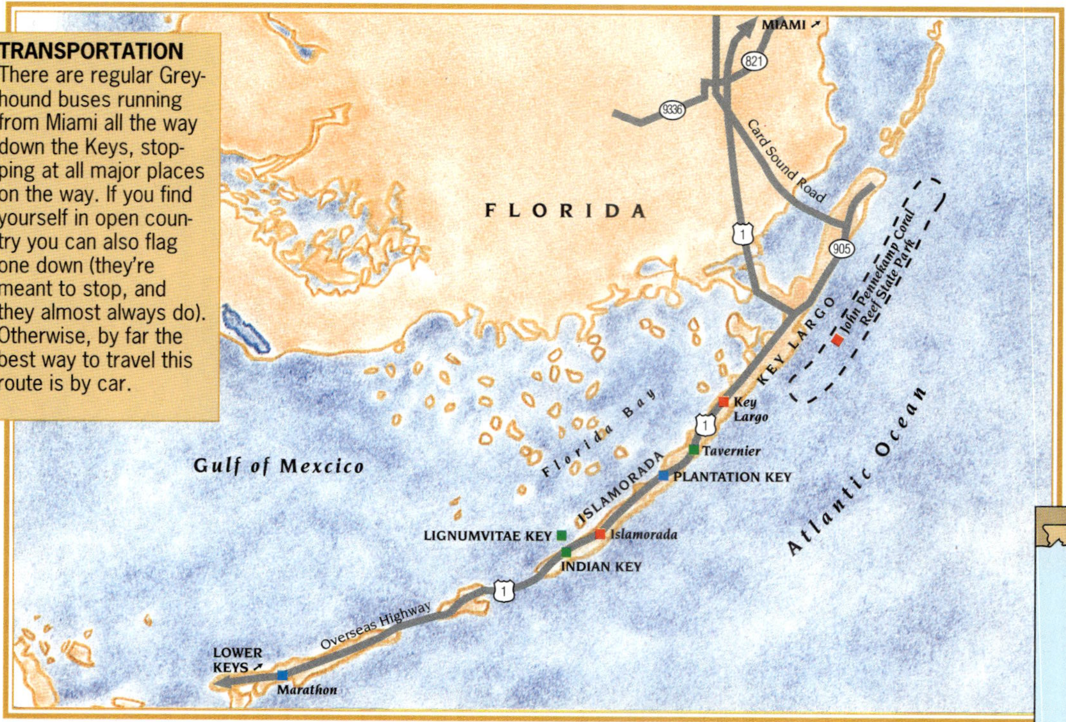

TRANSPORTATION
There are regular Greyhound buses running from Miami all the way down the Keys, stopping at all major places on the way. If you find yourself in open country you can also flag one down (they're meant to stop, and they almost always do). Otherwise, by far the best way to travel this route is by car.

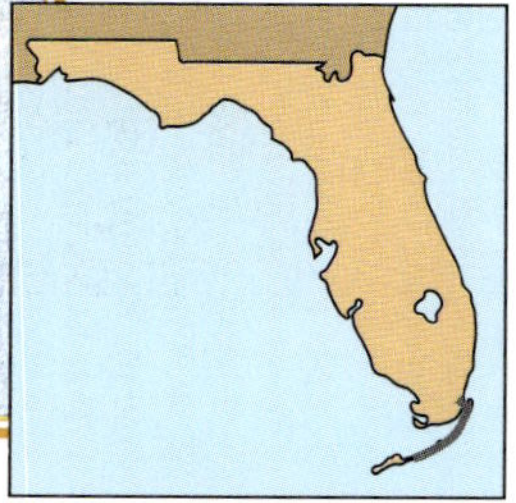

SIGHTS & PLACES OF INTEREST

INDIAN KEY

See Islamorada, below.

ISLAMORADA 🛏 ✕

Some 82 *miles* NE *of Key West on* Rt 1.
Islamorada is the collective name for a 20-mile strip of islands, which include Upper and Lower Matecumbe Key. It's also the name of the main town here. Judging from their names, you would think these were the islands of the dead. Though Islamorada in fact means "purple island," there is an old local legend that the word is a corruption of the Spanish for Dead Man's Island; and Matecumbe is a corruption of the Spanish word *matar* (kill) and *hombre* (man).

Some say these names derive from the reception given by the local Caribs and Indians to the first Spaniards who arrived here. Another legend has it that a notorious pirate was found dead here, after his crew had murdered him and run off with his treasure. That said, the nearest you're likely to come to death nowadays is after too many cocktails at one of the shoreside bars. (Under no circumstances try a genuine Killer Shark's Tooth, which used to be an Islamorada speciality during the Prohibition era, when anything but methylated alcohol was sometimes difficult to come by.)

Islamorada has everything from the tacky to the truly beautiful. Those who like to watch dancing sea lions and dolphins will thoroughly enjoy the Theater of the Sea (Mile Marker 84.5, Windley Key). Here you can even spend a half hour swimming with the dolphins – though from the look of it when I was here, the dolphins far preferred cancanning with their own kind. But if you want a fishy dancing partner, it'll cost you $80 per person, and be sure to book well in advance – tel. 305 664 2431. Others may prefer to take a less active role and watch the sharks feed, or visit the aquarium which has its own coral reef and all manner of brightly col-

BACKGROUND

The Florida Keys were discovered several millennia ago by the Seminoles and the Calusas, with occasional visits from the Caribs. Despite these visitors, the islands remained largely uninhabited. In 1513 the Spanish explorer Ponce de León arrived. For reasons best known to his analyst, he thought that these paradise islands looked like tortured holy men, and he named them *Los Martires* (The Martyrs). During the following centuries, notorious pirates such as Blackbeard, Captain Morgan and Lafitte used the hidden coves and bays of the Keys to ambush the galleons of the Spanish Gold Fleet sailing home from South America.

In 1819 the Americans took over Florida from the Spanish, and the islands, now known as the Keys, became the southernmost part of the United States. The name Key comes from the Spanish word *cayo*, which means small island. The Keys are in fact hundreds of small limestone islands, running in a 120-mile sweeping curve from Biscayne Bay to the reefs and atolls beyond Key West. They mark the dividing line between the Gulf of Mexico to the west and the Atlantic Ocean to the east.

They are protected to the east by the third largest coral reef in the world – the only living coral reef in America – which flattens out the ocean waves, resulting in little surf and few beaches on the eastern side of the chain.

The Keys remained largely uninhabited, apart from the remote island of Key West, which became a salvage and fishing center, as well as a haunt of wreckers who made fortunes salvaging ships that came to grief on the notorious reefs. Business prospered to such an extent that by the 1870s Key West was the largest city in Florida.

In the early years of the 20thC, Flagler (page 27) began building the railroad from eastern Florida down across the Keys to Key West, which it reached in 1912. (See Flagler's Folly, page 96.)

After Flagler's Overseas Railroad was destroyed by a hurricane in 1935, President Roosevelt rebuilt the bridges and turned it into a road

fans and collectors.

Afterwards you can go to **Water Mania**, where you can get soaked, lost (in a maze) or crazed (in an infernal games arcade). All this makes a great day out for the kids, and is considerably less expensive than most of the attractions in nearby Orlando. Then you can take them for a boat ride at **Lake Front Park.**

Kissimmee is a convenient, inexpensive base for visiting Orlando (see Recommended Hotels and Restaurants, pages 44 and 45).

ORLANDO 🛏 ✕

30 miles inland from the E coast in mid-Florida. Orlando is Florida's major tourist destination. This is the home of Walt Disney World, which claims to be "The World's Top Tourist Attraction," and receives more tourists each year than many countries.

Once upon a time, Orlando was a sleepy small town in the midst of Florida's lake district. The nearby pine woods had real Bambis, the citrus farms all had contented cats who lived off real mice, and the snoozing alligators in the swamplands could only dream of dolphin steaks.

Walt Disney World (full details in separate entry, pages 38-43) was Walt Disney's final dream. The site for this theme-park-to-end-all-theme-parks was chosen in utmost secrecy. Undercover buyers were dispatched to central Florida to purchase parcels of land. This process took years. After a series of astute purchases and much skillful bargaining, Disney finally owned a 42-square-mile plot (twice the size of Manhattan Island). Meanwhile, Disney's agents had managed to persuade the Florida legislature to grant powers to Disney's corporation usually reserved for independent kingdoms. Building on this kingdom-within-a-state was well under way when Walt Disney died in 1966. Walt Disney World opened in 1971, and central Florida was immediately transformed.

Over the years since Walt Disney World opened, Orlando has seen the building of several other major theme parks, and has attracted businesses from all over America. Orlando is an archetypal American success story. Yet unlike many other such, it has not sunk into a bathos of rampant exploitation. Orlando is a pleasant place, with green parkland, lakes and some interesting museums. Yet there's no denying the commercialization of the theme parks that remain its *raison d'être*. If you don't care for these, you shouldn't be here.

Orlando has a number of attractions less spectacular than Walt Disney World, which make for an enjoyable, unstupendous interlude:

Orlando Museum of Art

2416 North Mills Avenue; open 9 am-5 pm Tues-Sat, Sun afternoons only; admission free (expected donation $4). This has a fine collection of pre-Columban artifacts going as far back as the second millenium BC. There's even an interactive area for the kids, called Art Encounter, sponsored by Walt Disney World. My favorite is their collection of 19th and 20thC American art, which has a few real gems (as well as a few less polished items).

Orlando Science Center

810 East Rollins Street; open 9 am-5 pm Mon-Fri, Sat and Sun afternoons only; admission $6.50. Hands-on interactive science, showing it can be fun to learn how electricity is generated, how your body works, and other answers to the kids' endless "Why? How? What?" There's also a good planetarium show, and on weekends they have cosmic concerts with lasers splitting the darkness and rock music splitting your eardrums. Ideal for kids and grandparents (who can turn off their hearing aids).

Wet 'n' Wild

6200 International Drive; open daily, hours vary with the seasons; phone 1 800 992 WILD for details. In the heat of summer, when Orlando becomes Boilando, this is the place to be. Here you can splash, slide, gurgle and splutter your way through 25 acres of aquatic fun. The Sur is claimed as the biggest and best tube ride in the world. When you've survived this 580-foot slide, you're ready for the Black Hole, which is almost as long – only in the dark, and with a few surprises en route. The huge Surf Lagoon has waves you would expect to see in Hawaii, and, at Raging Rapids, you can plunge over a waterfall. There's even an area of sanity where adults can sunbathe in peace.

• *An inhabitant of Sea World.*

Ripley's Believe It Or Not!
8201 *International Drive; open 10 am-11 pm daily; admission* $8.95.This museum is just what you would expect. Your kids will probably love the five-legged cow, the Rolls Royce made of a million matchsticks, and the man weighing over 1,000 pounds. Aspiring artists will be fascinated by the painting executed on a grain of rice, and the Mona Lisa made out of toast. There's even a hologram of Robert Ripley himself.

SEA WORLD
About 5 *miles* SW *of downtown* Orlando, *at* 7007 Sea World Drive; *open* 9 *am*-7 *pm daily (later during summer vacation); admission* $32.95.

"The World's Greatest Zoological Park" is spread over 175 acres, with dozens of attractions laid out around a 17-acre central lake.

The park's most famous resident is Shamu, a performing killer whale who's had an entire stadium built for him. Shamu puts on a 20-minute show every afternoon, and if you want a seat you should arrive at least half an hour early. (For time of show, inquire at the main entrance.) Anyone who thinks that whales are sleepy, slow-moving creatures is in for a surprise when Shamu starts bouncing his way through the pool, splashing all, far and wide.

The best place to start is the Window to the Sea, a 20-minute multimedia show in the Seaworld Theater, which explains what the place is all about, and describes the serious ecological purpose behind all the commercialism. For example, stop at Manatees: The last Generation? Here you learn that there are now only 2,000 Florida manatees (sea cows) left. You can also learn how they live, and get a realistic assessment of their chances of avoiding extinction. Other more resilient species can be seen at Terrors of the Deep. Here you walk down a plexiglas tunnel through a tank of frightening creatures. Sharks slide by, eyeing their dinner, venomous eels elongate before your eyes, and poisonous puffer fish glide peacefully past. Even more disturbing is Mission: Bermuda Triangle, which simulates a dive in a research subma-

ored fish to go with it.

Just down the road, at Mile Marker 82, you come to the **Hurricane Memorial**. In 1935, during the infamous Labor Day Hurricane, a train was dispatched to pick up the men working on the Overseas Highway, many of whom were First World War veterans who had been unable to find jobs during the Depression. After the men had been rescued and the train was on its way back, it was hit by a tidal wave which derailed the train and drowned 423 of its passengers. They are now buried in a mass grave below the monument, which includes an artist's impression of the hurricane.

A little further down the road, off Highway 1 at Mile Marker 78, you can catch boats to Indian Key and Lignumvitae Key. Many of the more remote Florida Keys are maintained as nature and wildlife reserves, which are not open to the public. These two islands are the exception.

Indian Key, which lies on the ocean side of Islamorada, is much more exciting than the average nature preserve. It is thought to have been inhabited by pre-Columbian Americans – alternatively by Caribs and Calusa Indians – for several thousands of years. The Calusa Indians are said to have massacred 400 Frenchmen who paid them a visit in 1770.

In the early 1830s, Indian Key was bought by the prodigal Jacob Houseman, son of a wealthy New York ship owner. Jacob had stolen one of his father's ships and set off for Florida to set up as a wrecker. He installed himself and his crew on Indian Key, salvaging rich cargoes from the wrecks, and during leaner times occasionally hanging out lanterns to lure passing ships on to the nearby reefs. Houseman was so successful that within a

LIFE OR DEATH FOR THE CORAL REEF?

The coral reef that protects the eastern shores of the Keys from the ravages of Atlantic breakers is at present under threat. Though it is the only living coral reef in America, it may not remain so for much longer. In 1993, large quantities of sea grass began dying in Florida Bay as a result of an upset in the marine balance caused by pollution. This dying sea grass became clogged, forming into small seaweed seas, which drifted eastwards on the tides. Eventually masses of the sea grass became caught on the coral reef.

This will soon have a catastrophic effect, as it prevents sunlight from reaching the coral. Without sunlight, coral dies. The National Oceanic and Atmospheric Administration has put forward an emergency rescue plan, but this has been opposed by the local fishermen. The life (or death) of the coral reef at present depends on the outcome of this dispute.

– the Overseas Highway. This marked the southern end of Rt 1, which runs from Maine to Florida. During this period the largely uninhabited Keys were "tidied up" and made habitable, using methods which would have modern ecologists up in arms. Channels were dredged, swampy ground filled in and mosquitoes eliminated with a fierce barrage of chemicals. As a result, the Keys became a paradise – which was soon invaded by the sort of people who want to live in paradise.

Today, the Keys still have much of this mixed heritage. Stuck on a stifling summer's day in a traffic jam which seems to stretch from Miami to Key Largo is not the best introduction to the Keys. And even when you finally get started, Rt 1 seems to pass little more than a string of hamburger joints, garish motels and billboards disfiguring the beautiful shoreline. But don't despair, it's not all like this. Off the main road you'll find all sorts of enchanting vacation spots.

And the further down the Keys you go, the more their natural beauty returns. You can walk through subtropical jungle landscapes filled with exotic birds, and offshore you'll see desert islands just as they appear in the cartoons – a knoll of sand with a palm tree, surrounded by the blue-green ocean.

• *Night fishing in Islamorada.*

year he had accumulated the modern equivalent of more than $1 million. He immediately set about refurbishing his 10-acre island home, laying out streets, setting up warehouses to store his loot and even building a "hotel," where female visitors could be housed. Unfortunately, he conducted his trade a little too enthusiastically for the authorities, who withdrew his license after he had "salvaged" a ship that was still tied up at the dock.

After Jacob Houseman left, the island was bought in 1838 by the botanist Henry Perrine. He set about growing tropical plants on a commercial scale, with the idea of producing coffee, tea and hemp, as well as exporting plants to rich landowners in the southern states. But two years later the island was attacked by Seminole Indians, who set fire to every building in the place, killing all who didn't manage to flee. This put an end to Perrine's scheme. The island was abandoned, but his plants continued to flourish.

Your two-hour visit to Indian Key should include a walk through the ruins of the settlement and a tour of Perrine's still flourishing plants. There's not always a guide, but the paths are clearly marked. You can also see the remains of the grave of Jacob Houseman, who eventually died during a salvage operation off Key West, but had often expressed a wish to be buried back in what had once been virtually his own private kingdom. By a stroke of poetic justice, Houseman's original grave was vandalized by latter-day wreckers in search of treasure.

• *Underwater statue of Christ, off Key Largo.*

Lignumvitae Key has a less picturesque history, but is a more picturesque spot. The island is named after the *lignum vitae* (wood of life) tree, which acquired this odd name from the early Spanish visitors. They were convinced that this tree grew near the mythical fountains of youth. The *lignum vitae* has exceptionally hard wood, which is used nowadays for making bowling balls.

Lignumvitae Key is largely covered by virgin forest, and you'll find this is much more than just a load of potential bowling balls. The forest is filled with a veritable jungle of tropical flora and fauna, including the large Golden Orb spiders, whose webs can be seen hanging from the branches across the trails. My favorites are the Tourist Trees (so-called because of their peeling red skin). The real name of this tree is equally picturesque: gumbo-limbo. Along the shore you'll find all kinds of mangroves, some of which are so rare that I can't even remember their names. This landscape has a distinctly primeval feel, and looks much as it did before the first humans arrived in the Keys several thousand years ago.

In 1919 Miami businessman W.J. Matheson, who had made a fortune in chemicals, bought the island and built himself a hideaway home. He also laid out the trails which lead through the forest. You can still see his house – which was lifted lock, stock and barrel by the 1935 hurricane and dumped across the other side of the island. It has since been restored intact to its original site.

Aficionados of kitsch will find themselves in seventh heaven as they travel the Keys. One of the high points is at **Grassy Key** (Mile Marker 59). Here, on the north side of Highway 1, you will see a concrete sculpture over 30 feet high depicting the dolphin Theresa and her baby dolphin Nat. These grace the house of Milton Santini, the genius responsible for the first *Flipper* movies. Nearby is the **Dolphin Research Center**, where those intelligent mammals put on regular aquatic displays.

Islamorada town modestly claims to be the sport fishing capital of the world. And it probably is. This is where George Bush comes for his big game fishing. If you want information on this sport, go to the local Chamber of Commerce, which is housed in an old railway wagon at Mile Marker 82. But be warned: fishing for marlin is expensive – a boat and a skipper will set you back $350-550 a day. But you can join a party for a fraction of this sum. The best spots for big fierce tarpon and blue marlin are in the backcountry, across Florida Bay near the Everglades (see also below), and way out in the Atlantic Ocean at special spots known only to experienced skippers and inexperienced fish.

Holiday Isle Docks (Mile Marker 84) has the biggest concentration of fishing boats for rent. For something different, try joining a fishing party for a night trip, which will cost you about $30.

At Bud 'n' Mary's Dock (Mile Marker 80) there's a pleasant little **fishing museum**; and if you want to hear the best fishing stories, the place to go is the Harbor Bar by the marina at Whale Harbor.

There's also some good swimming in this area – especially for divers. Even if you only use a snorkel, you can still see the coral reefs and the wrecks. Details of all kinds of different trips are available at the various docks and marinas, or try the Chamber of Commerce. Try a boat trip to the backcountry, a region at the head of Florida Bay which has thousands of tiny islands. It's a favorite with fishermen and nature lovers alike. On a good day you'll see dozens of species of birds, many of them rarely seen outside this area.

JOHN PENNEKAMP CORAL REEF STATE PARK

See Key Largo, page 81.

KEY LARGO

Main town on first of the Keys S of the Florida mainland, on Highway 1, 55 miles from Miami. Key Largo became famous as a result of the 1948 Humphrey Bogart-Lauren Bacall film *Key Largo*. This amalgam of romance and crime, in which Bogie and his volatile sidekick took on a hurricane and Edward G. Robinson, summed up everyone's romantic idea of the Florida Keys. In fact, all but about five minutes of the film was shot in Hollywood, with only a few brief location scenes requiring the presence of Bogart and Bacall in the Keys. Worse still, the town now known as Key Largo was called Rock Harbor in those days. Such is the power of the movies (and the possibilities for the tourist business) that the citizens of Rock Harbor decided to adopt the name which had previously applied only to the entire island. (Its original Spanish name *Cayo Largo* means Long Island.)

The Caribbean Club (Mile Marker 104, Key Largo) is said to be the spot where the bar scenes in *Key Largo* were filmed. Inside, you'll find a classic film buff's shrine to movie heroes Bogart and Bacall, and great views (this is the place to turn the world upside down at sundown with those Tequila Sunrises).

More movie memorabilia is to be found at the Holiday Inn (Mile Marker 100), where the marina contains the original steamboat in which Humphrey Bogart dragged Katherine Hepburn through the reeds in *The African Queen* (another exotic location movie, this time with an African setting, which was filmed entirely at Shepperton Studios, just outside London). Here you can also see *Thayer IV*, the beautiful old wooden boat that was used in *On Golden Pond*, starring Henry Fonda and Katherine Hepburn, which was neither filmed, nor claimed to be filmed, anywhere near Key Largo – but what the hell.

Key Largo needs such attractions, because, quite frankly, the place itself is a mess. The main street is a litter of fast-food joints and fishing tackle shops. But there are things to see on the rest of the island.

At the northern end, near where Route 905 joins Route 1, is **Key Largo Hammock**. Here you drive for miles through woodlands of West Indian hardwood trees. This was what much of the Keys looked like before civilization arrived. The area does have its hazards, however. Some say that Key Largo Hammock is popular with drug dealers. And don't be tempted to leave your car and explore because these forests contain some *extremely* poisonous flora, including the Manchineel "devil tree," a bush whose foliage can blind or permanently disfigure.

Further down on Highway 1, just beyond Mile Marker 105, you will see the colorful design of the church of **St Justin Martyr**. Inside is a wall painting that depicts the Last Supper, and an altar table carved from a 2-ton block of finest Carrara marble shipped from Italy.

The big attraction of the island is the

POLITICALLY CORRECT
DOLPHIN
When you see dolphin on the menu, this is dolphin fish, not a retired inmate of the local dolphinarium.

POLITICALLY INCORRECT
PROTECTION
The authorities remain ever alert to the menace of mosquitoes, which once rendered the Keys uninhabitable. The entire length of the Keys is sprayed by planes twice a day. The authorities claim that this has no effect on human beings.

John Pennekamp Coral Reef State Park *Mile Marker 102.5, entry $4. per vehicle*, which lays claim to being the world's first undersea park. Don't be fooled: a large part of this 200-square-mile park is permanently above the surface, and none the worse for that. There are plenty of fine swimming spots in deserted creeks, and nature trails through the mangrove forests. You can snorkel and scuba-dive (equipment for rent), and explore by canoe. There's also an aquarium. And if this isn't enough, they also have an "authentically reconstructed" shipwrecked Spanish galleon.

But the main attraction at Pennekamp Park is undoubtedly the **coral reef**. This is the northern end of the natural barrier which protects the Florida Keys from the Atlantic. (The entire reef stretches for 150 miles – all the way down to the reefs beyond Key West.) You can take the two-hour glass-bottom boat tour, or the shorter snorkeling tour. For those who are qualified, there's also a scuba tour. Any which way, it's well worth it.

The reef itself is a wonder of fairytale fantasy and fishy life. Boring pedants will wish to know the arcane names of each exotic species. Art lovers, on the other hand, will recognize their fish at once. A Picasso fish, a pair of Mondrian, a shoal of Miros – all authentic, and as bright and colorful as the works of the great artists who plagiarized their plumage. You will also see a number of wrecks. These are indeed genuine shipwrecks, many of

• *The African Queen, Key Largo Marina.*

them more than a century old. The only trouble is, the actual shipwrecks took place somewhere else. A quarter of a century ago, Key Largo was sold these wrecks by an enterprising "marine landscape artist," who took the precaution of stripping them of anything valuable before transporting them to their present resting places. There's also an underwater statue of Christ, said to be an exact replica of the kitsch masterpiece by sculptor Guido Galletti, which is in the sea off Genoa on Italy's Mediterranean coast.

The sea at Pennekamp Park is one of the world's wonderlands, and within the park there are over 50 square miles of reef. There should be even more. Until recently, the locals used to dynamite the reef to produce souvenir lumps – but now that we're all ecologically correct this practice has ceased. So where does all the coral in the souvenir shops come from? This is shipped in from Third World countries (mostly in Southeast Asia) where dynamiting coral reefs is still considered a quaint local custom.

During the summer it's essential to book ahead for these reef tours. Phone 305 451 1621 at least a couple of days before your visit.

If you want to see authentic exhibits from local shipwrecks, try a visit to the **Maritime Museum of the Florida**

RECOMMENDED HOTELS

ISLAMORADA

Most accommodations are expensive in Islamorada, and you'll be lucky to find a place for under $60. Out of season you can often get a surprisingly worthwhile reduction, even at the pricey spots.

Checca Lodge, $$$; *Mile Marker* 82, *Islamorada* 33036; *tel.* 305 664 4651; *cards* AE, DC, MC, V.

Occupies 27 acres of Atlantic shore along Matecumbe Key. The grounds include a golf course, tennis courts and swimming pools. They have won big awards for their environmental policy. They host an annual dinner for the Cousteau Society, and there's even an old graveyard preserved amidst the landscaped premises. Extremely child-friendly. There are even ecology-trained counselors.

Holiday Isle Resort, $$-$$$; *Mile Marker* 84, *Islamorada* 33036; *tel.* 305 664 2711; *cards* AE, DC, MC, V.

One of the largest resort complexes in the Keys, but it aims to attract the budget-conscious customer, and you can often get great bargains. There are several hotels on the premises; the Harbor Lights Hotel has the best bargains and standard amenities. The complex has innumerable restaurants and bars, the most lively of the latter being by the ocean. This, the Tikki Bar, was where the Rum Runner cocktail was invented, and is still slaughtering them with its 150-proof rum and blackberry brandy. But don't expect a quiet stay – everyone is *very* friendly.

Key Lantern, $-$$; *Mile Marker* 82, *Islamorada* 33036; *tel.* 305 664 4572; *all major cards.*

As inexpensive as they come in Islamorada. Basic, but friendly.

If the above is full, try the nearby Chamber of Commerce at Mile Marker 82 (open 9 am to 5 pm, Mon to Fri; tel. 1 800 FAB KEYS). They're very helpful, and sympathetic to budget travelers.

KEY LARGO

Bay Harbor Lodge, $-$$; *Mile Marker* 97.7, *Key Largo* 33037; *tel.* 305 852 5695; *cards* DC, MC, V.

A real find, right by the shore. Huts and cottages set in a couple of acres of landscaped grounds. The big bonus here is the boss: Laszlo Smoga, who actually welcomes foreigners and speaks German. You can rent one of their canoes, and set off from their dock.

Economy Efficiency, $; 103365 *Overseas Highway*; *tel.* 305 451 4712; *cards* MC, V.

The name says it all. This is the best basic budget spot in Key Largo, but there's a snag. You have to stay *at least* a couple of nights. The other guests are friendly, and sometimes riotous.

Jules Undersea Lodge, $$$; *Mile Marker* 103.2, 51 *Shoreland Drive, Key Largo* 33037; *tel.* 305 451 2353; *cards* MC, V.

Many hotels claim to be unique, this one is. The name is no joke. The lodge consists of 600 square feet of former underwater research station, 30 feet below where most hotels usually begin. Said to be popular with subaquatic honeymooners. Once you're shown to your room, you're expected to stay there: your evening meal is delivered in a sealed container, and there's a video in the communal galley. Be sure to book at least a month in advance. It's not cheap, but it'll provide you with a story that will last a lifetime.

• *Marathon accommodations.*

MARATHON

Conch Key Cottages, $$-$$$; *turn off Overseas Highway at Mile Marker sign* 62.3, *Marathon* 33050; *tel.* 305 289 1377; *cards* MC, V.

This one is on its own little island, reached by a causeway. The ambience is all very away-from-it-all, amidst the bougainvillea and hibiscus. Prices vary considerably between romantic bungalows down by the water, with their own private beach, and less romantic caravans amongst the mangroves. They're installing a pool.

There are a number of more or less expensive motels along the Overseas Highway. The best for price and location is:

Sea Cove Motel, $; *Mile Marker* 54, *Marathon* 33050; *all major cards.*

Your basic motel, such as you can find by the road all the way up Highway 1 to Maine. But this one is right by the water. They even have rooms in a couple of houseboats moored at the pier. It's worth planning ahead to incorporate this one in your schedule, as you'll be lucky to find one cheaper anywhere between Miami and Havana.

Keys (Mile Marker 102.5, Key Largo). It's not very large, but you'll learn far more about the shipwrecks than you will from the displaced and denuded wrecks placed beneath the surface for decoration.

Eight miles down the road from the town of Key Largo (yet still on the island), you come to **Tavernier**. This has a small quarter of historic buildings, some of which are over a century old – making them almost pre-historic for these parts. Don't expect anything too special: the 20thC has no monopoly on tacky building.

LIGNUMVITAE KEY

See Islamorada, page 80.

LOWER KEYS

See Florida Overall: 5.

RECOMMENDED RESTAURANTS

ISLAMORADA

For your special night out, try:

Atlantic's Edge, $$$; *at Checca Lodge Hotel, Mile Marker 82, Islamorada; tel. 305 664 4651; all major cards.*

Gourmets view this as the best restaurant in the Upper Keys. Sophisticated decor, with a fine view out over the ocean, particularly atmospheric in the early evening. The menu is equally spectacular, with the emphasis on Creole and Caribbean dishes. Superb fresh local fish and seafood, in exotic sauces.

Islamorada abounds in overpriced restaurants, sometimes flashy, sometimes shoddy, which specialize in feeding tourists. Some pleasant exceptions to the rule are:

Green Turtle Inn, $$-$$$; *Mile Marker 81.5, Islamorada; tel. 305 664 9031; all major cards.*

This is the place where the celebs come for a slice of the local culinary action – and have been coming for nearly 50 years. A museum piece, by Keys standards: even the waitresses have been here for longer than they care to remember. Photos of famous diners line the walls, and the menu includes alligator steak and superb fresh grouper.

Manny and Isa's, $$; *Mile Marker 81.6, Islamorada: tel. 305 664 5019; cards* AE, MC, V.

Small cafe-restaurant with great atmosphere where they serve genuine Cuban cuisine. For something really special, try their lobster enchiladas. The only trouble is, they don't take reservations and there are only half a dozen tables – so get here early. Closed Tuesdays.

If you want to meet the locals, try:

Woody's Saloon and Restaurant, $-$$; *Mile Marker 82, Islamorada; tel. 305 664 4335; don't even think of credit cards.*

This is your genuine local saloon, complete with pool tables and video games. They even have their own resident group, led by Big Richard. A very friendly crowd, some with way-over-the-top opinions. For those who need something to soak up the beer, there are pizzas. For those who don't, there's always more beer.

KEY LARGO

Alabama Jack's, $; *5800 Card Sound Road; tel. 305 248 8741; no cards.*

Reached from Key Largo by way of the Card Sound toll bridge. A legendary end-of-the-line spot, famous for

MARATHON 🛏 ✕

On Highway 1, 59 *miles* NE *of Key West.* This a the large town of 7,000, and a distinctly ordinary spot. Away from the garish strip there's a jungle trail at Crane Point Hammock on 55th St. This has more than 60 acres of tropical landscape with well-marked trails, and a Museum of Natural History. If you feel like a swim, pick up your picnic goodies in Marathon and head for Sombrero Beach (turn off by Mile Marker 55), which has clear sea, sand and shaded tables. Otherwise, you're better off heading on down Highway 1 for the Lower Keys.

MIAMI

See pages 142-165.

PLANTATION KEY

About 3 *miles* SW *of Tavernier on Highway* 1, *at Mile Marker* 93. An unfashionable Key with an attraction which is often overlooked. Here you can visit the **Florida Keys Wild Bird Rehabilitation Center.** This is where the birds are sent after they've come into too close contact with us. If and when they recover fully they are set free – meanwhile you can visit and try to make amends. This is your best chance to see many rare species close up. The rarest bird when I visited was a seagoing ibis that had somehow found its way across the ocean from Africa. His supporting cast included various terns, bills and pelicans. As with all hospitals, entry is free, except for the patients, who have all paid in their own way.

TAVERNIER

See Key Largo, page 84.

its Country and Western, and its clog dancing. It's on a couple of barges, with views of the mangroves, and sometimes you'll see a crocodile swim past. Basic Keys food – including great conch chowder and conch fritters. Closes at 7 pm.

Italian Fisherman, $-$$; *Mile Marker* 104, *Key Largo; tel.* 305 451 4471; *no cards.*

The Keys Italian-style, with tasty homemade pasta and a range of local seafood dishes. Friendly service.

Mrs Mac's, $-$$; *Mile Marker* 99.4, *Key Largo; tel.* 305 451 3722; *no cards.*

Popular spot with the locals, who have contributed the myriad of empty beer cans and license plates that form the decor. You'll need some beer yourself to put out the fire from their chilli, otherwise try their great All-American meatloaf. Closed Sundays.

For your wild night out, try:

Coconuts, $$; *Mile Marker* 100, *Marina del Ray.*

Here you can be deafened by disco music, or run ragged by reggae.

More romantic types might prefer:

Horizon Bar, $$; *top of Holiday Isle Resort, Mile Marker* 84.

Great views and live golden oldie music.

MARATHON

Grassy Key Dairy Bar, $-$$; *Mile Marker* 58.5, *Marathon; tel.* 305 743 3816; *no cards.*

Don't be put off by the stone ice-cream cones outside. Here George and Johnny dish out everything from succulent seafood to sumptuous steaks, all at fair prices, too. The menu changes daily: Tuesday might be Tex-Mex, Saturday Southern, Friday, Italian. Closed Sundays.

Herbie's Bar, $; *Mile Marker* 50.5, *Marathon; tel.* 305 743 6373; *no cards.*

Best inexpensive seafood for miles around. The small, functional dining areas can get crowded – it's deservedly popular with the locals, who swear by the conch chowder. Closed all of October.

Seven Mile Grill, $-$$; *Mile Marker* 47, *Marathon; tel.* 305 743 4481; *no cards.*

You'll find this lively spot at the eastern end of Seven Mile Bridge. Great fresh fish, and "snacks" such as Irish-wolfhound-sized hot dogs. And as for the desserts – abandon hope if you're on a diet.

Florida Overall: 5

Southern Florida

Between No Name Key and Fort Jefferson
The Lower Keys

40 miles; map Hallwag Florida

Between the Florida mainland and Key West, the Overseas Highway (Rt 1) crosses 31 islands and 42 bridges. Most of these, and certainly most of the best ones, are on the stretch between Marathon and Key West.

Seven Mile Bridge, which links the Middle and Lower Keys, is a long, exhilarating drive over the blue ocean. At its western end lies Bahia Honda Key, whose 600-acre state recreation area has beaches and nature trails through subtropical forest.

Beyond here, at Big Pine Key, you can see the tiny Key deer, one of many examples of rare wildlife on the archipelago. Further down Route 1 you come to the Looe Key Marine Sanctuary, where you can dive at some of the most spectacular reefs you'll find anywhere.

Then, at the very end of the road, there's Key West.

The Conch Republic, as it calls itself, is as laid back as you'll get. The big social event of the day is the sunset. This is the southernmost point in the U.S. – here you're closer to Cuba than than you are to Miami.

You can tell always tell how far you are from the end of the road at Key West by the mile markers. These begin at 0 in Key West, and end up at 132 at the mainland. From Marathon to Key West along Rt 1 is just over 60 miles. You can easily do this in an afternoon. Some prefer to dawdle though the islands and take at least a couple of days seeing the sights. Others end up taking a lifetime.

• *Seven Mile Bridge.*

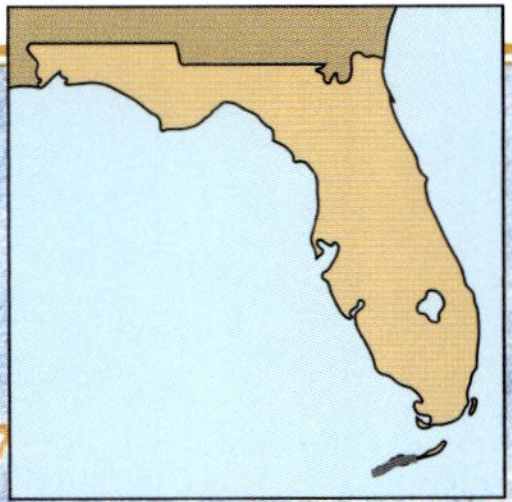

TRANSPORTATION
There are regular Greyhound buses running from Miami to Key West. These stop at every place of any consequence, and can even be hailed. There's a plane service from Miami to Key West. But by far the best way to see this spellbinding stretch of the Keys is to drive it.

• *Bahia Honda State Recreation Area.*

SIGHTS & PLACES OF INTEREST

BAHIA HONDA KEY

SW of Seven Mile Bridge, 62 miles NE of Key West. No, this is not the key which was recently bought by the Japanese. Bahia Honda means "deep bay" in Spanish, a description of the waters to the south-west of the island which were an anchorage for the passing galleons.

The island contains the 600-acre **Bahia Honda State Recreation Area**, which has some of the finest beaches and swimming places in the entire keys. The best beach is on the lagoon at the north-east end of the island, and is just like the travel posters. (Though, as with all beaches in the Keys, the water is shallow.) Inland there are well-marked nature trails, where you can stroll through tropical scenery. The birds here are as exotic as the plants: spoonbills and crested pigeons squawk and swoop among the satinwood trees and morning glory, beyond lies the deep, deep blue of the ocean.

Those who prefer more active pursuits should try the south-west of the island, which has great windsurfing and snorkeling. (Equipment can be rented at the local store.)

Honda Key marks the beginning of the less developed stretch of the Lower Keys. From here south-west there are strict laws about building. Off the beaten track you can search out your own hidden paradise.

BIG PINE KEY ×

About 45 miles E of Key West on Rt 1. Big Pine Key lives up to its name, but it is most famous as the home of the Key deer. This goat-sized deer arrived here in prehistoric times, when the Keys were part of the mainland, and is a distant relative of the Virginia white-tailed deer. For centuries its endearing appearance and friendly nature have warmed the hearts of all, from sentimentalists to venison lovers. The Key deer was so popular with hunters that by the 1940s only a few dozen were left, and it was in danger of becoming extinct. In 1954 the **National Key Deer Refuge** was established, and there are now nearly 400 deer. (These are culled at the rate of about 40 a year by passing drivers like you – so drive carefully.)

To reach the National Key Deer Refuge turn right at the stoplight on Rt 1, later fork left onto Key Deer Boulevard, and then follow the signs. There's a freshwater lake on Key Deer Boulevard called the **Blue Hole**, which is home to large soft-shelled turtles. A resident alligator welcomes swimmers to this idyllic spot.

If you want to see the Key deer in more remote terrain, drive to the unimaginatively named **No Name Key**, which is to the east of Big Pine Key. Like most of the local inhabitants, the deer tend to avoid the heat of the day, preferring the long shadows of early morning and evening.

FORT JEFFERSON

In the Gulf of Mexico, 68 miles W of Key West, on the Dry Tortugas. This is the spot for those who insist on going to the *very* end of the line. It's so far off the map that it's not even marked on many of them. Stuck out on a lonely

• *Fort Jefferson.*

atoll in the middle of the Gulf, well out of sight of land, lies the largest 19thC coastal fort built by the U.S. Its exact purpose is comprehensible only to the military mind. Building was started in 1846, but before it could finish even the military had begun to question the project.

So it was decided to turn the place into a prison. This became the U.S. answer to Devil's Island (which lies across the Caribbean, off the coast of French Guyana). It had all the qualifications: no fresh water, overbearing heat, fatal diseases, cut off from the mainland by miles of shark-infested, hurricane-raked seas – and superb sunsets. Unfortunately the guards weren't made of the same stuff as their French counterparts, and were soon as eager to leave as their charges. In 1874, after yet another outbreak of yellow fever, followed by the usual hurricane, the prison authorities decided to call it a day. The place was then declared a national monument (presumably to the folly of military and prison authorities). The lonely, abandoned fort stands on the optimistically named Garden Key, which is surrounded by forbidding reefs known as the **Dry Tortugas**. These were discovered as early as the 1500s, in the usual way that reefs are discovered. When the shipwrecked sailors were rescued by the Spanish explorer Ponce de León, he named the reefs Tortugas, in honor of the many turtles who inhabited them. They later acquired their prefix for obvious reasons – as a warning to thirsty, inexperienced sailors armed with a map.

However, when I visited the reefs they were all very wet, since it was raining heavily; and there wasn't a turtle to be seen. On the other hand, there were plenty of seabirds – several of which were members of extremely rare species. Yet I did see something even more rare. Normally the fort is abandoned and deserted, but at the time of my visit it was occupied by a Swiss couple, who assured us that they had come to study the wildlife.

The hexagonal fort has 50-foot high

• *Key West.*

walls and occupies almost the entire island. Because the military believes in doing something thoroughly, the fort is also surrounded by a symmetrical moat, which must be the most superfluous of its kind in the world. One of the towers has been converted into a lighthouse, with a patch of bedraggled palm trees growing inside. There is also a museum, whose contents are of little interest (but you don't tell anyone this, having come all this way). You can swim and snorkel from the beach.

Unless you own a boat, the only way to get here is by air from Key West. Contact Key West Seaplane at Murray's Marine, 5630 Junior College Road, Stock Island, tel. 294 6978, and expect to pay approximately $150. The flight is all part of the adventure, taking you over remote keys, tide-sculpted sandbars and coral reefs (some with shipwrecks) west of Key West. A great splurge, and a fund for tall stories for years to come.

KEY WEST 🛏 ✕

The southernmost town on Rt 1, *at the far end of the* Florida Keys. This is the end of the line, and my favorite spot in Florida. But be warned: it's also many other people's favorite spot – so expect crowds during the season.

Key West is closer to Havana than it is to Miami. Havana is 90 miles south, while Miami is 150 miles away up Rt 1. It's different from the rest of Florida, and more spiritually akin to California – with that added "away from it all" ingredient. Until as late as 1912, you could only get here by boat.

Everyone complains that Key West is changing, that it's becoming overwhelmed by tourism, that it's not like it was in the "good old days." Don't worry. People have been saying this for years – and still Key West has managed to retain its blend of laid-back atmosphere and eccentricity which makes it unique in the U.S.

The island has a population of approximately 30,000. Many of these are Conchs (pronounced Conks), named after the large attractive shells whose snails used to provide the staple diet for the first inhabitants. The original Conchs were white settlers who emigrated from the Bahamas. Those known as Freshwater Conchs are emigrants from all over mainland U.S. The remaining population is just as varied. It includes Bahamians, Cubans, military personnel from the nearby bases, hippies of the kind long considered extinct elsewhere, adventurers of every type, and of course, the gays, who now make

• *Opposite: Sailing in Key West.*

Fury

A SUITABLE HISTORY

The historian Wright Langley unearthed some ancient human bones at a dig on the Key West Naval Base, which lies west of the town center. This find led him to speculate that the first inhabitants of Key West were a primitive cannibal tribe. More orthodox historians say that the earliest inhabitants were Calusa Indians, who probably lived here for some centuries before the arrival of the Spanish.

But Wright Langley's theory may not be quite so outlandish as it sounds. Early Spanish explorers called the place *Caya Hueso*, meaning "island of bones," allegedly because they found the shores littered with human bones. It was the name *Caya Hueso* which became corrupted to Key West – the island is not the furthest west in the chain, only the westernmost of the inhabited keys.

The Calusa Indians disappeared from Key West in the 1700s, and are now extinct, though a persistent legend has it that they emigrated across the water to Cuba. After they left, Key West became the haunt of pirates, who used the place for spells of rest and relaxation. (Some say it has never got over this phase.)

In 1815 the Spanish governor of Florida granted the island to one of his officers, for unspecified services. The Spanish officer arrived to inspect his gift, but was not impressed. Evidently his unspecified services had not been quite up to par. Six years later the Spanish ceded Florida to the United States, and the hapless Spanish officer at last managed to unload the island. In a bar in Cuba he ran into an Alabaman entrepreneur named John Simonton and succeeded in selling him the deeds to the island for $2,000.

Simonton managed to make a quick buck by tempting three local settlers to buy into his venture, and everyone was happy. Then the U.S. Navy arrived and insisted on setting up a large base on the island. This high-handed American policy aimed to put an end to all forms of traditional business on the island, and it suceeded. Piracy was eliminated.

In the wake of piracy, American settlers established the related nautical trade of wrecking. Local sailors were soon earning a fortune rescuing cargoes and people from ships wrecked on the notorious Florida reef. Much of this was legitimate salvaging, but when trade became slack wreckers often took to luring ships onto the reefs with lanterns. Astonishingly, millions of dollars were made from the wrecking trade. Indeed, historians claim that by the 1850s Key West was the richest city in the entire U.S. By 1888 Key West had a population of 18,000, making it by far the largest city in Florida.

The next migrants to reach Key West were the Cubans, who brought with them the trade of cigar-making. Then the Greeks arrived and set up a lucrative trade harvesting sponges from the coral reef.

In 1912 the Overseas Railroad finally reached Key West, and its constructor Henry Flagler arrived on the first train with a brass band playing. Key West was now on the direct route from New York to Havana. (In those days a return ticket cost just $24.) The tourist boom began.

Twenty years later it was all over. Key West was hit by a succession of misfortunes that reduced it to one of the poorest cities in the United States. First the sponge trade collapsed, owing to a blight which quickly spread through all the sponge grounds. Then there was labor trouble in the Cuban cigar trade, which packed up and moved north to Tampa on the west coast of Florida. Then came the Stock Market Crash of 1929, and the Naval Base was closed down. As if all this weren't bad enough, the Overseas Railroad was destroyed by a hurricane in 1935. Soon 80 percent of the remaining hardbitten Conchs were on welfare. There was nothing to do but sit around all day, and nothing to eat but coconuts and

• *Conch shell.*

seafood. (To this day, you can sometimes still hear the odd disgruntled tourist echoing this complaint.)

As part of Roosevelt's New Deal, the Overseas Highway was built to replace the Overseas Railroad. Then came the Second World War, and the U.S. Navy returned. Key West was back in business. After the war, things began to look up even further. President Harry S. Truman took a shine to Key West and established his "Little White House" on the island. What was good enough for the president was certainly good enough for the people. Soon the visitors began to trickle back. The island had attracted Hemingway in the 1930s, and it now began to attract other artists and writers. The American philosophical poet Wallace Stevens stayed, and it inspired one of his finest works: "*Idea of Order at Key West*." Here is an extract:

The fishing boats at anchor there,
As night descended, tilting in the air,
Mastered the night and portioned out the sea,
Fixing emblazoned zones and fiery poles,
Arranging, deepening, enchanting night.

American genius Tennessee Williams also stayed in Key West and even wrote a few plays here. By now the tourists were flowing back, until by the 1980s the flow had become a gold rush. There was no need for the locals to go wrecking any more – the tourists came in and got wrecked all by themselves, handing over their precious cargo left, right and center. A good time was had by all, and so it remains to this day.

up at least 20 percent of the population. These disparate elements blend surprisingly well, giving the place a distinctive liberal ambience. Here anything goes, and people believe in appreciating the simpler joys of life. Where else would the sunset – *every* sunset – be considered one of the main events of the day?

The Conch Republic

In April 1982 Key West declared itself independent, and the "Conch Republic" was born. The trigger which fired this secession was a roadblock set up by the U.S. Border Patrol on Rt 1 just south of Florida City. Border Patrol began searching all cars and trucks coming from the Keys, and questioning their owners, in the hunt for imported drugs and illegal immigrants. The result was huge traffic jams for anyone wanting to drive to Miami.

• *Ernest Hemingway House and Museum, Key West.*

This was the beginning of the hot season, and everyone was soon steaming. The Florida Keys have a long tradition of arrivals by moonlight on hidden beaches; and the laid-back citizens of Key West bitterly resented being treated like foreigners and criminals in their own country.

The citizens of Key West resorted to unilaterally declaring their independence. They hoisted their own flag and issued their own border passes (but not to federal agents). They even printed their own currency. After declaring war on its powerful neighbor, the Conch Republic gracefully surrendered and petitioned for a large handout of foreign aid from Washington. This was all taken in good humor (though no foreign aid was forthcoming), and the U.S. Border

Patrol lifted the roadblock.

Now, every year in late April, the Conch Republic Celebration is held in Key West. A big open-air party is held in Mallory Square, and the Conch Republic flag is ceremonially raised. In the same month there's also a Conch Shell Blowing Contest, which is open to all comers. You'd be surprised at the noises that come out of some of those shells – though don't go expecting to hear a Mozart horn concerto.

The main sights

The best way to see Key West is on foot. It's seldom too hot for walking. The ocean breezes render the climate surprisingly moderate, considering it's fewer than 80 miles north of the Tropic of Cancer. Even at the height of the summer it usually remains 10 degrees or so cooler than Miami.

Key West is almost 5 miles long (and a couple of miles wide), but most of the main sights are concentrated around the **Old Town**, at the western end of the island. The Old Town stretches roughly from White Street in the east, west to the shorefront at Mallory Square and south as far as Truman Avenue. The main drag of the Old Town is undoubtedly **Duval Street**, which runs north from Truman Avenue to Mallory Square. This used to be the roughest street in Florida, and still has a number of old bars – including the celebrated **Sloppy Joe's** of Hemingway fame (see page 105). Some of the old buildings are in the original Conch style, and some bear Spanish and Deep Southern influences. But don't expect to find much "old style" behavior here nowadays. The shops are mainly stylish (and often expensive) boutiques catering to the aesthetically underprivileged – though there are a few tasteful exceptions. Much better fun than window-shopping is checking the passing crowd, which usually includes a fair percentage of all sexes who genuinely enjoy the attention. Duval Street takes you past the side streets leading to all the best sights.

Ernest Hemingway House and Museum, *907 Whitehead St, open 9 am-6 pm daily; entry $7.* One of the pleasantest houses in Key West, this superb spot was built in 1851 in Spanish Colonial style and was provided for Hemingway by his wife. Hemingway lived here

• *Hemingway souvenirs in a Key West store.*

mainly in the 1930s, and his drunken antics and exaggerated big-game fishing exploits did a great deal to put the place on the map during one of its poorest periods.

The house is surrounded by a balcony that looks down over a superb jungle garden, which also has a magnificent swimming pool. Like everything to do with Hemingway, this has a story attached – and it's well worth taking the guided tour, which includes a generous sprinkling of these.

When Hemingway lived here he had a six-toed cat, and nowadays its six-toed descendents aloofly prowl the house and garden. Anyone who leaves such a legacy can't be all bad. And the book he wrote about life in 1930s Key West, *To Have and Have Not*, is one of his better efforts.

By contrast, the superior artist Tennessee Williams lived in an inferior clapboard house just over a mile down the road at **1431 Duncan Street**. The house lived in by the author of *A Street-*

A BOGUS CLAIM?

The Conchs claim that Key West is the southernmost point in the U.S. But strictly speaking this isn't true. Hawaii is several hundred miles further south. The locals get around this by claiming that theirs is the southernmost spot in *mainland* U.S. Yet Key West itself is almost a hundred miles from the mainland.

car Named Desire is at present occupied by a couple named Paradise. It is not open to visitors.

To visit other famous locals, head to: **Key West Cemetery** at *Margaret and Angela streets, open sunrise-6 pm, entry free*. Key West is solid rock, so the locals have to bury their dead above ground in modest mausoleums. In true Key West style these are adorned with the immortal nicknames and witticisms of their inhabitants and those they left behind. There are vaults occupied by "Bean," and "The Tailor." One tomb is inscribed "I told you I was sick," and on another a long-suffering wife had her last say with: "At least I know where he's sleeping tonight."

There are even a few graves of favorite local pets. One has a statue of a Key deer. Unfortunately, there's so little space on the island that for the last half century or so the locals have taken to recycling the graves. Rumour has it that there are now more than 100,000 buried where there's only room for 15,000.

The **Lighthouse Museum** is at *938 Whitehead Street, open 9.30 am-5 pm daily; entry $4*. You can't miss this. It's 86 feet high, just south of the Old Town. The lighthouse went up in 1847, to the chagrin of the locals trying to earn their living as wreckers, and its light still works. Inside, there are 88 steps up to the best view in Key West. The museum itself has a number of nautical nicknacks, of interest to only the saltiest of old salts.

But to make up for any disappointment, try a walk through the streets of nearby **Bahama Village**. This occupies the streets close by, and is filled with old-style Caribbean houses still occupied by Bahamian and Afro-Cuban families. The wooden houses, in streets

FLAGLER'S FOLLY

Henry Flagler built the railway that opened up the east coast of Florida and in 1905 decided to extend it south through the Florida Keys to Key West. His idea was to construct a direct railroad-ferry route running from New York to Havana, Cuba. The railroad that ran through the Keys was known as the Overseas Railroad, and it was one of the greatest engineering feats of the era.

Thousands of laborers were shipped in to work on the project. At one stage Flagler is said to have chartered every U.S. merchant ship in the Atlantic to bring in materials. Dredgers were shipped from Liverpool, floating cranes from London and cement from Hamburg. The 2-mile Long Key Viaduct, which he built, is still in use. But his greatest feat was building Seven Mile Bridge, which links Marathon and the Lower Keys (see separate entry). These bridges had to be built to withstand hurricanes, and Flagler claimed that no expense was spared to ensure the safety of his Overseas Railroad. This may have been so of the railroad itself, but the workers on the project were ill-paid and housed in such appalling conditions that before it was finished more than 700 of them had died.

After the original Seven Mile Bridge was destroyed in a hurricane, the railway track was uprooted in favor of a roadway. This became a great favorite with socialites from New York and the South, heading for Key West and the ferry to prohibition-free Havana in the Thirties. In some places the road over the bridges was just over 20 feet wide, and cars would be forced to crawl at a snail's pace to avoid being blown off into the sea. There were several drawbridges enabling ships to pass between the Gulf and the Atlantic Ocean. Their mechanism would become rusted in the sea breezes, causing frequent hold-ups. On one occasion revelers returning from Cuba were held up for three days, and during the ensuing wild party, drank every drop of the contraband rum which they had smuggled into the U.S., while the police and customs agents grimly watched from the other side of the bridge.

Many of the old bridges can still be seen, crossing stretches of water alongside the present roadway. They are now mainly the haunt of fishermen.

well off the main tourist trail, have picturesque porches and faded paint. How much longer the neighborhood will be left alone is another matter. See it while you can, before the developers and "restorers" move in.

The little restaurant at the corner of Petronia and Thomas streets, **Blue Heaven**, used to be a bordello, and the locals also used to hold cockfights here. Behind the house there's even a small graveyard where the finest of the losing cocks were buried. (They were unfit to eat.) Hemingway is said to have refereed boxing matches here.

A word of warning: Bahama Village is a delightful place to walk during the day, but at night you should exercise caution.

Wrecker's Museum, *322 Duval Street, open 10 am-4 pm; entry $4*. The museum is housed in the home of the sea captain and celebrated wrecker Francis Watlington, who built the place in 1829. He had been a Florida senator, but resigned to join the Confederate Navy during the Civil War. He used his seafaring skills to make a fortune out of salvaging wrecks from the reefs of the Florida Keys. (According to maritime law of the period, the first to get a line aboard the wreck was entitled to all its contents, after rescuing anyone aboard.)

Upstairs there's a wonderful Conch-style **doll's house** which has eight rooms, and is filled with miniature furniture of the period. Other upstairs rooms display some fascinating cartoons. Among these is the famous one of the preacher who gave one too many sermons on the evils of drink, and was tossed into the drink by his long-suffering, hard-drinking parishioners.

There are several museums in town devoted to Key West's history. The best for treasure recovered from the wrecks is the **Mel Fisher Maritime Heritage Society Museum** at *200 Greene St, open 9.30 am-5 pm daily; entry $5*. The best collection of old photos of Key West is at **Old City Hall**, *open most days; entry free*.

Southernmost Point, *at the S end of Whitehead and South streets*, claims to be the southernmost spot in the U.S., and it is suitably marked as such with a brightly-painted sign, so you can have your photo taken beside it.

I have visited here twice, and each time the question has arisen as to where the other three points are. According to the person who won the bet last time, they are the Aleutian Islands; Barrow Point, Alaska; and the easternmost tip of Maine. In those spots they probably also have painted signs, but, unlike the one in Key West, I doubt if those proclaim that the spot they stand on is also in another country. The sign here firmly states that it is in the Conch Republic.

As you approach this spot, the shops and facilities state that they are "the southernmost gas station in the U.S."

• *Lighthouse Museum, Key West.*

KEY WEST LITERATI

No fewer than eight Pulitzer Prize-winners have lived at one time or another in Key West. Famous writers who have stayed here include novelists John Dos Passos, Gore Vidal and Kurt Vonnegut; playwright Tennessee Williams and poets Wallace Stevens, Elizabeth Bishop and Robert Frost. Key West's most celebrated literary inhabitant, Ernest Hemingway, won the Nobel Prize. Every year on his birthday, July 21, they hold a Hemingway lookalike contest, a fitting tribute to his unique talent.

• *Sunset Celebrations in Key West.*

and so on. These notices are all genuine. What most people don't realize is that the actual brightly painted sign is misleading. The *real* southernmost point in the U.S. is through the wire to the right, in the naval base. You can *see* it, but you can't actually get to it – and don't try.

This geographical confusion continues when it comes to the **Southernmost House**. There are two of these. The stylish Georgian structure at 1400 Duval Street is my choice as the genuine one. The second claimant, at 400 South Street, may have been built over a century later, but it's much more interesting. This was where Thelma Strabel lived while writing her novel *Reap the Wild Wind*, which is all about Key West during the wild old days of the wreckers. Sadly, neither house is open to the public.

Just round the corner at the end of Duval Street you'll find the **Southernmost Beach**, where you can have your indisputably southernmost swim.

To experience the Mallory Square Sunset, turn left at the top of Duval Street. For those who must know these things, this square is named after Stephen Mallory, secretary of the Confederate Navy, who also ran the Mallory Steamship Line. This will probably be unknown, and of little interest, to the hundreds of people who turn up here every evening to take part in the **Sunset Celebrations**. Yes, Key West is that sort of place – and this is the big event of the day. The hawkers and bead sellers turn up, as do all kinds of survivors from that distant age when high had nothing to do with altitude and everyone was peaceful and loving (except occasionally at anti-Vietnam demonstrations). The fabulous tropical sunset, which is absolutely free of charge, fills the whole of the western sky with glorious crimson, streaked with gold and all the colors of your favorite ice cream. It's so sensational that people gasp – some actually applaud; others leap and dance, others take photos of the fire-eater against the sky, that has just eaten the sun. Don't miss it, whatever you do. (But be warned: no one else wants to miss it either – in the season it can get so crowded that they really ought to have a second showing.)

During the day, Mallory Square is a quaint, old-fashioned tourist market, where you'll see may superb examples of that colorful sunburnt species undergoing their traditional ritual, known locally as the "rip-off."

Little White House, in the **Truman Annexe**, west of the top end of Whitehead Street, is an ordinary little house that was the vacation home of the ordinary little man who became one of the great U.S. presidents: Harry S. Truman. He first came here in 1946, and returned many times. The house is now a museum, and contains the usual mementoes, some of which (especially the photos) are of genuine interest.

For Harry Truman, holidays meant trips with his political cronies and long morning dips in the pool. These presidential swims were something of a trial to his staff. Such was the eccentricity of Key West plumbing during this period that no one was allowed to go to the lavatory while the president was in the pool.

The **Truman Annexe** was the site of the naval base which was set up in 1822 to combat piracy in the Gulf of Mexico and the Caribbean, after Florida became part of the United States. During the Second World War nearly 20,000 military personnel and staff lived and worked here. Later it was decommissioned, and in 1986 it was bought lock, stock and barrel for $17 million by the developer Pritam Singh.

This could have been the occasion for having yet another historic spot transformed into a magnificent luxury nightmare – which would have completely destroyed the entire character of old Key West. But Pritam Singh proved to be a rare man, and set about creating an integrated community of (moderately) inexpensive family homes

• *A Key West hotel.*

• *Stylish car in Key West.*

and condominiums with landscaped gardens. It is undeniably designer-suburban, compared with much of old Key West, but so far the area has managed to remain exciting, popular and tasteful. This is as much a welcome rarity as the man who is responsible for it. Pritam Singh first arrived in Key West in the 1960s as a penniless hippy. Later he converted to the Sikh religion and decided to become a multimillionaire hippie. As with quite a few who underwent a similar transformation (The Beatles, Peter Norton, Charles Branson) he remained a recognizable human being with a sense of fun.

Audubon House, *205 Whitehead Street, at Greene Street, open 9.30 am-5pm daily; entry $7.* This was the home of James Audubon, the celebrated naturalist and author whose illustrated *Birds of America* is among the classics in its field. He visited Key West in 1832, looking for exotic species which he had not yet drawn, and at the same time, ironically, shooting large numbers of less exotic species for fun. (Audubon saw nothing anomalous about his sporting hobby.) After a few weeks of enjoyable sketching and hunting, he left. The present house, which was built over a decade later, has absolutely nothing to do with Audubon, except for the fact that it houses a collection of his ornithological engravings.

The man who built the house was another of Key West's celebrated wreckers, John Geiger. Besides the Audubon engravings you can also see the Geiger family photos. The Geiger family was quite interesting. John and his wife produced 12 children, and John was in the habit of bringing back children he had rescued from the wrecks, as well as the abandoned wives of sailors who had been left destitute. Look closer at one or two of those faded family snaps, use a bit of imagination, and a whole era of human life comes into being before your eyes.

This was the first of the old Key West mansions to be completely refurbished, and it set the trend. Be sure to take a stroll through the fabulous tropical gardens which surround the house.

Curry Mansion, *511 Caroline Street, open 10 am-5 pm; entry $5.* The mansion was built in 1855 by Milton Curry, the first millionaire in Florida; or in 1899 by Milton Curry, the *son* of the first millionaire in Florida. The history books provide alternative versions – and you take your pick. This 20-room mansion was Curry's rendition of a house in Paris, though why he chose this particular model was not discovered – either by local historians, or by his wife. You can wander about many of the rooms, and there is an interesting brochure. The house has been completely restored, in an eclectic combination of styles. There is a grotesque Frank Lloyd Wright lamp, a comforting Chinese commode and much banal glass – a combination of character that remains unfailingly stimulating. And those who enjoy the ambience of a stimulating environment will be pleased to know that they can stay here. The present owners, Al and Edith Amsterdam, have turned part of the building into a tasteful up-scale bed-and-breakfast spot.

Despite its distant echoes of Paris, Curry Mansion is now considered one of the finest examples of Conch architecture. You'll see more modest examples of this distinctive local style along Caroline Street, and just north (Greene Street). These also exhibit a sweet-and-sour mixture of styles. They were built in the 19thC by locals, often cheaply and speedily constructed to house the people who were building them. Yet there's no denying the imagination and inventiveness that went into their design. Nowadays, almost all of them have been painted, and gone is the rough-and-ready charm of their original unpainted appearance. Even so, their appeal and inventiveness remain – and their inordinate cost ensures that those who buy them have enough cash to maintain them in their modern colorfully painted Conch-reincarnation style.

Key West Aquarium, *1 Whitehead Street, directly opposite Mallory Square, open 10 am-6 pm daily; entry $6.* Built in 1934 as the world's first open-air aquarium, it took the prize as the world's first indoor open-air aquarium, when it was covered over some decades later. The inmates include a wide range of the species to be seen in the Keys. If you want to stroke a sea slug, shake hands with a starfish or poke the home of a hermit crab, this is the place for you.

Less hardy specimens are to be found at **231 Margaret Street**. The building used to be an old turtle-canning factory renowned for its turtle soup. In the 1970s the Florida Marine Conservancy turned it into a **Hospital for Sea Creatures,** *open noon-11 pm daily; entry free*. Besides the usual aquatic infirmary of malingering minnows, sick scampis and out-of-sorts sea urchins, they also look after injured seabirds. There's a large pool, which contains sharks who are tossed suitably gory remnants at feeding time. (Curiously, in the same building you'll find the Turtle Kraals Restaurant, where one hopes visiting relatives of those in the hospital don't end up on the menu.)

For further information on Key West and free brochures, call at the Greater Key West Chamber of Commerce on Wall Street, near Mallory Square. There's also a **Conch Tour Train** which leaves Mallory Square every half hour or so for a 90-minute tour of all the main sights ($15). On the other hand, if you're feeling energetic you can rent a bike. Many hotels either rent them, or have an arrangement with a nearby rental shop. For something different, try Moped Hospital, at 601 Truman Avenue, where you can rent brightly colored bikes with balloon tires.

To find out what's going on in town, pick up a free copy of the weekly *Island Life*. For events of interest to the gay community, check *What's Happening*.

LITTLE TORCH KEY 🛏

See Recommended Hotels, page 103.

LOOE KEY 🛏

Some 5 miles offshore from Ramrod Key, which is at Mile Marker 27.5 on Rt 1. The **Looe Key National Marine Sanctuary** is the Lower Keys' rival to John Pennekamp Coral Reef State Park up on Key Largo. In my view, it's even better.

Catch the boat from Ramrod Key, 4 miles west from Big Pine Key, or try Strike Zone Charters, which operates out of Big Pine Key at Mile Marker 28.5, tel. 305 872 9863. Four-hour trips, including rental of snorkel equipment, cost about $30 (double this for experienced divers renting oxygen tanks).

At Looe Key you'll find 5 miles of spectacular coral reef with all kinds of weird and wonderful formations, and *hundreds* of different species of tropical fish. When I was last here I saw a largish octopus, and later a much larger ray gliding menacingly through the rainbow shoals, before flapping gently off into the translucent blue yonder.

The sanctuary is named after the British warship HMS *Looe*, which ran into the reef and sank here in 1744. Its wreck is still visible, as are the remains of other wrecks. (Whether the latter are authentic, or imports, like the ones at John Pennekamp Park, I couldn't discover.)

NO NAME KEY

See Big Pine Key, page 88.

PIGEON KEY

See Seven Mile Bridge, below.

SEVEN MILE BRIDGE

Carries Rt 1 on its link between Marathon and the Lower Keys. The original bridge was the greatest engineering feat on the Overseas Railroad – often known as Flagler's Folly (see page 96). Although the bridge was built to withstand hurricanes, it was unable to survive the Labor Day Hurricane which hit it on September 2, 1935. The modern bridge cost nearly $50 million, has 546 concrete piers, and rises to over 70 feet above the sea at its apex. You can still see parts of the original bridge running alongside.

It's worth stopping to take a look at the old bridge. As you head south down Rt 1, turn right just before the modern bridge, and park on the lot below the bridge. From here you can walk out for several miles along the old bridge. This is the only way you can get to **Pigeon Key**, which was used in the early years of the century as the camp for the laborers who built the bridge. You can still see the huts which housed them – at press time they were being transformed into a museum.

Pigeon Key was used recently as a location for the film *True Lies* starring Arnold Schwarzenegger. Towards the end of the bridge the University of Miami has its Institute of Marine Science, which is not open to the public.

SUGARLOAF KEY 🛏 ✕

See Recommended Hotels and Restaurants, pages 103 and 104.

SUMMERLAND KEY ✕

See Recommended Restaurants, page 105.

UPPER KEYS

See Florida Overall: 4.

RECOMMENDED HOTELS

BAHIA HONDA KEY

Bahia Honda State Park, $; *Mile Marker* 29.5; *tel.* 305 872 2353; *cards* MC, V.

There's a campsite here, which also has half a dozen cabins. These are a bargain, if there are four or more of you. The state park attracts crowds, but you can easily lose them in 600 acres. Set out along the trails and find your own deserted tropical beach.

BIG PINE KEY

Deer Run Bed and Breakfast Lodge, $-$$; *Long Beach Drive, Big Pine Key* 33043; *tel.* 305 872 2015; *no cards.*

This is the place to come if you want to see the deer. Run by friendly Sue Abbot, who will tell you all the best places in the neighborhood. This spot really does have a home-away-from-home atmosphere. Be sure to book ahead. The inn has three rooms. Non-smokers only.

KEY WEST

Key West is a great place to stay, but it can be expensive. The season lasts from December to May, and during these warm winter months you'll be lucky to find a room under $90 a night. In the off-season you might find a few places with rooms for under $60.

Because Key West is a popular spot for gays, there are a number of exclusively gay motels and hotels. Almost everywhere, you're welcome regardless of sexual orientation – and your hosts will expect you to be equally tolerant of your fellow guests.

The most inexpensive hotel in town that I know of, is:

Tilton Hilton, $$; 511 *Angela Street, Key West* 33040; *tel.* 305 294 8694; *cards* MC, V.

The only resemblance this spot has to a Hilton is its name. A friend of mine described the decoration as "fundamental." Only a short walk from Mallory Square.

For only a little more money you can stay in a charming mini-paradise:

Key Lime Village Motel, $$; 727 *Truman Street, Key West*; *tel.* 305 294 6222; *all major cards.*

Small cabins and rooms amidst the palm and mango trees. (They also have some cheaper rooms with shared bathroom.) Just five minutes walk from Duval Street. Has a marvelous small swimming pool surrounded by jungle.

The best of the inexpensive guest houses is:

Wicker Guesthouse, $$; 913 *Duval Street, Key West* 33040; *tel.* 305 296 2475; *all major cards.*

This consists of four traditional old Conch houses, complete with porches (which are not just for show: there's no air-conditioning, only fans). As it's a guest house, you also get a free breakfast.

More pricey accommodations include:

Duval House, $$-$$$; 815 *Duval Stret, Key West* 33040; *tel.* 305 294 1666; *cards* AE, MC, V.

Twenty rooms with period furnishings around a subtropical garden, complete with swimming pool. Rooms vary in price, but those without too many antiques, four-poster beds, and so on offer value for money.

Eaton Lodge, $$-$$$; 511 *Eaton Street, Key West* 33040; *tel.* 305 294 3800; *cards* MC, V.

The rooms here also overlook a garden, and most have balconies. The lodge is on the National Register of Historic Places, but the plumbing does not belong to this prestigious class. If you're coming from the airport, they'll pick you up in their very own London taxi, which will deliver you to the chandeliered lobby. All as pleasant as it sounds.

La Concha Holiday Inn, $$-$$$; 430 *Duval Street, Key West* 33040; *tel.* 305 296 2991; *all major cards.*

Being Key West, this is no ordinary

Holiday Inn. It was built in 1925, and on can picture "Papa" Hemingway sipping cocktails here when it was the center of the social whirl. After the 1939 hurricane it was abandoned, and for years existed simply as a ghost hotel. Then in 1987 Holiday Inn sent in the ghostbusters and turned it into a great hotel. It's in the heart of the old town, has some of the greatest views on the island, and a large swimming pool.

Try The Top, a bar where you can enjoy a mind-blowing cocktail to match the mind-blowing sunset.

If the price doesn't matter, *the* place to stay in town is:

Marriott's Casa Marina Resort, $$$; *1500 Reynolds Street, Key West 33040; tel. 305 296 3535; all major cards.*

This was built by Flagler in 1921 to house the stream of stars, socialites and snappy spendthrifts who came in on his railway. The resort covers 13 acres and has more heiresses to the acre than anywhere else in town. Loll in wicker chairs beneath the bronze ceiling fans of the beamed lobby.

Its 150 rooms are housed in several buildings overlooking the lawns and private beach, complete with 80-foot swimming pier. Many rooms have balconies overlooking the ocean. Like any such spot, it has its own history of famous and infamous moments. Apart from the usual Tallulah Bankhead yarns, my favorite is the one about the general who moved in during the Cuban missile crisis and had his own personal anti-aircraft missile-launchers installed on the beach. The place is soon to be remodeled.

Those who want to stay at one of the exclusively male gay spots, should try:

Curry House, $$; *806 Fleming Street, Key West 33040; tel. 305 633 7439; cards* MC, V.

Not to be mistaken for the Curry Mansion (see page 100), where the ambience is unintentionally campy. A delightful spot. They also know the name of a female gay guest house.

In season, Key West gets sold out. It's always worth phoning ahead. If you're having difficulty in finding a place, call Key West Chamber of Commerce at 402 Wall Street (near Mallory Square); tel. 305 294 2587.

LITTLE TORCH KEY

Little Palm Island, $$$; *Mile Marker 28.5, Little Torch Key 33042; tel. 305 872 2524; all major cards.*

Exclusive resort complex on Little Munson Island. Once the haunt of presidents (when presidents could afford this kind of vacation). Thirty suites housed in scattered thatched villas – 3 miles across the water from the reception lobby on Little Torch Key. A genuinely inaccessible hideaway on a 5-acre tropical island. Just the place for your second honeymoon, or another first one.

LOOE KEY

Looe Key Reef Resort, $$; *Mile Marker 27.5; tel. 305 872 2215; cards* MC, V.

Ideal base for visits to the nearby marine sanctuary (see page 101 – Looe Key). They also run trips out to distant deserted atolls. A major scuba and snorkel center, it even has its own fully equipped shop.

SUGARLOAF KEY

Sugarloaf Lodge, $$-$$$; *Mile Marker 17, Sugarloaf Key 33044; all major cards.*

A motel with a difference – this one even has a lagoon with its own adopted, friendly dolphin named Sugar. Straightforward accommodations, but in a superb location. Nearby there's a marina which rents boats and offers trips.

Also has an excellent, inexpensive restaurant, Maximillions Diner, which serves a corned beef hash fit for a maximillionaire.

RECOMMENDED RESTAURANTS

BIG PINE KEY
Island Jim's, $-$$; *Mile Marker 31.5, Big Pine Key; tel.* 305 872 2017; *no cards.*

All-American breakfasts, and great steaks. Friendly clientele who are likely to give you the wrong directions with the very best of intentions.

This island also has the best bar for miles around (though the competition isn't exactly stiff). If you want a few beers and some lively live music, head down to the No Name Pub at the beginning of Watson Avenue (east).

KEY WEST
Unlike lodging, eating in Key West won't cost you an arm and a leg. There are plenty of places where you can pick up a light, inexpensive snack – or just have a drink and watch everyone who wants to be watched parade by. One of the best of these is:

Croissants de France, $-$$; 816 *Duval Street; tel.* 305 294 2624; *no cards; closed* Wed.

Right on the street where all the action is. Great breakfasts and exotic fruit juices, choice crêpes and succulent salads – all served on the veranda in leafy shade.

In the evening it becomes an excellent French restaurant (**$$-$$$**).

If you want great-value fresh seafood try:

Half Shell Raw Bar, $-$$; 920 *Caroline Street; tel.* 305 294 7496; *no cards.*

Idyllic spot, at the very end of Margaret Street overlooking the water. Sit on the dock with your sangria watching the sun go down, then go inside for their superb stone crabs and mustard sauce. A lively, very friendly spot.

For excellent seafood amidst romantic sophistication, try:

Cafe des Artistes, $$$; 1007 *Simonton Street; tel.* 305 297 7100; *cards* AE, MC, V; *evenings only.*

French cuisine with a Caribbean touch by chef Andrew Berman. He won an award for his Lobster Tango Mango, which more than makes up for its name. (Ingredients include lobster flambé, shrimp in mango and saffron *beurre blanc.*)

You can dine inside among the paintings, or outside beneath the stars. Now generally considered to be the best restaurant in Key West. The building was said to have been built in 1935 by Al Capone's accountant, whose first-class cooking skills were practised in a different sphere.

Pier House Restaurant, $$$; *at the* Pier House *Hotel,* 1 Duval *Street; tel.* 305 296 4600; *all major cards.*

In the old days, the ship for Havana put in at the pier here. A legendary spot, which was a great favorite with Tennessee Williams. You're right over the ocean, and their dishes are as dramatic as the setting – with much *nouvelle cuisine* flourish in the presentation. Their Key West yellowtail snapper is justly renowned.

Yo Sake, $-$$; 722 *Duval Street; tel.* 305 294 2288; *all major cards; dinner only.*

Japanese cuisine amid Japanese decor, but with a zippy difference. Long sushi bar, and other more intimate areas. All your usual favorites, and more. Perhaps it's the influence of Key West, but the place has an infectiously happy ambience.

SUGARLOAF KEY
Mangrove Mama's Restaurant, $-$$; *Mile Marker* 20, *Sugarloaf Key; tel.* 305 745 3030; *cards* DC, MC, V; *closed Sept, the odd* Thur.

Legendary spot, in a shack which survived even the great 1935 hurricane that destroyed the railway. Great fresh local seafood at mouth-watering prices. Dine inside amid the atmosphere and the locals, or out under the shade of a banana bush.

SUMMERLAND KEY
Monte's Restaurant and Fish Market, $$; *Mile Marker* 25, *Summerland Key* 33043; *no cards*.

Here you can choose your own fresh fish from the day's catch on the slab, and it tastes as good as you'd expect. Their fresh shark is something else – but they also do a great spicy crayfish pie. As for the decor – forget it (a plastic disaster). People come here from miles around for the food.

WORLD-FAMOUS WATERING HOLES OF KEY WEST
No visit to Key West would be complete without a visit to:

Sloppy Joe's, 201 *Duval Street; tel.* 305 294 5717.

Raunchy, raucous bar where they have great live performers belting it out. The walls are hung with all kinds of Hemingway memorabilia because Sloppy Joe's is *said* to have been Papa's favorite bar.

And it really was. Trouble is, the original Sloppy Joe's was down the road. The place where Papa and the fishermen used to hang out and tell each other their macho fishing fibs is now called Captain Tony's. But Papa obviously got soused in them all, so who cares.

• *Duval Street, Key West.*

Captain Tony's, 428 *Greene Street; tel.* 305 294 1838.

Run by the redoubtable Cap'n Tony himself. Or rather, when I was last here it was being run by what he swore was his thirteenth daughter who was probably the only person on planet Earth who could handle her dad. Cap'n Tony is getting on a bit now, yet he's still a Key West legend, and deservedly so. But beware, he's no tame parrot in his grizzled beard and sailor cap. Out of season, when it's less crowded, I can still see why this used to be my favorite bar south of the Mason Dixon Line.

Florida Overall: 6

Northern Florida

Between Cape Canaveral and Jacksonville

The North-Eastern Coast

60 miles; map Hallwag Florida

This is Florida old and new. St Augustine is the longest continuously inhabited settlement in the U.S., pre-dating Jamestown by more than 40 years, and one of the most historically interesting. By contrast, Daytona Beach is one of the wildest resorts in the U.S., attracting a brash, fun-loving crowd. This is the home of the famous Daytona 500 stock-car race, and during Spring Break it attracts thousands of students from all over the U.S.

The beaches along this stretch of the coast are among the finest in Florida, and bring in more than 8 million visitors every year. The best way to travel through is along Rt A1A, where you're never far from the ocean. From New Smyrna Beach in the south to Jacksonville Beach in the north is just over a hundred miles and can easily be covered in a leisurely day's drive. But you should allow at least a couple of days for exploring St Augustine. The old quarter here is a living museum of Florida's colonial past, with elements dating from British and French as well as Spanish rule.

Daytona has "The World's Greatest Beach," where 70 years ago the fastest drivers in the world flirted with death in their attempts to break the World Land Speed Record. Twenty miles south at New Smyrna Beach, you can see the 200-year-old ruins of an early colony, which came to grief through the greed of its unscrupulous owner.

In summer this area takes off with a vengeance. Out of season, its empty shoreline can be appealingly desolate.

TRANSPORTATION
Regular bus service links all the main towns, but the best way to see this stretch is by car.

SIGHTS & PLACES OF INTEREST

ANASTASIA ISLAND

See St Augustine, page 114.

DAYTONA BEACH

About 55 miles S of St Augustine on Rt 1. **Daytona Beach** is so long and wide and flat that cars once broke the world land speed record on it. From Ormond Beach in the north down to the Ponce de León Inlet, "The World's Greatest Beach" stretches for 23 miles. It is the most popular piece of coastline in Florida, a world of boardwalks, amusement parks, high-rise beachfront hotels, wet T-shirt competitions and all the fun of the fair. There's always something going on at Daytona Beach.

January marks the start of the stock-car qualifiers for the famous **Daytona 500**, which takes place a month later. March includes Motorcycle Week, when the bikers hit town. Then comes Spring Break in April, when college students from all over America come to Daytona to do what students do when they're on vacation by the sea. This mayhem is followed by Speedway Racing, which comes to a climax in June with the Firecracker 400. And on it goes.

These events take place at the **Daytona International Speedway** – "The World Center of Racing" – at *1801 Volusia Avenue, off Rt 92* beyond the airport. If you want to find out more about these events, stop at the Daytona Beach Convention and Visitors Bureau, 126 East Orange Avenue, open 9 am to 5 pm Monday to Friday.

For some background historical information about Daytona Beach's long love affair with souped-up engines, try a visit to the **Birthplace of Speed Museum** at *160 East Granada Boulevard, open 1 am-5 pm Tues-Sat; entry $1*. Daytona types aren't big on museums, so don't be surprised if you find this one doesn't quite live up to your expectations. The best things here are the photos of the old heroes of speed, and a replica of a Stanley Steamer: the car that hurtled into the ocean at 197 mph in 1907.

Something of a contrast is the **Museum of Arts and Sciences**, *1040 Museum Boulevard; open 9 am-4 pm Tues-Fri, 12 noon-5 pm Sat and Sun; entry $3 adults, $1 children and students.* Primitive types have long been a feature of Daytona Beach, but even during Motorcycle Week you won't see a hairy monster to match the million-year-old giant sloth on display here. The Daytona region has produced many fine fossils and skeletons of beasts who never made it into the Speedway era, and this is where they've ended up.

The museum has exhibits of all kinds. But best of all is the superb collection of **Cuban art.** When Cuban dictator Generalissimo Batista fled the island in the 1950s, this is part of the loot he

SMASHING RECORDS

In 1902 R.E. Olds wowed them all by roaring down Daytona Beach at a speed of 57 mph. Oldsmobiles were soon smashing through to 70 mph. In 1907 Fred Marriott came within a whisker of breaking through the 200 mph barrier before his car veered off the sand in an inadvertent attempt at the Water Speed Record.

After this there was a long lull: it looked as if the 200 mph barrier was unbreakable. Then, in 1928, the British millionaire speed fanatic Sir Donald Campbell arrived at Daytona with a car powered by an aircraft engine, which finally crashed through the barrier at 206 mph.

Campbell was launched on the career which would bring him to the brink of bankruptcy, returning to Daytona to crash the Land Speed Record again and again. The Wall Street Crash came and went as Campbell roared on into the record books. Finally, in 1935, he clocked 276 mph, the highest speed ever achieved on Daytona Beach. In order to keep breaking the Land Speed Record, Campbell needed not only more speed and more money, but more land. Even "The World's Greatest Beach" was now too small.

Today you, too, can drive your car down the beach, but you have to stick to the 10 mph speed limit and pay $3. The best time is in the early evening, when hundreds join the parade.

brought with him. Like many an out-of-work Latin American dictator, Batista set up home in Florida. And when he died, he gave his collection to his hometown museum. This is probably the finest collection of Cuban art outside Cuba, and will quickly convince you that there's plenty more to Cuban culture than Havana cigars and Cuba Libre.

FORT CAROLINE

See St Augustine, page 110.

JACKSONVILLE AND JACKSONVILLE BEACHES

See Florida Overall: 7.

NEW SMYRNA BEACH

About 20 miles S of Daytona Beach. Archaeologists claim that New Smyrna Beach may have one of the oldest Indian settlements in the country. The site of this settlement is at Turtle Mound, and has yet to be fully excavated.

By the early 1500s, New Smyrna Beach had become the Indian village of Caparaca. It is believed that this is where the Spanish explorer Ponce De León first set foot on the Florida mainland in 1513.

The first European settlers arrived here in 1756, led by Scottish doctor Andrew Turnbull. He named the place New Smyrna after his Greek wife's birthplace (which is now called Izmir, in Turkey). Turnbull brought with him 1,500 impecunious Greek, Italian and Minorcan settlers. These were expected to dig canals and drainage ditches

• *Daytona Beach.*

for rice fields, as well as clear the land and work the maize, sugar and cotton plantations.

Turnbull exploited and overworked these settlers so badly that eventually most of them fled up the coast to St Augustine.

Many of the old drainage canals from Turnbull's settlement are still being used today. At the **Turnbull Ruins** you can see the remains of the colony, including its mill, wells and the foundations of Turnbull's house.

Nothing much happens in New Smyrna Beach these days, but it has a huge wide sandy beach stretching for 8 miles. Alas, New Smyrna Beach has succumbed to World's Greatest Syndrome. It claims that its beach is "The World's Safest." When I questioned my local informant about figures to support this, and how they were gathered worldwide, I was told that New Smyrna's world supremacy was a "scientific fact." He explained how a vast rock formation 40 miles offshore has "a baffling effect" that prevents powerful undercurrents from dragging waders along the beach and swimmers far out into the ocean.

He made up for my bafflement by taking me to the **Atlantic Center for the Arts** at *1414 Art Center Avenue*. This is a gem. It has regularly changing shows by good artists, and literary workshops run by writers of the caliber of Edward Albee.

ORMOND BEACH

See Daytona Beach, page 108.

• *Cuban art at the Daytona Museum of Arts and Sciences.*

ST AUGUSTINE 🛏 ✕

Some 32 miles SE of Jacksonville on Rt 1.

St Augustine really is historic. Europeans had set up residence here more than half a century before the Pilgrim Fathers arrived at Plymouth Rock. This is the oldest continuously inhabited settlement in the U.S.

Ponce de León, the earliest Spanish explorer of Florida, put ashore here in 1513 in search of the legendary Fountain of Youth. He had an ugly encounter with a group of painted braves and decided to push on. More than 50 years later the Spanish Admiral of the Fleet (and former smuggler) Pedro Menendez de Aviles arrived here on September 8, 1565, with a thousand settlers and a priest. He named the place after the saint of the day, who happened to be St Augustine of Hippo. (The latter half was sadly dropped in order to prevent scholars confusing it with the North African town.)

But Menedez' motives were far from saintly. The French had already staked their claim to establishing the oldest continuously inhabited settlement in America, by founding **Fort Caroline** 30 miles north at the mouth of the St Johns River. Menendez quickly erased French hopes of entering the record books by sacking Fort Caroline and massacring its inhabitants. He then returned and set his thousand settlers to work building a settlement, and nine wooden forts, along the coast. Meanwhile the priest was dispatched to the interior to convert the locals to the Roman Catholic faith. Here he encountered Timucuan tribes, who already had a thriving animistic faith of their own. This featured several extremely painful sacrifical rites, which, fortunately for the priest, only worked if they were practiced on fellow members of the faith. The priest returned to St Augustine disgusted by the spiritual primitivism of these native Americans, who had resisted his attempts to convert them to the faith of the Inquisition.

The nine wooden forts fared even worse. The few that weren't flattened by storms, struck by lightning or raided by pirates, were finally burnt to the ground by the English Admiral of the Fleet (and former pirate) Sir Francis Drake. St Augustine now had to put up with the hostile attentions of the English, as well as the usual difficulties which beset any fledgling settlement in this part of the new continent (plague, typhoid, hurricane, lightning, pirates, native raids, famine, syphilis, potato blight, and so on).

The Spanish decided to protect themselves by building a fine fortress in the latest indestructible style (diamond-shaped battlements with turrets extending from each corner). Building on the

Castillo de San Marcos was started in 1672, and this exercise evidently proved of such therapeutic value to the inhabitants of St Augustine that the fortress was only completed 84 years later in 1756. This was just in time to hand it over to the British, who took over in 1763.

Ironically, this was a peaceful takeover. The Spanish simply swapped the entire Florida peninsula for the town of Havana, whose nightlife was considered far too good to be left in British hands. In this way, the *Castillo de San Marcos* laid the foundations for its proud boast – which remains true to this day – that it has never suffered a military defeat. However, the same cannot be said for St Augustine. Throughout the course of the 18thC, it was held successively by the British, the French, and again the Spanish, as well as enduring many a long siege by any one or two of these three. (Presumably surrender didn't count as a military defeat in those days, at least as far as the *Castillo de San Marcos* was concerned.)

During the American War of Independence, St Augustine backed the wrong side, but no one seemed to mind. The Americans weren't interested in fighting for a subtropical swamp such as Florida, and it was left in Spanish hands. Within 40 years the Americans changed their mind and began making cross-border raids. Rather than risk the reputation of their indefatigable fort in St Augustine, the Spanish decided to sell Florida lock, stock and barrel to the United States and leave for Spain.

By the time the Americans took over in 1821, St Augustine was almost a ghost town, having suffered from a disastrous outbreak of yellow fever. The population was little more than 1,500, a third of whom were African American and native American slaves.

Things hardly looked set to improve with the outbreak of the Seminole War, when the native Americans refused to be evicted and threatened to take over the state. Yet, ironically, this marked the beginning of St Augustine's reversal of fortune. The port became a major center for the importing of arms, as well a base for ships ferrying munitions and supplies up and down the coast. The profits were used to fix the place up. Fortunately, the locals didn't have enough money to build from scratch, so they restored many of the old buildings from the Spanish period. The result was a curiously quaint little city, which looked as if it belonged on the shores of the Mediterranean.

It was not long before the first few tourists began to arrive, seeking to escape the cold northern winters. This source of revenue was interrupted by the American Civil War, when once again St Augustine backed the wrong side. In 1862, St Augustine surrendered to the Union forces (thus enabling the illustrious record of the *Castillo de San Marcos* to remain intact).

• *Ramparts of Castillo de San Marcos.*

• *Old-style transport in* St *Augustine.*

A year after the end of the war, oil tycoon Henry Flagler arrived in St Augustine on his honeymoon. He was so impressed by the charms of the city that he initiated his development of Florida as a vacation destination. Flagler's new railway brought rich winter tourists, and he built the magnificent Ponce de León Hotel to house them. But Flagler's railway soon passed on down the coast, and St Augustine never really took off as a luxury society resort, becoming instead a pleasant historic backwater.

Yet the citizens remained proud of their city. Through the years the gradual restoration of St Augustine continued, with the result that today there is nowhere quite like it in the rest of the country. The picturesque narrow streets and balconied houses of the old city are beautifully preserved, down at the waterfront there are pleasant cafes, and across on the barrier islands there are miles of fine beaches.

A walk through old St Augustine

In order to avoid the crowds, which can be considerable during the vacation season, I suggest you start this walk early in the morning, or late afternoon. Allowing for time to stop in at the various sights, it should take you just over a couple of hours.

Start from the **Visitors Center**. This is at 10 Castillo Drive, where it meets San Marco Avenue, *open 8.30 am-5.30 pm, later in summer.* Here you can pick up a map of St Augustine, and there's also a small museum with a few historic odds and ends.

Just across the road is the most unhistoric museum in St Augustine: **Ripley's Believe It or Not,** *open 9 am-6 pm, closing 9 pm in summer; entry* $7.50. This collection of monuments to human ingenuity and inanity (one of several worldwide) is housed in a suitably zany Moorish-style castle. The exhibits were collected by the celebrated cartoonist Robert Ripley on his travels around the globe in the 1920s and 1930s.The height of absurdity is achieved by a model of the Eiffel Tower constructed with 110,000 toothpicks. The low point is reached with an African mask made out of flayed human skin. The sublime is reduced to the ridiculous with a Van Gogh painting reproduced in jelly beans; the reverse is achieved with a mummified Egyptian cat which has not purred for more than 2,000 years. Videos exhibit world-class achievement in its most desperate form (the man who hammered nails with his fist and pulled them out with his teeth, and so on).

Having survived this titillating insight into the human condition, you now turn south down San Marco Avenue.

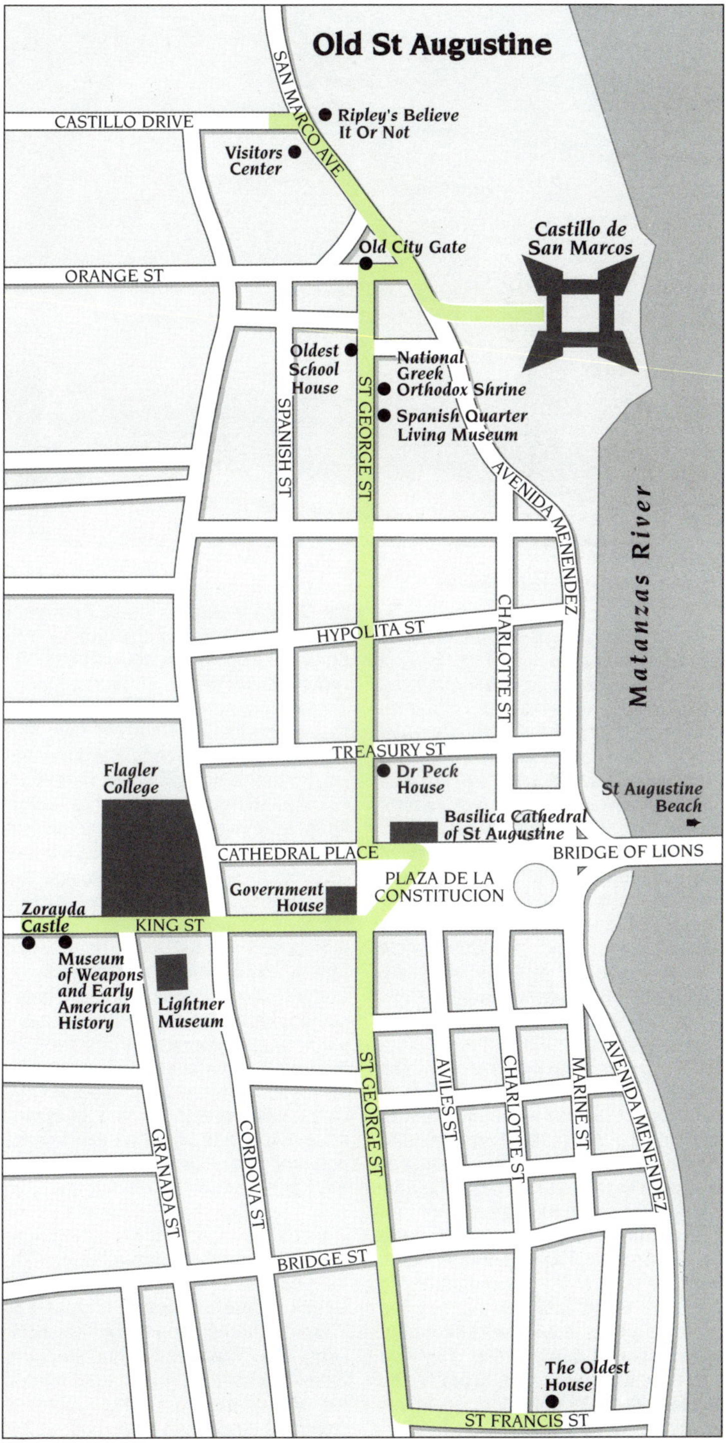

Old St Augustine
CASTILLO DRIVE
SAN MARCO AVE
Ripley's Believe It Or Not
Visitors Center
Castillo de San Marcos
Old City Gate
ORANGE ST
Oldest School House
National Greek Orthodox Shrine
Spanish Quarter Living Museum
SPANISH ST
ST GEORGE ST
AVENIDA MENENDEZ
Matanzas River
CHARLOTTE ST
HYPOLITA ST
TREASURY ST
Dr Peck House
Flagler College
St Augustine Beach
Basilica Cathedral of St Augustine
CATHEDRAL PLACE
BRIDGE OF LIONS
PLAZA DE LA CONSTITUCION
Government House
Zorayda Castle
KING ST
Museum of Weapons and Early American History
Lightner Museum
AVILES ST
MARINE ST
GRANADA ST
CORDOVA ST
BRIDGE ST
The Oldest House
ST FRANCIS ST

• *Oldest School House, St Augustine.*

On your left you will see the **Castillo de San Marcos**, *open* 8.45 *am*-4.45 *pm daily, extended hours on Sun and in summer; entry* $2. The castle is in predictably good condition, given its undefeated record and the way in which it maintained this (see page 111). It was built of shell-rock blocks quarried on nearby Anastasia Island. Initially its walls were covered with plaster, which was painted white and red (the ancient Spanish colors) so that no passing Spanish ship would fire on it by mistake, and any aggressors would know precisely whom they were attacking (and adjust tactics accordingly).

The castle has a square center, with acute-angled ramparts extending from each corner. These enabled the inmates to direct extra firepower, or to get a better look at the enemy before surrendering. Inside there are a number of storerooms, an uninviting prison cell and several ancient cannons. The central area was used as a prison camp for native American prisoners during the Seminole War. There are fine views from the surprisingly low ramparts. On one side these look out across the rooftops of the city which the castle once defended. On the other, they look over the waterway that brought the ships to which the defenders would surrender.

As you leave the castle, you will see the **Old City Gates.** These date from the 1700s, guarding the entrance to San Augustino Antiguo (the Old Quarter) and its central artery, St George Street. This was barely wide enough for horses to pass each other in the old days, and is now pedestrianized. The street is lined with Spanish-style balconied houses, all in authentic colonial style. Unfortunately, owing to St Augustine's violent history, many of the originals were destroyed. The present buildings are for the most part heavily reconstructed, but none the worse for that.

Proceed south down St George Street, and 50 yards on your right you come to No. 14, which is the **Oldest School House**, *open* 9 *am*-5 *pm, closes* 8 *pm in summer; entry* $2. This wooden building is well over 200 years old. Inside you can see wax models of the oldest teacher and pupils, including a traditional dunce. You can also see the dungeon where those who had misbehaved contemplated running away to sea.

Continue south down St George Street, and on the opposite side at No. 41 you can see the small **National Greek Orthodox Shrine,** housed in St Photios Chapel, *open* 9 *am*-5 *pm daily; entry free.* This commemorates the Greeks who fled from commercial exploitation in New Smyrna (70 miles down the coast, see page 109) at the end of 18thC. The typical homely chapel is in the Byzantine style. Inside there are frescoes, icons and recorded Orthodox chants, as well as a display outlining the monstrous episode which brought the Greeks to St Augustine. (For further details, see New Smyrna Beach, page 109.)

Further down St George Street, on the same side, you come to No. 29 Triay House, the entrance to the **Spanish Quarter Living Museum,** *open* 9 *am*-5 *pm daily; entry* $5. This consists of several colonial-style houses dating from the 1700s. The houses have been meticulously reconstructed to form a living museum, complete with locals in fancy dress going about their 18thC business. The blacksmith even lives above his old smithy, and tells you the secrets of his trade. There's a glimpse of bygone thirsts in the **Geronimo de Hita y Salazar House,** which houses an ancient tavern.

A couple of hundred yards further down St George Street on the same side, at the corner of Treasury Street, No. 153, **Dr Peck House**, is said to have housed the city Treasury, *open* 10.30 *am*-4.30 *pm, Sun afternoons only; entry* $1.50. In 18thC Spanish colonial times this house became the center of St Augustine society. In 1837 it was bought by Dr Peck from New England, and his descendants lived on here until 1931. Items of Dr Peck's original furniture remain on display.

About 50 yards further on, St George Street enters the Plaza de la Constitucion. As early as the 1500s this was the market place and commercial hub of the settlement. The square is overlooked on the north side by the **Basilica Cathedral of St Augustine,** *open* 5.30-*to* 7 *pm daily; entry free*. Although this church was largely rebuilt just 30 years ago, it is a suitably faithful facsimile of the 18thC original. It contains the oldest parish records in America.

Across the plaza, on the corner of St George Street and King Street, is **Government House**, *open* 10 *am*-4 *pm; entry* $2. The first Spanish governor of St Augustine lived in a house on this site in the 1500s. The present building houses a museum where you can learn about St Augustine in the bad old days, and how they built the *Castillo de San Marcos* which was meant to herald the beginning of the good old days.

Continue west down King Street, and on your left you'll see the imposing façade of the **Lightner Museum,** whose twin towers overlook a pleasant fountain, a large fish pond and palm

• *Flagler College, St Augustine.*

• *Stained-glass window, Lightner Museum.*

trees; *open 9 am-5 pm daily; entry* $4. This was built by Flagler in 1889 as a luxury hotel to house the society tourists brought in by his new railway. The old Alcazar Hotel went bust in the Depression, and now houses the decorative arts collection of Chicago publisher Otto C. Lightner, who acquired most of his collection cheaply from fellow tycoons who suffered the same fate as the Alcazar Hotel.

If you're interested in anything from Egyptian mummies to Tiffany lamps, this is an ideal spot to browse. You probably won't have time to see everything, so it's best to choose ruthlessly. My first choice is the superb **Venetian glass** collection. On the way up to this on the second floor, you may well catch a glimpse of things which will bring you back another day.

On the opposite side of the street is **Flagler College,** which was originally Flagler's Ponce de León Hotel. This extravagant monstrosity is now a liberal arts college. Take a walk around the campus, and – for an insight into the absurdity of Victorian era grand hotel architecture – look inside the main building, *open 10 am-3 pm; entry free.*

Further down King Street on the opposite side is the **Museum of Weapons and Early American History,** *open 10 am-6 pm; entry* $2. This contains the usual collection of gruesome weapons with which the pioneers did their best to eliminate bison and native Americans. If weapons don't interest you, head for the riveting and authentic **Civil War diaries.**

Just down the street on the same side is another prime example of 19thC architectural bankruptcy. **Zorayda Castle,** *open 9 am-5.30 pm; entry* $4. This was intended as a copy of the wonderful 13thC Alhambra Palace, Granada, Spain. The version seen here was eventually bought by an eccentric Egyptian millionaire, who used it to house his Sacred Cat Rug, which dated from 300 BC and was said to inflict a hideous curse on anyone who set foot on it.

Retrace your footsteps down King Street until you arrive back at the Plaza. Here continue south down St George Street for 300 yards and turn left into St Francis Street. On the left at No. 14, you will see **The Oldest House,** which dates from 1723; *open 9 am-5 pm, entry* $5. In fact, the original house on this site was built more than a century before this, but was razed to the ground by the invading British around the turn of the 18thC. The rooms are in various styles, reflecting different eras of the house's occupancy. Its most illustrious occupant was Mary Peavett, wife of a paymaster in the British garrison. She supervised the addition of a second storey to the building, and opened a shop. She then turned the place into a tavern, at the same time filling in as a midwife. In 1783, when the British were turned out, she converted to Catholicism so she could remain in Spanish St Augustine. Three years later her husband died. Within a year, the 53-year-old widow had married a handsome 28-year-old wastrel named John Hudson, who ran up debts all over town and did his best to spend all her money. Eventually Hudson was sentenced to a stretch in the Castillo cooler for ripping down an official proclamation and using it for "the indecent gesture of wiping his backside." Hudson was eventually banished from St Augustine, leaving Mary to savor the memories and count her pennies in The Oldest House.

Retrace your footsteps down St Francis Street, turn right back up St George Street, and you arrive at the central Plaza.

RECOMMENDED HOTELS

DAYTONA BEACH

Fact of life: during special events at the Speedway track, or during Spring Break (March-April), rooms are likely to be double, triple (or more) their usual price. The good news is that during the summer prices plummet. For an inexpensive night at the heart of the action, try:

Econo Lodge, $-$$; 301 *South Atlantic Avenue, Daytona Beach* 32018; *tel.* 904 255 6421; *all major cards.*

On the ocean close to the pier at Broadway. When the surf gets too rough, there's a good pool, which attracts a friendly crowd.

Howard Johnson Hotel, $$; 600 *North Atlantic Avenue, Daytona Beach* 32081; *tel.* 904 253 7543; *all major cards.*

Attractive Art Deco block on the ocean front. Get a high room and look down at night as the cars cruise the beach.

ST AUGUSTINE

Howard Johnson, $$; 137 *San Marco Avenue, St Augustine* 32084; *tel.* 904 824 6181; *all major cards.*

North of downtown, just half a mile from the old quarter. Pleasant pool; delightful courtyard with centuries-old oak tree, complete with Spanish moss. Standard motel rooms.

Many of the places out at the beach only rent by the week. An exception is:

Beacher's Lodge, $-$$; 6970 Rt A1A, *St Augustine Beach* 32086; *tel.* 904 471 8849; *cards* DC, MC, V.

More than a hundred rooms, near the sea. A friendly spot, where you get free orange juice and a newspaper in the morning.

RECOMMENDED RESTAURANTS

DAYTONA BEACH

Checkers, $-$$; 219 *South Atlantic Avenue, Daytona Beach; tel.* 904 239 0010; *no cards.*

This serves a great all-you-can-eat dinner. If you think *you* can eat, get down here when the bikers are in town to see how it's *really* done.

For something slightly more upscale, try:

Sophie Kay's Waterfall Restaurant, $$; 3516 *South Atlantic Avenue, Daytona Beach; tel.* 904 756 4444; *all major cards.*

Amid the palm trees and the greenery, a waterfall cascades into a goldfish pond. Local TV cook Sophie is famous for her imaginative seafood. The atmosphere is so exotic that John Travolta even brought his mother here for her birthday.

ST AUGUSTINE

Raintree, $$; 102 *San Marco Avenue, St Augustine; tel.* 904 824 7211; *all major cards; open for dinner only, between 5 pm and 10 pm.*

Their wine list wins awards, their cuisine wins finger-kisses, and their ambience wins hearts. And this needn't cost too much, if you go for one of their superbly imaginative crêpes.

For a romantic nightcap, try a final brandy amid the greenery on the delightful brick patio.

Santa Maria, $-$$; 135 *Avenida Menendez, St Augustine; tel.* 904 829 6578; *all major cards.*

Family-run institution down on the waterfront, famous for fresh seafood. Friendly clientele includes locals as well as tourists.

Northern Florida

Between Jacksonville and Tallahassee

Jacksonville and the North

150 miles; map Hallwag Florida

This section covers northeastern Florida, and inland along the Georgia border to Tallahassee. Jacksonville, the largest city in the state, sprawls for miles along both banks of the St Johns River, but has a number of sights that make up for its unpromising industrial ambience. Nearby, on the coast, are a number of lively resorts with superb stretches of pristine white sandy beach.

North-east of Jacksonville is Amelia Island, another fine vacation spot often overlooked by visitors.

Inland, the countryside is largely unspoiled, and feels much more like the traditional Deep South than the vacation state of Florida. Here, at Olustee, you can see the site of one of the great battles of the Civil War. Nearby is the wilderness woodland of the Osceola National Forest, which has miles of trails and some of the best fishing in the region at Ocean Pond.

East of the Osceola National Forest, you encounter the meandering course of the Suwannee River. It was made famous by the 19thC songwriter Stephen Foster, who never in fact set eyes on the river. You can learn about the poignant life of this supremely gifted artist at the Stephen Foster Folk Culture Center in White Springs. The area contains a number of state parks, and, because it is, on the whole, off the beaten track, these are just the places to go if you want to get away from it all.

You can drive from Jacksonville to Tallahassee in a morning, but it is worth allowing a couple of days to explore, and you'll probably want to spend at least a day enjoying the coast.

TRANSPORTATION
Regular Greyhound buses connect Jacksonville and Tallahassee, stopping at the main towns. There's also a daily train between these two cities, which gives you a chance to see what life is like on the slow track. However, by far the best way to explore this region is by car.

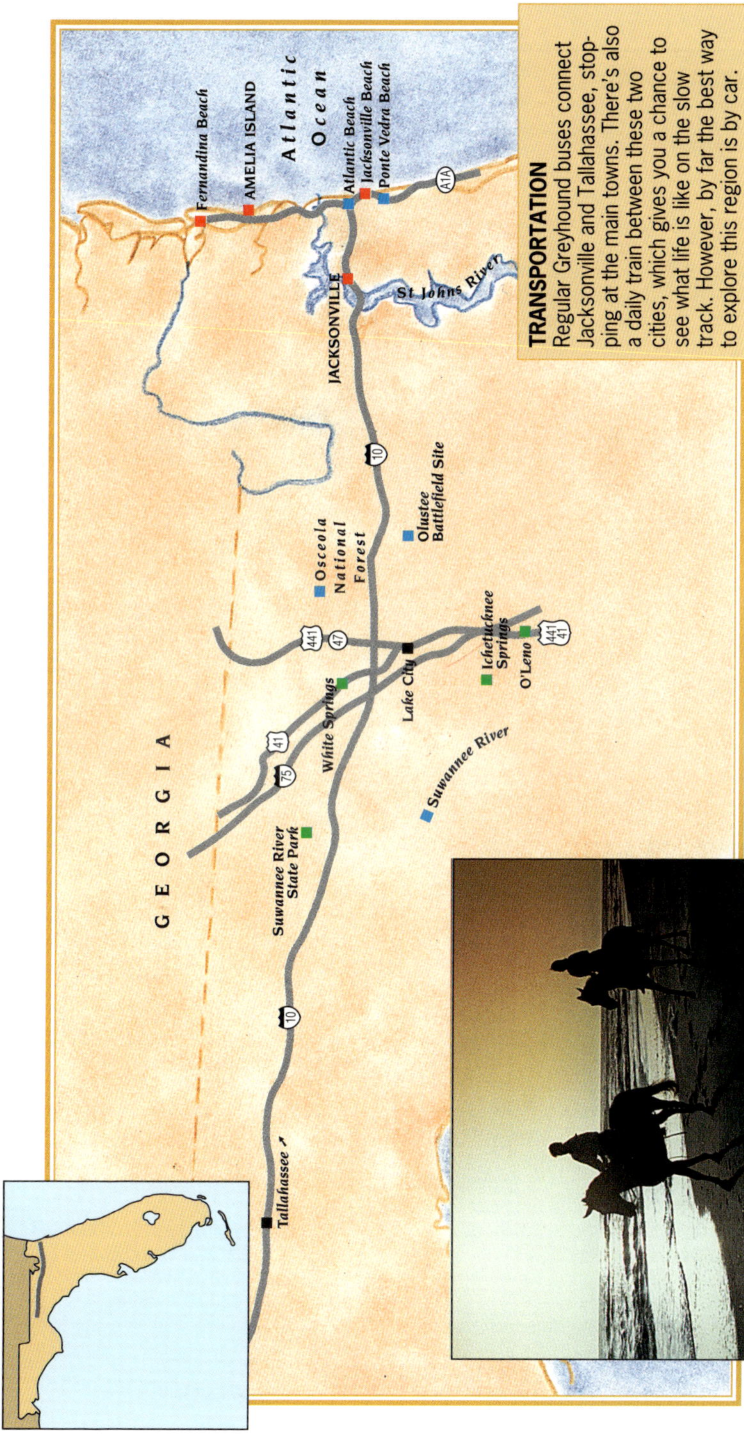

SIGHTS & PLACES OF INTEREST

AMELIA ISLAND 🛏 ×

Some 29 miles NE of Jacksonville, at the end of Rt A1A. This 15-mile long island lies up against the state border with Georgia. It has a long and varied past; no fewer than eight different flags have been raised over it since it was discovered by Europeans in the 1500s, which makes it unique in U.S. history. The flags are: the Spanish (twice); the French; the British (several times); the flag of the American "Patriots of Amelia Island" (which flew for all of a day, in 1812); the Green Cross of Florida (an alternative patriotic group, which lasted only a little longer); the Mexican; the Confederate and finally the Stars and Stripes.

The island's main town is **Fernandina Beach**, once a pirate stronghold. At the beginning of the 19thC, when the island was still in Spanish hands, it became the main smuggling centre for goods going in and out of the United States. President Monroe, who had placed an embargo on foreign vessels trading with America, characterized Fernandina Beach as a "festering fleshpot" - which naturally caused an immediate upsurge in the city's popularity.

Don't miss the **Old Town** of restored houses, some of which were built almost 150 years ago. These are around Centre Street. They insist upon keeping the old English spelling. The way the locals have it: the Spanish named the town, but the English named the streets – and according to an ancient local Indian legend, the pelicans brought the sun. Many of these houses have gables, turrets and porches typical of the finest American architecture of the period. Watch for the **Tabby House** and **Fairbank's Folly**, an Italianate fantasy which bankrupted its owner and horrified his wife.

Also worth visiting is the **graveyard**, where you'll see a wide range of European names that reflect the polyglot population of the period, and where the local worthies of Centre Street and the ex-pirates lie side by side.

Be sure to visit the **Museum of History**, *233 South Third Street, open 11 am-3 pm, Mon-Fri; entry free but voluntary donation invited.* This is housed in what was once the local jail, and has some interesting maps and photos, which will mean much more if you've already seen Centre Street district in its present state.

The Old Town dates from the era when **Fernandina Beach** was the main port on Florida's east coast and the wealthiest city in the state. It was also the terminus for the cross-state railroad, which ran all the way down to Cedar Key on the Gulf coast (a modern nowhereville). The old railway depot is now the Amelia Island-Fernandina Beach Chamber of Commerce.

There are over 10 miles of beach on Amelia Island. You'll find the **town beach** at the end of Atlantic Avenue. From here you can see the Amelia Lighthouse, which dates from 1839. Like all the beaches in this region, it is excellent, and seldom becomes too crowded. Indeed, Fernandina Beach is something of a well-kept secret. Except during the height of the summer season, it's usually fairly quiet.

About 3 miles north of here is **Fort Clinch State Park**, *open 8 am-sunset daily; cars $4.* The U.S. government started to build this fort early in the 1800s, after they bought Florida from the Spanish. The idea was to deter pirates and smugglers from entering the harbor, but soon the smugglers, the pirates, the builders and even the local garrison lost interest – and the place was never completed. Despite this lack of military decorum, the place witnessed a minor skirmish in 1864 during the Civil War. History recalls this as very much a half-hearted effort by all concerned; nonetheless it is today regularly re-enacted with inauthentic vigor. In summer there's an excellent candle-lit tour of the fort (enquire at the Fernandina Beach Chamber of Commerce for details and reservations).

The surrounding park contains an animal preserve (largely birds and gators), a nature trail, a beach and a fishing pier. From here you can see across to **Cumberland Island** (in Georgia, and accessible only from Georgia – by way of a 30-mile detour to St Marys). Cumberland Island is part of the protected national shoreline, and it is said that you can sometimes see its resident wild horses galloping along the beach.

FERNANDINA BEACH

See Amelia Island, above.

ICHETUCKNEE SPRINGS

Off Rt 27, just over 3 miles NW of Fort White, which is 20 miles S of Lake City; open 8 am-sunset; entry $4 per car. This is the source of the Ichetucknee River, whose waters eventually become part of the celebrated Suwannee River, which is just 8 miles west of here. A pleasant picnicking and canoeing spot. You can swim, too, but the water can be chilly. More adventurous types should try the **tube-rafting** course, while those who prefer quieter pursuits will enjoy making their way along the banks on foot, keeping an eye out for otters and beavers.

There are more nature trails and fishing opportunities down Rt 27, just north of High Springs, at **O'Leno**.

JACKSONVILLE 🛏 ✕

By the coast at the mouth of the St Johns River. With a population of more than 600,000 and spreading out over more than 840 square miles, this industrial city is the largest in Florida, as well as the second largest in area in the entire U.S. (Only Los Angeles sprawls further.) The Indians called the first settlement to occupy this site *Wacca Pilatka*. In the 1700s the British translated this as Cow Ford. After the U.S. bought Florida, surveyors laid out a town plan here in 1822. The city was named after Andrew Jackson, the governor of Florida at the time (who was later to became the seventh president of the U.S.). Despite the Seminole War and the Civil War, Jacksonville flourished. This was largely owing to its natural deep-water port, which supported docks and shipyards, also serving as an outlet for St Johns River trade.

In the 19thC Jacksonville became known as a winter resort center: surprising, because the place has a distinct winter of its own.

Then in 1901 Jacksonville Place, an area on the north bank of the St Johns River, burned down, rendering over 10,000 people homeless. The town which rose from the ashes became the center of the new U.S. film industry. But the stolid local citizens believed in hard work and heavy industry – they weren't interested in this kind of tomfoolery. So the film industry moved to California. Jacksonville lost its chance to become tinseltown, and chose instead to become a tin-roof factory town.

At the risk of offending more than half a million people, one has to say that modern-day Jacksonville isn't much of a place for travelers. But it does have several quite interesting sights, and there are some pleasant nearby stretches of beach. (See separate entry: Jacksonville Beaches, page 124.)

For further information about Jacksonville, contact the Convention and Visitors Bureau, 3 Independent Drive, open 8 am to 5 pm Mon to Fri, tel. 904 798 9184).

The main sights in town are:

Jacksonville Art Museum

South of the river at 4160 Boulevard Center Drive; opening hours vary - ask at the Visitors Bureau; entry free. This gallery has two utterly disparate attractions (which may require two separate visits).

Their **pre-Columban collection** extends well beyond works of art. Some of the exhibits are more than 5,000 years old, and have been gathered from as far afield as Peru. Be sure not to miss the intriguing carved Mayan stones outside in the sculpture garden. The other big draw is the museum's collection of **modern art**. As with most such collections off the main art trail, it contains the usual array of hits and misses by several big names – including Picasso and Lichtenstein.

The supporting galleries of Korean porcelain, photography and so forth are much as you'd expect.

If it's too grey outside to visit the beaches, and you need to see more art, try :

Cummer Gallery of Art

829 Riverside Drive, on the other side of the river from the Jacksonville Art Museum; opening hours vary - ask at the Visitors Bureau; entry $3.

This is a worthy collection of a wealthy local, including several works by European masters. By far the most interesting paintings are the fresh and unmasterly early American works, which show what the country was really like before Hollywood fed us the reconstructed version. Even better are the leafy gardens where Baron Cummer used to stroll alongside the river. The fountains, pools and statues here are modeled on those of the Villa Gambera-

ia outside Florence.

For a genuine artistic oddity, head out to:

Delius's cottage – Jacksonville University Campus
On the S bank of the river by University Boulevard. At the age of 28 the British composer Delius ran away from England to write music in Florida. He set up shop in a dilapidated orange grove on the banks of the St Johns River. Here he was deeply impressed by the music of the African American orange pickers, strains of which found its way into his early *Florida Suite*. The cottage where he lived has now been completely restored, and can be visited on the campus. (Stop at the Visitors Center for details.)

Other more down-to-earth attractions include:

Anheuser-Busch Brewery
111 Busch Drive, Jacksonville 32207, N of the river towards Oceanway, off Rt 95 for the airport; open 9 am-4 pm, Mon-Sat; entry free. A long, inspiring tour instructs you in the secrets of the liquid which makes life bearable during a Florida heatwave. Anheuser-Busch has been brewing for almost as long as Jacksonville has existed, and has acquired quite a bit of history. At the end, after all the thirsty propaganda, you get two small samples.

Jacksonville Zoo
8605 Zoo Road, N of the river, off Rt 95 heading N by Heckscher Drive; open 9 am-5 pm daily; entry $4. Jacksonville Zoo has a modern, cageless design and the expected interest in endangered species. The white rhinos have even started breeding in captivity – a rarity for this species.

Those who are dying to see what an alligator can *really* do should attend their feeding at 2 pm. The snoozing logs suddenly wake up to become thrashing monsters. Equally thrilling is the shark aquarium, where *Jaws* understudies glide about in menacing style through 35,000 gallons of clear empty water – which remains so, except for *very* brief moments at feeding time.

• *Exhibits in the Cummer Gallery of Art, Jacksonville.*

Fort Caroline National Memorial
2713 Fort Caroline Road, on the S bank of the river, 6 miles E of downtown off Monument Road; open 9 am-5 pm daily; entry free. This is the site of a 16thC fort which played a significant role in the settlement's bloody early history. In 1562 the French Huguenot (Protestant) sailor Jean Ribault sailed up the St Johns River and decided to found a colony here. This was just the place to establish a Huguenot settlement, away from Catholic persecution in France. Ribault built a column, which claimed the territory for France, and then set sail back to France to collect Huguenot colonists and supplies.

When he arrived home, he discovered France was in the middle of a civil war. The Huguenots were far too busy fighting the Catholics to be interested in sailing off to found a colony. So instead Ribault sailed to Protestant England, but Queen Elizabeth I was unimpressed with his ideas and locked him up in a dungeon.

Meanwhile, the Huguenots in France had decided that they *did* want to found a colony after all. In 1564 several hundred of them set sail for Florida and established a pioneer settlement on the spot Ribault had found for them. This they named La Caroline, after King Charles IX. (The feminine gender was not intended as an insult to Charles. According to the strict rules of the French language, a colony's name had to be feminine.)

But the colonists soon became fed up with colonizing such a pleasant and sunny spot. They had set sail with dreams of Eldorado, but there was no gold and the local food was inedible. Just as they were about to abandon the colony, relief arrived in the form of Ribault (who had been released from his dungeon and sent back to France). Ribault brought with him another 600 colonists and the colony soon began to thrive. When Philip II of Spain got wind of this, he was outraged that the French had gained a foothold in Florida (which he insisted should be an exclusive preserve of the Spanish). He immediately dispatched Admiral of the Fleet Pedro Menendez de Aviles to expel the French. Menendez landed at St Augustine, just down the coast. Immediately

Ribault set sail to attack St Augustine, but his fleet was caught by a hurricane and his ships were wrecked on the shore. Seizing his chance, Menendez sailed for Fort Caroline, took the unprotected colony, and massacred more than a hundred of its defenders. On his way home, his ship laden with bounty and bountiful Huguenot women, Menendez spotted Ribault and his 300 shipwrecked sailors. He at once put ashore. Just in case they were thinking of starting another Huguenot colony on the beach, he massacred the lot. For a while after this, the French decided to adopt an entirely different approach to founding colonies in America – starting at the other end of the continent, in Canada.

The present Fort Caroline is an "authentic replica" of the original, whose site can still be seen.

Nearby you'll find a large park with woodlands (**The Theodore Roosevelt Area**). A 2-mile trail takes you through what was Indian territory for longer than 1,000 years, and where bald eagles still live in the wild.

A walk around Jacksonville

If you just want to walk around Jacksonville, head for Riverwalk, on the south bank of the St Johns River in the heart of downtown. The boardwalk along the riverside here is over a mile long, and gives you a fine view of the city skyline. Along the way there are restaurants, various memorials (including one to those who died in Desert Storm) and a Maritime Museum. After a stroll along the river, cross Main Street Bridge, and on your left at 2 Independent Drive you come to Jacksonville Landing. This large shopping complex overlooks the river, and includes branches of more than 50 stores, as well as open-air stalls, cafes, and bars. The Landing also stages all kinds of events throughout the year. (Call the Visitors Center for the latest details.)

If you want to get back to Riverwalk Landing, you can take a water taxi: they usually run 11 am-10 pm, shorter hours in winter, $2 one way.

JACKSONVILLE BEACHES 🛏 ✕

On the coast, 12 miles directly E of downtown Jacksonville. The coast opposite Jacksonville is part of a long stretch of uninterrupted sandy beach.

There are three main beach resorts. The first one you come to on Rt A1A heading north up the coast is **Ponte Vedra Beach**, at the eastern end of Rt 202 from Jacksonville. This is millionaires' territory, with exclusive homes overlooking the ocean and the golf course. The local residents have purposely made it difficult to get to the beach - but it's worth making the effort. There's just one way in, from Ponte Vedra Boulevard, which forks off Rt A1A by Mickler Landing. Here you're far from the madding crowd.

A couple of miles up Rt A1A you come to **Jacksonville Beach** (at the end of Beach Boulevard – Rt 90 – if you're traveling east from Jacksonville). In summer this is a lively resort center, with crowds spilling in from the city on weekends. It has a fishing pier which juts over a thousand feet out into the ocean, and a pavilion flying the flags of all 50 states in the Union. Here you'll find hotels, restaurants and a festive atmosphere.

Neptune Beach, just north of here on Rt A1A, is much quieter. Another mile or so north again and you come to **Atlantic Beach**, which was the first resort to be developed on this stretch of coast. It was laid out as early as 1901 by Henry Flagler, the man who built the railway. This, too, is a lively spot.

Beyond Atlantic Beach you can continue north up Rt A1A to **Mayport**, where there's a big naval station. Ship watchers should keep an eye open for huge aircraft carriers, and the large freighters heading out to sea from the wide mouth of the St Johns River.

You can catch a ferry here across the river if you want to drive on up Rt A1A to see Amelia Island – see page 120.

LAKE CITY

About 55 miles W of Jacksonville, off Route 10. One of those places that just *exists*. It sprung up by the junction of Interstates 10 and 75, and was originally named Alligator. According to the local story, this name derived from an Indian chief named Halpeter-Tustennuggee. The founders of the town chickened out of using his real name, and instead decided to use the chief's nickname: "Alligator." (Some say he acquired this nickname by wrestling an alligator to death in his youth, others maintain he got it because he looked like an alligator.)

Nowadays, Lake City is merely the home of **Alligator Town, U.S.A.** – a gator farm established by Ross Allen. This was the man responsible for setting up the celebrated Reptile Institute at Silver Springs, just outside Ocala. Otherwise, there's nothing of interest in Lake City. However there are a few worthwhile attractions just down the road, including Ichetucknee Springs, the Osceola National Forest, and the Olustee Battlefield – see separate entries.

O'LENO

See Ichetucknee Springs, page 121.

OSCEOLA NATIONAL FOREST

NE of Lake City. This protected woodland area covers 200 square miles. There are extensive, well marked trails, and Ocean Pond is one of the best fishing spots in the area. Ocean Pond is also near the Olustee Battlefield Site – see below.

OLUSTEE BATTLEFIELD SITE

Some 12 miles E of Lake City off Rt 90; site open 9 am-5 pm daily; entry free.
During the Civil War, the Florida Panhandle was one of the Confederates' main strongholds. In February 1864, 5,000 Union troops began marching inland from Jacksonville intent on attacking the Panhandle. They were confronted here, at the pinewoods outside the small town of Olustee, by a large Confederate force. The two sides joined battle, and by the end of the day 300 men had lost their lives, and each side had more than 1,000 wounded. Afterwards both sides claimed to have won. This was the only major engagement in the Civil War which took place in Florida, but it was the second largest battle in the entire war – only Gettysburg was on a bigger scale.

There's a **monument** commemorating the battle, and a **center** where you can learn details of what went on. Afterwards you can follow a trail which leads you over the battlefield. The battle is re-enacted every February by a cast of several hundred, all dressed in period Confederate and Yankee uniforms.

SUWANNEE RIVER

Everyone has heard the famous song: "Way down upon the Swanneeee River..." The song's proper name is "Old Folks at Home," and it has now been adopted as the state song of Florida.

The Suwannee River, in fact, rises across the state border, in Georgia. After draining out of the Okefenokee Swamp, it meanders for 250 miles down through northern Florida, before finally emptying into the Gulf of Mexico at the town of Suwannee.

The river's present name is thought to be a corruption of San Juannee (Little St John) as it was pronounced by the early slaves in the region.

For much of its length the Suwannee River flows through unspoiled countryside. Along with its main tributary, the Santa Fe River, it passes by no fewer than four state parks, and there are frequent campsites and piers along its banks. The **Suwannee River State Park** is off Rt 90, 20 miles south-east of Madison, just above Ellaville, with fishing, canoeing, and nature trails.

Thirty miles upstream from the Suwannee National Park lies **White Springs** (11 miles north-west of Lake City). Seventy years ago this used to be one of the most fashionable spas in America, and people came from all over the South to take the medicinal spring waters. These were said to cure you of almost anything. Maybe they did – because in the end fewer and fewer people came back, and today all you can see are the remains of the vast pool which was filled by the warm spring waters.

However, White Springs now has another (equally questionable) claim to fame. It's the home of the **Stephen Foster Folk Culture Center**. Stephen Foster was the man who wrote that celebrated song. As a matter of fact, he lived in Pittsburgh, never saw the Suwannee River, and even spelled its name wrong in the song. Foster only used it because he wanted a name that would evoke the feeling of the old Deep South, and also fit in with the music. Amazingly, his first choice was the Pee Dee River, which actually runs through South Carolina. But somehow "Way down upon the Pee Dee River..." didn't evoke quite what he had in mind.

Despite the fame of the final version, Stephen Foster was much more than

• *The Suwannee River.*

just a one-song man. One hundred and fifty years after he wrote them, several of his songs are still perennial favorites. Some which you may recognize are: "My Old Kentucky Home", "Oh! Susanna", "Jeanie with the Light Brown Hair", "Beautiful Dreamer" and "Camptown Races." A cluster of golden oldies sufficient to keep him in bourbon until a ripe old age – or so you would have thought. But things went wrong for Foster, and he was forced to sell the copyright for many of his hits. Despite this, he still persisted in his avowed aim to become "the best Ethiopian songwriter" (composer of minstrel ballads). But unfortunately he took to drink, and was soon turning out sentimental ballads with such titles as "Poor Drooping Maiden." He died in 1864 at the age of 38, a penniless alcoholic in New York.

Foster is now universally recognized as one of the first great American songwriters, and his fame is celebrated to this day at White Springs. Here a carillon of a hundred bells rings out a succession of his best-known tunes, and you can take a ride on a mock riverboat called "Belle of the Suwannee." The maudlin sentimentalist who penned "Poor Drooping Maiden" would probably have loved it; the magic tunesmith who knew the difference between Pee Dee and Suwannee might well have congratulated himself on remaining in Pittsburgh.

• *Olustee Battlefield Site.*

Every May on Memorial Day Weekend they hold the **Florida Folk Festival** here at the Folk Culture Center. It's worth going out of your way for this one – the musical standards are high, the Deep Southern food is great, and a wild old time is had by all. Yaaa-hoo.

SUWANNEE RIVER STATE PARK

See Suwannee River, page 125.

TALLAHASSEE

See Florida Overall: 8, *page* 136.

WHITE SPRINGS

See Suwannee River, page 125.

RECOMMENDED HOTELS

AMELIA ISLAND

For something different, try:

1735 House, $$-$$$; *584 South Fletcher Avenue, Amelia Island* 32034; *tel.* 904 261 5878; *cards* AE, MC, V.

Old bed-and-breakfast inn, all decked out in authentic New England style – complete with ancient sea chests and nautical bric-a-brac. Many rooms with views out over the ocean. But if you want a *real* view of the ocean, try a night in their lighthouse. Be sure to book *well* in advance for this one.

1735 House is south of Fernandina Beach, and nearby is a selection of inexpensive accommodations on Fletcher Avenue. The best of these is:

Seaside Inn, $-$$; 1998 *Fletcher Avenue; Amelia Island* 32034; *tel.* 904 261 0954; *no cards.*

Friendly motel, popular with vacationers and families.

JACKSONVILLE

In general, the closer you are to downtown the more expensive the accommodations get. The best range of inexpensive motels is out near the airport, 7 miles north of town on Rt 95. Here you'll find:

Airport Motor Inn, $-$$; 1500 *Airport Road, Jacksonville* 32256; *tel.* 904 741 4331; *no cards.*

Your basic friendly motel, where the guests tend to look like Zsa Zsa Gabor and one of her husbands traveling incognito.

An inexpensive exception to the rule, somewhat closer to the center of Jacksonville, is:

Motel 6, $; 8285 *Dix Ellis Trail, Jacksonville* 32256; *tel.* 904 731 8400; *all major cards.*

Off Rt 1, 5 miles south of downtown. Over a hundred standard rooms at standard rates, with the standard Florida bonus of a pool.

Highly recommended is a bed-and-breakfast inn a couple of miles south of the city center on the river:

House on Cherry Street, $$-$$$; 1844 *Cherry Street, Jacksonville* 32256; *cards* MC, V.

Carol and Merril Anderson are more like friends than hosts by the time you leave, and they've given each room its own ambience. Some have fine views over the river, some have four-poster beds, and all over the place you can see their collection of decoy ducks. Make friends with your hosts and the other guests on the patio with a free glass of wine and hors d'oeuvres at 6 pm. And if you are interested in tennis, be sure to quiz the Andersons – they've refereed in the big tournaments. Only snag (for some): the entire place is a nicotine-free zone.

The best reasonably priced place in the center of town is:

Marina Hotel at St Johns Place, $-$$; 1515 *Prudential Drive, Jacksonville* 32207; *tel.* 904 396 7154; *all major cards.*

Right by the Riverwalk in the best part of downtown. Tasteful decor and classical music soothe the nerves of workaholics (who are all out of the way well before you're up). But be warned: prices soar if you insist on having a room overlooking the river.

JACKSONVILLE BEACH

Prices rise considerably during the summer, when you must book ahead and expect to pay at least $50 for a room. In winter, on the other hand, you'll find bargains here.

Comfort Inn Oceanfront, $$; 1515 *North 1st Street, Jacksonville Beach* 32250; *tel.* 904 241 2311; *all major cards.*

Looks classy, and is – but the prices are surprisingly reasonable. Directly opposite the superb beach.

For something less pricey, try further down the same street:

Surfside, $-$$; 1236 *North 1st Street; tel.* 904 246 1583; *no cards.*

Friendly service. Acceptable, though basic, amenities.

• *Centre Street, Amelia Island.*

RECOMMENDED RESTAURANTS

AMELIA ISLAND

The best area for eating places is Fernandina Beach's Old Town around Centre Street, where there's a choice of restaurants in all price ranges. For a great steak, try:

1878 Steak House, $$; 12 *North 2nd Street, Fernandina Beach* 32034; *tel.* 904 261 4049. *Most major cards.*

If you are a foreign visitor and want to discover why American steaks are (deservedly) world famous, eat here.

JACKSONVILLE

Ciao Gianni Ristorante, $-$$; *Jacksonville Landing,* 2 *Independent Drive; tel.* 904 353 2626; *cards* AE, MC, V.

The name says it all. Informal Italian cuisine in informal Italian setting: pasta and pizzas.

The best restaurant in town is undoubtedly:

The Wine Cellar, $$$; 314 *Prudential Drive; tel.* 904 298 8989; *cards* AE, MC, V.

Superb French cuisine stylishly served in a romantic candle-lit atmosphere.

If you feel like letting your hair down, try:

Crazy Horse Saloon, 5800 *Phillips Highway.*

The entry charge of $2 gets you into both clubs. One is a disco, the other a country-and-western saloon. In the latter, many of the customers get into the swing of things by dressing up as cowboys - in the former, they dress up as themselves (which is often *much* weirder). Both stay open until 2 am. On Wednesday nights women get free admission, and free drinks until 9 pm. On Tuesday nights you can watch them making the famous TV show *Hitkicker Cowboy* in the Crazy Horse Saloon (the country-and-western section). Nothing fit for the nation's screens goes on in Masquerade, the disco section, which usually plays the very latest hits.

Crazy Horse Saloon is near the university and popular with students. You have to be over 21 to get into both places. And you must be able to provide *proof* if necessary.

JACKSONVILLE BEACHES

This popular vacation strip comes alive during the summer. For food and music, try:

Ragtime Tavern and Taproom, $-$$; 207 *Atlantic Boulevard, Atlantic Beach; tel.* 904 241 7877.

New Orleans-style restaurant and beach bar, with jazz and creole cooking. Friendly staff and lively clientele. They even brew their own beer.

For a night on the town that you won't remember in the morning try:

Baja Beach Club, 222 *Ocean Front,* where you can bop until you drop.

Northern Florida

Between Tallahassee and Pensacola
The Panhandle Coast

200 miles; map Hallwag Florida

The Florida Panhandle is the narrow strip of territory running west from Tallahassee between the Gulf of Mexico and Alabama. The atmosphere here is much like that of the Deep South.

There are two main cities here: Tallahassee, the state capital, and Pensacola, which can claim to be the earliest settlement in America. Both cities have historic districts of old mansions, in styles which include Spanish Baroque, New Orleans French, Victorian British and Georgian Georgian.

Outside Tallahassee lies the Apalachicola National Forest, the largest in the state. This huge wilderness area has hiking trails and canoeing, as well as excellent fishing. For great sea fishing you should head down to Destin, on the Gulf. In the old days, the fishing was so good here it was known as "The World's Luckiest Fishing Village."

The Gulf Coast of the Panhandle has everything from remote barrier islands with turtles and rare birds to the rip-roaring resorts of the so-called Redneck Riviera. These are popular with vacationers from Georgia and Alabama, as well as students who come from all over the South for their springtime blowout. The beaches along this coast are pristine, white and sandy; and the Gulf sunsets are an event.

You can easily drive from Tallahassee to Pensacola in a day along the coastal road (Rt 98). In order to take in some of the sights on the way, allow a couple of days.

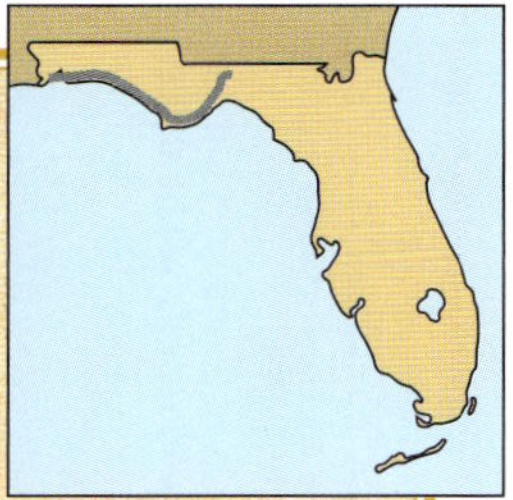

• **Bridge at Port St Joe.**

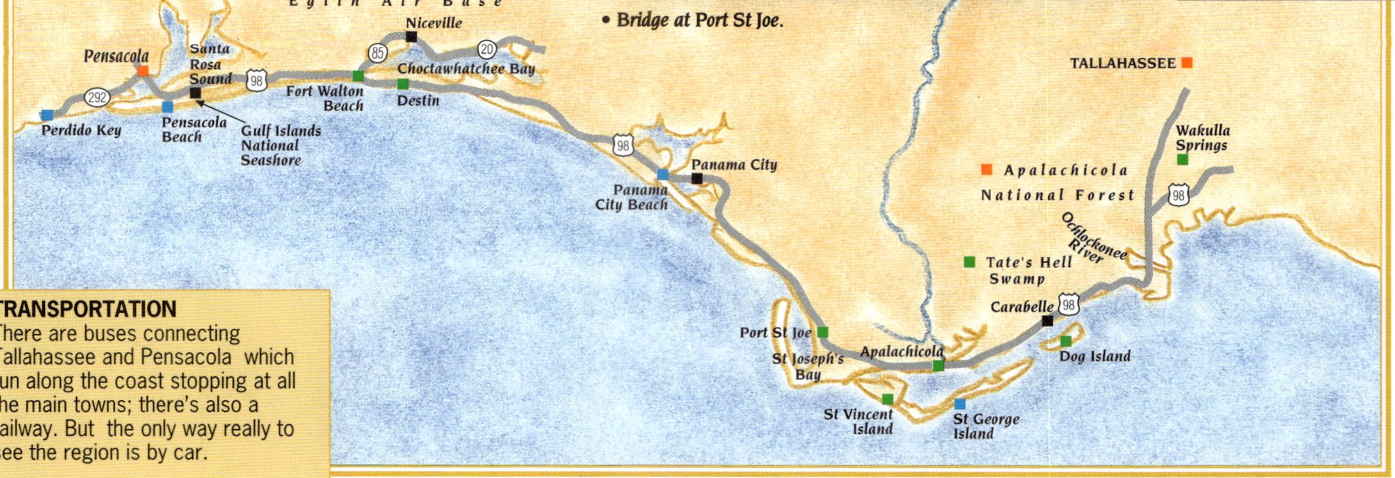

TRANSPORTATION
There are buses connecting Tallahassee and Pensacola which run along the coast stopping at all the main towns; there's also a railway. But the only way really to see the region is by car.

SIGHTS & PLACES OF INTEREST

APALACHICOLA 🛏 ✕
About 70 miles SW of Tallahassee on Rt 98, at the coast. The oyster capital of Florida. Over 90 percent of the oysters eaten in the state come from the beds in Apalachicola Bay. The town was the home of Dr John Gorrie, who built the first commercial ice-making machine. He foolishly didn't bother to patent this wonder, as he thought its only use was cooling the sickrooms of his malaria patients. There's a **museum** here with a replica of his epoch-making machine, the harbinger of the cocktail era.

APALACHICOLA NATIONAL FOREST
Extending SW of Tallahassee for about 50 miles. Florida's largest national forest, the great wilderness area of the Panhandle, covering nearly half a million acres. Several roads run through it. Rts 375 and 67 cross the Forest north-south either side of the Ochlockonee River, and there are more remote side roads off Rt 65 to the west.

There are several fine **lakes** in the forest, where you can picnic and swim, and then head into the woods along a trail. The lakes closer to Tallahassee tend to become overrun on summer weekends. Those further into the forest often remain idyllic, even at the height of the season.

There's a superb **canoe trail** which runs down the Ochlockonee River for nearly 70 miles, from one end of the National Forest to the other. The forest has nature trails, fishing and swimming spots – but there's no lodging here other than camping. For further details, contact the Visitor Center in Tallahassee.

DESTIN 🛏 ✕
On Rt 98, 45 miles E of Pensacola on the strip of land separating Choctawhatchee Bay and the Gulf of Mexico. Founded in 1830 by a sea captain from New England named Leonard A. Destin, for decades Destin was the only settlement on this stretch of the coast. It remained a small fishing village until it was discovered by anglers in the 1930s. The fishing was so good here that Destin soon had the largest charter fleet on the Florida Gulf coast, and had begun calling itself "The World's Luckiest Fishing Village." Then came the huge Eglin Air Base on the other side of Choctawhatchee Bay; then came the developers and the condos. The old-time residents now refer to themselves as "Fish Heads," some proudly, others ruefully.

Now Destin is just another resort, but not a bad one. Film buffs will be thrilled to know that *Jaws II* was filmed on the beach near here.

DOG ISLAND
See Detour – St George Island, page 136.

FORT WALTON BEACH ✕
On Rt 98, 37 miles E of Pensacola.
This spot was named after a Confederate army camp set up here in 1861 to guard the approach to Pensacola. The camp never contained more than a dozen or so soldiers, and as soon as some Yankee troops began shelling them from across the water on Okaloosa Island, they fled. But the name stuck. And more than that: it eventually took on an entirely unforseen lease of life.

When archaeologists began excavating the local Indian Mound they found that that this area had once been a major religious center. Several unique artifacts were discovered, and these are now classified as belonging to "Fort Walton Culture."

Nowadays, outside the museum, Fort Walton Culture may appear something of a contradiction in terms. Fort Walton Beach stands just outside the huge 700-square-mile Eglin Air Base. Tourists and the military have increased the population from 100 (in 1940) to 80,000.

And what of Walton himself? Who was this man after whom the fort was originally named? According to the history books, Walton was a colonel who once became deputy military governor of the western region of the Panhandle – such are the heights to which we must aspire to achieve immortality.

GULF ISLANDS NATIONAL SEASHORE
See Pensacola Beach, page 135.

NICEVILLE
On Rt 85, 48 miles E of Pensacola at the head of Choctawhatchee Bay. This used to be a sleepy little settlement where the locals passed their days fishing for mullet in the bay. In those days it was

THE TIME ZONE

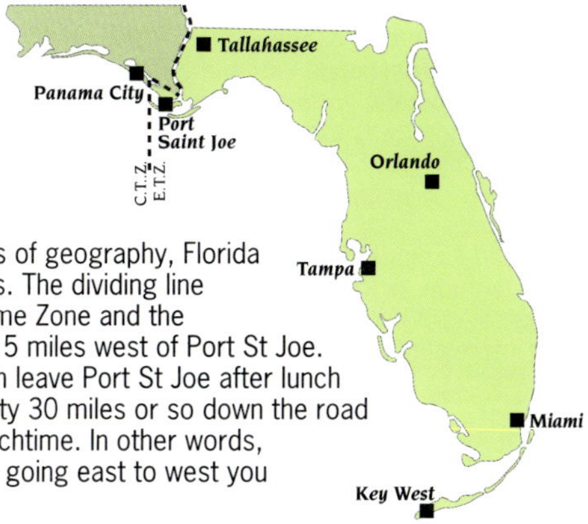

By one of those oddities of geography, Florida falls into two time zones. The dividing line between the Eastern Time Zone and the Central Time Zone runs 5 miles west of Port St Joe. This means that you can leave Port St Joe after lunch and arrive in Panama City 30 miles or so down the road in time for a second lunchtime. In other words, when you cross the line going east to west you *gain* an hour.

called Boggy. Then in 1938 the place received a charter granting it city status. "Boggy City" didn't project quite the right image, so the locals chose the present name. Surprisingly, it *is* quite nice here, away from the main tourist centers of Fort Walton Beach and Destin across the bay. However, the new Mid-Bay Bridge may soon change all this.

PANAMA CITY

See Panama City Beach, below.

PANAMA CITY BEACH 🛏 ✕

On Rt 98, 95 miles E of Pensacola. This is Florida's answer to New York's Coney Island. In honor of all the Georgians and Alabamans who flock here to whoop it up in the summer, it even calls itself the "Redneck Riviera." And it looks like it, too. Aficionados of kitsch will find themselves in seventh heaven, aesthetes should avert their eyes and drive on beyond the city limits.

If you want a good time, amid a wild crowd, this is the place for you. Students from all over the South flock here to do what students do – to joyous excess – during the spring break (March and April). They're an exceptionally friendly crowd, and you're usually welcome to join them – at your peril.

The **beach** here stretches almost 15 miles and has two piers. The main part of town is the **Miracle Strip** along the front. Here you can play "Goony Golf," hang around the machines in the arcades, eat hot dogs and ice cream, ride the rollercoaster, buy T-shirts ("Wet T-shirt Miss World"), and attempt to drink the place dry. There is no opera house, but operatic extras abound (and leap) all over the place. Yet for some reason, they haven't yet found a way of commercializing the beach, or the ocean which washes up on it. These remain as marvelous as ever. Those who want to work off the night's excesses can join in the beach games; those who can't even face going outside behind dark glasses can try visiting an exhibition that mirrors their state of mind. The **Gallery of Crime and Punishment,** *8500 Thomas Drive, open 9 am -6 pm daily; entry $3.* Displays include an electric chair, photos of characters who ended up sitting in one, and a wide range of ghoulish accessories.

The activities I have described take place during the "Hundred Magic Days" of summer. At other times, an uncanny air of normality returns, and the place has all the charm of an out-of-season resort (which never gets really cold). I've had a pleasant swim here in late November, followed by a quiet chat about the world monetary system over a few beers in a ghostly silent bar. Either love it, or leave it – there's not much else to say about Panama City Beach.

If you feel the need to escape, you'll find relative calm east of town at the St Andrews State Recreation Area. Here there's miles of beach, woodlands and nature trails through the dunes. There's also a ferry across to **Shell Island** at the mouth of the bay. This, too, has huge stretches of sandy beach, and is great for collecting shells. Even these spots can get overrun during the height of the season – but the further you go, the further you get away from it all.

Panama City itself is a port and lumber center 7 miles to the east across Hathaway Bridge. It is said to have received its name because it's on the same latitude as its namesake in Latin America – but it isn't. This is by far the most interesting thing about Panama City, Florida.

PENSACOLA 🛏 ✕

Western limit of the Panhandle on Rt 98, right by the Alabama border. Despite the claims of St Augustine, Pensacola is in fact the oldest European settlement in America. Don Tristan de Luna arrived and planted the flag of Philip II of Spain here as early as 1559. His intention was to found a colony, but things went wrong from the start. The colony was struck by a series of hurricanes, and the colonists quickly became disillusioned with their living conditions. After two years, Tristan de Luna decided to call it a day. The chance that the colony would one day take on its founder's name – and thus be called Lunacy – was lost. Also lost was Pensacola's chance of calling itself the oldest *continuously inhabited* settlement in America (the title now claimed by St Augustine, which wasn't founded until four years after Pensacola was abandoned).

The Spanish returned and raised the flag at Pensacola in 1698. Since then, the city has flourished under no fewer than five different flags. The Spanish, the French, the British, the American, and the flag of the breakaway Confederate Republic during the Civil War.

The city still reflects this varied past, in its architecture, ambience and street names. The British built grandiose Victorian homes, the Spanish gave the streets names such as Cervantes and Tarragona and the French gave the place more than a few echoes of New Orleans.

Pensacola is now a busy port (the nearest beaches are 5 miles away), but it still has its historic districts and a number of sights. For a map of these, see the Pensacola Visitor Information Center, at 1401 East Gregory Street (next to Pensacola Bay Bridge, and open 8 am to 5 pm daily). But a word of warning: stick to the main tourist trail, and don't wander off the beaten path at night: Pensacola is no small town.

The Historic Districts

The **Palafox District** (around the southern end of Palafox Street) grew up largely as a result of something which never happened. In the early years of the 20thC, many expected that Pensacola would experience a boom in trade once the Panama Canal opened. Numerous fine houses were erected in this area, but the boom never happened. Today these buildings possess the elegance of distant age, with their Mediterranean architecture and New Orleans balconies. Don't miss the ornate Iberian-style **Saenger Theater**, once a cinema and now the home of the Pensacola Symphony Orchestra.

On Government Street you can see the **Empire Building**. When it was built in 1909, this was the tallest building in the entire state of Florida.

Half a mile east of here you come to the **Seville District**, which has many fine Creole, Spanish and Victorian mansions. The main feature here is the **Historic Pensacola Village,** *open 10 am-4 pm daily; entry $6*. Here you can see so-called "living history characters" wandering the streets as if they've lost their way to the ball. Much more interesting than the extras for the film-that-never-was are the many museums inside the restored old houses. These cover the entire history of the city, and include some eye-opening photos of the city after early hurricanes.

Don't miss **Julee Cottage**. This was built in 1809 and belonged to Julee Panton, a freed black slave who became such a successful businesswoman that she ended up with a slave of her own. An example to her contemporaries, she loaned money to other slaves so they could buy their freedom (but appears to have forgotten that charity begins at home).

The **North Hill Preservation District,** north of the Palafox district, has some old mansions still occupied by descendants of the original owners. Being authentic, these folk feel no need to dress up and invite passing tourists into their homes, which are not open to the public. At the junction of LaRua and Palafox there's a **plaque** which marks the spot where Fort George once stood. This was the site of the Battle of Pensacola, where the 2,000 British soldiers defending the fort lost to the invading Spanish.

A couple of museums you shouldn't miss in Pensacola are:

Pensacola Museum of Art
At 407 Jefferson Street, open Tues-Fri 10 am-4 pm; entry free. Houses a permanent exhibition of varying interest. The best thing here is usually the traveling show of modern art, likely to feature anything from contemporary U.S. art to obscure European Impressionists. The museum is housed in the old mission-style building which served as the city jail for almost 50 years until 1954.

Civil War Soldiers Museum
108 Palafox Street, open 10 am-4 pm Mon - Sat; entry $4. If you want to see what it was *really* like to be a soldier in the Civil War, this is the place to come. Anyone who is under the illusion that the senseless carnage of war is a 20thC invention is in for a shock. And the carnage didn't just take place on the battlefield, judging from the medical implements on display. There's also a bookshop which contains a wide range of titles. These mostly describe different aspects of this conflict which all but divided the United States into two countries just 70 years after it had come into being.

Out of town there's another museum of particular interest to juvenile males of all ages:

National Museum of Naval Aviation
At the Eglin Air Base 7 miles E of Pensacola on Rt 98, open 9 am-5 pm daily; entry free, but you have to show identification. The base was founded in 1915 and is the largest in America. Its museum appears to contain an example of everything the U.S. Navy has managed to get airborne since that date. Here you can see everything from pioneer machines flown by the Wright brothers to a modern space module. You can climb into many of the planes and sit in the pilot's seat.

This base turns sailors into fully trained pilots at the rate of more than a thousand a year. It is also the home of the Blue Angels demonstration team, which often puts on spectacular eardrum bursting displays. For details, contact the Pensacola Visitor Center.

• *Pensacola, elegant architecture*

PENSACOLA BEACH 🛏
About 5 miles S from Pensacola, across the bay and over Santa Rosa Sound, on Santa Rosa Island. This is where Pensacola comes to enjoy itself by the sea – a crowd which includes plenty of sailors from the Eglin base. A lively spot.

If you want to get away from the crowds, head east or west on Rt 399 along the **Gulf Islands National Seashore**: miles and miles of beaches and dunes.

PERDIDO KEY
Take Rt 292 heading SW out of Tallahassee for 15 miles in the direction of Gulf Beach. Long, long stretches of dazzling white beaches, two of which are regularly voted among the top ten in the U.S.

PORT ST JOE
On Rt 98, 22 miles W of Apalachicola, on the coast at St Joseph's Bay. This sleepy fishing village was once "the richest and wickedest city in the south-east." In 1839 it was the site of the constitutional convention which brought official statehood to Florida. It was known originally as Saint Joseph, and soon became a booming port exporting cotton all over the world. Shippers made fortunes, and erected grandiose mansions. The town had a casino, a racetrack and even a theater. Saint Joseph was riding high, busily establishing its wicked reputation – but Fate had it in for the town. Yellow fever struck, wip-

ing out 80 percent of its inhabitants within a year. Next a forest fire burned much of it to the ground. As if this weren't bad enough, the following year a tidal wave came in from the sea, washing away the wharves and warehouses of the port, and burying the remains of Saint Joseph under the sand.

The few remaining locals decided to try again on the same spot. Only this time it would be different. They rechristened the place Port St Joe, and chose to do without such celebrated displays of riches and wickedness. Which is why it is now an ordinary little spot, where nothing of any interest ever happens.

Across the bay is the 12-mile spit which forms the **St Joseph Peninsula State Park,** *open 8 am-sunset; entry $4 per car.* This area is largely unspoiled. You can walk right to the northern end of the point. The sunsets are particularly spectacular on the southern end at Cape San Blas. The spit is bisected by the time zone divide (see page 133). According to a young Einstein I met here, this means that the sun is setting into the sea an hour earlier than you see it happening. "That's Relativity for you," he assured me.

DETOUR – **ST GEORGE ISLAND**

Off the coast opposite Appalachicola, which is 70 miles SE of Tallahassee on Hwy98. Island reached by causeway from Eastpoint, 7 miles E of Apalachicola. St George Island is one of the barrier islands 5 miles or so off the coast, and stretches for over 30 miles. The beach is sandy and largely deserted, and the views of the Gulf are superb. The island is on a major migration route for several species, and also has a varied resident population of wildlife, including scores of raccoons. There's a bed-and-breakfast inn where you can stay overnight (see Recommended Hotels, page 139), as well as a few restaurants in case you get hungry after your long walk along the shore. The eastern end of the island is occupied by a state park, with a hiking trail.

The two nearby barrier islands can only be reached by boat. **Dog Island**, to the east, is reached by boat from Carabelle on the mainland. **St Vincent Island**, to the west, is a nature reserve with loggerhead turtles and bald eagles.

ST VINCENT ISLAND

See Detour – St George Island, above.

TALLAHASSEE

On Rt 98. Founded in 1824, Tallahassee is the state capital of Florida. When the United States bought Florida from the Spanish in 1821, Florida's two main cities were St Augustine on the east coast and Pensacola at the western end of the Panhandle. Most of the rest of the state remained swamp and jungle. The authorities decided to establish a state capital midway between the two main cities. Two surveyors set out, one from each city, and they met in the foothills at a Tamali Indian settlement called Tallahassee, which meant "old fields." The authorities decided that this was just the place for the new state capital, evicted the Indians who had been here for more than a thousand years, and set up three log cabins. The inaugural Florida government met in one of these cabins in 1823, the administration occupied another, and the living quarters were in the third.

Tallahassee quickly grew, both in size and importance. The first railway in Florida was built from Tallahassee to St Marks on the Gulf Coast, as an outlet for the cotton trade.

In 1861 Florida ceded from the Union and joined the Confederates in the Civil War. The Panhandle became a Confederate stronghold. When the Confederate army stopped the advancing Union army at Olustee (see Florida Overall: 7), Tallahassee remained the only Confederate city east of the Mississippi.

Today, Tallahassee remains the state capital, and not much else. It's a provincial backwater compared to the bustle of Miami or the sophistication of Palm Beach, but there's no denying its charm. Here you'll find Deep Southern mansions, leafy walkways alongside the sunny streets and a sense of history. The city's *raison d'être* is the administration, but its 170,000 inhabitants are far from all being boring bureaucrats.

The city has a couple of universities, and more than 25,000 students, which makes for a lively nightlife.

It also has a host of things to see:

The Capitol Buildings

Tallahassee's **Old Capitol Building** stands at the end of Apalachee Parkway. It dates from 1845, and looks much as you'd expect an old Deep South capitol building to look. The steps lead up to its white neoclassical pillared façade, and it is topped by a domed tower whose flagpole flies the Stars and Stripes. It's utterly unoriginal, but on a pleasantly human scale. In other words, exactly the opposite of its next-door replacement: the **New Capitol Building**, whose brash modernism dominates the city skyline.

This was erected in 1977 for almost $45 million, with the apparent aim of outraging the locals. It was wildly successful in its aim, but it has also been a success in its secondary goal: housing the administration of a modern state. Bureaucrats don't function well if they're crammed into a delightful old building – they need space, modern air-conditioning, and bright offices high above mundane reality if they're to govern and tax people properly. Head up to the 22nd floor observatory, and you can't escape the feeling of dominating the city below. On a bright sunny day you can see even see the distant blue-green sea of the Gulf. This building is open from *8.30 am-5 pm Mon-Fri and Sat afternoon; entry free; there are also free guided tours, beginning on the hour.* If you're here when the State House of Representatives is in session (April and May), be sure to take in the public gallery on the fifth floor. When I last visited, they were debating the state waterways with all the vigor and enthusiasm you'd expect to be devoted to such a fascinating topic – and I spotted at least a dozen representatives who were quite definitely wide awake.

The Old Capitol, which is said to have exercised even greater soporific powers on its inhabitants, is *open 9 am-4.30 pm daily and afternoons on weekends; entry free.* Here you can see an exhibition devoted to the history of the State of Florida, which has had sufficient scandals to render this an intriguing topic. Nearby is the equally august and ancient building of the **Union Bank**, which was featured in some of these scandals. They did more than just cook the books here: on one occasion after the bank had gone bust, they turned it into a bakery. Its halls, once filled with the rich cooking aroma of current accounts and currant buns, are *open mornings Tues-Fri, afternoons on weekends.*

At the Visitor Information Center in the West Plaza foyer of the New Capitol (*open 8.30 am-4.30 pm daily*) you can pick up a city map, which will guide you to the other main sights.

Historic districts

If you want to visit some of the city's historic ditricts, head a couple of blocks north from the New Capitol. Here you'll come to **Park Avenue**, with its tree-lined old streets and Deep South mansions. Originally this had the rather unprepossessing name of 200 Foot Street, but a formidable inhabitant with social pretensions decided this was not quite right for her son's wedding invitations – so the name was changed.

At 301 East Park Avenue you'll find the columns and portico of **Knott House**, which dates from 1843 and is open to the public (ask at the Visitors Center – hours vary). This was the home of the eccentric Mrs Knott, who decorated the staid furniture with examples of her poetic ability. It is now known affectionately as "The House that Rhymes." Despite its staid appearance, this house has a curious history. It was built by a freed slave, and was later lived in by the first African American doctor in the state. The proclamation declaring the end of slavery in Florida was read from the steps of the house in 1865.

At Park Avenue and Bronough Street you'll find the **Old City Cemetery** and the **Episcopal Cemetery**. Among the social equals of these twin cemeteries, the only truly egalitarian society on earth, you'll find a prince and princess (relatives of Napoleon), some early slaves, soldiers killed in the Civil War (from both sides) and many others who wouldn't have been seen together in life.

Nearby is the **Calhoun Street historic district**. This spot was even more prestigous than Park Avenue, and used to be known as "Gold Dust Street."

Museum of Florida History
If you're interested in learning more about the state's past, visit here. There are some fascinating exhibits relating to the first Indian settlements, plus all kinds of information about early pioneers, Flagler's railway (see A brief history of Florida, page 27) and the like; it continues right up to date with coverage of the space era. Their mascot is Herman the mastodon, who roamed these swampy regions long before humanity was even a gleam in a gorilla's eye.

FAMU
Those who would like to learn about an apsect of Florida's past which is often glossed over should head just over a mile south-west of downtown to the **Florida Agriculture and Mechanical University** (known as FAMU). This was founded in 1887 and is Florida's main African-American university. The Black Archives Research Center and Museum here is *open 9 am-4 pm Mon-Fri; entry free*. Take a look at the leg-irons to see what slavery was really like, and read Martin Luther King's letters to understand how little had changed in the segregated Deep South, even in the 1960s. But for me the real gem in this museum is the tape collection. The recordings here contain the voices of several elderly African Americans speaking about the old days. Just listen, and an all-but-forgotten history is poignantly evoked.

THE CANOPY ROADS
For a taste of Deep South magic, try a drive down the Canopy Roads, which are mostly within easy reach of Tallahassee. These old country roads are bordered by oak trees. The branches of the trees are covered with Spanish moss and meet above the road, forming canopies that often last for miles. The best of them is the **Old Bainbridge Road**, which goes from outside Tallahassee past the Lake Jackson Indian Mounds and on up to the picturesque old town of Havana. For details of further Canopy Roads (there are miles and miles of them) see the Visitor Center in Tallahassee.

Lake Jackson
Three miles north of downtown (off Rt 27) you come to Lake Jackson, a popular local fishing and boating spot. On the west shore of the lake are the Lake Jackson Indian Mounds, *open 8 am-sundown; entry free*. Nearly a thousand years ago this was the site of a large tribal religious center. Excavations have unearthed ritual figures and ceremonial breastplates. The largest of the mounds are over 200 feet square and nearly 40 feet high. There's not much more to see, but it's worth wandering down the nature trail to try and get a sense of what this region must have been like around the time when the Vikings were putting in their first appearance at the other end of the continent.

TATE'S HELL SWAMP
Southern region of Apalachicola National Forest. As evil as it sounds, this 150-square-mile swamp is the home of the deadly moccasin water snake. The swamp was named after a local farmer who ventured in while pursuing a panther. A week later, despite having been bitten by snakes, he finally emerged. And in the words of the famous local folk song:

When Tate was discovered, these words he did tell:
"My name is Old Tate, boys, and I've just been to hell!"
These few spoken words were the last that he said.
His spirit had left him, Old Tate he was dead.

Archaeologists who have dated local fossils say that there has been a swamp here for more than 10,000 years. Some of the trees preserved in its mud are more than 600 years old. No point in venturing into such a spot, but you can see it inland from Rt 98 after it reaches the coast near Lanark Village.

WAKULLA SPRINGS
By Rt 61, 19 miles S of Tallahassee. Said to be the world's greatest natural springs, producing over half a million gallons of mineral water a day. Just the place for a cool dip, or you can take the glass-bottom boat trip above the cavernous source.

RECOMMENDED HOTELS

APALACHICOLA

Useful as a base for exploring the barrier islands if there's no lodging available on St George, also within easy reach of the Apalachicola National Forest.

Gibson Inn, $$; 57 *Market Street, Apalachicola*,32401; *tel.* 904 653 2191; *no cards.*

Friendly bed-and-breakfast inn which also has an excellent restaurant (**$$**) serving great seafood and the oysters for which Apalachicola is famous.

DESTIN

Village Inn, $$; 215 US 98E, *Destin* 32541; *tel.* 904 837 7413; *all major cards.*

One of the few worthwhile, yet comparatively inexpensive, spots in Destin. More than a hundred rooms, and a short walk from the beach. Ideal for fishermen, and they go out of their way to provide entertainment for children.

PANAMA CITY BEACH

Prices tend to shoot up here in the summer season, when there often isn't a room to be had on weekends unless you have reservations. In general, the east end of the beach tends to be livelier. In the off-season rates drop considerably, and you can often pick up a real bargain.

Sunset Inn, $-$$; 8109 *Surf Drive, Panama City Beach* 32413; *tel.* 904 234 7370; *cards* AE, DC, V.

Lives up to its name, with great sunsets visible from rooms with views over the Gulf. Also has a larger-than-usual pool, and is far from the hullabaloo.

PENSACOLA

The big event of the year here is the Fiesta of the Five Flags which takes place in June. Be sure to reserve early if you're planning to visit any time during this month.

Days Inn Downtown, $-$$; 710 *North Palafox Street, Pensacola* 32501; *tel.* 904 438 4922; *all major cards.*

Motel, complete with pool, right by all the main sights. They have nearly 150 rooms, but even so, be sure to phone ahead in season.

For a budget deal, try:

Motel 6, $-$$; 5829 *Pensacola Boulevard, Pensacola* 32501; *tel.* 904 477 7522. *Most major cards.*

More than a hundred rooms – sometimes has vacancies when everything else is full.

PENSACOLA BEACH

Barbary Coast Motel, $$; 24 *Via de Luna Drive, Pensacola Beach* 32561; *tel.* 904 932 2233; *cards* MC, V.

Pleasant motel, right by the beach. You pay extra for a room with cooking facilities, but the best place to meet people is at the barbecue.

ST GEORGE ISLAND

The only hotel on the island is:

St George Inn, $$; W *of causeway*, St *George Island*; *tel.* 904 670 2903; *no cards.*

Pleasant bed-and-breakfast spot with just half a dozen rooms. Booking *well* ahead is *essential.*

TALLAHASSEE

Accommodations can get a little scarce when the state legislature is in session (April and May), but even then it quiets down on the weekends. The most extensive range of inexpensive accommodations is on North Monroe Street (Rt 27 leading north-west out of town in the direction of Havana). The best here is:

Shoney's Inn, $-$$; 2801 *North Monroe Street, Tallahassee* 32303; *tel.* 904 386 8286; *all major cards.*

A free cocktail when you arrive, a pool, rooms with a Deep South garden view, and complimentary breakfast. Great for the price.

If you're after a bargain, but want to stay in downtown, you can always try the Florida State University (FSU) campus residence:

Osceola Hall, $; 500 *Chapel Drive, Talahassee* 32301; *tel.* 904 222 5010;

no cards.

Obviously this is only available during the summer vacation. Student-style rooms, with all that this implies – ie you don't get free cocktails thrown in. A real bargain, and you'll find your fellow guests are likely to be interesting, too. (When I stayed, I met up with a young French professional clown, whose father was a well-known politician.)

Also downtown, but much more upscale, is:

Holiday Inn University Center Downtown, $$; 316 *West Tennessee Street, Tallahassee* 32301; *tel.* 904 222 8000; *all major cards.*

An 11-floor Holiday Inn, with views out over the city from the highest rooms; however, the best views are from their rooftop Viking Lounge.

Not to be mistaken for the other Holiday Inn in Tallahassee, which is a mile or so east of downtown at 1302 *Apalachee Parkway* (Rt 27), *tel.* 904 877 3141; *all major cards,* and is less expensive, **$$**.

The best place in town is undoubtedly:

Governor's Inn, $$$; 209 *South Adams Street, Tallahassee* 32301; *tel.* 904 681 6855; *all major cards.*

Although it's named after Andrew Jackson, Florida's first governor, this spot only opened ten years ago. But the building is much older: it is described as "a historic warehouse" but I was covertly informed that it was actually a stable. Despite this, you won't find a more elegant spot in the whole of the Panhandle. The suites here are named after former governors of Florida, and even the "ordinary" rooms boast tasteful antiques and four-poster beds. It's in the center of a brick-paved historic street just around the corner from the Capitol. This is where the political wheelers and dealers hang out when the state legislature is in session.

RECOMMENDED RESTAURANTS

APALACHICOLA

No visit here would be complete without sampling the famous local oysters. The best place to go for these is:

Boss Oyster Bar, $-$$; 125 *Water Street*; *tel.* 904 653 8139; *no cards.*

DESTIN

Captain Dave's on the Harbor, $$; 314A US 90, *Destin*; *tel.* 904 837 6357; *cards* MC, V.

This is where the stars and crew used to eat when they were filming *Jaws II* on the beach nearby. The fresh seafood is landed at the harbor right outside, and if you're lucky you can even turn the tables on Jaws (he's best steamed).

For those who just want to snack and watch harbor life go by, **Captain Dave's Oyster Bar** is next door.

If you're here at night, try:

Hog's Breath Saloon; 1239 *Siebert Street, Destin*; *tel.* 904 244 2199.

Lively company and raunchy rock music.

FORT WALTON BEACH

For good meal, or just a few beers, try:

Pandora's, $-$$; 1120 *Santa Rosa Boulevard, Okaloosa Island*; *tel.* 904 244 8669; *all major cards.*

Across the water from Fort Walton Beach on the barrier island (Okaloosa). Here part of the dining area is a grounded yacht (with views out to where it ought to be). Romantic nautical atmosphere. Great ribs and fresh local fish. Live bands play in the bar to appreciative, friendly clientele.

PANAMA CITY BEACH

There's a range of big, cheap eateries, which often serve surprisingly good seafood. Many offer "all you can eat" deals for $7 or so.

Just a few notches up the scale is:

Boar's Head Restaurant, $$; 17290 *Front Beach Road, Panama City Beach*; *tel.*

904 234 2239; *all major cards; closed* Mon *in winter.*

The large "thatched cottage" exterior announces that this is sheer Hollywood Ye Olde England, and the inside lives up to these expectations, complete with beams and fireplaces. But the food is no joke. The prime-rib is great, the seafood imaginative and tasty. They even serve wholesome game in winter.

If you want to see (or take part in) the celebrated "Hunk Shows" and wet T-shirt contests, head on down to:

The Spinnaker; 8795 *Thomas Drive, Panama City Beach; tel.* 904 234 7822; *no cards.*

Free entry into an inferno of bars and discos which stay open until after 3 am most nights. At 25 you're ancient here.

PENSACOLA

If you're looking for a lively night out, with entertainment and a pleasant crowd, try:

McGuire's Irish Pub, \$-\$\$; 600 E*ast Gregory Street, Pensacola; tel.* 904 433 6789; *all major cards.*

Basic Irish grub, and plenty of it. Try their Irish Seafood platter for a real treat. Raucous Irish music. They also brew their own beer on the premises: this is Pensacola's oldest brewery. Guaranteed good time. To show your appreciation, sign a dollar bill and contribute to the decor – as more than 80,000 others have before you.

If you want to dine in a little more style, try:

Jamie's, \$\$-\$\$\$; 424 E*ast Zaragoza Street, Pensacola; tel.* 904 434 2911; *cards* AE, MC, V.

Gourmet French cuisine in a restored old mansion in the historic Seville District. The superb wine list and classic dishes make it the best in town.

TALLAHASSEE

The best restaurant in town is:

Andrew's Second Act, \$\$\$; 228 *South Adams Street, Tallahassee; tel.* 904 222 2759; *cards* AE, MC, V.

Classic cuisine in the heart of downtown. Intimate spot with a maze of underground candle-lit dining areas – romantic enough for lobbyists to woo politicians, and discreet enough for lovers to lobby each other. Their French dishes are masterly, but the adventurous should try the chef's speciality of the day (and ask him to recommend a wine to go with it).

Andrew's Second Act is part of a complex of restaurants. **Andrew's Upstairs, \$-\$\$,** serves great steaks, and Andrew's **Adams Street Cafe** specializes in light lunches served at tables outside.

The best budget seafood restaurant in town is:

Barnacle Bill's, \$-\$\$; 1830 *North Monroe Street, Tallahassee; tel.* 904 385 8374; *cards* AE, MC, V.

Everything from fresh Apalachicola oysters to mouth-watering steamed mullet. All the fun of a fair with live golden-oldie music, and outside dining in summer.

With nearly one fifth of the population students, Tallahassee has a healthy nightlife. The younger crowd tend to hang out at:

Flamingo Cafe Lounge, 525 *West Tennessee Street; tel.* 904 224 3534; *no cards.*

Lively live music until late.

Oldies (such as the over thirties) will probably feel more at home at:

Club Park Avenue, 115 *East Park Avenue; tel.* 904 599 9143.

A lively, informal night club on two floors which has speciality nights midweek (phone ahead so you don't turn up as a cowboy on Indian night).

More upscale is:

The Moon, 1020 *East Lafayette Street; tel.* 904 222 666.

Nightclub featuring live bands. The rhythm-and-blues here can be as good as you'll hear anywhere.

Miami and Miami Beach: *introduction*

Miami is a phenomenon. It looks like one, and it feels like one. Miami's downtown architecture is among the most futuristic and beautiful in all America, its cruise liners moored along the Port of Miami look as exotic as spaceships, and its overhead railway snaking through canyons of tinted glass is the stuff of science fiction.

Miami has long been renowned for both its crime and its culture. In the early 1980s it had a growing number of surreal skyscrapers, and the highest murder rate in the U.S. Yet tourism boomed, attracted by the pastel scenery and designer clothes of TV's Miami Vice. Fortunately, nowadays tourism has largely won out over crime.

And the culture? Miami's islands have been wrapped in pink by Christo, the Art Deco district of Miami Beach has the appearance of a preservation area from Raymond Chandler's pre-war California, and a theater in Coconut Grove put on the first U.S. performance of Samuel Beckett's *Waiting for Godot*.

Miami has always been ambitious. And it has certainly stamped itself on the world map. Everyone has heard of Miami. Yet curiously, it is only the second largest city in Florida (industrial Jacksonville, 300 miles to the north, is the largest), and it's not even the state capital (this is at Tallahassee).

Large sections of Miami's population come from such disparate locations as Cuba and the Bronx, Latin America and Haiti. In the course of my visits, I've been befriended by such diverse characters as a Castilian waiter translating *Don Quixote*; two deserters from the French Foreign Legion running a youth hostel; a Haitian voodoo priest; a CIA agent who

had worked in the Kremlin during the Stalin era; a former London banker running a fish and chip shop; a New York taxi driver who had just driven a British rock star all the way from Broadway; and a security guard who was on the run from a Texas state penitentiary.

Miami now has a population of two million and covers 2,000 square miles. It spreads over 30 miles along the coast, from North Miami Beach to Cutler; and covers a score of islands. More than 80 percent of Miami is within 5 miles of the ocean: a real seaside city with more than 15 miles of beaches. It's seldom too hot, and never too cold – with an average temperature of 76 degrees Fahrenheit. The radio forecasters start the morning "It's another day in paradise..." Yet the last time I woke up there on a still, sunny morning, with an endless blue sky above, the forecaster added: "Today is the start of the hurricane season." It all happens in Miami.

Some spend their entire vacation in Miami. There's certainly enough to keep you occupied for at least a couple of weeks. Even if you don't want to stay this long in one place, you should allow at least three days to see the sights, sample the scene and hit the beaches.

USING THIS SECTION

Greater Miami is huge – like Los Angeles, it is a collection of large population centers rather than one city.

We therefore introduce you to the area as a whole by describing it neighborhood by neighborhood on pages 151-155.

The main sights and places of interest are then covered on pages 156-158.

Walking is a good way to see parts of Miami, and on pages 158-161 you will find two walking tours which enable you to explore on foot and take in some of the most interesting architecture and landmarks.

Otherwise, your best way around the city is to drive between districts, taking in the spectacular scenery on the way; or use one of the excellent local rail systems – see Metrorail and Metromover, below.

ARRIVING

Miami International Airport is the tenth busiest in the world, but it's efficient and user-friendly.

All the main car rental firms have desks immediately outside the arrivals gate.

Otherwise the best way into town is by taxi. The fare to Downtown is about $20, Coconut Grove will cost a couple of dollars more, and South Miami Beach is just under $25.

There are several mini-van services which cost about half as much. The best of these are SuperShuttle and Red Top. You'll see their reps by the arrivals gate.

It's even cheaper to take a bus into town, but it takes time: No. 7 bus takes just over half an hour to reach Downtown; the J bus will get you to Miami Beach in under 45 minutes.

INFORMATION

Miami has several tourist information offices. The **Greater Miami Convention and Visitors Bureau** is at *701 Brickell Avenue, open 9 am-5 pm, Mon-Fri.*

On Miami Beach there is the **Miami Beach Chamber of Commerce** at *1920 Meridian Avenue, open 9 am-5 pm, Mon-Fri, 10 am-4 pm Sat.* The best listings magazine is *New Times*, which comes out weekly. It is available free at most big hotels, restaurants, bars and also at street machines.

ORIENTATION

Miami consists of the twin cities of Miami (on the mainland) and Miami Beach (on the barrier island to the east across Biscayne Bay). These are linked by causeways, which also link up the islands.

If you plan to travel around Miami, you'll need an adequate street map. The best of these is the *Trakker*, which comes complete with a street index and costs $2.50 at any news-stand.

Miami is laid out on a grid pattern. The numbered avenues run north–south, and the streets run east–west. The low numbers begin in Downtown and fan outwards.

These are further divided according to the sector of the city. For example, if you're on North East 5th Street, you're a few blocks north-east of Downtown, and if you're on South West 5th Street you're on an entirely different street across the other side of Downtown. This may sound complicated, but it is in fact very logical and very helpful. You always know where you are in relation to Downtown.

There are *of course* a few difficulties. Several main streets just have names – such as Miami Avenue and Flagler Street. Also, various roads run diagonally across the grid; and in Coral Gables everything is named differently.

Also, just to keep you on your toes, the numbering system in Miami itself doesn't quite match up with the numbers in Miami Beach. For example, when you drive from 36th Street on to the Julia Tuttle Causeway across the bay, you arrive on Miami Beach at 41st Street. This may sound complicated, but once you get the hang of it, the whole thing becomes simple.

METRORAIL AND METROMOVER

The Metrorail, a single line elevated railway, runs from north Miami to south Miami, passing through Downtown. Downtown itself is ringed by the Metromover monorail system. Both of these provide some spectacular views of Downtown, but otherwise are of little use to most visitors as a means of getting around.

ACCOMMODATION GUIDELINES

If you are looking for sea views and beach life, the best place to stay is out at Miami Beach, page 157. South

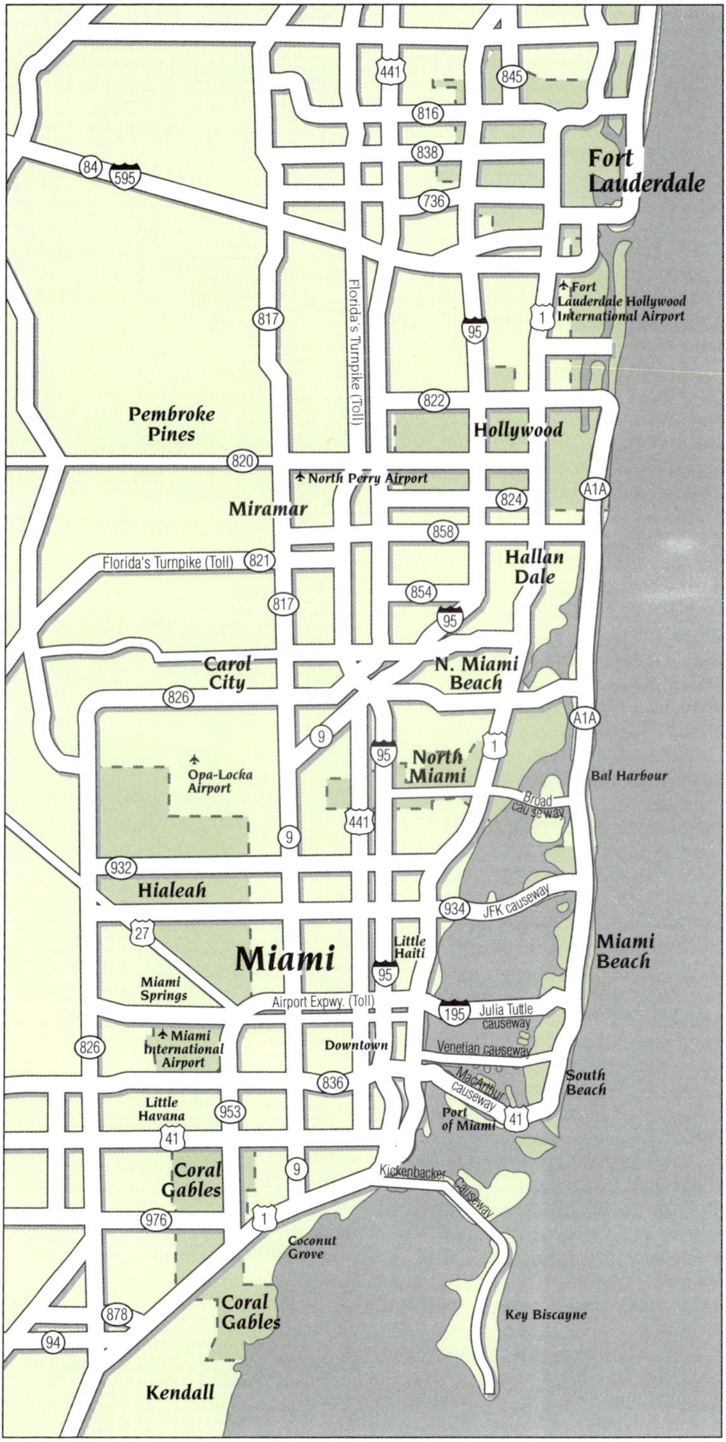
Fort Lauderdale
Fort Lauderdale Hollywood International Airport
Pembroke Pines
Hollywood
North Perry Airport
Miramar
Hallan Dale
Florida's Turnpike (Toll)
Carol City
N. Miami Beach
Opa-Locka Airport
North Miami
Bal Harbour
Broad causeway
Hialeah
JFK causeway
Miami
Little Haiti
Miami Beach
Miami Springs
Airport Expwy. (Toll)
Julia Tuttle causeway
Miami International Airport
Downtown
Venetian causeway
MacArthur causeway
South Beach
Little Havana
Port of Miami
Coral Gables
Kickenbacker Causeway
Coconut Grove
Key Biscayne
Kendall
441
845
816
838
84
595
736
817
95
1
822
820
A1A
824
858
821
854
826
9
932
934
27
195
836
953
41
976
878
94

Beach has the famous Art Deco hotels along Ocean Drive. The only snag is that you'll be 5 miles from the center of Miami.

Downtown Miami has a number of classy hotels amidst the high-rise wonders, and further south there's classy Coconut Grove, which has some superb, but comparatively expensive smaller hotels.

For further details on accommodations in general, see page 22; also see *Charming Small Hotel Guides* Florida, published by Duncan Petersen in the U.K. and Hunter Publishing in the U.S. This is a very worthwhile collection of all the most interesting places to stay in Florida – with many great new discoveries by the authors, Paul Wade and Kathy Arnold, and includes some of the whackiest hotels anywhere on Earth.

CYCLING

This is an excellent way to see certain parts of Miami. The best way to find out about cycling opportunities in the city is to get *Miami on Two Wheels*, which is available free at any tourist office (see Information, page 144). The three areas which cater to cyclists are Miami Beach, Coconut Grove (including Coral Gables), and Key Biscayne. Don't try cycling anywhere else.

To see these districts by bike, you can rent at Cycles on the Beach, 713 5th Street (Miami Beach); Dade Cycle Shop, 3216 Grand Avenue (Coconut Grove); and Key Biscayne Bicycle Rentals, 260 Crandon Boulevard. Cycles usually cost $3.50 per hour or $20 a day.

NEIGHBORHOODS TO AVOID

Especially avoid walking in Downtown at night, and indeed anywhere else, except South Beach and Coconut Grove, which are generally safe for walking at night, but still require caution because even in these respectable districts there are incidents from time to time.

At all costs, avoid Liberty City and Overtown – don't even drive through them. Be cautious about entering Little Havana or Little Haiti by car at night unless you know precisely where you are going.

For further essential safety information, see page 19.

• *Modern Miami*

BACKGROUND

Much of Miami looks as if it began yesterday, and much of it did. Yet even a city as modern-looking as this has its history. Miami's name comes from the old Tequesta Indian word *mayaime*, which means very big. However, when Julia Tuttle, the "Mother of Miami," arrived here in 1875, the place was nothing but an insignificant Indian trading post.

Julia Tuttle was the energetic widow of a Cleveland industrialist. She had money, she had drive, and she loved Miami. She moved into a nearby abandoned army post called Fort Dallas, whose site is now occupied by the parking lot of the Downtown DuPont Plaza Hotel, the fort itself having been moved lock, stock and barrel to Lummus Park, where it was rebuilt in 1924.

The northern part of the state, particularly the resort area along the St Johns River, was already a popular vacation spot when Julia Tuttle arrived. This was also a thriving citrus region. Julia Tuttle knew that if her dream of turning Miami into a thriving city was to succeed, it needed a railway link. For years she pestered railroad magnate Henry Flagler to extend his railway from northern Florida, but he refused to listen. His railway was already making a fortune out of the citrus trade and the tourists.

Then in 1895 there was a freak winter. Frost struck the whole of northern Florida, reaching as far south as Palm Beach. The tourists went home early, and over 90 per-cent of the citrus crop was ruined. Julia Tuttle seized her opportunity in a subtle but telling way. She sent Henry Flagler a sprig of orange blossom from Miami. Flagler got the message, and immediately started extending his railway south. It reached Miami in time for the winter season of the following year, 1896. In the same year, Miami was given its city charter.

Yet even when Flagler arrived on the first train into Miami, and stepped off to be greeted by the customary brass band, he remained unconvinced of the wisdom of his investment. Southern Florida was still very much unknown territory

Within a year he was completely won over. The tourists followed the railway to the warm south, and Miami quickly became a boom area. Flagler built the Royal Palm Hotel to accommodate the flood of visitors.

By 1910, Miami's permanent population had mushroomed to 5,000. A couple of years later the Indianapolis financier Carl Graham Fisher began developing the sandy barrier island across the bay, and Miami's twin city, Miami Beach, was born.

By the 1920s the Florida land boom was under way with a vengeance, with plots of land occasionally changing hands twice in a day. The millionaires began moving in. John Deering built himself a Renaissance palace near Coconut Grove. Further south, George Merrick built an entire city suburb, complete with grandiose entrance gates, in the Mediterranean style. The advertising campaign he launched to sell his villas was the largest the world had ever seen. In no time, everyone knew about Miami, and tourists flocked in from far and wide. By 1925 the city had 10,000 inhabitants, and was attracting over a third of a million visitors a year.

Then it suffered the first of a series of setbacks. The trouble began with the Mafia and the con-men: a large number of small investors found when they arrived that the land they'd been sold simply didn't exist. Word of this shadowy side lurking behind the sunny façade of Miami quickly spread. Then in 1926 there was a major hurricane. These two factors caused a number of larger investors to pull out, quietly shifting their assets elsewhere. The boom continued, though less bullishly, and with weaker financial underpinning. Then came the Wall Street Crash of October 1929 and the long years of the Depression.

Despite the bad times, development didn't cease altogether. Merrick continued to build his dream Mediterranean suburb at Coral Gables, and a few optimistic financiers continued to develop other parts of the city. But the millionaires weren't the only ones with faith in Miami. As part of the building program undertaken by Roosevelt's WPA (Workers Project Administration), the first Art Deco hotels began appearing at the southern end of Miami Beach. This faith in the city eventually paid off, and by the end of the 1930s the tourists were coming back to the tune of over three quarters of a million a year.

Miami's subsequent history has followed this pattern of boom and bust. Disaster has been followed by transformation, and each time the city has moved into an unexpected new phase. America's entry into the Second World War deflated the tourist boom. There were stories of German submarines off the coast, even rumors of invasion. These were poo-pooed at the time, and have subsequently been dismissed out of hand by historians. Yet there is conclusive evidence that at least one German reconnaissance party put ashore from a submarine at North Miami Beach.

Meanwhile, thousands of servicemen were billeted in the empty hotels of Miami Beach, and spent long days training on the beach. These servicemen came from all over America: most had never even heard of Miami Beach before. And after several hours training in the sand under a blazing sun, most of them never wanted to hear of the place again. Or so you'd have imagined. But after the war, these same GIs remembered Miami, and came flooding back for their vacations. Others came and studied on the GI Bill at the university. The post-war boom had started. Then came another setback.

Miami had quickly attracted the attention of organized crime. In the end, even Al Capone took up residence – at 93 Palm Avenue, Palm Island. "I came for the hot weather," he boasted to the press. Al Capone died in Miami in 1947 (his old home is still there on Palm Island, just north of the MacArthur Causeway across from Miami Beach). Around the same time, a U.S. Senate Committee opened hearings on organized crime. Miami became a persistent focus of their investigations, and its reputation as the place to be seen took a beating.

The late 1950s saw an exodus from nearby Cuba after Fidel Castro took power. The nearest city to Havana was Miami, and from this time on Miami has had a sizeable Cuban population. The first great influx of Cubans exacerbated racial tensions, especially in the African American community.

In 1968, Miami Beach received a huge boost when it hosted the Republican National Convention, but this plus quickly became a minus when riots erupted in the ghettos of Liberty City. The press, on hand for the convention, rushed to bring pictures of the riots to the nation's TV screens.

Then something even worse happened for Miami Beach. It began to lose the very reason for its existence. By the early 1970s the combined effects of construction work and tidal erosion had all but stripped Miami Beach of its sand. The authorities took this threat so seriously that they even called in the army. For four years, and at a cost of more than $50 million, military engineers supervised a rescue operation. This involved shipping vast quantities of highest quality sand from Alabama. In the end, enough sand was imported to have carpeted the whole of Long Island. As a result, Miami Beach now has far and away the largest urban beach in the world. For 10 miles of shoreline, the beach is over 300 feet wide.

As part of his ongoing tussle with the U.S., Castro opened the jails of Cuba and another wave of Cuban boat people arrived in Florida. Crime became rife amongst the new immigrant community in Miami. The murder rate per capita became the worst in the U.S., and race relations took an ominous turn. In 1980 riots broke out, and by the time they had finished, an estimated quarter of a billion dollars worth of damage had been done.

But once again, Miami bounced back. Downtown was undergoing a remarkable transformation. Mirrored and tinted cubist fantasies were sprouting into the sky.

At the same time, Miami's exotic image was being emblazoned across the nation's TV screens in *Miami Vice*. The viewers paid little attention to the bad guys, or what they were up to. The designer outfits of the good guys, and the designer locations of Miami, were far more interesting. Miami was real: it was on TV. This was where it was at. The tourists poured in from all over the U.S. – and began flying in from Europe in large numbers, too.

Despite its most recent setback (in the form of Hurricane Andrew), Miami is still riding high. The city conceived by the "Mother of Miami", Julia Tuttle, a little more than a century ago is now firmly established as one of the world's prime locations.

As a recently arrived Nicaraguan taxi driver once explained to me: "Without Miami there wouldn't *be* no Florida, man."

• *Miami Beach hotels.*

• *Fourth of July celebrations, Miami.*

COCONUT GROVE

A couple of miles S of Downtown, on the shore opposite Key Biscayne. This was once the Greenwich Village of Miami, and still has artistic associations. The Coconut Grove Playhouse, which opened in 1926, remains one of the best-known theaters in America. (As early as 1956, it staged the first U.S. performance of Beckett's *Waiting for Godot.*)

Nowadays the literati have been replaced by the glitterati, but the area retains a lively informal atmosphere, with many cafes, bars and clubs. Things tend to rev up in the evening – especially around **Grand Avenue** and **McFarlane Road.**

There's also a large Bahamian population here, which centers around Charles Street. Here you can still see a few authentic old wooden Conch houses. Every June the Bahamians stage their **Goombay Festival**, with costumed processions and Caribbean-style bands.

The Bahamians first arrived here at the turn of the century. It was several years later before the first artists and writers arrived. According to a story I was told, the Bohemians moved in because they misheard when they were told: "That's where the Bahamians live."

CORAL GABLES

See Florida Overall: 3, page 64.

DOWNTOWN

Center of town, N of the Miami River, opposite South Miami Beach. Walk the busy, vibrant streets of Downtown Miami, and you could be in Rio or Buenos Aires. The rich mix of the city's population is apparent everywhere you look. Haitians, Cubans, Bahamians, retired New Yorkers and perspiring executives, as well as visiting Europeans, Australians and Japanese, all swarm along the sidewalks. Here you can buy bargain ghetto blasters and even louder T-shirts, fiery Cuban cuisine or cool tropical fruit juice.

But Downtown also has more formal shopping at a fine shopping mall (**Bayside Marketplace**), as well as various culture and arts centers, and a museum (see page 156).

The tallest of the many tall buildings in Downtown is the **CenTrust Tower**, which has nearly 50 floors, a height surpassed only by the tallest Chicago and New York skyscrapers. On the eastern shore of Downtown is **Bicentennial Park**, which has fine views of the Port of Miami and its string of winged and

• *Crandon Park Beach, Key Biscayne.*

fluted cruise liners. (Amongst its several world titles, Miami lays claim to being "Cruise Capital of the World.") Walking in Downtown Miami in the sun may be hot and tiring, but it is safe. This is not the case after dark.

Head south over the drawbridge across the Miami River (South East 2nd Avenue Bridge) and you come to **Brickell Avenue**, lined with spectacular tinted and mirrored high-rise buildings. Much of this fantasy land was built with fantasy money: the sudden rise of many of these buildings coincided with the drugs boom of the late 1970s and 1980s.

This district is now the nation's largest international banking center outside Wall Street. It was here that insecure Latin American presidents used to place their money. (Many indeed retired to Miami.) Further south from the banks you come to a series of even more spectacular condominiums. These are an experience in themselves – built in a style given such names as Beach Bauhaus, Coconut Corbusier and Florida Flow. The most spectacular is probably the **Atlantis Building** at No. 2025, which is now ashamed to admit that it is over ten years old. The apartments, rents, and often the tenants, are exotic. I'm told the apartment once owned by the ex-president of Chile is now occupied by an Indian guru.

KEY BISCAYNE

The large barrier island S of Miami Beach, opposite Coconut Grove, accessible from the mainland by way of the Rickenbacker Causeway. On a still spring night, with a full moon dappling the waters of the ocean, Key Biscayne still lives up to the promise of its name. Biscayne comes from the Indian word *bischiyano,* meaning "favored path of the rising moon."

This is millionaire territory, a green and pleasant land of beaches and golf courses, woodlands and bicycle trails: just the place to get away from the blare and bustle of Miami.

First stop on the 4-mile-long Rickenbacker Causeway (toll $1) is **Virginia Key**. This has a fine beach on the south-eastern side of the island facing the ocean, and by the western shore is the **Seaquarium,** *open 9.30 am-5.30 pm daily; entry $20.* Just where the causeway enters the island is the Miami Marine Stadium, which hosts "Pops by the Bay" concerts.

Next you come to Key Biscayne itself, which is 4 miles long. The eastern upper side of the island is occupied by **Crandon Park Beach**. It has miles of beach, with palm trees. You can see pelicans skimming the waves and occasionally even dolphins leaping offshore beyond the sandbar as you stroll along the deserted sands. Then comes the weekend, and the crowds.

Further south on Crandon Boulevard (the main road from the causeway), you come to where Richard Nixon established his winter White House. The golf course in this part of Key Biscayne is one of the finest in the country, and hosts its own classic international championship. The annual tennis tournament staged here is one of the major events of the U.S. season.

Further on, at the southern part of the island, you come to the **Bill Baggs Cape Florida State Recreation Area,** *open 8 am-sunset, entry $3.50 per*

STILTSVILLE

From the south of Key Biscayne, you can still see the last remnants of this legendary settlement sticking up out of the sea.

In the 1940s, some fishermen decided to declare themselves free of the local tax authorities. They built a group of houses on stilts in the ocean, just outside the limits of the authorities' jurisdiction. For a while, all went well. The authorities played their part by being furious, and the fishermen lived happily in their tax haven. Then came the hurricanes, and life on the ocean wave became more difficult. The authorities unsportingly brought in a law forbidding the fishermen to carry out any repairs on their sea homes. One by one the citizens of Stiltsville returned to the land of tax returns.

I'm told that just one of the original inhabitants of Stiltsville remains in obstinate residence. The other increasingly tumbledown dwellings are sometimes squatted by aquatic hippies and occasionally a boatload of revelers puts in for a wild party. Rumor has it that Stiltsville will soon disappear from the map altogether. What excuse will they find for razing it? A fire hazard, perhaps? Look out for this spot while you can: these were the first tax deductible homes in the U.S.A.

Other artificial structures of note in Biscayne Bay include the **Spoil Islands**. There are more than a dozen of these scrub-covered, uninhabited islands. They were formed when dredgers deepened the channel for the Intracoastal Waterway, which runs between the barrier islands and the mainland. Carl Graham Fisher ("the man who made Miami Beach") chose one of these islands to build a memorial column to Henry Flagler, whose railway put southern Florida on the map. Other islands were more recently given vast surrounding collars of pink plastic, when Romanian-American artist Christo fulfilled his promise (threat?) to wrap them.

car. This has almost 500 acres of woodlands, a great beach (on the eastern side of the island), excellent fishing (along the sea wall on the western side), nature trails and bicycle paths. At the southern tip of the island you come to the **oldest lighthouse in Florida**, which was built in 1825.

The 100-foot-high lighthouse is now a mere navigational beacon, but if you join the tour you can climb the 120 steps to the top, where you giddily emerge to a superb, spinning view.

LITTLE HAITI

Between Biscayne Boulevard and Interstate Rt 95, from 41st Street N as far as 80th Street. This rather run-down area used to be known as Lemon City. The first Haitians began moving in during the late 1970s, refugees from the terror regime of the notorious Papa Doc. Since then, thousands more Haitian boat people have made the perilous trip across the Caribbean. There are now almost a quarter of a million Haitians living in Miami, and 100,000 of these live in Little Haiti.

The Haitians speak Creole patois or French, and English is usually their second (or even their third) language. They brought with them a colorful culture, which contains many echoes of their African past. Voodoo is still very much alive here, and along 54th Street you can see shops selling objects which feature in the spooky ceremonies.

At 5927 North East 2nd Avenue, there's a **Caribbean Market** where you can buy crafts and some fine tapes of Haitian music. Keep your eye open for paintings, which fall into the category of so-called naive art. Some of these are very good, but they're increasingly sought after by dealers, so don't expect them to come cheap.

LITTLE HAVANA

Beyond Coral Gables, 3 miles W of Downtown.

This neighborhood centers on what is officially called South West 8th Street. You would hardly expect Cubans to accept such a mundane name for their main thoroughfare, so they've rechristened it Calle Ocho, a translation of 8th Street.

Little Havana lives up to its name. The ambience is unmistakably Cuban, and in some of the shops you'll even

• *Making cigars in Little Havana.*

THE MIAMI CUBANS

The first big wave of refugees began arriving from Cuba in the late 1950s, after Castro took over. They've been arriving ever since. There are now well over half a million Cubans permanently settled in Miami, and most of them live in and around Little Havana (see page 153). The first to arrive were comparatively affluent – mainly middle-class Cubans who had good reason to suspect that their future in Castro's Cuba would not be rosy. The second big wave arrived in 1980 and were very different from their predecessors. Many were poor and illiterate, and one in four of them had been released from Castro's jails. Some were political prisoners, but others were criminals who naturally sought to continue their chosen trade when they arrived in the Promised Land.

I've encountered several Cubans who have done time in Castro's jails – all of whom informed me that they were of course political prisoners who had fallen foul of the regime on idealistic grounds. Perhaps I've just met an unrepresentative cross-section.

encounter people who only speak Spanish. All the signs are in Spanish, the odor of Cuban cigars hangs in the air, and the music you'll hear played along the streets has unmistakable Latin American rhythm (and volume). When you visit Little Havana you'll hear stories about the "old days" in Cuba – pre-Castro times. But whatever you do, don't become involved in a political discussion about Cuba. People still occasionally die on the streets of Little Havana for expressing the "wrong" views. (Shades of political opinion vary only in the extremity of their anti-Castro stance.)

On Calle Ocho near 12th Avenue you can see the **Brigade 2506 Memorial**. This commemorates the disastrous Bay of Pigs invasion of Cuba in 1961, in which many Cuban exiles lost their lives.

South of here on Memorial Boulevard there's a **monument to Jose Marti**, who died in 1865 attempting to liberate Cuba from the Spanish. Nearby 12th Avenue has been renamed Ronald Reagan Avenue, in recognition of the former president's tough anti-Castro stance.

At 1001 South West 12th Avenue, there's a small restaurant called **La Esquina de Tejas,** which has a signed photo of Reagan on the wall. Reagan stopped here for a bite during his 1983 re-election campaign. This proved such a vote-winner with the large Cuban electorate that George Bush repeated the gesture four years later, but didn't get a street named after him.

Every year in early March Calle Ocho plays host to the **Little Havana Festival**, a noisy celebration of all that it means to be Cuban. This festival is almost audible in Havana itself.

SOUTH BEACH

S *end of Miami Beach island.* This is the home of the famous Art Deco district, with its 1930s- and 1940s-style pastel hotels. The best of these are along Ocean Drive, overlooking the palm trees, the wide stretch of beach and the ocean. (Early in the morning, when the sunlight is glassy clear and the beach is empty, the view from your room is uncannily like a Hockney painting.)

In all, there are several hundred Art Deco buildings in the district. Though they all reek of a certain period, the style was never static. The motifs show distinct evolutions, which often depend upon the passing fashion of the year in which they were built. For example, some are strictly angular, others rounded; some have patterns, others figures. If you wish to impress your friends with your knowledge of this esoteric subject, be sure to visit the **Art Deco District Welcome Center** at 1001 Ocean Drive. Alternatively, there's an excellent walking tour which leaves from outside the Leslie Hotel, 1244 Ocean Drive. It starts 10.30 am Saturdays, lasts 90 minutes, and costs $6.

But be warned, parking can be a nightmare in this district, especially on the weekends. And tow trucks are in constant evidence. The best time to get here is early on a weekday morning.

Further north on Miami Beach you come to the mammoth hotels lining the ocean. These modern blocks in no way match the delicate beauty of the Art Deco hotels. The greatest of these structures is the Fontainebleau Hilton Resort which even has a huge *trompe l'oeil* mural by Richard Hass, claimed as "the world's largest." Presidents, Hollywood royalty, and James Bond stay here, and Miss Universe used to be crowned here. (See Recommended Hotels, page 162.)

CAPE FLORIDA LIGHTHOUSE

This lighthouse has quite a history. A dozen years after it was built, it was beseiged by Seminole Indians. The two keepers barricaded themselves in and held out as best they could. But eventually the Seminoles tried to smoke them out. In desperation, the keepers tossed down a barrel of gunpowder, which almost blew the base of the lighthouse to pieces. The Seminoles retired and regrouped, preparing for the final charge. But fortunately for the keepers, the explosion had alerted a passing ship, which put in and rescued them.

A quarter of a century later, Confederate desperados doused the lights in an attempt to wreck passing Union ships. As a result, a Dutch schooner running guns to the Confederates was wrecked along the coast, and its entire cargo was lost.

• *Art Deco hotel, Miami Beach.*

SIGHTS & PLACES OF INTEREST

AMERICAN POLICE HALL OF FAME AND MUSEUM

3801 Biscayne Boulevard; open 10 am-5.30 pm daily; entry $6. Once upon a time Miami had the worst crime figures in the U.S., and it's all recorded here. This museum will be of interest to anyone who has watched police shows on TV. Patrol car No. 3801 rides up the outside front wall, and inside it's all just as gung-ho. There's even a genuine electric chair, and leg-irons such as are still worn on chain gangs in Tennessee.

BACARDI ART GALLERY

2100 Biscayne Boulevard; open 9 am-5 pm, Mon-Fri; entry $4. This museum is often overlooked by tourists, mainly because its exhibitions vary so much. They might be showing a lesser-known modern European master or works by contemporary American artists. Check the latest issue of *New Times* to see what's on tap when you're in town. The outside of the museum is covered with a large blue-and-white tiled mosaic which is almost as good as the shows inside.

BASS MUSEUM OF ART

2121 Park Avenue, South Beach; open 10 am-5 pm, Tues-Sat, 1 pm-5 pm Sun; entry $5. This has an unexpectedly prestigous collection of European art – from the 16thC to the moderns. There are fascinating works by Dürer and Rembrandt, as well as temporary exhibitions which tend to be very good.

CORAL CASTLE

See Florida Overall: 3, page 64.

FAIRCHILD TROPICAL GARDENS

See Florida Overall: 3, page 71.

FRUIT AND SPICE PARK

See Florida Overall: 3, page 71.

HAULOVER BEACH PARK

10800 Collins Avenue; off the beaten path, N of Miami Beach. Here you'll find a long stretch of sandy beach, backed by dunes with some pleasant walking trails. On weekdays it is sometimes completely deserted.

HMS BOUNTY

401 Biscayne Boulevard; open 10 am-5 pm Mon-Fri; entry $5. This life-size replica of an 18thC British man o' war is moored at Bayside Marketplace in Downtown. It was constructed for the film *Mutiny on the Bounty* and is remarkably authentic, right down to the usual nautical confusion of ropes which make up the rigging. There's even a mutinous crew on board. These consist of present-day American pirates pretending to be mutinous British Jack tars, and are as authentic as Marlon Brando's hilarious English accent in the film itself. But the film was great, largely owing to Brando, and your visit here will be great, largely owing to a jolly crew.

HOBIE BEACH

By the Rickenbacker Causeway, which leads across to Key Biscayne from just N of Coconut Grove. This is generally considered to be the best windsurfing beach in Miami – but it's no more than that. If you want a good swimming beach, you're far better off heading across the causeway to Key Biscayne (see page 152).

MATHESON HAMMOCK PARK

See Florida Overall: 3, page 71.

METRO-DADE CULTURAL CENTER

101 West Flagler Street; open 10 am-5 pm daily, afternoon only Sun; entry $4. A post-modern architectural classic in the so-called Mediterranean style, by Philip Johnson. As with all such hugely expensive classics, it also has its classic error. The focal piazza, intended as an informal meeting place, remains as empty as the Sahara Desert. Why? Because it's almost as *hot* as the Sahara Desert. A pity – because the rest of the Center has plenty going for it.

There are two main features: the Historical Museum of Southern Florida and the Center for the Fine Arts.

Like the short history of Southern Florida itself, the **Historical Museum of Southern Florida** is filled with much Indian lore. *Open 10 am-5 pm daily, afternoon only on Sun; entry $4.* Easily the most interesting exhibits are the photos – of everything from Seminoles to visiting stars. It's also intriguing to see what the people who made Southern Florida actually looked like. Henry Flagler, Julia Tuttle, Carl Graham Fisher, Al Capone – they're all here.

If there's a world-class art exhibition

in town, it'll be on display here at the **Center for the Fine Arts**, *open 10 am-5 pm Mon-Sat, afternoon only on Sun; entry* $5. Check the free weekly listings magazine *New Times* to see what's current.

METROZOO

See Florida Overall: 3, page 71.

MIAMI BEACH BEACHES

Along the E shore of the barrier island which forms Miami Beach, facing the ocean. This wide, seemingly endless beach stretches for miles along the shore. It all looks much the same, though the hotels backing it range from the arty to the traditional.

Different sections of this beach attract different groups. For instance, the beach around 1st Street is popular with surfers. Further north attracts the local retired crowd. At Lummus Park you get plenty of families by the children's play area. A bit further north, there tend to be European tourists who are used to sunbathing topless. This is illegal in America, but in areas such as this the authorities tend to turn a blind eye.

The beach around 12th and 13th Streets is popular with gays. And it is claimed that this is where Marilyn Monroe swam, when she visited Miami Beach.

Way up at 46th Street, by the Hilton, the beach is occupied by a lively crowd from the University of Miami.

MIAMI SEAQUARIUM

See under Key Biscayne, page 152.

MONKEY JUNGLE

See Florida Overall: 3, page 72.

MUSEUM OF SCIENCE AND SPACE TRANSIT PLANETARIUM

3280 South Miami Avenue; open 10 am-6 pm daily; entry $6. State of the art, with plenty of interactive exhibits. This is the sort of place where you can learn what blinding lights, flashing electricity and all kinds of noise *really* are – as distinct from the mere nuisance you always supposed them to be. A great spot for the kids – and for adults too, once they begin to unwind a bit. Also has an interesting planetarium (regular shows, price included in ticket), and a fascinating wildlife center.

NIGHTLIFE AND BARS

Miami has a lively (rather than wild) night scene. South Miami Beach has the best selection of clubs and bars. The venues here are constantly changing – see *New Times* for the latest listings. **Bash,** run by Madonna's old flame Sean Penn at 655 Washington Avenue, is good for a musical mind-bend. If you want to do this with booze alone, head for the **Clevelander Bar** beside the pool at 1020 Ocean Drive.

Another good bet is Coconut Grove. Dancers will enjoy the **Baja Beach Club** at 3015 Grand Avenue, drinkers will prefer the Tavern in the Grove at 3416 Main Highway. For a club with that Latin beat, head down to Calle Ocho in Little Havana, to **El Inferno** at 981 South West 8th Street (week- ends only).

If you just want to watch some great dancing, try **Ballet Flamenco la Rosa** at 1008 Lincoln Road, Miami Beach. For classical music, try the **Gusman Center for the Performing Arts** at 174 East Flagler Street, Downtown, which has two resident orchestras. The best **theater** in town is without doubt the celebrated **Coconut Grove Playhouse** at 3500 Main Highway, Coconut Grove. *New Times* will have details of what's currently playing at these spots, as well as all other places of interest.

ORCHID JUNGLE

See Florida Overall: 3, page 72.

PARROT JUNGLE

See Florida Overall: 3, page 72.

VILLA VISCAYA

3251 South Miami Avenue; open 9.30 am -4.30, pm; entry $4. When Chicago tycoon James Deering chose to build himself a winter home on the edge of Coconut Grove, he decided to do it in style. It didn't particularly matter which one.

Deering's architect was set to work on a Renaissance Italian villa, which was given a Spanish name. The interior designer was sent to France for chandeliers, Germany for antiques, Portugal for carpets, Britain for bound leather books. The gardens were laid out in the formal French style, with Tuscan flourishes, and a neoclassical seaside promenade looked out towards a stone ceremonial Venetian barge. It could have been a disaster, but James Deering had taste, and made sure that those who worked for him also possessed this rare quality. James Deering had made his fortune out of combine harvesters, and his ability to combine apparently disparate elements was not limited to the factory. Villa Viscaya is a gem, which far outshines many European villas.

The gardens are a delight, and the inside of the villa is now maintained as a museum. (It always was, in the disgruntled view of his wife.) The main rooms each epitomize a certain style – such as the gentlemanly **English library** (Adams), and the (rather over-the-top) **Rococo Salon**. Fortunately, lapses of taste such as the latter are rare. Worth seeing if you see nothing else in Miami.

WEEKS AIR MUSEUM

See Florida Overall: 3, *page* 73.

A walk around South Beach

Start towards the southern end of Ocean Drive, at the junction with 5th Street. 5th Street is the continuation of the main road on to the southern end of Miami Beach island, which runs from the mainland across the MacArthur Causeway past the ocean liners at the Port of Miami.

Here, to your east, are the palm trees and greenery of Lummus Park, with the beach and the ocean beyond. Lining the west side of Ocean Drive are the cafes and frontages of the Art Deco hotels. Proceed north up Ocean Drive (with the ocean to your right) doing your best to avoid falling into the arms of some fashionably attired rollerblader pirouetting his (or her) way down the pavement.

You will pass fashionable cafes, and their trendy clientele. As you proceed up Ocean Drive, you'll see hotels in a constantly changing variety of styles – all within the Art Deco mode. At 850 Ocean Drive, you'll see the **Waldorf Towers**. This dates from 1937, and its famous "lighthouse" tower quickly became established as a local landmark. Further up, at 960, is the **Edison**, a classic of the Spanish-American Revival style.

To your left you can still see the palm trees, with the beach and the ocean beyond. You may recognize this as the backdrop for several photographs in Madonna's wildly over-hyped aluminium-covered book *Sex*. Overhead you can sometimes catch a glimpse of the Concorde flying in to Miami Airport.

At 1116 Ocean Drive you will see the Spanish-American Revival façade of the **Amsterdam Palace**, which was built in 1930. This is said to echo the 16thC Colonial style house built by Diego Columbus (brother of Christopher) on the island of Hispaniola.

At 1244 you can see the **Leslie Hotel**, whose refurbishment and brilliant color scheme were the inspiration of Barbara Hulanicki (who in the swinging sixties ran London's trendy store *Biba*). Hulanicki's gaudy colors depart from the traditional pastel tones of the Art Deco district – some consider these to be an interesting development, others view them as a desecration.

On the corner of 13th Street and Ocean Drive are the bilious pastel shades of the **Carlyle**, and opposite at 1300 the superb **Cardozo** (also the work of Hulanicki). Call in and have a look at the lobby, which featured in the 1959 Frank Sinatra film, *Hole in the Head*.

Now head inland down 13th Street until you come to Collins Avenue. Here you'll see the **Almanac**, whose barrel tile roof is a further example of the Spanish-American Revival style.

Continue west down 13th Street to the junction with Washington Avenue. Across Washington Avenue to the north (right), you'll see the **Post Office**, with its pink marble entrance steps. This

LOST?
If you get lost, it's easy to find your bearings in South Beach. The streets run from east to west, with 1st Street at the southern end of the island and the Art Deco Welcome Center at 10th Street. The avenues run north–south, with Ocean Drive running alongside the eastern beach shore. Collins Avenue is the next inland, and Washington Avenue runs a block further west.

was built in 1937, in the so-called Depression Moderne style, and is still in use. Be sure to take a look at the fine interior with its murals.

Now turn south (left) down Washington Avenue. At 1130 (on your right) you come to the **Old City Hall**, with its fine columns, which dates from 1927.

On the other side of Washington Avenue, at the corner of 11th Street, you can see the archetypical 1950s **11th Street Diner**, which was shipped all the way from Pennsylvania.

Further down Washington Avenue, on the left at the corner of 10th Street, is the large **Washington Storage Building,** in the Hispano-Baroque style. This dates from 1927, and was used by winter visitors to store their furniture and buckets and spades while they went back home. It now contains the **Wolfsonian Museum**, a collection of modern cultural artifacts and some curious propaganda artworks; *open 1 am-5 pm Mon-Fri; entry* $1.

Turn east (left) down 10th Street back towards the ocean. At the crossing with Collins Avenue, you will see the Essex Hotel, whose classic interior is well worth a look.

Continue east along Tenth Street until you come to Ocean Drive. Here you can turn right, and in a few blocks you'll find yourself back where you started. Or better still, you can cross over Ocean Drive, head straight for the beach, and reward yourself with a refreshing swim in the sea.

A stroll through Coconut Grove

Start in the heart of Coconut grove, at the junction of Grand Avenue, Main Highway and McFarlane Road. Just opposite, at 3015 Grand Avenue, you will see **CocoWalk Mall**. This is where people come to see and be seen (while getting in a little power shopping). This multi-level mall has brick courtyards and terraces lined with shops and restaurants.

From the main intersection head south-west down Main Highway, lined with cafes and boutiques. Watch out for **Ouch Boutique** at 3415 on the left. This is where Sylvester Stallone and Madonna buy their gear, and outside you can see one of the few remaining street murals in the area.

Further down on the same side you come to **The Barnacle**, the park that contains the home of the first European to settle in Coconut Grove. In 1891 Commodore Ralph Monroe built the house which still stands on this site (*tours every 90 minutes from 10 am-2.30 pm Thur-Mon; entry* $2). The house still has many of its original furnishings, and a pleasant view out over Biscayne Bay.

The first street leading left off Main Highway after The Barnacle is known as **Millionaire's Row**.

On the other side of Main Highway, you can see the beige Spanish Rococo front of the **Coconut Grove Playhouse**, which was rebuilt in 1927. This has a justly renowned reputation as one of the finest theaters in America, often hosting plays on their pre-Broadway run.

Charles Avenue runs west off Main Highway, just north of the Coconut Grove playhouse. A couple of blocks down this street the first African American settlers of Coconut Grove made their homes in the late 1800s when they worked in the original coconut groves. The Bahamian-style wooden houses here are reminiscent of the Conch houses of Key West. (A word of warning: don't stray too far up this street into the run-down district at its end.)

Back on Main Highway, continue south-west to the corner with Devon Road. Nearby is the **Plymouth Congregational Church**, which dates from 1916. Its walls are covered with vines, and its oak door is almost four centuries old. (This originally came from a monastery in the Pyrenees mountains in northern Spain.)

From here you can retrace your steps back up Main Highway to the center of Coconut Grove. Then, if you wish to explore further, try strolling west along Grand Avenue (and south down Commodore Plaza) for some good people-watching. Or head south-east down McFarlane Road for Peacock Park, and then turn north along South Bayshore Drive to see the huge **Coconut Grove Exhibition Center**. Its site was renowned as an exhibition center long before one was built here. This was where, at the old Dinner Key Auditorium, Jim Morrison of The Doors stripped off his trousers for the exhibition that put an end to his 1969 tour of Florida.

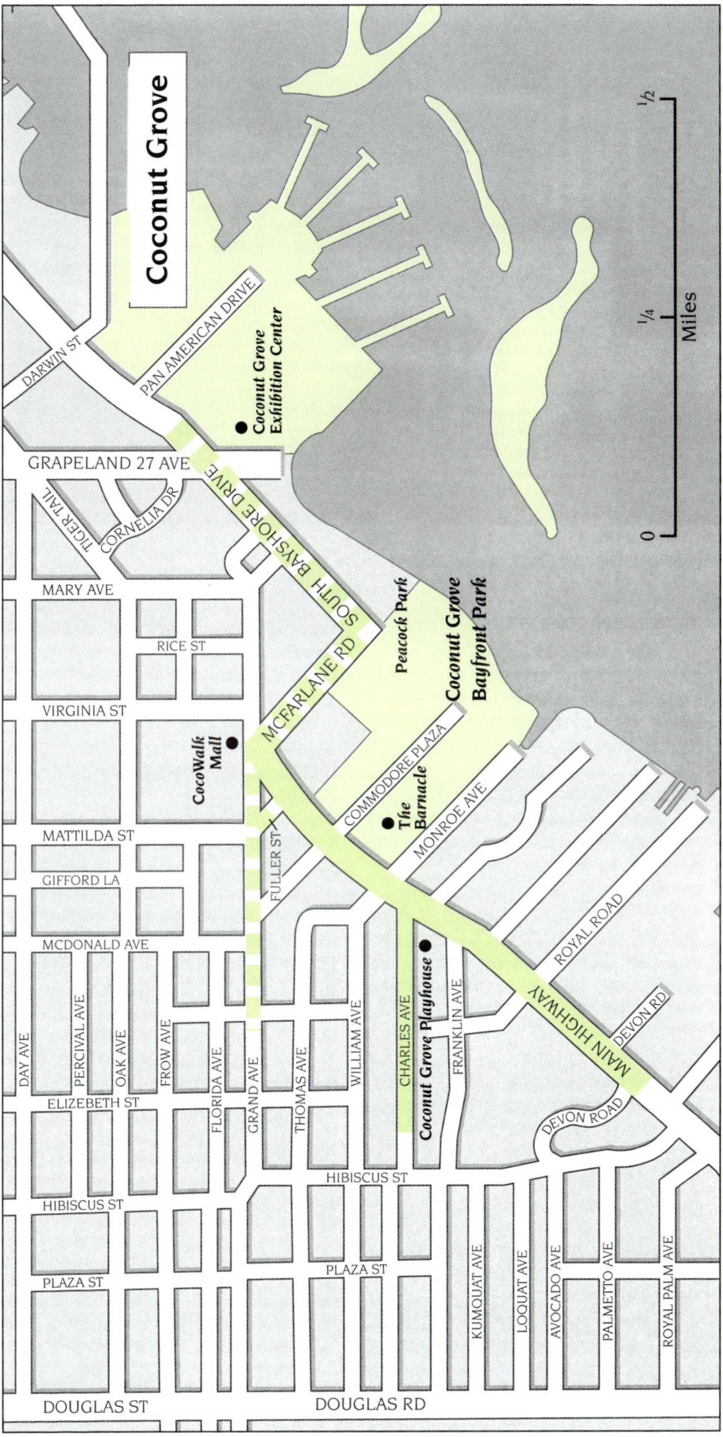
Coconut Grove
Coconut Grove Exhibition Center
PAN AMERICAN DRIVE
DARWIN ST
GRAPELAND 27 AVE
SOUTH BAYSHORE DRIVE
TIGER TAIL
CORNELIA DR
MARY AVE
RICE ST
VIRGINIA ST
MCFARLANE RD
Peacock Park
Coconut Grove Bayfront Park
CocoWalk Mall
COMMODORE PLAZA
The Barnacle
MONROE AVE
MATTILDA ST
GIFFORD LA
FULLER ST
MCDONALD AVE
Coconut Grove Playhouse
ROYAL ROAD
MAIN HIGHWAY
DEVON RD
DEVON ROAD
DAY AVE
PERCIVAL AVE
OAK AVE
FROW AVE
FLORIDA AVE
GRAND AVE
THOMAS AVE
WILLIAM AVE
CHARLES AVE
FRANKLIN AVE
ELIZEBETH ST
HIBISCUS ST
PLAZA ST
KUMQUAT AVE
LOQUAT AVE
AVOCADO AVE
PALMETTO AVE
ROYAL PALM AVE
DOUGLAS ST
DOUGLAS RD
0
1/4
1/2
Miles

• *Center for the* Fine Arts, *Metro-Dade Cultural Center.*

RECOMMENDED HOTELS

You can usually find a place to stay in Miami. Most of the hotels are in Miami Beach, where there are always vacancies of some sort along Collins Avenue. In Miami Beach, proximity to the beach will affect the price of the room as much as the quality of the hotel. As far as prices are concerned, the season lasts anywhere from the start of November to the end of April. Outside this period you'll find prices reduced, sometimes by as much as 30 percent. Even so, prices in Miaimi tend to be high. There are irritating state and city taxes (more than 10 percent), and sometimes obscure parking or service charges. Be sure to find out whether these are included in the price you have been quoted. The best place for inexpensive motels is way out in South Miami at Homestead; see also Florida Overall: 3.

Days Inn – Miami Airport, $-$$; 3401 *LeJeune Road, Miami; tel.* 305 871 4221; *no cards.*

Relatively inexpensive accommodations out by the airport, in case you're unexpectedly delayed. More than 150 standard rooms, and a pool.

Doubletree Hotel at Coconut Grove, $$$; 2649 *South Bayshore Drive, Coconut Grove* 33133; *tel.* 305 858 2500; *all major cards.*

More than 150 rooms, heated outdoor pool and lit tennis courts. Upper rooms have stunning views out over the bay.

Everglades Motel, $-$$; 605 *South Krome Avenue, Homestead; tel.* 305 247 4117; *no cards.*

Your genuine, no-frills inexpensive motel. About as inexpensive as you'll get in Miami (and if it's full there are others further up along North Krome Avenue). But the snag is, you're 20 miles from Downtown. Useful if you're on your way back from the Keys or the Everglades, and don't want to waste money in Miami.

Fontainebleau Hilton Resort and Spa, $$$; 4441 *Collins Avenue, Miami Beach* 33140; *tel.* 305 538 2000; *all major cards.*

This is the biggest hotel on the front, with more than 1,500 employees, and a similar number of rooms. It opened in the early 1950s and quickly acquired legendary status – numbering presidents, James Bond, and so on, among its guests. And they

• *Downtown Miami skyline.*

can't help it if Frank Sinatra also has his own suite. Rooms have superb ocean views. The pool has to be seen to be believed. If you want to splurge during your stay in Miami beach, this is the place to come. The "Fountain-Blue" (as it's called) is the most famous hotel on the beach. Its only serious rival in the entire Miami area is the Biltmore – see Florida Overall: 3, page 72.

Leslie Hotel, $$$; 1244 *Ocean Drive, Miami Beach* 33139; *tel.* 305 534 2135; *all major cards.*

The classic Art Deco hotel, built in 1937 by Albert Anis. It's comparatively small (just 70 rooms), but it looks as fine inside as it does outside. The service matches the surroundings, and you're on Ocean Drive right by the beach. The view from the rooms is also exactly right: classic minimalist – sea, sky, beach, palm tree. Be sure to reserve early in season. If they don't have rooms, they'll recommend the Cardozo just down the street at 1300 Ocean Drive, which is run by the same management and is almost as good.

Howard Johnson, $$-$$$; 200 *South East 2nd Avenue, Miami* 33131; *tel.* 1 800 327 0200; *all major cards.*

Nothing special, but the best deal you'll get in Downtown Miami.

Kenmore Hotel, $$; 1050 *Ocean Drive, South Beach* 33139; *tel.* 305 532 1930; *all major cards.*

Best value for the money in pricey South Beach, just a three-minute walk from the beach. Free breakfast in the friendly spacious lobby, and there's even a pool out front.

If this one is full, try their sister hotel a couple of doors down Washington Avenue, the **Park Washington**, (also **$$**, and good value.

Kent Hotel, $$; 1131 *Collins Avenue, South Beach* 33139; *tel.* 305 531 6771; *cards* AE, MC, V.

Pleasant Art Deco hotel in the heart of the district, just a block from the ocean.

Paradise Inn Motel, $$; 8520 *Harding Avenue, Miami Beach* 33141; *tel.* 305 865 6216; *all major cards.*

As inexpensive as you'll get up at this end of Miami Beach. Basic motel rooms, but only a block from the ocean.

RECOMMENDED RESTAURANTS

There's a rich mix of cuisines plentifully available in Greater Miami. Naturally, the Cuban and Haitian cooking is among the best you'll find anywhere. Latin American, Chinese, Caribbean, Creole, and Southern are all excellent. Even the local American cooking has its own distinctive flavor – relying heavily on seafood, citrus and salads. There's also choice across the entire price spectrum – with prices often lower than you might expect.

Bijan's Fort Dallas Restaurant and Raw Bar, $-$$; 62 *South East 4th Street, Downtown Miami; tel.* 305 381 7778; *most major cards.*

Overlooking the Miami River close to the sight of the original settlement (where Julia Tuttle took up residence). Lively spot, particularly at night when they sometimes have live music.

Joe's Stone Crab, $$; 227 *Biscayne Street, Miami Beach; tel.* 305 673 0365; *all major cards.*

A Miami Beach classic since before the First World War (which is prehistoric, as far as this area is concerned). There are more than 400 seats, but you may still have to wait in line, especially on the weekends. (They don't accept reservations.) The famous stone crabs are freshly caught, freshly cooked, and served cold, with a mustard-mayonnaise sauce. Joe's invented this dish, and nowhere is it served better.

This restaurant's reputation rests so firmly on its stone crabs that it closes when they're out of season (early June to early October). And this reputation is so well established among the regulars that when Joe's opens they know it's the start of the Miami beach tourist season, and when it closes... time to go home, folks.

Las Tapas, $-$$; *Bayside Marketplace,* 401 *Biscayne Boulevard, Downtown Miami; tel.* 305 372 2737; *no cards.*

Just the place to put your feet up and enjoy an authentic Spanish snack with a glass of Sangria, after your morning's power shopping in the Downtown mall.

Le Pavillon, $$$; 100 *Chopin Plaza, Downtown Miami; tel.* 305 577 1000; *all major cards; open evenings only,* Mon-Sat.

American cuisine served amid the atmosphere of a gentleman's club. The menu constantly changes, featuring dishes from different parts of America, as well as several Florida specialities. The wine list has some American classics and a supporting cast from Europe. Discreet, understanding service.

Mark's Place, $$$; 2286 *North East 123rd Street, North Miami; tel.* 305 893 6888.

The chef owns this one, so he can choose what he *really* wants to cook. And when it's a chef of the caliber of Mark Militello, you can be sure you're in for something special. His speciality is New American cuisine.

You will see why gourmet critics consider this the best restaurant in the state. Snazzy decor with brass railings and avant-garde art; and an even more avant-garde menu. Scotch-whisky-and-mango barbecue sauce, fennel-and-tangerine vinaigrette – and the like. But these combinations work, and there's an imaginative wine list to complement them. Mark pays such attention to detail that he even has some of his devoted staff growing organic vegetables for him.

No foodie's trip to Florida will be without a visit to this shrine of haute cuisine.

News Cafe, $-$$; 800 *Ocean Drive, South Miami Beach; tel.* 305 538 NEWS; *cards* AE, MC, V.

The trendy place on Ocean Drive, the showplace of the Art Deco district. It can get very crowded, especially on weekends. But be sure to get a seat outside on the terrace, where everyone comes to see and be seen.

The menu is trendy, healthy, and low-cal.

Señor Frog's, $$; *3008 Grand Avenue, Coconut Grove; tel. 305 448 0999; all major cards.*

One of the liveliest night spots in Coconut Grove, and very popular on the weekends with actors and students. The menu is Mexican, the music is Mariachi, and the drink is Margaritas. Expansive portions and ecstatic clientele.

Versailles, $-$$; *3555 South West 8th Street, Miami; tel. 305 444 0240; cards* DC, MC, V.

This is *the* place to come for Cuban food, right in the heart of Little Havana on the famous Calle Ocho. The large menu here has all the Cuban favorites, at favorite prices. This is where the locals come when they're thinking of home.

SHOPPING

Shopping is taken so seriously in Miami that they even talk of the "shopping scene." Much of this boils down to what designer sunglasses to wear with your almost non-existent (but exquisitely designed) beachwear.

Those who are seriously into this kind of thing, should head for **Alice's Day Off** at 5900 Sunset Drive, South Miami. Other mere fashion mortals will probably prefer to do some window shopping at the malls before making their choice.

The best of the malls is certainly **Bayside Marketplace** at 401 Biscayne Boulevard, in Downtown. This has more than 100 shops on 16 acres of prime waterfront. If you're having serious problems getting rid of your (or your partner's) money, head for **Bal Harbor** at 9700 Collins Avenue, Miami Beach. Gucci, Cartier and the like are all here: top of the line, at top prices.

More down-to-earth shoppers should head for the Lincoln Road Mall, on Washington Avenue at 16th Street. Forty years ago, this was what Bal Harbor Mall is today, and it was known as "the Fifth Avenue of the South." At the western end of this, you'll find the **Lincoln Road Arts District**, an enclave of galleries, artists' studios and cafes that is often overlooked.

Those who prefer their art in the form of classical statues amid tropical greenery should head for **Mayfair-in-the-Grove** at 3000 Florida Avenue. This is the Coconut Grove mall with Coco Chanel prices.

Miami's old-time shopping institution is **Burdine's** at 22 East Flagler Street in Downtown. This department store is almost 60 years old – an age which very few admit to in Florida these days.

If you feel the need to bargain hunt, head for the **Opa-Locka Flea Market** at 12705 North West 42nd Street, in Hialeah. Here, from Friday to Sunday, there are literally hundreds of stalls selling all kinds of goods, bads and uglies.

If you're into antiques, try **One Hand Clapping** at 432 Espanola Way, South Miami Beach, where they specialize in Art Deco objects. The best bookshop in Miami is **Books & Books** at 296 Aragon Avenue, Coral Gables. There's always B. Dalton in the Bayside Marketplace at 401 Biscayne Boulevard, Downtown.
The best place to replenish your CD stock is **KowTow Music**, 1249 Washington Avenue, Miami Beach. For authentic Cuban sounds, try **Lily's Records** on Calle Ocho in Litte Havana (1260 South West 8th Street).

SOCCER

Miami has at least two good Spanish-speaking TV stations. On weekends both of these screen soccer matches live from Latin America. All you've heard about matches in Brazil, Argentina and other South American countries is true. The acting is terrific, and the soccer is out of this world. This is your chance to hear a legendary Spanish-language commentator making his trademark call: GOOOOOOOOOO-LLLLLLLLLL.

Central Florida

South from Orlando

120 miles; map Hallwag Florida

This region is worth exploring if you have some time to spare after visiting Walt Disney World and Orlando. It's off the beaten track, and thus provides a pleasant contrast to your more hectic times with Mickey and his goofy pals.

My favourite sight here is the Florida Southern College at Lakeland. This was built by the celebrated architect Frank Lloyd Wright, and was one of his last great projects.

The Cypress Gardens, near Winter Haven, are one of the horticultural wonders of the state. But their proximity to Orlando means that their tourist potential is exploited to the full. Press on south down Rt 27 and you come to Lake Wales, which is renowned for its annual passion play. This takes place in the open air during February and March. Nearby you will find the delightful Bok Tower Gardens, with the sensational Singing Tower. Further down Rt 27, you come to Sebring, home of the famous Sebring Motor Racing Track. Beyond, at Palmdale, is the Gatorama, where the alligators live. Those with time to spare should be sure to drive a few miles on to Lake Okeechobee, America's second largest inland lake.

You can easily drive across this region in a day. Allow a couple of days if you want to take in some of the sights.

TRANSPORTATION
There are infrequent buses between the main towns, but the only practical way to explore is by car.

SIGHTS & PLACES OF INTEREST

BARTOW

About 12 miles SE of Lakeland. If you think tourist over-development has ruined Florida, go to Bartow. Here you'll see that we are capable of doing far worse things to the environment than covering it with condominiums. Bartow is the center of the phosphate mining industry.

Florida produces a quarter of the world's phosphate, the main ingredient of many fertilizers. The industry earns Florida a massive $3.5 billion a year. This means that millions of tons of Florida are dug up, shipped out, and turned into evil-smelling substances that are scattered over fields throughout the world.

What's left after this operation looks like the surface of Mars after the acid monsoon season. Mile upon mile of barren ashen hillscape, dotted with deathly green lakes (locally known as slime pits). The worst region is Bone Valley, along Rt 60. Apparently, big efforts are being made to reclaim this land, and put it to some use. Now for the good news. In the course of phosphate mining, many superb fossils have been unearthed in **Bone Valley** (hence the name). Phosphate is essentially pre-historic alluvial waste, and ideal for preserving fossilized skeletons of such extinct species as mammoths and sabre-toothed tigers. These can be seen east of town at the **Bone Valley Exposition.**

CYPRESS GARDENS

Head for Winter Haven, 17 miles E of Lakeland, and you come to the gardens just SE of town on Rt 540; open 9.30 am-5.30 pm daily; entry $25.

Once upon a time, this was all unspoiled swamp. Now it's a massive 200-acre floral theme park. After you've gotten over the entry fee ($25), you're not likely to be surprised by anything you'll see in here. Walking through the gardens are women dressed as southern belles, waving fans and flouncing their hooped skirts. On **Lake Eloise** the **Greatest American Ski Team** performs synchronized water-skiing and paragliding shows. And it's not just the humans who engage in such high jinks.

Further on you can see the **Feathered Follies**, which include roller-skating parrots, and parrots playing basketball. You'll also see humans making noises like parrots, while parrots make noises like humans. And be sure not to miss **Cypress Roots**, the local museum which shows photos of famous visitors to the park. (Yes, Elvis on water-skis.) After this, a visit to **Hug Haven** is a must. Here you can thrill to the sight of your child hugging a panther (admittedly a small one).

By now you're ready for the **Wings of Wonder**, a 5,000-square-foot conservatory where hundreds of butterflies flutter about your head. And now it's time for a visit to the 150-feet-high **Island in the Sky**, where you can survey all that you have survived.

The flowers and trees at the Gardens can be truly superb. The variety of flowers on display is awesome: dozens of hibiscus, scores of poinsettias, hundreds of roses, thousands of jasmine, millions of chrysanthemums. Such is the claim. The flowers easily outlast the florid hyperbole.

HAINES CITY

On Rt 27, 30 miles SW of Orlando. A must for all baseball fans is **Boardwalk and Baseball**, which is 9 miles north of town at the intersection of Rts 4 and 27, *open 9 am-9 pm daily; entry $20.* Here there's a **National Baseball Hall of Fame** exhibit, and you can see a film which covers the entire history of the game. You can also try out your batting, and have a go at a pitching machine. Non-aficionados can while away their time at the funfair and the Wild West Show.

LAKE ALFRED

On Rt 92, 12 miles E of Lakeland. This is the kitsch capital of Polk County. On Haines Boulevard you'll find shops selling all kinds of American kitsch and out-and-out junk. (Those who don't know the difference might as well stay away.) Great spot for picking up unusual baseball caps, defunct 1950s milk-shake shakers, and other such prime cultural items.

LAKELAND

On Rt 4, 45 miles SW of Orlando. Lakeland is essentially a working city, and its attempts at mainstream tourist attrac-

FRANK LLOYD WRIGHT
America's greatest architect, and considered by many to be the foremost architect of the 20thC. Frank Lloyd Wright was born in Wisconsin in 1867. He studied engineering at the University of Wisconsin before working as an architect. By his late twenties he had already developed his own ideas about architectural style. He believed in using modern materials, and adapting them to modern living. His Midwestern style became known as Prairie School. In 1912 he designed the first "slab" skyscraper, though this was never built. In all he designed more than 800 buildings, though less than half of these were ever built. Among his greatest successes was the Imperial Hotel in Tokyo, which generated considerable controversy, but vindicated Lloyd Wright when it withstood a major earthquake.

Wright was a charismatic figure who lived a turbulent emotional life and endured more than his fair share of disaster. His mistress was murdered by a madman, who set fire to his house, Taliesin. After he rebuilt Taliesin, it was struck by lightning and burned to the ground once more.

The Florida Southern College at Lakeland was one of Lloyd Wright's last major projects (1940-1949) and was undertaken at the same time as the building of his Guggenheim Museum in New York, which remains his best-known masterpiece. He died in 1959 at the age of 91.

• *Annie Pfeiffer Chapel.*

• *Stained glass, Denforth Chapel.*

tion are doomed to be outshone by the delights of nearby Tampa and Orlando. But more discriminating visitors will be well rewarded by a visit to **Florida Southern College** – south-west of downtown at McDonald Street and Ingraham Avenue. This contains the largest collection of buildings by the 20thC's greatest architect, Frank Lloyd Wright.

This project was commissioned

• *The Legend of Spook Hill.*

when Lloyd Wright was in his early seventies, and the building was largely undertaken by the students themselves. Many of the original buildings have now been added to, or adapted to uses for which they were not designed. Despite this, it is possible to discern much of Lloyd Wright's original idea. Pick up a free map from one of the boxes in the covered walkways, and follow the tour. Don't miss the **Annie Pfeiffer Chapel**, and the stained-glass effects which rain colored light between the buildings.

Of course, Lloyd Wright didn't supervise the local students who were set to work building his project, with the result that many of his advanced architectural ideas were sometimes rather freely translated.

For example, despite the heat, Lloyd Wright insisted on there being no air-conditioning in his buildings, as this would destroy their "organic architecture." However, the inhabitants of these buildings had other ideas. Judge for yourself whether the pros win out over the cons.

Another place where the pros contest with the cons is the **Polk County Museum of Art** at *800 East Palmetto Street, open 10 am-4 pm Tues-Sat, Sun afternoons only; entry free.* Here you can see a changing exhibition of works by young Florida artists. These range from the good to "good heavens!"

LAKE OKEECHOBEE

For the sights around Lake Okeechobee, including the Brighton Seminole Indian Reservation and Belle Glade, *see Florida Overall: 2, page 57.*

LAKE WALES 🛏 ✕

On Rt 27, 40 miles S of Orlando. Lake Wales is in the high Sierras of Florida – it's all of 250 feet above sea level. Train buffs will want to visit the **Lake Wales Depot Museum** at *325 South Scenic Highway, open 9 am-4 pm, closed Sun; entry free.* Here you can see all kinds of old locomotive memorabilia and other odds and ends, including a collection of fruit company crate labels.

Drive on to North Avenue and defy gravity at **Spook Hill**. Here your car will obligingly roll *up* the hill. (All right, try it and see.)

Lake Wales is famous for its annual **Black Hills Passion Play**. Outdoor performances take place in February and March at the local amphitheater. Call 813 676 1495 for details.

At the local **Masterpiece Gardens** you can see a mosaic of The Last Supper which contains almost a third of a million pieces.

A couple of miles north of town, off Rt 27A, are the **Bok Tower Gardens**, *open 8 am-5 pm; entry* $3. Edward Bok was born in Holland and emigrated to America where he worked his way up from being an office boy to editor of *Ladies Home Journal*. In 1920 he published his autobiography, which won the Pulitzer Prize. With his loot he bought the local mountain: so-called Iron Mountain, which soars to 287 feet. As a mark of gratitude and self-esteem, Bok turned this very Dutch mountain into a "sanctuary for humans and birds." On top of the mountain he built a 200-foot-high pink tower, which might even have

• *Bok Tower Gardens.*

made Sigmund Freud blush. The Bok Tower Gardens were opened in 1929 by Bok's pal, President Coolidge. Mr Bok is buried at the foot of his remarkable tower.

The 130-acre gardens are filled with shady walks beneath palms trees, magnolias, pines and all manner of arboreal wonders, where the birds chirp and coo quietly amid the foliage. The peace of this woodland idyll is disturbed once every half an hour by the 53-bell carillon which rings out from the tower (known on account of this as the Singing Tower). Less raucous concerts are occasionally performed on summer evenings in the gardens.

• *Sculptural detail of Bok Tower.*

Further into the gardens there's the **Pine Ridge Trail**, which leads you through untended woodland to a viewing hut, where you can observe the local wildlife.

Also a couple of miles north of town, but on Rt 17, is the celebrated **Chalet Suzanne**. This was founded in 1931 by the redoubtable Bertha Hinshaw. Her husband had just died, and the Depression had left her broke. She built the free-form chalet and opened it as a restaurant where she cooked according to her own free-form recipes. The result was a huge success. Curious gourmets with cast-iron digestions flocked in from far and wide to taste Bertha's concoctions in her oddly concocted house, whose brightly colored walls reel like a Cubist painting.

Bertha's famous Romaine Soup is canned here. This is so highly esteemed that in 1973 the crew of Apollo 15 even took a can with them to the Moon.

Twelve miles down Rt 60 to the east of town, you come to the **Lake Kissimmee State Park,** *open 8 am-sunset; entry $3.50 per car*. This has the usual nature trail, parts of which are particularly picturesque; and you can go canoeing on the lake. More unusual is a reconstruction of an early Florida cattle ranch, complete with genuine Florida cowboys, who used to be known as crackers, because of their whips.

ORLANDO

See Florida Overall: 1, page 33.

PALMDALE

On Rt 27, 14 miles S of Orlando. South-west of town, off Rt 27, is the famous **Gatorama,** *open 8 am-6 pm daily; entry $4.50*. This is, in fact, a working alligator farm, and fully licensed as such. (You can't just keep one of these charming creatures in the tub as a pet – you need a license.) Here you can view thousands of toothsome gators basking in the sun, all waiting to have their tails turned into succulent steaks and their skins transformed into politically incorrect handbags. Nothing much happens – except at feeding time, when all hell breaks loose.

SEBRING

Off Rt 27, 70 miles S of Orlando. Home of the famous **Sebring Motor Racing Track**, which is 8 miles south-east of town off Rt 98. Every year in March the **12 Hours of Sebring** endurance race is held here. For a couple of days, thousands of motor racing fans descend on this out-of-the-way spot from all over America (and you won't be able to find a room). Otherwise, it's just a sleepy little town.

The town was founded by George Sebring, who planted an oak tree here in 1912. The oak tree is still standing, and the streets fan out in a semicircle from this central landmark.

South-west of town on the other side of Lake Jackson is the **Highlands Hammock State Park,** *open 8 am-sunset; entry $3.50 per car*. This has a pleasant walking trail through the sub-tropical swamp.

WINTER HAVEN 🛏✕

See Cypress Gardens, page 168 and Recommended Hotels and Restaurants, page 173.

RECOMMENDED HOTELS

LAKELAND

The best place to stay in town is:

Lake Morton Bed and Breakfast, $-$$; *817 South Boulevard; tel. 813 688 6788; no cards.*

Friendly welcome. Also serves great breakfasts, where you can discuss with your fellow guests what ought to be done about the ravages of the local phosphate mining (see Bartow, page 168). The most original suggestion I heard was to import camels and turn the entire area into a desert theme park.

If you just want somewhere to lay your head, try:

Scottish Inn, $-$$; *244 North Florida Avenue, Lakeland; tel. 813 687 2530; no cards.*

As authentically Scottish as McDonalds, but none the worse for that.

LAKE WALES

Chalet Suzanne, $$$; *Box AC, Rt 17, Lake Wales 33859; tel. 813 676 6011; all major cards.*

Best known as a resturant (see also Recommended Restaurants, and Sights & Places of Interest, page 172) this whacky spot also has a few rooms. These live up to the eccentric promise of the exterior. The best rooms look out over the lake. This conventional view gives a soothing respite from the vividly contrasting interior views.

WINTER HAVEN

Ranch House Motor Inn, $-$$; *1911 Cypress Gardens Boulevard, Rt 27A, Winter Haven; tel. 1 800 366 5996; no cards.*

Helpfully situated right outside the famous Cypress Gardens. Also makes a useful base for exploring the surrounding region. Standard motel, nothing fancy.

RECOMMENDED RESTAURANTS

LAKE WALES

Chalet Suzanne, $$-$$$; *Box AC, Rt 17, Lake Wales 33859; tel. 813 676 6011; all major cards.*

The most original restaurant in central Florida. The regulars swear by it – they even fly in to eat here, landing at the local air strip. Eccentric atmosphere and imaginative cuisine according to the original recipes of the famous Bertha Hinshaw. (See also Recommended Hotels, and Sights & Place of Interest, page 172.)

The Gardens Cafe, $-$$; *Bok Tower Gardens, Rt 27A, Lake Wales; tel. 813 676 1408; no cards.*

Pleasant open air cafe in the famous gardens, with fine view. Ideal for a light meal, or just to drop in for a coffee and a cake while you rest your weary legs after the rigors of the day's sightseeing.

WINTER HAVEN

Ranch House Motor Inn Coffee Shop, $-$$; *1911 Cypress Gardens Boulevard, Rt 27A, Winter Haven; tel. 813 294 4104; no cards.*

All that you'd expect of a good motel coffee shop. This one is handy because it's just outside the famous Cypress Gardens, and much less expensive than the overpriced and overcrowded eateries inside. (For details on accommodations, see Recommended Hotels.

Local Explorations: 2

Central Florida

The Gold Coast

50 miles; map Hallwag Florida

Florida's Gold Coast originally received its name from the gold washed on to the beaches from Spanish treasure galleons wrecked offshore. Now most of the gold is found on shore in the houses that line the beach.

The stretch of coastline from Fort Lauderdale to Palm Beach is arguably the wealthiest in the world. Even Malibu, the Hamptons and the French Riviera can't compete with Palm Beach, America's swankiest "old money" resort - whose Worth Avenue is the world's most expensive shopping district. Nearby Boca Raton is also in the polo belt. Fort Lauderdale may be less rarified, but its claim of being the "Venice of America" is fully justified, with so many miles of inland waterway that it even has water taxis.

This region is largely millionaire territory, and the beaches are marvelous. But most of the coast is built up, with only the occasional stretch of unspoiled shoreline. If you want wide open spaces, you have to head inland to the Loxahatchee Wildlife Refuge.

There are three main routes through this part of Florida. The inland Florida Turnpike (Rt 95) is the fastest. Rt 1 follows the Intracoastal Waterway, has long strips of hamburger joints and neon, and is often crowded. Best of all, if you have some time, is Rt A1A which runs along the barrier islands.

From Fort Lauderdale to Palm Beach is just 50 miles, and can easily be covered in a morning. If you want to take in the beaches, see some of the sights, and explore the social Himalayas of Palm Beach, it's worth allowing a couple of days for this region.

TRANSPORTATION
There are regular buses connecting all the main towns on this route, but these don't take in the sights, and often leave you stranded far from the beach. The only practical way to explore this region is by car.

• *Whitehall Palm Beach.*

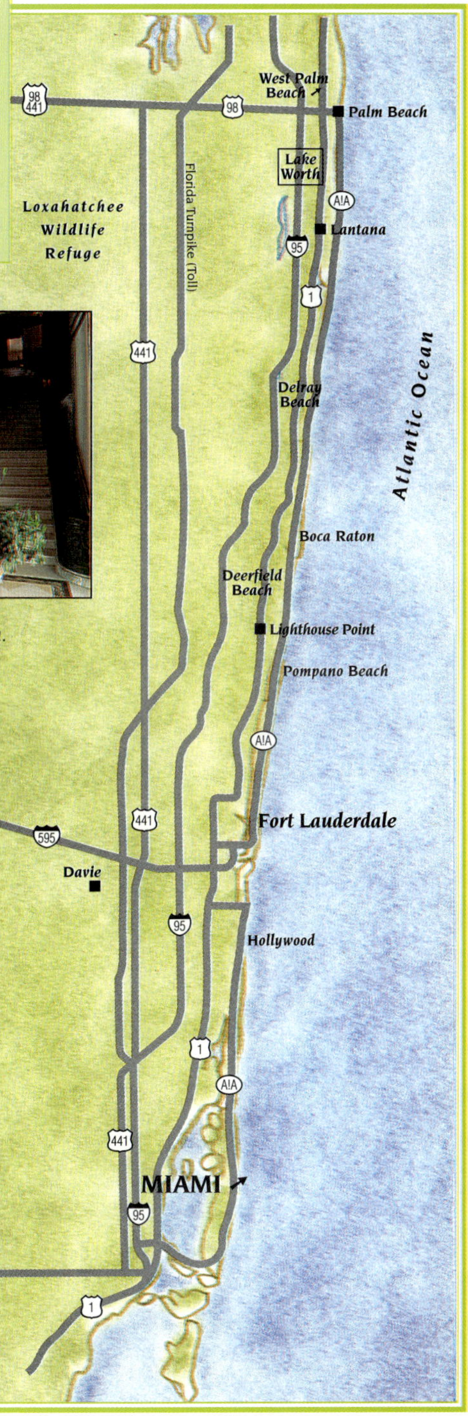

• A *typical* Mizner *house*, Fort *Lauderdale*.

SIGHTS & PLACES OF INTEREST

BOCA RATON

On the coast 24 *miles* S *of* Palm *Beach*. The first European to reach this part of the coast was the Spanish explorer Ponce de León in the early 1500s. His sailors are thought to have named this spot Boca de Raton – which means rat's mouth – because of the sharp rocks in the harbor.

Nothing of much note happened here until the 20thC. Then, in the 1920s, the eccentric Addison Mizner arrived from Palm Beach. Mizner was an ex-boxer turned architect who had made money building houses for the rich in Palm Beach, but had finally exasperated his clients by his cavalier attitude toward detail. (They didn't mind the grand staircases that wound up nowhere, this was all part of the fun. But when there was no kitchen, or he refused to include any bathrooms because "they didn't fit with the overall scheme," it was time for him to move on. For further details, see Palm Beach, page 185.)

Addison Mizner moved on to Boca Raton, and brought with him a suitably grandiose plan. He intended to build a Utopian community for the rich, which would be "beyond realness in its ideality." The Florida land boom was in full swing, and the scheme soon attracted rich backers. These included the socialite perfumier Elizabeth Arden and a Vanderbilt chum of hers.

Mizner's design included a large lagoon, a Grand Canal, and gondolas. Yes, Mizner wanted to turn Boca Raton into "the Venice of Florida" – despite the fact that Florida already had one Venice (Venice, Florida) and "The Venice of America" (Fort Lauderdale). Mizner immediately set to work building a million-dollar hotel; the canal and the lagoon were dug, and the foundations were laid for a magnificent cathedral (which was to be dedicated to his mother). But while the gondolas were being shipped across the Atlantic, the Wall Street Crash occurred. The gondolas (complete with an instructor gondolier) arrived to find a long ditch, empty of water, leading to the empty shell of the Cloister Inn Hotel, complete with its peach-colored tower and marble columns. (This is now occupied by the stylish Boca Raton Resort and Club – see Recommended Hotels, page 188.) Mizner had gone bust. Once again, it looked as if nothing was going to happen for 400 years in Boca Raton.

But it did. And this time the local authorities wisely decided they would lay down strict rules about any architecture within the limits of their jurisdiction. Surprisingly, they endorsed Mizner's "Venetian" style (officially known as Mediterranean Revival). From now on, they decreed, building in Boca Raton would have to conform to this style. Planning permission for buildings without ornate entrance gateways, arches and loggias were likely to be turned down. Buildings over a certain size were expected to incorporate bell towers (though in keeping with the Mizner ethos, these did not have to include a working set of bells). The result was architecturally second-rate and unimaginative. And Boca Raton continued to prosper – in its own quiet way. (Which certainly wouldn't have been the case if there had been bells in all those towers.)

Further prosperity arrived in the 1970s in the form of IBM, who set up their headquarters in Boca Raton. Nowadays, the polo players at the Club include both the idle rich and the workaholic executive.

There are several sights worth seeing in Boca Raton:

Boca Raton Museum of Art

801 West Palmetto Park Road (due to move soon to the Boca Raton Museum Center, 700 Banyan Trail). Phone 407 395 2500 for information. Open 10 am-4 pm Mon-Fri, 12 noon-4 pm weekends; entry free (donation welcomed).

This is rapidly gaining a reputation as one of the best small museums in the state. The core of what's on display is the **Mayers Collection**, which contains drawings and lesser works by many of the modern greats – including Degas, Picasso, Matisse and Modigliani. The artists may be greats, but not all the works on display are. Yet precisely because they are lesser works, this sometimes makes them even more interesting in relation to the artist's successful works. Indeed, look hard and you begin to see how difficult it is to get it right.

There is also an African collection.

Singing Pines Children's Museum

498 Crawford Road; open 12 am-5 pm Tues -Sat. Housed in a modest bungalow with an absurd pillared portico, the building is said to be the oldest wooden structure in Boca Raton, and may even be as much as 80 years old. Yet whereas most other buildings here try to look old, this one looks refreshingly modern. Inside they have kids' exhibitions, games, and sometimes even little plays in which your kids can take part while you sit in the audience. Good fun, and the younger ones really do enjoy it.

Mizner Park

Mizner Boulevard, off North East 5th Avenue (Rt 1). This exclusive shopping mall was opened in 1991, and faithfully echoes the work of its namesake. It's designed largely for the rich to demonstrate precisely how rich they are, in an otherwise inoffensive setting. This is where you marvel at the price it is possible to pay for a simple T-shirt (which may cost more than the limit on your credit card). As Socrates said when walking down a similar street in 4thC BC Athens: "How many things I can do without."

But of course it's always great fun to sit in the shade of one of the cafes, and watch it all going on.

In a fitting tribute to Mizner Park, The **World Museum of Cartoon Art** is transferring here. Besides stocking over 50,000 original cartoons, the museum will exhibit more than a hundred hours of cartoon movies. But be warned: once here, the kids may wish to see nothing else during their entire stay in Florida.

Royal Palm Polo Sports Club

Clint Moore Road. This is the exclusive social hub of Boca Raton. Alas, there are no polo ponies for rent – so if you haven't brought your string along, you'll have to make do with watching the locals perform as best they can.

This is the home ground of Royal Palm, one of the best teams in Florida. The players here, and in the Palm Beach region, are as good as any in the world (though they have a tough time of it when the Argentinians come over to contest the International Gold Cup – the unofficial world championship which takes place in March).

Polo may be a rich person's game, but it's often very exciting to watch.

Games are played on Sundays only, at 1 pm and 3 pm. The season lasts from January to April. For further details phone 407 471 3995.

Old Floresta

If you want to see the houses Mizner designed, there are plenty of these in Old Floresta, the residential district off West Palmetto Park Road, north of the Museum of Art. There are also guided tours of the Boca Raton Resort and Club, which grew out of Mizner's original Cloister Inn. For details phone 407 395 8655.

Other Mizner buildings are scattered here and there (the ones that look most like his are invariably imitations). For details, contact the Chamber of Com-

merce, which is on the Old Dixie Highway, half a mile or so north of the Mizner shopping mall (on the same side).

Walking and swimming
There are several pleasant spots for walking and swimming in Boca Raton. My favorite swimming beach is **South Inlet Park** at 400 Ocean Boulevard (Rt 1). A couple of miles further north on the same road is **Red Reef Park**. Here there really is a reef, and inland there are trails through the semitropical woods. A mile further north is **Spanish River Park**, which has a beach, nature trails beyond the tunnels (beneath Rt 1), and an observation tower, whose high viewing platform will confirm for you that this region is just as flat as it looks from ground level.

DAVIE

Inland, 8 miles SW *of* Fort *Lauderdale.* This is the Wild West, Florida style. Davie began in 1910 as a cowboy town, when they herded cattle in this part of Florida, rather than tourists. Today it's still a cowboy town, and many of the locals ride around dressed like extras from a western movie. You can even tether your horse outside McDonald's, where there's a "ride-thru" window. Even the Town Hall has swinging saloon doors. If you want to pick up the right gear to show off in front of your pardners back home, head for 6211 South West 45th Street and hitch your horse outside

• *Boca Raton Resort and Club.*

Grifs Western. Here they sell some great boots, genuine ten-gallon hats, and even saddles. Should you be passing through Davie in November, you can see the Florida State Championship Rodeo.

If your plans don't include the Everglades National Park (see Florida Overall: 3 and Local Explorations: 4), you can still sample the swampland experience by taking an airboat ride through alligator land at the **Everglades Holiday Park and Campground** at 21940 Griffin Road, a mile south of Davie on Rt 441.

DEERFIELD BEACH

On the coast 2 miles S *of* Boca *Raton.* Of little interest, apart from **Deerfield Island Park**, a superb 50-acre enclave of countryside which has somehow remained immune to Gold Coast condomania. Once upon a time, Al Capone decided to buy this island. Al's casino – which was naturally its owner's favorite gambling spot – was just across on the mainland. Unfortunately, as soon as Capone laid down the cash to buy the island, the tax authorities demanded to know where these used bills had come from. Capone was most miffed, and felt obliged to make a hasty tactical withdrawal. Intensive inquiries were made as to how the tax boys could have got wind of this deal, and concrete boots were ordered for the island's owner, but these were never used. Anyway, as a result Deerfield Island was never developed. The Deerfield Island Park has some fine views over the water, and two superb **trails** – one by a mangrove swamp, and another along the inner shore. The island's permanent residents include foxes, armadillos and racoons.

To get to the island, turn off Rt 810 at the Chamber of Commerce, and continue to the quay at the end of Riverview Road. The Riverview Restaurant, on this road, used to be Al Capone's joint. There's a free ferry across to the island only on Wednesday and Saturday mornings. Phone 305 428 3463 for details.

DELRAY BEACH

On the coast 19 *miles* S *of* Palm *Beach*. This is an enclave of financial sanity between the horror-story prices of Boca Raton and Palm Beach. It also has a pleasant beach, and suitably humble beginnings.

The place was started by a retired postmaster from Chicago. When he arrived at this stretch of coast in the early 1890s, it was completely empty – apart from mangrove swamps, alligators, snakes and the like. The ex-postmaster turned developer bought the mangroves, snakes and so on for a song. He then began selling off plots of land at $5 each in newspapers throughout Michigan – and he soon had enough money to clear the land before the buyers turned up to view their property.

There's just one place of real interest in Delray Beach, **The Morikami Museum and Japanese Garden**, 4000 *Morikami Park Road* (5 *miles inland*); *open* 12 *noon-*5 *pm* Tues-Sun; *entry* $4.25. This is the site of one of Florida's more curious historical episodes. In 1905, a group of Japanese farmers (sponsored by railway magnate Flagler) arrived here and set up a colony, which they called Yamoto. The idea was that they would farm silkworms and grow tea. Having quickly discovered that neither of these could survive Florida's climate, the resourceful colonists turned to cultivating pineapples, which flourished. Until they were all ruined by a blight in 1908. And that was the end of Yamoto Colony.

The site is at present maintained by a more successful group of Japanese business people. The 200-acre site has been turned into a veritable little Japan. There's a model of an imperial villa, a Shinto shrine, and, of course, a tea house. These are set amidst a beautifully landscaped Japanese garden – which even has a bonsai section of dwarfed plants indigenous to Florida. Most interesting of all is the museum, which contains everything from memorabilia of the original colonists to an audio-visual introduction to Japanese culture.

FORT LAUDERDALE ×

Ten miles N *of Miami*. After Miami, this is the most popular seaside resort in Florida. And that's the trouble. Fort Lauderdale suffers from the Canada-Belgium-New Zealand syndrome: the illu-

• *Davie* McDonald*'s*.

sion that there's something similar but far better next door. To compensate for this inferiority complex, Fort Lauderdale collects titles. It's "The Venice of America," "The Yachting Capital of the World," "The Tennis Capital of the World," "The Most Popular Beach Resort in Florida" and, finally, "The Second Greatest Cruise Capital in the World." Wow.

So what are we to make of these stupendous claims? The "Venices of America" are of course Venice, Florida and the other half-dozen or so Venices scattered throughout the country. But Fort Lauderdale does have a point. There are over 350 miles of navigable waterways in the city, six rivers, all kinds of pleasant creeks, beautiful riverfronts, harbors and artificial canals. In fact, Fort Lauderdale has a good deal more water than Venice.

Nearly 50,000 craft are moored along Fort Lauderdale's waterways – and a large portion of them are yachts. Which brings us to the "Yachting Capital of the World" title. There's no denying that Fort Lauderdale is big on the international yachting scene. The Whitbread Round the World Yacht Race put in here in 1994. It's also the place where they build those super-yachts for Saudi princes and media moguls.

And the "Tennis Capital of the World"? Well, Chrissie Evert was born here - and she went on to become one of the greatest women's tennis players in the world. Miami may be bigger, but much of Fort Lauderdale is better – in a well-groomed suburban way.

But this wasn't always the case. Fort Lauderdale has a short but checkered past. It all started in the 19thC, during the Seminole War. In 1838 a certain Major William Lauderdale from Tennessee put up a fort here to protect the locals living on nearby plantations. The war finished, and for the next 60 years nothing much happened.

In 1896 Flagler's railway arrived. This was to change the face of Southern Florida and transform Miami into a boom resort. But no one got off at Fort Lauderdale. By the time the place was granted city status in 1911, it had only 175 inhabitants. (By this stage Miami had more than 5,000 residents and was attracting nearly 100,000 visitors a year.)

Not until the Prohibition years did Fort Lauderdale come into its own - and even then it had to suffer the indignity of becoming famous under a different name. Rum runners bringing in illegal liquor from the Bahamas earned it the nickname "Fort Liquordale." Long after Prohibition, the legend lived on – attracting college students from all over Florida who came to whoop it up during spring break. In 1960 they even made a teeny-bopper film about Fort Lauderdale, called *Where the Boys Are.* And after that Fort Lauderdale really *did* become famous. College kids from all over the South began flooding in during the spring break. The booze flowed – and there was even some time for sex and rock and roll. Word soon spread, and college kids began homing in from even further afield. By 1985 over a third of a million college kids from all over the country were arriving for the spring break mayhem. They'd even heard of Fort Lauderdale in Wisconsin and Montana. The trouble was that soon nobody except students wanted to come anywhere near the place. This left Fort Lauderdale rather empty for long stretches during the year. So the authorities decided to up the legal drinking age. The students quickly got the message and moved further up the coast to spots such as Daytona Beach. Nowadays only a few thousand students turn up during spring break – and they're usually from parts of Montana or Wisconsin where news of recent developments has yet to penetrate.

Fort Lauderdale is now a civilized place, with one-and-a-quarter million inhabitants. It's popular with retired couples and young executives – who share a passion for sailing. And, of course, the tourists flock here too. The seafront along Atlantic Boulevard now has bright sidewalk cafes and restaurants, and the riverfront has been similarly transformed.

There are several things worth seeing in Fort Lauderdale:

Bonnet House

900 *North Birch Road; open May-Nov only; morning tours* $7.50; *reservations necessary; tel* 305 563 5393. This haven of calm was built by artist Frank Clay Bartlett, who moved here from Chicago in the 1920s. There are 35 acres of superb tropical gardens, complete with Frank's

sculptures, scampering monkeys, and a pond of gliding swans. Last I heard, his widow Evelyn was still living here – more than 100 years old, and as enchanted as ever by her private paradise.

Hugh Taylor Birch State Recreation Area

3109 East Sunrise Boulevard; open 8 am-sunset daily; entry $4 per car. This 200-acre haven of wilderness is in the midst of urban Fort Lauderdale. A century ago it was the winter home and estate of Chicago lawyer Hugh Taylor Birch, who left it to the city on the condition that it was not to be developed. There are nature and canoe trails, and all kinds of tourist-friendly wildlife: rabbits, racoons, rare birds, and various exotic rodents.

International Swimming Hall of Fame

1 Hall of Fame Drive (off Sea Breeze Boulevard); open 9 am-7 pm daily; entry $3. A poignant display of medals and memorabilia of the swimming greats. There's even a statue of Johnny Weissmuller, the first screen Tarzan – and an Olympic gold medalist.

Adjacent is the **Aquatic Complex**, which has two Olympic-sized pools where you can attempt to emulate the feats of your heroes.

Museum of Art

In the heart of Downtown at 1 East Las Olas Boulevard; open 10 am-5 pm Tues-Sat, Sun 12 noon-7pm; entry $3.50, free on weekends. Inside this postmodernist structure, there's one of the best art collections you'll see anywhere in Florida. The show is stolen by their collection of works from the unjustly neglected **CoBrA Group**. After the war a group of like-minded modernist artists living in Copenhagen, Brussels and Amsterdam joined forces (and the names of their cities) to form a loosely Expressionistic movement. They believed that the violence of modern society demanded a violent artistic response. Few great names emerged, though the Dane Asger Jorn is increasingly receiving the recognition that is his due. This is the finest collection of CoBrA Group works you'll find outside Europe.

Also of interest are paintings by the early 20thC American William Glackens, a member of the Revolutionary Black Gang (Ashcan School), America's first real artistic movement.

Museum of Discovery and Science

401 South West 2nd Street; open 10 am-5 pm Mon-Sat, Sun afternoon only; entry $6.

This $30 million palace of science as entertainment was opened in 1992. Here you can learn all kinds of things you never knew about ecology, space and nutrition in interactive, painless fashion. There's even a section which tells you about your own home, and the effect this ecologically disastrous dwelling is having on the environment. The star exhibit is the **IMAX Theater** with its 4,000-square-foot screen and six-channel sound.

Stranahan House

335 South East 6th Avenue (Las Olas Boulevard); open 10 am-4 pm Wed, Fri and Sat; $3 guided tour. Frank Stranahan arrived in Fort Lauderdale in 1892 as a pioneer, and began trading with the Seminoles. This house was his general store, and the place where he stored the alligator skins and exotic feathers he got from the Indians when he went trading up river. Later he made the place into his home and married Ivy, the local schoolmistress.

Today you can see precisely what it was like to set up house in the backwoods of Florida during the early years of the 20thC. The inside of the house has been preserved with all its nicknacks – as well as mementoes of two lives which belong to a closed history, and yet remain in living memory. Frank Stranahan began speculating in property, but went bust when the Florida land boom collapsed at the end of the 1920s. He drowned himself in the river, but Ivy went on living here in a time warp until as late as 1971.

Fort Lauderdale by boat

If you really want to see Fort Lauderdale, the best way to get around is by water taxi: tel. 305 565 5507. These stop up and down the Intracoastal Waterway at landing stages and restaurants, some even delivering as far north as Pompano Beach (one way ticket $6, all day pass $14).

Fort Lauderdale isn't "The Venice of America" for nothing. Here you can also hire a gondola. This is of course motor-

• *Rollerblading in Fort Lauderdale.*

ized. For your neo-Venetian experience, contact Gondolas of America, tel. 305 522 3333, located at the Bahia Mar Yacht Center. Here you can also take a three-hour cruise on the *Jungle Queen*, a Mississippi-style riverboat. Highlights of this trip include views of mansions, fascinating snippets of local history, and a visit to a recreated Indian village. This is the genuine tourist experience.

HOLLYWOOD

About 4 miles S of Fort Lauderdale.
This was founded by Californian entrepreneur Joseph W. Young at the height of the Florida land boom in the 1920s. Young came from Hollywood and wanted to make his development just like home. Fortunately he failed. There are no superstars here, but there is a 2-mile long broadwalk along the ocean.

Hollywood is popular with French-speaking vacationers from Quebec province in Canada – said to be a tradition which dates from the 1920s when Young hired Quebecois to build the place. Unfortunately, this Gallic ambience appears not to have carried over to the local restaurants.

LANTANA

About 10 miles S of Palm Beach. Lantana's claim to fame is that it produces the world's largest selling weekly newspaper – the *National Enquirer* – available at supermarkets from the Aleutian Islands to Key West.

LOXAHATCHEE NATIONAL WILDLIFE REFUGE

On Rt 441, 15 miles SW of Palm Beach, in the direction of Coral Springs; open dawn to dusk; entry $3 per car. This is the vast sawgrass swampland between Lake Okeechobee and the coast. It's utterly flat and largely featureless, so there isn't much spectacular scenery. But this is where to come if you want to get away from the hustle and bustle of the coast. There are a couple of walking trails, and on these you're likely to see a range of birds, the ubiquitous alligators, and even some snakes. There's an observation tower with a view over miles of flat swamp, so be sure to bring your binoculars. More adventurous souls should try the 7-mile canoe trail; others will probably prefer their airboat tours.

LIGHTHOUSE POINT

Some 2 miles N of Pompano Beach. One of those spots which you pass through on your way up the coast. Anywhere else it would be a knockout, but here it just blends in with the rest of the spectacular scenery. Same old sea, same old pelicans, same new vacation homes.

But if you've got time to spare, try a visit to **Cap's Place**, a legendary bar which can only be reached by boat. During the Prohibition era, an old soldier turned smuggler named Cap Knight took over a couple of beached barges on the island, and turned them into a speakeasy. Cap only brought in

• *International Swimming Hall of Fame.*

the very best booze from the Bahamas, and was soon attracting the very best boozers. Look on the walls and you'll see photos of many of the great achievers of the era, steeling themselves in preparation for their great achievements: King Edward VIII (gearing up to abdicate), Winston Churchill (gearing up for the Second World War), Jack Dempsey (gearing up to defend his title) and President Roosevelt (gearing up to get rid of Prohibition). It's not easy to find unless you keep an eye out for the signs. These lead you off Rt A1A to Cap's Dock, where you pick up the boat (flash your lights if it's not in).

MIAMI
See pages 142-165.

PALM BEACH
On the coast, 80 miles N of Miami. Palm Beach likes to think of itself as one of the most stylish places on Earth. Despite this, the place has a mixed history. It all began in 1878, when a Spanish ship ran aground on the island, leaving its crew marooned with a hundred barrels of wine and a wreck full of coconuts. The Spanish were not fit to bargain when a canny local happened upon the scene, and offered them $20 for the lot. The locals drank the wine, but soon got fed up with the taste of coconut. So they simply dug a trench and buried the 20,000 they hadn't eaten. In the early 1890s the magnate Henry Flagler was prospecting the new route south for his railway, and noticed this paradisical offshore island lined with coconut palms.

Flagler decided to transform the aptly named Palm Beach into an exclusive resort for his fellow magnates. In 1894 he completed the Royal Poinciana Hotel, at the time the largest wooden structure in the world, and the largest hotel in America. In this case, quantity was not sacrificed for quality. Lovers of the biggest and the best were soon flocking to the Royal Poinciana. (In those days the railway brought them across to the island, and right to the front door.) The visitors' book soon began filling up with names such as Vanderbilt, Astor, Rockefeller, and William (princes only sign their first name).

Things went so well that Flagler quickly had to build another couple of hotels, and create an entire township across on the mainland at West Palm Beach to house the hotel staff. Most of the menial work in these hotels was done by African Americans, who transported the guests around the hotel grounds in pedal-powered "Afromobiles." In the evenings they would put on a "Darktown Strutter's Ball" or a "Golliwog Show," performing minstrel numbers and cakewalks while the guests chatted on the terrace over their cocktails. Old Palm Beach hands fondly refer to these times as the good old days.

In 1918 a 280-pound ex-boxer turned architect named Addison Mizner arrived in Palm Beach. At the time he was unemployed, but his arrival could not have been more opportune. The rich were beginning to tire of Flagler's opulent hotels. They may have been on vacation, and things may have cost a bit (Flagler made sure of this), but they wished to spend their money more energetically. And what better way to do this than to get some local architect with extravagant ideas to build you a huge mansion? Mizner quickly evolved a style to meet these requirements, and began building mansions for the rich. The idea caught on, and soon everyone was having mansions built in what soon became recognizable as the Palm Beach Style. This was described by one unkind critic as "not so much a style as a lack of one." This remark was both unoriginal and incorrect. In fact, Mizner's style was a cocktail of styles. Even he described it as "a little bit of Seville and Alhambra, a dash of Madeira and Algiers." The architectural world was stirred, but not shaken.

The 1920s saw the arrival of High Society in its purest form. Cornflake heiress Marjorie Merriweather-Post built herself a $7 million dollar winter palace called Mar-a-Largo (a name which no one even dared to suggest might describe its owner). This Moorish-Italian monsterpiece had more than a hundred rooms, and a 20-acre estate. From here Marjorie Merriweather-Post ran the Palm Beach "season" for almost half a century. The season's participants were kept busy with society balls and charity lunches. Vast sums were raised for charity as Palm Beach's finest gathered in mutual admiration of their stratospheric social status.

During the following giddy decades the outside world went through the occasional setback (in the form of a Depression, World War and so on) but the Palm Beach season struggled on. In time, the Woolworths and the Kennedys faded graciously, and foreign imports such as Arndt Krupp von Bohlen und Halbach and the Duc de Doudeaville arrived on the scene.

You'll find that little has changed. During the season (mid-December to

MIZNER: PALM BEACH'S ARCHITECT

Addison Mizner, the "Aladdin of Architecture," was the man who gave Palm Beach its architectural style.

When Mizner arrived in Palm Beach in 1918 he weighed over 280 pounds and was out of a job. Previously he had worked as a miner, then a prizefighter, before turning his talents to architecture. The limitless blue skies and limitless bank balances of Palm Beach quickly inspired Mizner to invent a "Medieval-Mediterranean-Moorish" style of architecture which he considered suitable to this Shangri-La.

Paris Singer, heir to the Singer sewing machine fortune, was so impressed by Mizner that he decided to back his ideas. Mizner was hired to build a rest home for wounded soldiers returned from the First World War. The result was a Spanish monastery with medieval towers – doubtless the only military establishment of its kind in the land.

After the war this building was turned into the **Everglades Club**, which became the exclusive social hub of Palm Beach. Soon everyone wanted to get into the Everglades Club (according to one wit, because they couldn't face the sight of the outside of it). But the wit was wrong. In no time every Vanderbilt and Rockefeller wanted a home in the new style. Mizner was soon building houses all over Palm Beach. His Medieval-Mediterranean-Moorish style soon began taking on Algerian, Ancient Greek and even Roman flourishes. As if this wasn't enough, Mizner also tried to give his creations a "historic lived-in" look. Stucco walls were splattered with condensed milk to add patina, shotguns were fired into oak beams to give them a worm-eaten appearance and tiles were laid quaintly askew for that genuine olde worlde look. Style makes sheep of us all, but the wooliest are the stylish. Soon everyone was following Mizner's style. As a result, Palm Beach is an architectural wilderness. The money and the opportunity to build a showcase of modern styles – during one of the most exciting architectural periods of the 20thC – was lost.

Having put his stamp on Palm Beach, Mizner set off in 1925 to do the same for Boca Raton, 20 miles down the coast. He launched a nationwide advertising campaign, describing Boca Raton as "the Greatest Resort in the World." The fact that Boca Raton didn't yet exist was dismissed as irrelevant. And despite this awkward fact, Mizner is said to have made more than $3 million dollars in contracts and land deals during the first week of his advertising campaign. Heartened by such widespread belief in his dream, Mizner set to work. Within no time he had constructed the $1.5-million shell of a hotel, laid out a number of estates, built some houses, dredged acres of huge ditches for a Grand Canal and Lagoon – and then the Florida land boom collapsed. Mizner went bust, and "the Greatest Resort in the World" came to a standstill. This time there was no need to age the buildings artificially. They were ruins before they'd even been completed. And their owners were ruined too.

Even so, Mizner's legacy remains to this day. The "Aladdin of Architecture" had given the world a style which truly looked as if it had been produced by a genie from a magic lantern. What would have made a great background in an epic Disney cartoon now became the foreground of Palm Beach and Boca Raton. See also Boca Raton, page 176.

mid-April) the only other people driving compact cars like yours will be the paparazzi. During the rest of the year, Palm Beach's mansions are deserted, apart from the architects, interior decorators, landscape designers.

Besides the exotic local flora and fauna, there are several sights worth seeing in Palm Beach:

Whitehall

Cocoanut Way and Whitehall Way; open 10 am-5 pm Tues-Sat, Sun afternoons only; entry $5. In 1901 Henry Flagler made the Florida legislature an offer it couldn't refuse, and the state divorce laws were altered so that the 71-year-old magnate could marry his third wife, Mary Lily Kenan. As her wedding present, Flagler's 34-year-old bride received this 73-room mansion (what the Florida authorities received is not recorded). Mrs Flagler III immediately set about entertaining her friends in the grand style, while the old man would disappear off up his secret staircase to ponder schemes for increasing his fortune, presumably so as to keep up with the bills. One of these schemes can still be seen laid out in his office – the extension of his railway from Miami down to Key West.

• *Society of the Four Arts.*

The entrance to Whitehall has half a dozen white pillars. Inside, the 100-foot long hallway is said to be modeled on St Peter's in Rome. The other rooms display a similarly tasteful megalomania. The vast music room contains an organ with more than 1,000 pipes, the ballroom echoes Louis XV's at Versailles, and other *salons* and antechambers display a random selection of Grand European styles.

At the back of Whitehall is Flagler's personal railway carriage, The Rambler, which he used when he wished to get further away from his wife's social gatherings. It's worth taking the tour of the house, which is conducted by a guide who knows more about Whitehall than its original inhabitants probably did.

Whitehall was originally next door to the Royal Poinciana Hotel, Flagler's first hotel at Palm Beach. The hotel had more than 2,000 rooms and was topped by the customary bell tower. Nothing now remains but a commemorative plaque.

Society of the Four Arts

Four Arts Plaza; open 10 am-5 pm Mon-Sat, Sun afternoons only, Dec-mid-Apr; entry $3, *donation suggested.* This is Palm Beach's culture club. They often have interesting art shows, lectures and films. There is also a sculpture park and gardens. Phone the Palm Beach Convention and Visitors Bureau, tel. 407 471 3995, to find out what's going on here, and at other venues.

Worth Avenue

The world's most expensive shopping street. Indeed, this spot is so exclusive that a number of its establishments only open by appointment. The street is surprisingly small; it runs for just a few hundred yards. It's lined with stratospherically expensive shops, a few art galleries containing art so rarified it's almost invisible, and a number of restaurants where it's cheaper to buy the silver than the hors d'oeuvre you eat with it. At this level, shopping becomes voyeurism for mere mortals. However, there is a small two-storey arcade of shops called **The Esplanade**, where prices dip to bankrupting level in shops such as Saks of Fifth Avenue.

Curiously, there *are* bargains (of a

kind) to be had in Palm Beach. No Worth Avenue shopper would be caught dead wearing the same outfit twice – but not all of these discarded items are banished to the back of the wardrobe. Just a few end up at **Thrift Store Inc**, 231 South County Road. Here you may encounter bargain prices of a sort you have never experienced before – but there's no denying they're real bargains compared to Worth Avenue.

The Kennedy Compound

This is at 1095 North Ocean Boulevard, north of the Palm Beach County Club, but you can't see much of where the notorious shenanigans took place.

• *Whitehall, Palm Beach.*

Cycling

North-east of the Kennedy Compound at Lake Way is the **Palm Beach Cycle Trail**, which takes you along Lake Worth and palm-shaded roads past a string of exclusive mansions. You can rent bikes at the Palm Beach Bicycle Trail Shop, 23 Sunrise Avenue, at around $4 per hour.

Beach

The only real **public beach** in Palm Beach is off South Ocean Boulevard by Royal Palm Way.

For further nearby sights and places of interest, see West Palm Beach in Florida Overall: 2, page 58.

POMPANO BEACH

Some 6 miles N of Fort Lauderdale.

Another resort, this time with a an even more obtrusive rash of high-rise condos and hotels than others on this stretch of coast. There's Fisherman's Wharf, with some genuine fishermen, and there's a coral reef you can wade out to and snorkel along. The local Hillsboro Lighthouse claims to be "the brightest in south-east Florida."

WEST PALM BEACH

See Florida Overall: 2, page 58.

RECOMMENDED HOTELS

BOCA RATON

Boca Raton Resort and Club, $$$; *501 East Camino Real Drive, Camino Real 33431; tel. 407 395 3000; all major cards.*

Addison Mizner's original Cloister Inn (which first put Boca Raton on the map) has now been incorporated as part of this 350-acre resort, which extends from the inland shores of the Intracoastal Waterway to the Atlantic shore. There are two other residential complexes, as well as a 27-storey tower added to the original Cloister Inn complex. This is *the* place to stay in Boca Raton, and it has all the facilities you'd expect of a first-class resort – including golf course, five pools, lit tennis courts, and staff who have been trained to maintain their cool even in the face of celebrity behavior.

In all, the resort has nearly 1,000 rooms – but it's still wise to book ahead in season.

There's not much inexpensive accommodation in Boca Raton, and as usual the closer you are to the beach the higher the price. The best motel near the beach is:

Shore Edge Motel, $$; *425 North Ocean Boulevard, Boca Raton 33432; tel. 407 395 4491; cards* AE, MC, V.

Despite its name, this is in fact across the road (Rt A1A) from the beach. The sort of standard Florida motel which seems so ordinary in the middle of your vacation – but is the stuff of dreams once you get back home. Everything you'd expect: right down to the friendly welcome, the pastel walls and the pool.

DELRAY BEACH

Riviera Palms, $$; *3960 North Ocean Boulevard, Delray Beach 33483; tel. 407 276 3032; no cards.*

Standard motel, but has a good pool. Just across from the beach. It only has 20 rooms, so be sure to make a reservation.

FORT LAUDERDALE

Bahia Cabana Beach Resort, $$; *3001 Harbor Drive, Fort Lauderdale 33316; tel. 305 524 1555; all major cards.*

More than 50 tropical-style rooms, some of which reduce in price considerably off-season. The resort also has a very lively bar overlooking the marina – where you're likely to find professional ocean-going crews "resting up" between trips.

Venetian Court, $-$$; *71 Isle of Venice, Fort Lauderdale 33301; tel. 305 524 8444; cards* DC, MC, V.

Pleasant, friendly spot overlooking the canal, complete with pool. Be sure to book ahead in season (Dec-Apr).

PALM BEACH

The Breakers, $$$; *1 South County Road, Palm Beach 33480; tel. 407 655 6651; all major cards.*

A Palm Beach institution, dating from the early years of the century. This is the last of the three great hotels which Flagler built (the other two burned down). Guests once included presidents, Rockefellers and Vanderbilts – and they even let in Randolph Hearst (the newspaper magnate who featured in Orson Welles' *Citizen Kane*). Built to resemble a Renaissance palace, with 200 acres of grounds, it retains that rare ingredient – class. It has even survived the usual $50 million renovations, which seem to take place with the regularity of presidential elections.

The ballroom is a venue for charity balls when the season is in full swing. Traditional facilities include two golf courses (on land where a fair-sized divot costs almost as much as your entire home) and a private beach.

If you're looking for an inexpensive place to stay in Palm Beach, forget it. Head back across the water to West Palm Beach (see page 59). If you must stay on the island, the nearest you'll come to a reasonably priced hotel is:

Palm Beach Historic Inn, $$-$$$; *365 South County Road, Palm Beach 33480; tel. 407 832 4009; no cards*

A real find, but it's been found by a few others as well – so you'll have to book well in advance. Friendly bed-and-breakfast accommodations.

RECOMMENDED RESTAURANTS

BOCA RATON
If you're doing things in style, *the* place to dine at in Boca Raton is:

La Vielle Maison, $$$; 770 *East Palmetto Park Road, Boca Raton; tel.* 407 391 6701; *all major cards.*
This house dates from the 1920s. (It was originally built by Mizner, but has been "improved" so many times that the style is now eclectic. The dining area is filled with romantic nooks, and the kitchen is filled with temperamental cooks. Guaranteed no disappointments. The cuisine is French, with a few international flourishes – and the wine cellar wins awards.

Those who wish for a hearty meal rather than an expensive aesthetic experience, should try:

Tom's Place, $-$$; 7251 *North Route* 1, *Boca Raton; tel.* 407 997 0920; *no cards*
Mainly steaks and ribs, but also a few seafood dishes, all served with friendly informality. This is the place where Joe Frazier and the American football stars come to stoke up. And the barbecue sauce is so good you can buy it by the bottle.

FORT LAUDERDALE
Shooter's, $-$$; 3033 *North East* 32*nd Avenue, Fort Lauderdale; tel.* 305 566 2855; *all major cards.*
One of the best bar-restaurants in the entire region. They're famous for their large helpings of seafood, but they also do good pasta and steaks. In the beach area right on the Intracoastal Waterway.

Pier Restaurant, $; 2 *East Commercial Boulevard, Lauderdale-by-the-Sea; tel.* 305 776 1690; *no cards; closes around* 4 *pm.*
Quite frankly, the food and the decor aren't much. It's the location that's great – on the pier. Try lunching on one of their pancakes, with a "genuine" milkshake, after a hard morning on the beach.

Rumour has it they're soon going to turn the famous **Elbo Room** bar on The Strip into a hamburger joint. Stop in for a beer before it's too late, and relive your crazy youth. It's here they shot *Where the Boys Are* – the film which transformed 1960s Fort Lauderdale into spring break Mayhemsville for generations of college kids. And they still turn up at the Elbo Room.

PALM BEACH
The present "in" spot in Palm Beach is:

Bice, $$$; 313½ *Worth Avenue, Palm Beach; tel.* 407 835 1600; *all major cards.*
First of all, the name is pronounced in the Italian style – *Bee*-chay. Sit outside at the green marble tables for Italian cuisine as stunning as its price. The pasta is perfect, and the seafood highly sophisticated.
The sidewalk cafe where the celebs are seen is:

Chuck & Harold's, $-$$$; 207 *Royal Poinciana Way, Palm Beach; tel.* 407 659 1440; *all major cards.*
You'll see the occasional tanned face you recognize, but can't quite name, lurking among the potted begonias on the terrace. Celebrity birthdays are marked on the blackboard, along with the specialities of the day.

Local Explorations: 3

<u>*Central* Florida</u>

Ocala and Region

40 *miles; map* Hallwag *Florida*

The area around Ocala is filled with lakes, springs and woodlands. East of the city is Silver Springs, which claims to be the largest group of artesian springs in the world, and Florida's first tourist sight. Further east you come to the Ocala National Forest, whose lakes, woodlands and canoe trails range over 366,000 acres.

South-east of the forest you can visit the upper reaches of the St Johns River where, during the 19thC tourist boom, paddle steamers shuttled between the resorts. You can take a trip in a paddle steamer from Sanford, just 10 miles north-east of Orlando. To see what Florida looked like in those days, head west from here to the small town of Mount Dora, whose old houses remain just as they were more than a century ago.

Ocala has a number of disparate attractions. Specialists in American culture won't want to miss the Don Garlits Museum of Drag Racing, a gem of its kind. Gems of another kind, a well as works of art, can be found at the Appleton Museum of Art, where, unlike at Ocala's other museum, visitors can view the exhibits without the accompaniment of a Wurlitzer jukebox.

Ocala is one of the main racehorse training and breeding centers in the United States, and you can visit several of the neighboring establishments.

You can easily drive around in a day, but it's worth allowing a couple of days so you can explore whatever catches your interest.

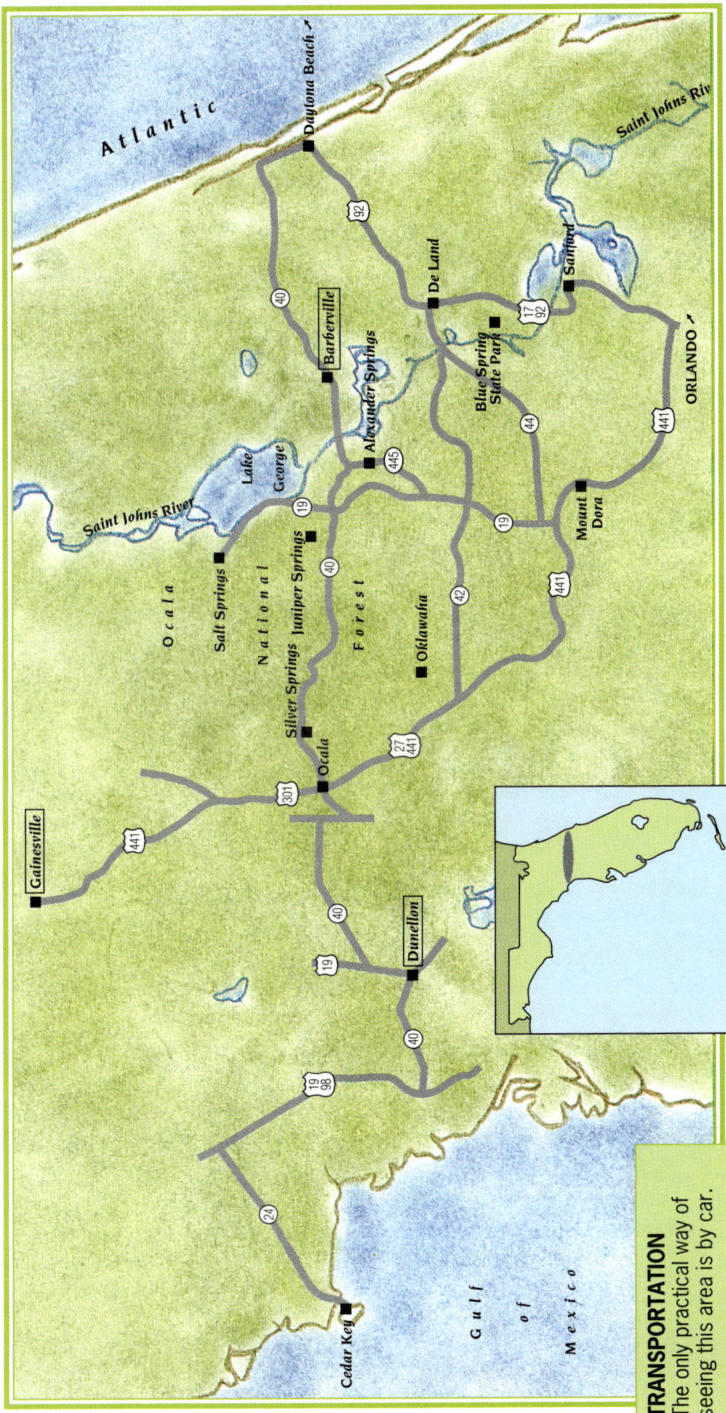

TRANSPORTATION
The only practical way of seeing this area is by car.

SIGHTS & PLACES OF INTEREST

BLUE SPRING STATE PARK

About 10 miles SW of De Land off Rt 44; the park is open 8 am-dusk; entry $3.50 per car. In winter the warm waters of Blue Spring attract hundreds of manatees from the cooler waters of the adjoining St Johns River. This is an endangered species, and when you see so many of them flopping about in the water, you can see why. They must have proved irresistible to Indians and hunters who wanted real turtle soup for dinner.

Nearby you can see **Thursby House**, a pioneer dwelling which dates from 1872, where they doubtless enjoyed manatee soup regularly for dinner on cold winter nights. It's also worth taking the free ferry trip to **Hontoon Island**. A hundred years ago this spot was a thriving port. It had a busy dock and paddle steamers from the St Johns River visited regularly to pick up passengers and the orange crop.

INDIAN RIVER GRAPEFRUIT

These citrus trees, originating in China, were first imported to Florida more than three centuries ago by the Spanish. But it wasn't until the end of the 19thC that citrus fruit became a commercial crop. This was largely due to a Chinese immigrant named Lue Gim Gong, who settled in De Land. He developed a strain of citrus that could withstand the occasional winter cold spells in Florida. This was a huge success and caused the rise of the Florida citrus business. Lue Gim Gong was honored by having a grapefruit named after him. There are still groves of Lue Gim Gong's grapefruit in commercial production. They are labeled Indian River, and are sold in super-markets all over Europe and America.

Among his botanical experiments, Lue Gim Gong also developed a currant the size of a cherry. This, too, was a great success, until people decided that they preferred currant-sized currants.

You can stay overnight in cabins both at Blue Spring and on the island: see Recommended Hotels, page 197.

CASSADAGA

About 15 miles N of Sanford, just E of Rt 4. These are the terrestrial directions we mere mortals must follow if we wish to reach Cassadaga. Others arrive by more ethereal routes. This is a community of spiritualists who are in constant communication with those who have departed this vale of tears before us.

And don't imagine that this is just a passing oddity. Far from it. The serious and sober citizens of Cassadaga moved here well over a hundred years ago, and have been plugged in to the Beyond ever since. And they're willing to let you in on an extension. A half-hour session with your departed Uncle Harry, quizzing him on where he buried the family silver, will set you back about $40. For details, stop in at the Andrew Jackson Davies Building on Stevens Street. This also has a bookshop, and they hold occasional talks on UFOs, ghosts and visitors from other worlds. Visitors from so-called reality, like you, should approach Cassadaga in the right spirit, or not at all.

CEDAR KEY

As the crow flies, 60 miles W of Ocala. Take Rt 40 W out of Ocala, then Rt 19 N, then Rt 24 SW. Cedar Key is at the end of the line, on Florida's west coast. This stretch of coast is known as The Big Bend. One look on the map and you'll see why. Unlike the rest of Florida's coastline, it remains utterly undeveloped. The reason? Because there's not a beach in sight, and the shore is a tangle of mangrove islands. In other words, it's mostly not much better than a swamp. This remoteness has protected it from the tourist trade.

Cedar Key is virtually the only spot worth visiting on this coast. It even began as the end of the line: 150 years ago the trans-Florida rail route ended here. (It started at Amelia Island: see Florida Overall: 7.)

Nowadays, Cedar Key remains little more than a sleepy fishing village. Efforts have been made to bring in the tourists, but they seem to be having little permanent effect. However, if you are here in October, they do have a lively small seafood festival featuring their great local oysters.

DAYTONA BEACH

See Florida Overall: 6, page 108.

DE LAND

On Rt 92, 23 miles inland from Daytona Beach, or 67 miles E of Ocala by Rt 40. The original De Land was a dealer in baking powder. After making a fortune raising cakes, he decided to raise a city. De Land was duly founded in 1876, and billed as "the Athens of Florida." Alas, the city produced no Acropolis and no Plato, and is now only "the De Land of Florida" – a rather ordinary, but pleasant, spot. Almost as old as De Land itself is its celebrated **Stetson University**, founded by the man who made his fortune selling the cowboys their hats. There are a few century-old buildings on campus, and also the justly renowned **Gillespie Museum of Minerals**, which is at the corner of Michigan Avenue and Amelia, *open Mon-Sat 9 am-4 pm; entry free; closed winter.* This is one of the largest collections of minerals and gemstones in America, and has examples from all five continents.

MOUNT DORA

On Lake Dora 20 miles NW of Orlando, off Rt 441. If you want to see what this region looked like at the turn of the 20thC when it was Florida's great tourist center, head out to Mount Dora. This is Old Florida, complete with old-fashioned balconies and fancy woodwork. Nowadays, many of the downtown shops have been taken over by antique dealers, and they're popular on the weekends with bargain hunters from Orlando. Stop at the Chamber of Commerce at 341 Alexander Street if you want a map showing the most historic houses in the village.

OCALA

On Rt 40, 67 miles inland from Daytona Beach. Ocala is famous throughout the U.S. as a racehorse breeding and training center, almost on a par with Kentucky. There are nearly 500 such establishments in Marion County, and you'll see them all over the countryside as you approach Ocala. They look much like racehorse breeding and training places the world over – neat white fences, green grass, aristocratic stallions resting between sessions.

To see what it's like out in horse country, try the drive to **Just a Farm** at Dunellon (20 miles southwest of Ocala, take Rt 40, then Rt 41), which is open to the public. Somewhat closer is **Fairview Farm**, at Candler, which is 4 miles southeast of Ocala on Rt 464. But be sure to call ahead to the Ocala Breeders' Sales Company and Training Center, tel. 904 237 2154, *before* you set out, to make sure they're open for

• *Don Garlits Museum of Drag Racing, Ocala.*

visitors on the day of your visit.

Ocala itself has two cultural highspots worth seeing. Both are museums. One features art, the other drag racing.

The Appleton Museum of Art is east of downtown at *4333 East Silver Springs Boulevard; open 10 am-4.30 pm and Sun afternoons, closed Mon; entry $3.* This houses the collection of the industrialist Arthur I. Appleton, who made his fortune in Chicago and moved down here to breed horses. The collection displays Appleton's unmistakable taste. There are more than 4,000 displays, and they range from pre-history to the present century. Don't miss the Etruscan collection or the superb South American water-containers. There's also the inevitable Rodin *Thinker*, without which no aspiring collection of the period was complete.

Having had your art, and a good lunch in town, you're now ready for the **Don Garlits Museum of Drag Racing**. This is *8 miles W of town at 13700 South West 16th Avenue; open 10 am-5 pm daily; entry $8.* Culturally deprived souls who have never been to a drag race will learn plenty here.

Here's your chance to see a Swamp Rat – the stretch limo of the racing scene. In the hands of local hero Don Garlits, it was capable of reaching 270 mph. Forty years ago he was renowned throughout America for his deeds on the track. At the museum you can relive those times – with mementoes, video shots, press clippings. And, of course, the cars. Besides the Swamp Rats you can also see several classic U.S. motors of the 1950s, including Buicks and Chevvys. These are all displayed in a suitably reverential atmosphere with golden oldie hits thumping out on a Wurlitzer jukebox (which only by accident wasn't a car).

• *Silver Springs.*

OCALA NATIONAL FOREST

Just W of Barberville on Rt 40, or just E of Ocala on Rt 40. The Ocala National Forest covers over a third of a million acres of Central Florida. Here you'll find a lake as large as a city (Lake George), islands, miles of unspoiled waterways, isolated hiking trails and some lively country resorts.

Ocala National Forest is not known as The Big Scrub for nothing. Within its limits you'll find the largest sand pinewood in the world, patches of semi-desert with sand dunes, thousands of deer, and the occasional bear.

There are three main regions of the Ocala National Forest:

Juniper Springs

Off Rt 40, 25 miles E of Silver Springs, N of the main road. A canoeing center, in the heart of the forest. Try one of their many canoe trails, or rent an inner

tube. There are also hiking trails through the woods, or you can try a dip in the clear mineral water pool. Phone ahead, on 904 625 3147, for further details.

Alexander Springs

A dozen or so miles SE of Juniper Springs off Rt 445, which runs S from Rt 40 at Astor Park. This spot is of special interest to swimmers and sub-aqua enthusiasts. The waters are glassy clear and perfect for even the most inexperienced snorkelers. There are also canoe trails. For up-to-the minute information, phone 904 669 3522.

Salt Springs

In the N sector of the Forest, 15 miles N of Rt 40. Though this is the most recent of the forest's resorts, it's also the most developed. This is fishing territory, where huge catfish are hauled in regularly. But there's also good swimming, and a few canoe trails. One of these takes you across Lake George and up the St Johns River. For details, phone 904 685 2048.

A word of warning: during the summer season these resorts can become overrun with vacationers and campers. You need ingenuity, and energy, to get away from it all. At other times, it's all yours.

There's a famous 60-mile-plus **hiking trail** through the forest. Alternatively you can drive through the forest along relatively remote roads, such as Rts 464 and 445. Details of all activities, maps, and friendly advice can be obtained at the Visitor Information Center at the start of the forest on Rt 40, tel. 904 625 7470.

OKLAWAHA

Off Rt 301, 15 miles SE of Ocala, on the N shore of Lake Weir. A quiet little town which had its 15 minutes of fame on January 16, 1935. On that day the FBI finally managed to track down and corner the notorious Ma Baker and her son Fred. For years Ma Baker's gang had ruled the roost in this part of Florida. If you didn't pay up, you got a visit from Ma herself. Others counted themselves lucky to be merely kidnapped, trussed up and delivered in a barrel.

Fifteen FBI agents tracked Ma Baker down to a cottage by the lake. In the ensuing shoot-out, they fired over 1,500 rounds – before they dared to go in and see what was left of Ma and her son. The cottage still stands, but the present owners decided to fill in the holes.

ORLANDO

See Florida Overall: 1, page 33.

SANFORD

On Lake Monroe, 50 miles SE of Ocala, or 10 miles NE of Orlando. You've heard all about the old riverboat days on the St Johns River. This is your chance to try for yourself. Head down to **Captain Roy's Riverboat Fleet**, which you'll find at the Sanford Boat Works on Rt 415. During the tour your guide fills you in on local history, and even manages to catch a glimpse of all that rare wildlife which you can never quite make out lurking in the undergrowth on the bank.

Sanford was founded just a century ago by a retired diplomat. After the tourist boom collapsed in this part of the country, it became known as Celery City. There are a few dozen buildings dating from the boom era, and you can pick up a map guiding you to these at the Chamber of Commerce, *400 East 1st Street, open 9 am-5 pm weekdays.*

The **Shelton Sanford Museum** has a range of exhibits and mementoes showing what it was like in the good old days. Others might be more interested in the **Seminole County Historical Museum** at *300 Bush Boulevard, open 9 am-1 pm weekdays, afternoons only weekends; entry free.* This displays all kinds of historical oddities which have been picked up over the years throughout the county.

SILVER SPRINGS

E outskirts of Ocala, off Rt 40; entry $21.95. This is said to be the oldest tourist attraction in the state of Florida. The entry fee is an outrageous $21.95. This said, if you've got money to burn it's not a bad place to spend the day.

It is claimed that this is the largest group of artesian springs in the world, and it may well be. However, young children may be more impressed by the animals, which include a giraffe and a robotic dinosaur. Included in the ticket price is a glass-bottom boat ride, a cruise into the wildlife forest, a jungle safari and entry to their museum of vintage cars (which features the Mercedes once owned by the real Maria von Trapp of *Sound of Music* fame).

If you spend an entire day here doing everything and seeing everything, it becomes much more like value for money.

The other attraction in Silver Springs is **Wild Waters,** *open 10 am-5 pm daily; entry* $10; *closed winter.* This is a water theme park, complete with giant water rides, giant waves and a giant pool.

RECOMMENDED HOTELS

BLUE SPRING STATE PARK

Cabins, $-$$; *Blue Spring State Park, 2100 French Avenue, Orange City; tel.* 904 775 3663; *no cards.*

You rent a fairly basic cabin, and it sleeps up to four. The big bonus is when you go for a walk in the early morning. There are also similar cabins on nearby Hontoon Island (same price range and phone number). Be sure to book ahead, especially for weekends.

DE LAND

The special spot in town is:

Holiday Inn De Land, $$-$$$; 350 *International Speedway Drive, De Land* 32724; *tel.* 904; *all major cards.*

This is the place where the celebrities stay, when they're in De Land. Celebrities? In De Land? How about Tom Cruise?

A real find, this one – and the less prestigious rooms aren't as expensive as you'd expect. A sophisticated hideaway: guests are allowed into the local De Land Country Club.

OCALA

Ocala Hilton, $$-$$$; 3600 *South West 36th Avenue, Ocala* 32674; *tel.* 904 854 1400; *all major cards.*

Towered pink hotel set in picturesque landscape. Bonuses here include a fine outdoor pool, large rooms and live entertainment.

The inexpensive motels are east of downtown on Silver Springs Boulevard (Rt 40). Try:

Horne's Motor Lodge, $-$$; 3805 *Silver Springs Boulevard, Ocala* 32671; *tel.* 904 629 0155; *no cards*

A friendly welcome, and the prices come down sharply out of season.

RECOMMENDED RESTAURANTS

DE LAND

For a treat, try:

Pondo's, $$; 1915 *Old New York Avenue, De Land; tel.* 904 734 1995; *cards* AE, MC, V.

Once the romantic nook where the wartime pilots training at the nearby base took their dates. The ambience remains, and the cuisine is now as imaginative as the conversations used to be. Superb seafood, as well as meat dishes.

OCALA

The widest range of inexpensive restaurants is out by the motels along Silver Springs Boulevard. However, you may find that in Central Florida, off the tourist trail, your budget stretches further than elsewhere.

Richard's Place, $$; 316 *East Silver Springs Boulevard, Ocala; tel.* 904 351 2233; *no cards.*

Here the menu displays a little imagination, and their steaks are perfectly cooked.

Local Explorations: 4

Southern Florida

From Naples South

140 miles; map Hallwag *Florida*

The extreme southwestern corner of Florida has two major attractions, but they could hardly be more different.

Naples is the most sophisticated resort in western Florida – often called the Palm Beach of the Gulf Coast. Here you can visit the boutiques and art galleries of Olde Naples where the prices look as if they're being quoted in Italian lire. But the superb palm-lined beach and the historic pier are both free, and the seafood restaurants on picturesque Naples City Dock won't give you financial indigestion.

In the northwestern section of the Everglades, head for Everglades City, where you can take an airboat ride along the waterways far into the national park, or out through the mangrove maze of Ten Thousand Islands.

You can drive across this region in a morning. It's only just over 100 miles from Naples to Miami along the Tamiami Trail (Rt 41). But it's worth allowing a day or two to explore the Everglades, and to reward yourself with a spell back in civilized Naples.

TRANSPORTATION
Greyhound buses connect Miami and Naples, but the only realistic way to see the rest of this region is by car.

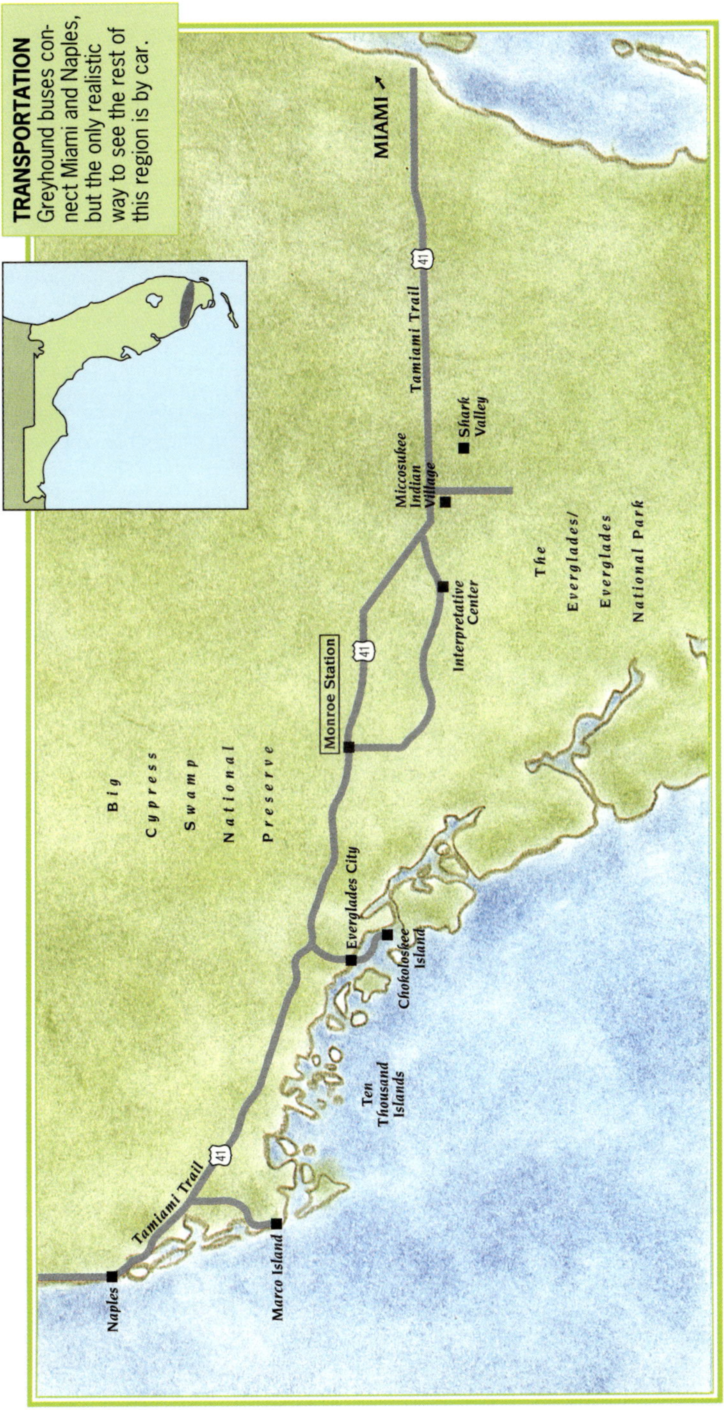

SIGHTS & PLACES OF INTEREST

CHOKOLOSKEE ISLAND

See Everglades City, page 201.

THE EVERGLADES

This huge national park occupies the extreme SW corner of the Florida peninsula. The Tamiami Trail (Rt 41) runs along the N boundary of the park, giving access to Shark Valley and the Miccosukee Indian Village (see entries). The turn-off S from Rt 41, along Rt 29, takes you to Everglades City (see page 201). There is no road from Everglades City into the park, but from here you can take boat trips into the park along the unspoiled Everglades shoreline.

Important: For the history of the Everglades, and for information on access via the main eastern entrance to the southern region of the park, see Florida Overall: 3, page 66.

Big Cypress Swamp National Preserve

Huge area N of Rt 41, to the NW of Everglades City. To drive into it, head for Monroe Station, which is on Rt 41 17 miles E of Everglades City. Here you can drive S on a loop road through the preserve, which brings you back on to Rt 41 30 miles or so later (close to the Miccosukee Indian Village and just over 35 miles from Miami).

Eighteen miles along the loop road, you come to an **Interpretive Center**, where you can learn all about the different ecosystems which you're passing through.

Unfortunately, the balance of this entire region was upset by the building of the **Tamiami Trail** (Rt 41) in the 1920s, which led to the commercial felling of vast swathes of bald cypress trees in the previously inaccessible hinterland.

The occasional homesteads along this road are inhabited by a rustic breed who like to think they are still living in the pioneer era, and don't like the illusion shattered by approaching tourists.

TAMIAMI TRAIL

This runs through remote but tough territory. Until recently, isolated general stores were expected to supply all local needs, and frequently did so free of charge (when they were held up at gunpoint). Years ago I remember seeing a sign outside one store: "Armed Security Guard on duty 3 nites a week – take your pick." Another advertised: "Marriages performed here: bring $10 and a woman."

Miccosukee Indian Village ✕

Off Rt 41, 25 miles E of Monroe Station; open 9 am-5 pm daily; entry $5. This tourist replica is virtually all that is left of the home of the proud and independent people who once inhabited the Everglades. It may look like a tawdry tourist trap – but this only underlines what has actually happened. The Miccosukee are a cousin tribe to the once mighty Seminoles. Nowadays they make their living off tourists – producing traditional craft objects, organizing airboat rides through the sawgrass and putting on alligator wrestling shows.

Their harsh yet noble way of life lasted for thousands of years in Florida, and has been destroyed in less than a century: the human price that has been paid for Florida to become today's vacation paradise.

It's difficult to know what else to say, except: be sure to buy a few souvenirs at the shop. Some of these are good and some...aren't.

Shark Valley

On Rt 41, just over 1 mile E of Miccosukee Indian Village. When I was last here it looked like the Sahara Desert, but I was told this was a purely temporary state of affairs. Normally, this is mile upon mile of grassy swamp territory.

You can take a **14-mile tram ride** right into the heart of the Everglades, and stop at an **observation tower** with views out over the unending flat countryside. Bring your binoculars if you want to see the animals properly. When you go walking along one of the trails, don't be afraid of the alligators. But don't approach them. With regard to tourists, these sleepy creatures believe in a live-and-let-live policy. If awakened unnecessarily they tend, like humans, to be irritable. But unlike grumpy humans who have just been chased out of bed, they can move *incredibly* fast.

EVERGLADES CITY 🛏 ✕

At the end of Rt 29, 35 miles SE of Naples

off the Tamiami Trail (Rt 41). Back in the early 1920s, advertising tycoon Barron Collier owned more than a million acres of land in south-western Florida. Most of this was uninhabitable swamp, and those bits along the coast that were habitable could only be reached by sea. But Collier had big ideas. He decided to build the Tamiami Trail, linking Miami on the east coast to Naples on the west coast. Collier dredged a navigable waterway through the mangroves of Ten Thousand Islands, and created Everglades City as his construction base. When the trans-state Tamiami Trail was finally completed, it opened up the southwest coast. In gratitude, the state even named the local county after him.

Collier wanted Everglades City to be more than just a construction base, and laid out an ambitious grid of streets. But Everglades City never really took off as a big resort. People pressed on along the Tamiami Trail, more interested in getting to the spectacular beaches of the west coast. Everglades City remained a pleasant backwater, popular only with big game fishermen. Nowadays it also provides a useful base for visitors to the north-western region of the Everglades (see separate entry).

Everglades City is a great place for taking **airboat rides** out along the waterways of the Everglades, and also into **Ten Thousand Islands**. The latter is a virtually unchartable region of countless mangrove-lined islands, and is as enchanting as it sounds. It's home to a huge variety of wildlife. The larger airboats charge about $15 a trip; but if you can afford it, take a private ride to experience the labyrinthine solitude of this huge natural wilderness. Cost: about $60 an hour.

If you want to see what this region was like in the old days, head south out of Everglades City for 4 miles, across the causeway to **Chokoloskee Island**. Here on the waterfront you can visit **Ted Smallwood's Store**, which has been turned into a museum, *open 10 am -5 pm daily, reduced hours during summer; entry* $2.50. This clapboard trading outpost was put up by pioneer Ted Smallwood in 1906, when this spot bore some resemblance to the Wild West, and a tourist would have been greeted with astonishment. The waterfront is also famous for being the place where a character was gunned down in a novel: locals not only remember the character's name, but the name of the man who wrote the novel – Ed Watson and Peter Mathiessen, respectively. Yet curiously, the names of the actual men who really were gunned down here have long been forgotten.

THE MANGROVE
Mangrove trees flourish by the millions along this stretch of the Florida coast, turning much of it into impenetrable jungle. The mangrove is one of the few trees that can survive (and thrive) in the sea. However, it doesn't live on salt water: the roots of the tree manage to purify the salt water into fresh water. Many scientific attempts have been made to emulate this natural process, but none has suceeded in doing it as efficiently as the mangrove.

MIAMI

See pages 142-165.

MARCO ISLAND

At the end of Rt 951, *which leads off* Rt 41 20 *miles* S *of* Naples. As early as 2,500 years ago this island was inhabited by Calusa Indians. A few years ago, the island was threatened by a rather more primitive tribe, in the form of developers. Fortunately, the planning authorities acted quickly, with the result that the designers of the condos and resort complexes were forced to pay attention to the environment. Judge for yourself how successful they've been. Note in particular the artificial bald-eagle nests put up by the developers in an attempt to induce this rare species to nest in the vicinity of human dwellings.

Hints of what Marco Island used to be can be seen in the two remaining villages at either end of the island: **Marco** (north) and **Goodland** (south). Both have a few old houses dating from the period when human beings were the endangered species on this island.

But there remains one thing the developers haven't managed to touch. This is **Tigertail Beach**, on the west coast of the island, with miles of superb sand. There's also a sandbar, which forms a stretch of lagoon. This is a great windsurfing spot – especially for absolute beginners. The water is shallow, and there's usually just a gentle wind.

NAPLES 🛏 ✕

On Rt 41, 32 miles S of Fort Myers.

Naples is the Palm Beach of the Gulf Coast – a sophisticated resort which comes into its own when the beautiful people move south during the winter season, from November to April.

Just over a century ago, less than a dozen people lived here. Then a syndicate of rich businessmen from Kentucky moved in, bought the best part of 10,000 acres of land, laid out an exclusive vacation resort, and began selling off building plots. They even built a 600-foot-long pier, where the steamers could berth. In those days the only way to this part of the coast was by sea. Potential buyers soon began making the steamer journey to Naples. They liked what they saw, bought up plots and started building. The mansions along the beach front became Millionaires' Row, and winter visitors to Naples soon ranged from presidents to opera singers.

A second wave of development began after the Second World War, and this too was conducted in the best possible taste, with an eye to the society market. The result is as you would expect, especially Olde Naples – mainly expensive boutiques, gourmet restaurants and art galleries. Pastel Cadillacs and open limousines with groomed poodles to match the white leather upholstery drift up and down the street in the relentless pursuit of conspicuous consumption.

Head for the sea, and you'll find the democracy of the beach, with its pristine white sand between the tall palm trees and the pale lapping waves of the Gulf. Pelicans perched on the jetties provide a free show as they dive for fish.

Yes, Naples is certainly "beautiful," in the well-manicured sense of the word - but it needn't be expensive. Head for the **City Dock** in the evening, and you'll find several worthwhile but inexpensive seafood restaurants overlooking the water. Have a drink at the bar, and you'll find yourself among a friendly,

• *Big Cypress Swamp National Preserve.*

COOPERTOWN'S
Air Boats
60th ANNIVERSARY

laid-back crowd. The conversation can range from the eye-opening to the ear-bending.

Naples covers a surprisingly large area, and many things aren't where you'd expect them to be. For instance, the dock is on the opposite side of town from the beach. To get your bearings, stop for a map at the Naples Area Chamber of Commerce, 3620 Tamiami Trail, on Rt 41 into town. Here you'll learn that Naples too insists on being a capital of the world: "The World's Golf Capital."

A few other things to see in town:

Art lovers should try a round of the **commercial galleries** in Olde Naples. Amid some tough opposition, my favorites are the **Harmond-Meek Gallery** at *386 Broad Avenue South* (modern U.S. artists); the international shows at the **Helios Gallery** (*363 12th Avenue South*); and the **Naples Art Gallery** in the *Windsor Plaza*, which features contemporary shows.

Both children and collectors will appreciate the **Teddy Bear Museum** at *2511 Pine Ridge Road*, which has more than 2,000 well-stuffed bed companions on display; *open 10 am-5 pm Wed-Sat, Sun afternoon only; entry $5.*

For more grown-up children, there's the **Collier Automotive Museum** at *2500 South Horseshoe Drive, open 10 am-5 pm daily, reduced hours May -Nov; entry $6.* Advertised as the best sports car collection in America, it has all the classics of the species as well as one or two superb mavericks. You can see the first Ferrari ever made (though I'm told another contender exists in a private collection in Milan), and some dream MGs. Star vehicles include the Dusenberg SSJ owned by Gary Cooper, and racing Bentleys from the Brooklands era when all racing drivers were gentleman cowboys at heart. The guides also fall into this category, and are among the most knowledgable you'll come across in any museum devoted to works of post-Victorian art. Challenge them on technical details at your peril.

Those who enjoy hands-on experiences should visit **Jungle Larry's Zoo Park** at *1590 Goodlette-Frank Road.* Here

• *Olde Naples.*

you can stroke an alligator (and get your hand back), and even tickle a snake behind the ears. There are shows with tame lions, tame tigers and what look like almost-tame trainers. A tram ride takes you and your untamed children on a guided tour of the hundreds of animals. The children love it, and even the animals don't seem to mind too much.

No trip to Naples would be complete without seeing the famous **pier**. The original, built in 1886, was destroyed by a hurricane. Its several replacements have suffered from hurricane, fire and a colliding ship; each time, the citizens of Naples have insisted on building their landmark anew. Now the pier is classed as a state historic site. It's popular with fishermen, pelicans and sunset watchers. You'll find the pier at the end of 12 Avenue South, on the Gulf shore; *open* 9.30 *am*-11.30 *pm*; *entry* $11.

TEN THOUSAND ISLANDS

RECOMMENDED HOTELS

EVERGLADES CITY

Rod and Gun Lodge, $$; *Riverside Drive at Broadway*, Everglades City 33929; *no cards.*

This was once the hunting lodge of Barron Collier, the millionaire who constructed the Tamiami Trail. Collier would entertain his classy guests on the game he'd shot, which would be prepared by the former chef to Kaiser Wilhelm. No fewer than three presidents have stayed here. More interesting guests include Gypsy Rose Lee and Mick Jagger. And it's much less expensive than you'd expect.

NAPLES

Finding somewhere expensive to stay in Naples is easy. The inexpensive motels are across on the eastern side of the Tamiami Trail. Your best bet by the beach is:

Tides Motor Inn, $$; 1801 *Gulf Shore Boulevard North*, *Naples* 33940; *tel.* 813 262 3055; *cards* AE, MC, V.

Motel with pool, right by the beach, and round the corner from exclusive Olde Naples. Book *well* ahead during the winter season.

RECOMMENDED RESTAURANTS

EVERGLADES CITY

The Oyster House, $-$$; *Chokoloskee Causeway* (Rt 29); *tel.* 813 695 2073; *cards* MC, V.

Best fresh seafood, cheerfully served amid a litter of Everglades bric-a-brac.

MICCOSUKEE INDIAN VILLAGE

Miccosukee Restaurant, $-$$; *Tamiami Trail* (Rt 41), *Miccosukee Village*; *tel.* 305 223 8380; *all major cards.*

Just opposite the entrance to the village, on Rt 41. Paintings on the wall illustrate traditional Indian scenes. The menu is much more like the real thing. Interested in authentic Everglades frogs' legs? If not, go for an Indian burger or pumpkin bread.

NAPLES

For that romantic night out that your partner (and your bank manager) will never forget:

Sign of the Vine, $$$; 980 *Solana Road, Naples*; *tel.* 813 261 6745; *cards* AE; *dinner only*; *closed May, June and July*.

International cuisine classics, and imaginative home-grown creations, served by candlelight in a converted local mansion. Where the movers and shakers come to see and be seen.

Otherwise head for the picturesque City Dock, where **The Dock at Crayton Cove,** *tel.* 813 263 9940, *all major cards*, has great inexpensive seafood and great company.

Local Explorations: 5

Southern Florida

The Shell Coast

80 *miles; map* Hallwag Florida

The Shell Coast of southwestern Florida has long attracted the discerning visitor. Centuries ago, the wild-eyed pirate Jose Gaspar chose Captiva Island as home for his harem. The great inventor Thomas Edison set up his winter home in Fort Myers when it had fewer than four hundred residents, and a few decades later Henry Ford established a winter hideaway next door. Meanwhile, just south of town, the Koreshan religious sect founded their own Garden of Eden. And mystery writer Mary Roberts Rinehart discovered her own version of paradise on Cabbage Key – a spot which later so enchanted songwriter Jimmy Buffet that he was inspired to write "Cheeseburger in Paradise." These visitors may have had little else in common, but they all agreed that the Shell Coast was as near to paradise as they could find.

Nowadays, things have changed a little. For a start, more of us have discovered the wonders of beach life on these barrier islands. For sunset freaks, shell collectors, or beach bums, this place is still as good as any – whether you prefer the luxury of life at the South Seas Plantation on Captiva Island, or the more gregarious pleasures of Fort Myers Beach. Inland, you can discover what Florida was really like before anyone arrived here. Head for the Babcock Wilderness and the Corkscrew Swamp Sanctury and you'll find timeless nature at its best.

You can easily drive through this region in a day, but you should allow a couple of days at least if you want to explore.

TRANSPORTATION
The only practical way to get around this area is by car.

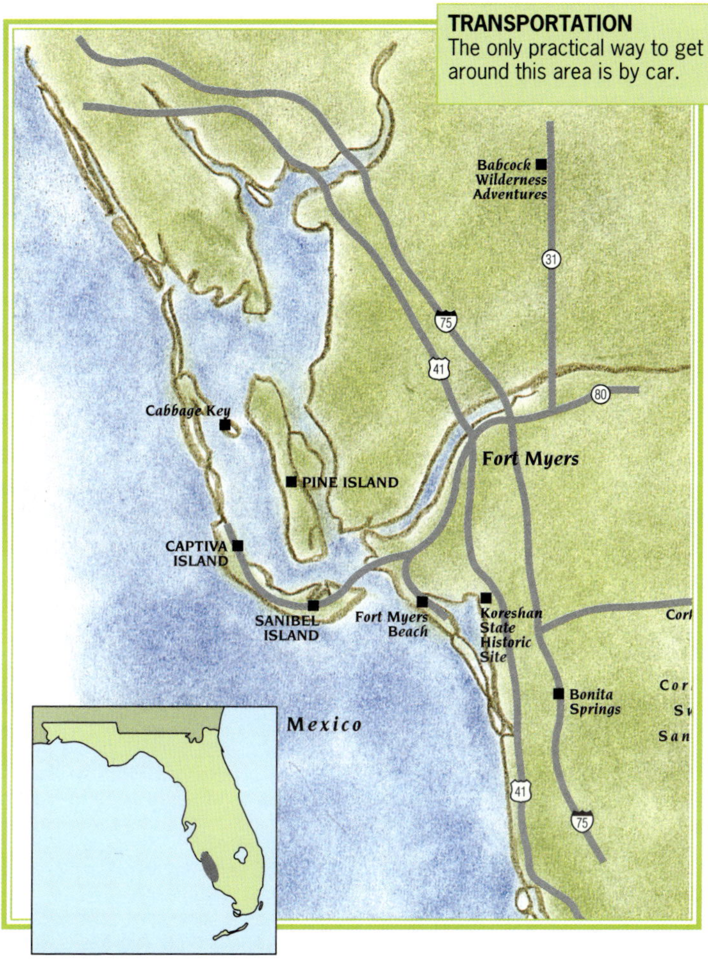

SIGHTS & PLACES OF INTEREST

BABCOCK WILDERNESS ADVENTURES

Off Rt 31, NE of Fort Myers; entry by appointment only, tel. 813 489 3911; closed Mon. In the old days this area used to be known as Telegraph Swamp - because conditions were so bad that even the telegraph wires had to bypass it. Then, in 1914, 90,000 acres of Telegraph Swamp were bought by timber magnate E.V. Babcock. In no time it looked as if a giant razor had shaved away the stubble of trees. Then Babcock decided he would turn the place into a wilderness. Nowadays, it is an amazing wildlife preserve. Untamed inhabitants include a herd of bison, the dreaded turkey vulture, deer, snakes, alligators and a rare breed of local cowboy – all of whom are permitted to roam freely through the untouched wilderness. There are even some cougars, who are kept in their own mountain lion enclosure, though they remain sadly deprived of any actual mountains.

You're taken in a 30-seater swamp buggy on a 90-minute journey into the heart of the wilderness: a chance to see what it was really like in Florida before civilization arrived. Only a few centuries ago, Miami was a jungle just like this.

BONITA SPRINGS

On Rt 75, 24 miles S of Fort Myers. A few years ago this was the fastest growing residential area on the Shell Coast – and it shows. There's not much to see here, not much to do here, and not much reason to stop unless you want to buy a plot of land (which is comparatively cheap now that the south-west Florida land boom has been hit by the recession). If you find yourself stuck at this unpromising locale, you're much better off heading down the road for the **Bonita Beach.**

CABBAGE KEY

Barrier island on Pine Island Sound, in the Gulf approximately 20 miles W of Fort Myers. Reached by boat from Pine Island, or from Captiva Island (see entry for details). This little laid-back paradise has been attracting the wealthy for several decades now. Mystery novelist Mary Roberts Rinehart arrived here in the 1930s and built herself an island home, using an old Calusa shell-mound for its foundations. Today, this sturdy clapboard house is the **Cabbage Key Inn**, and her library has been turned into a bar. This is said to have the most expensive wallpaper in the world: it's covered with more than 30,000 dollar bills, each one signed by a benevolent boozer. The restaurant here serves such local delicacies as beer-steamed shrimp, but it was the cheeseburgers which inspired songwriter Jimmy Buffet to compose his never-to-be forgotten hit "Cheeseburger in Paradise." See Recommended Hotels, page 212.

Wander round the **tropical garden**, climb the **water tower** for views across the sound to the other keys, or follow one of the paths around the 100-acre island, and you'll soon find there are more inspiring things about this tropical hideaway than the cheeseburgers.

CAPTIVA ISLAND

See Sanibel and Captiva Islands, page 214.

CORKSCREW SWAMP SANCTUARY

Some 5 miles S of Bonita Springs turn E on to Rt 846, and follow it for 17 miles; open 8 am-5 pm daily; entry $6.50. This is what the swamps of south-western Florida used to look like, before the logging industry arrived in the early years of the 20thC, and began pillaging entire forests of 500-year-old trees. The 10,000-acre preserve consists of swamplands and big cypresses, many hanging with Spanish moss, some of which started growing before Columbus arrived. Home of a number of increasingly rare storks and egrets, which were formerly hunted for their feathers. You can follow a 1.5-mile trail along a boardwalk which leads through the wilderness just out of reach of the alligators. Unfortunately, even this protected region is at present under threat owing to a seemingly unstoppable lowering of the water level.

FORT MYERS

On Rt 41, 82 miles S of Sarasota. Fort Myers was once the home of a genius. With characteristic prescience, he declared, way back in 1914: "There is only one Fort Myers, and 90 million people are going to find it out." The

• *Cabbage Key.*

genius was Thomas Edison, and for once he was wrong. Not that Fort Myers is entirely undiscovered – but then it isn't entirely overrun, either. Fort Myers has just about managed to weather the south-west Florida boom. (In the 1970s Fort Myers was the fastest expanding city in the entire United States – almost doubling its size, mushrooming by 92.4 percent.)

With the arrival of the recession, things have calmed down somewhat, although there's no denying the developers have left their mark. Despite this, Fort Myers is still a beautiful riverside spot, with its main streets pleasantly fringed by shady palm trees. Nearby there are more than a hundred islands (some mere dots in the ocean, others with mile upon mile of shining sandy **beaches** – great for swimming, sunbathing, shell-gathering and fishing). And when you grow tired of the simple beach life, there are several sights worth visiting in Fort Myers itself (see below).

Fort Myers has a history which long pre-dates the arrival of Edison. When the Spanish sailed into San Carlos Bay and up the Caloosahatchee River in the early 1500s, they noticed that the masts and wooden sides of their ships began sprouting thin shafts of wood with feathers on the end of them. The Spanish quickly understood that they were not the first to discover this pleasant spot.

In the following centuries, the Seminole Indians took to grazing their herds of cattle in the surrounding countryside. Then, in the early 1800s, the U.S. Army set up a fort, in the process giving the place a much-needed name. After the Seminole Wars, the victors unscrupulously appropriated the Seminole herds, and Fort Myers became a cowboy town. For a couple of decades, this was Florida's answer to the Wild West, complete with "high noon" shoot-outs, saloons and the usual collection of low-down varmints. Then came the Civil War, and everyone in town rallied to the Confederate flag. Once again Fort Myers became an army town.

In 1865, after the Civil War, the army moved out, taking everything with them. For almost a year Fort Myers was a ghost town. This sad and spooky state of affairs was remedied by the arrival of four new pioneer settlers, followed by a wave of Dutch immigrants. Making use of the warm climate, and the horticultural skills they'd learned in the tulip fields of their native land, the Dutch began cultivating flowers. They also cultivated a well-known talent from their adopted country: thinking big. In no time, Fort Myers was known as "The Gladiolus Capital of the World." No less. This was 1885, and by now Fort Myers had a population amounting to all of 350.

The year 1885 also saw the arrival of Thomas Edison. He was 38 and had already created many of the inventions which brought him widespread fame and wealth. Edison's doctor had advised him to come to Florida for the sake of his ailing health. The moment Edison set eyes on Fort Myers he knew this was just the spot he'd been looking for. He built himself a modest home, together with a large laboratory, and spent every winter here until his death 46 years later. Meanwhile, the secret of Fort Myers had been passed on to another man who was to transform the face of the 20thC. The plot next door to Edison's was bought by Henry Ford, who also built a winter retreat.

Today, you can still see the houses of both these remarkable men.

Edison Winter Home

At Seminole Lodge, 2350 McGregor Boulevard; open 9 am-4 pm Mon-Sat, Sun afternoons only; entry $8. This is the real thing. Edison's laboratory is just as he left it when he died almost 70 years ago. You can still see jumbles of test tubes, chemical bottles, apparatus in a state of mid-invention. Shining down are the original carbon filament lamps which Edison installed. (Unlike the later "improvements" on Edison's invention which we are forced to use, these light bulbs have continued to burn for 12 hours a day, year in, year out.)

Outside are the gardens where Edison set his mind to work on various horticultural experiments. There are examples of the weed, giant goldenrod (*Solidago Edisoni*), which Edison strove for many years to turn into a rubber-producing plant, and the African sausage tree upon which he conducted other more obscure (but seemingly unsuccessful) experiments. Geniuses, like the rest of us, are prone to error, but like any wise gambler, Edison played the percentage game. During his life he patented 1,096 inventions, among them the movie projector and the electric light bulb – so he could afford some flops.

At the back of Edison's laboratory there's a **museum** which displays many of his inventions. Unfortunately, this has also been closed for long periods recently, owing to the increasing fragility of its exhibits, which include many of Edison's actual inventions. There are some real gems, including the world's first gramophone record. When this precious strip of tin foil is played, you can just distinguish the strains of "Mary had a little lamb." You'll also see the model T Ford, given to Edison by *its* inventor, his next-door neighbor Henry Ford.

Edison's home is not open to the public, but you can explore his garden. After his move to Florida, Edison became an enthusiastic botanist. He planted the first palm trees which line the streets of Fort Myers. (The idea caught on to such an extent that Fort Myers changed its title from "The Gladiolus Capital of the World" and began calling itself instead "The City of Palms.") Edison collected more than 6,000 subtropical trees from all over

• *Thomas Edison's laboratory,* Edison Winter Home.

THOMAS EDISON

One of the great inventors of all time, Thomas Alva Edison was born in 1847 in Milan, Ohio. By the age of 12 he was working as a newsboy. After he saved the life of a stationmaster's child, the grateful father gave him lessons on how to operate a telegraph machine. This first encounter with science stimulated a lifelong interest in the practical application of scientific principles. Edison invented an automatic transmitter and receiver for the telegraph. At the age of 22 he was able to give up being a telegraph operator, a job which had taken him to cities all over North America. He set up a laboratory in a barn in New Jersey and devoted himself to his inventions, investing the money he made from his successes into research for future inventions. In this way, he invented and financed the research for a ticker-tape machine, a vote-recorder, the phonograph (the early gramophone), and the incandescent electric lamp (the first light bulb).

At the age of 38, suffering from ill health as a result of overwork and the death of his first wife, he came to rest in Florida on doctor's orders. One day he arrived on the steamboat at Fort Myers, then a dreamy settlement on the banks of the Caloosahatchee River with a population of just 350. He was so taken with the spot that he bought 14 acres for a winter home. He then returned to Maine, built the house, and had it shipped down to Florida in prefabricated sections on a succession of schooners. (The same schooners later took examples of these first pre-fabricated houses around Cape Horn to Hawaii, where they transformed the local architecture.)

Edison's doctor had given him just a few years to live when he advised winters in Florida. The inventor took his advice, also a second wife, and lived to 84 – continuing with his experiments to the end.

• *Henry Ford Winter Home.*

the world, and is said to have spent more than $100,000 assembling the plants for his garden. But it was more than just a garden, of course. Besides trying to turn the sap of weeds into aircraft tires, he also had a go at turning bamboo into filaments for his light bulbs.

The garden also contains the first modern swimming pool in Florida, which Edison built in 1900 with his own patented cement. It was empty when I last saw it, but its sides had no sign of any cracks, and I was assured that it has never leaked. (See also box, this page.)

Henry Ford Winter Home

Next door to Edison's home, you can see Mangoes, the surprisingly modest two-storey wooden house built in 1915 by Henry Ford. *Opening times and entry charge same as Edison Home; combined tickets $10.*

Henry Ford built the first mass-produced motor car, the model T Ford, known affectionately as the Tin Lizzie. Previously he had worked as chief engineer for the Edison Illuminating Company, which Edison had set up to manufacture his revolutionary new light bulb. When Ford described his ideas for the mass production of motor cars, with a mobile assembly line which began with nothing and ended up with completed cars rolling off one after another, everyone laughed. Only his friend Thomas Edison took him seriously. Ford's ideas were to revolutionize the entire manufacturing industry, and arguably had more effect on the 20thC than the revolutionary concepts of Marx and Freud. Ford never forgot Edison's encouragement, and built his house in Fort Myers for the sole purpose of spending his winters close to his friend.

The Shell Factory

At 2787 North Tamiami Trail (Rt 41) N *of Fort Myers.* The barrier islands around Fort Myers are famous for their shells, attracting many collectors. If you want to know what a great shell collection looks like, head for The Shell Factory, which claims to have the largest collection of shells in the world, laid out over 65,000 square feet. The shells range from humble sand dollars to weird and wonderful examples of nature's sculpture from all over the world. In fact, this is a shell supermarket – you can buy what you see.

FORT MYERS BEACH 🛏 ✕

On Rt 865, 7 *miles* S *of Fort Myers, across*

RECOMMENDED HOTELS

Accommodations on the Shell Coast tend to be expensive, especially during the winter season, November to April. There's a scarcity of inexpensive motels, especially on the islands. Out of season, prices drop somewhat.

CABBAGE KEY

Cabbage Key Inn, $$; PO *Box* 200, *Cabbage Key, Pineland* 33945; *tel.* 813 283 2278; *no cards.*

Historic hotel in the former home of mystery writer Mary Roberts Rinehart (see also page 208). They have just six rooms, and six cottages, so you have to book *weeks* in advance. But it's worth a try. The bar is a legend (and has played host to many legendary characters). The only way to Cabbage Key is by boat from Pine Island or Captiva Island (see text).

CAPTIVA ISLAND

There are no accommodations on this island, except in the luxury class. The famous example of this is:

South Seas Plantation Resort and Yacht Harbor, $$$, and rising; PO *Box* 194, *Captiva Island* 3924; *tel.* 813 472 5111; *cards* DC, MC, V.

This is what became of 19thC pioneer Clarence Chadwick's failed copra plantation, and you can still see a few of the remnant coconut palms dotted over the 330-acre estate. At this price, you can't expect anything other than a cliché paradise.

You dine in the old plantation workers' canteen, but happily neither the food nor the decor are authentic any more.

Off-season, you might be lucky and pick up a room here for only just over $200, otherwise you can pay up to three times this price – if you're willing to put up with the celebrities across the lawn.

FORT MYERS

Prices go down in summer.

Tides Motel, $-$$; 2621 *First Street, Fort Myers* 33903; *tel.* 813 334 1231; *no cards.*

Standard Florida motel close to downtown, with plenty of others nearby on the same street.

FORT MYERS BEACH

Beach House, $-$$; 4960 *Estero Boulevard, Fort Myers Beach* 33931; *tel.* 813 463 2372; *all major cards.*

Close to the local Times Square and the heart of the action.

SANIBEL ISLAND

There's no avoiding the fact that the islands, especially this one, are expensive.

Jolly Roger, $$-$$$; 3201 *West Gulf Drive, Sanibel Island* 33957; *tel.* 813 472 1700; *no cards.*

About as inexpensive as you'll get, around here. Even so, it's fairly standard. But it's by the ocean, and the million-dollar sunsets are free.

the causeway on Estero Island. This is the Coney Island of the Shell Coast, with a wild and whacky beach life, and a nightlife to match. Further down Estero Island, sanity returns, and the beaches become a little less populated. The big bonus here is that prices tend to be lower than on the nearby islands.

For something different, try a cruise on the schooner *Island Rover*, which sails from Sky Bridge. For around $12 you can take a daytime cruise in search of wildlife around Estero Bay, a sunset cruise in search of romance, or a moonlight cruise which *is* romance; telephone 813 765 7447 for details.

• *Sign for The Shell Factory.*

KORESHAN STATE HISTORIC SITE

On Rt 41 at Estero, 15 miles S of Fort Myers; open 8 am-dusk; entry $3.50 per vehicle. Cyrus Reed Teed was a U.S. Army surgeon in the 1800s. One day he experienced a vision which confirmed the true nature of the entire universe. As a result of his "great illumination," Teed saw that everyone else – including the scientists, philosophers throughout the ages and the founders of the world's great religions – had got it wrong.

Teed's remarkable vision turned his view of the world inside out, literally. According to Teed, the surface of the world on which we live is the hollow *inside* of the globe, which has the sun at its center. As a result of this vision, Teed decided to change his name to Koresh, and he founded a religious sect called the Koreshan Unity Movement – whose members were all expected to subscribe to this inside-out view of the world.

The Koreshans were originally based in Chicago, but their concave beliefs soon began to irritate their con-vexed neighbors. Eventually, in 1894, Teed decided they should quit city life and set up a paradise on earth which would "prove" their beliefs. In those days Florida was pure wilderness – just the place for a latter-day Garden of Eden. In 1894 the Koreshans bought a 300-acre site at the mouth of the Estero River and set about establishing a Utopian self-supporting community.

They put their beliefs into practice: equality for women, communal property and celibacy outside marriage. They produced a blueprint for a New Jerusalem – a city of ten million saved

RECOMMENDED RESTAURANTS

FORT MYERS

The Chart House, $$; *2024 West 1st Street, Fort Myers; tel.* 813 332 1881; *cards* AE, MC, V.

Superb views out over the Caloosahatchee River, with some of the freshest, most imaginative seafood in town. The prices are reasonable.

FORT MYERS BEACH

Plaka, $$; *1001 Estero Boulevard, Fort Myers Beach; tel.* 813 463 4707; *cards* MC, V.

Great Greek cuisine under the stars above the beach. Their moussaka is as good as you'll get in Athens.

SANIBEL ISLAND

McT's Shrimp House and Tavern, $-$$; *1625 Periwinkle Way, Sanibel Island; tel.* 813 472 1033; *cards* MC, V.

Gulf view and Gulf cuisine making use of interesting Caribbean ingredients. Also has a bar, where you can pick up "lite bites."

souls, all living without lust or property. They even marked out the 30-foot-wide boulevards, which would one day be lined with skyscrapers (such as those which had just begun appearing in Chicago).

Meanwhile, the population remained stubbornly below the 200 mark, and the only way to reach the settlement was by fighting your way past the alligators along the Estero River. Teed died in 1908, and the community began to dwindle. But it didn't peter out entirely. New members continued to trickle in. The last one arrived in 1940, a refugee from Hitler's Germany. The Koreshan community lasted until he finally died in 1982.

The present-day site is all that remains of this brave community. Some of the original buildings have been restored. You can also see Teed's residence, and the **Planetary Court**, home of the committee which coordinated the running of the community. It consisted of seven women, each named after one of the planets. During the Lunar Festival in April they also bring out the celebrated Rectilinator, the machine which proves that when we feel on top of the world we're mistaken. At the **Museum**, they'll take you on a guided tour (minimum indoctrination and fascinating photos, including some of Steed himself). They even publish their own newspaper, *The American Eagle*, which is filled with an unusual blend of intriguing whimsy.

SANIBEL AND CAPTIVA ISLANDS

The barrier islands across San Carlos Bay from the Caloosahatcheee River estuary and Fort Myers. Reached by way of Rt 867 leading SW out of Fort Myers and along the 3-mile long Sanibel Causeway ($3 return toll).

NO CONNECTION
The name of Koresh (formerly Teed) and the Koreshans has recently been blighted by a hideous coincidence. They have absolutely nothing whatsoever to do with the religious leader David Koresh – whose headquarters in Waco, Texas burned down while he and the surviving inmates had a shoot-out with federal agents, who had come to collect unpaid taxes.

Sanibel is like a South Sea island paradise off the coast of America. Main Street is called Periwinkle Way, and that just about sums it up. Here you're in a different world from the condos and the Coney Island crassness which increasingly mar so many of Florida's resorts.

The island was discovered almost 500 years ago by Ponce de León, who named it after Queen Isabella of Spain. Santa Isabella Island remained largely uninhabited, except when pirates put ashore for rest and relaxation. Then, in the 1890s, the island was settled by some English farmers, who changed the island's name while attempting to change its landscape. Fortunately, these new immigrants weren't very competent farmers. The copra plantation failed and the limes all grew an exotic subtropical fungus, leaving a pleasant wilderness of coconut palms and fragrant citrus trees.

In 1899 the Bailey family arrived and opened a shop. Although times were hard, the shop managed to survive – to such an extent that you can visit **Bailey's General Store** today.

For years, the inhabitants of Sanibel lived the quiet life, until plans were announced to join the island to the mainland by a causeway. The locals resisted, taking legal action. The case went all the way to the Supreme Court, but the islanders lost out, and the causeway was eventually built in 1963. Despite this, the locals have managed to limit the damage done by developers by enforcing some strict planning and conservation laws. As a result the island remains largely unspoiled.

Today, the **beaches** of Sanibel remain some of the best spots for shell hunting anywhere in the world. "Shunters" (local name for shell-hunters) flock here from all over, scouring the beaches for rare finds. You can see them roaming the beaches, bent down over the sand – suffering from what's become known as the "Sanibel Stoop." The best time for shell-hunting is low tide after a storm, and the best spot is **Bowman's Beach** on the northwestern shore of the island. The best months are said to be January and February, and according to a local fanatic I encountered, more than 200 different types of shell have been found here. Sometimes you can still find the occa-

sional rare spiny oyster or royal Florida miter, and there are usually plenty of cowrie, conch, paper nautilus and limpets. (You can pick up a shell identification chart at the local Chamber of Commerce, which is just past where you leave the causeway.)

Even here the locals have managed to enforce a measure of conservation. You're only allowed to collect two examples of any species of shell with a live occupant. Transgressors can be fined up to $500, or even sent to jail.

At the southern tip of the island there's a **wooden lighthouse**, which dates from 1884. The main road leads through the pleasantly wooded center of the island (mainly pine, banyan and other subtropical species).

The central land-facing coast of the island is occupied by the **J. N. "Ding" Darling National Wildlife Refuge,** *open dawn to dusk, closed* Fri; *entry* $4 *per car*. This 5,000-acre wilderness contains alligators, water snakes and otters, but the main attraction here is the **birdlife**.

In late autumn you can see flocks of migrating ducks, which are truly a wonder to behold. They tend to fly in during the late afternoon, but I was told by an early riser that they're even better just after sunrise. At all times of year you can usually see flamingoes, various

• A *few examples from the huge* Shell Factory *collection.*

rare and stately herons, as well as some superb (and some ridiculous) spoonbills. There are also canoe trails, hikes and a guided train tour. But it's worth the 5-mile drive even without these extras.

At the northern end of the island, the road crosses to the more remote but equally picturesque **Captiva Island**. If Sanibel was paradise, Captiva must have been hell. Centuries ago this was where the fearsome pirate Jose Gaspar kept his harem of captive women – hence the island's name. Captiva may have been a treasure island as well. According to legend, Jose Gaspar buried his treasure here – though sporadic digs have unearthed not a single Spanish doubloon.

The road runs along the western shore and ends up at a fine **beach**, which is celebrated for its sunsets.

There are many **other islands** to the north and east of here. You can see these by taking a boat trip from the South Sea Plantation. Prices start at $20, though some of the longer trips can be at least triple this. For details phone 813 472 5300. This is also an embarkation point for Cabbage Key (see page 212).

Local Explorations: 6

Northern Florida

Gainesville and Region

60 miles; map Hallwag Florida

Gainesville is the civilized heart of unspoiled central Florida. You won't find many other tourists up here, yet the region is not without interest. Gainesville is the home of the University of Florida. It's both lively and friendly. It's also the home of the famous Gators, the University football team, and turns into a carnival on the weekends when they're playing at home. During vacation time, the place is a sunny ghost town.

Down the road at Cross Creek, you can see the home of Marjorie Kinnan Rawlings. What Faulkner was to Mississippi, Rawlings was to Florida. (Read her masterpiece *The Yearling* to get the true flavor of this rural region.)

The St Johns River runs 50 miles or so to the east of Gainesville, and this too once had echoes of Mississippi. A hundred years ago this was the resort area of Florida, where rich northerners had their winter villas, and paddle steamers ploughed the river between Palatka and Green Cove Springs. The visitors have gone, but you can still see their grand mansions.

You can drive through this region, and cover the major sights, in a day or two on your way between Orlando and the Panhandle.

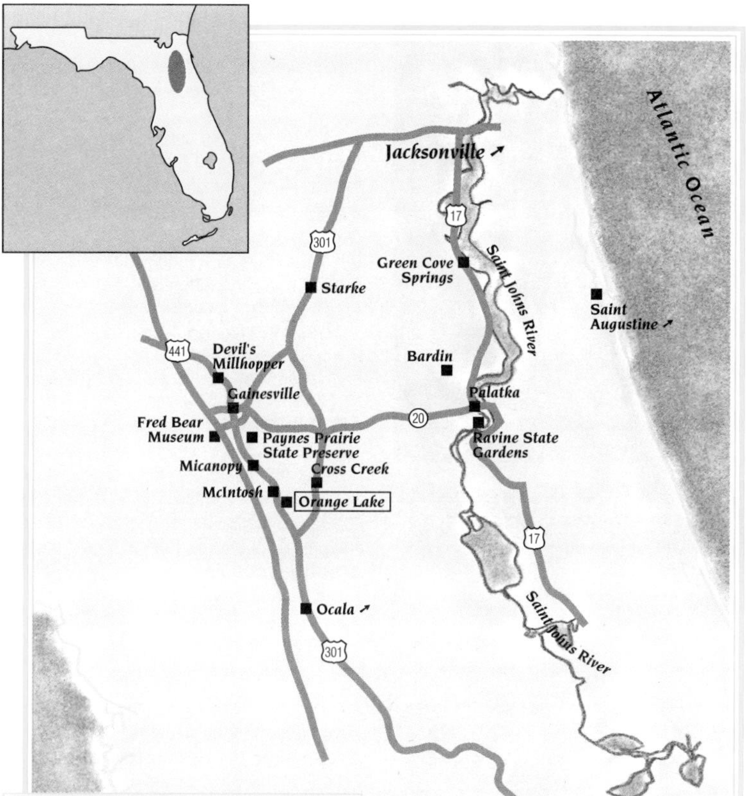

TRANSPORTATION
There are buses which link Gainesville and Palatka to the main nearby cities, Ocala, Jacksonville and St Augustine. But by far the best way to see this rural area is by car.

• A *Gainesville mansion.*

SIGHTS & PLACES OF INTEREST

BARDIN

About 10 *miles* NW *of Palatka.* Bardin is a tiny dot on the map in the middle of nowhere. It has nothing to recommend it. Nothing, that is, but a legendary creature called the Booger. According to locals who have seen this beast, it's half human, half animal, covered in hair and over 7 feet tall. It's said to resemble the Himalayan Yeti and the Sasquatch (see below). It roams elusively through the nearby woods, fighting shy of investigative journalists or anyone with a camera, but leaping out of the undergrowth every now and again to frighten the wits out of some unsuspecting local.

Drop in, and they'll tell you all about it. (Scoffers will find the odd sympathizer, but are not, as a rule, welcome.)

CROSS CREEK ✕

By Orange Lake, 30 *miles* SE *of Gainesville. Take* Rt 441 S *and turn off* E *onto* Rt 346 20 *miles from town.* Cross Creek is famous as the home of the writer Marjorie Kinnan Rawlings. She lived here and wrote about the people who lived here. Her book, *The Yearling*, was published in 1938 and won the Pulitzer Prize. You can visit her house on Rt 325; *open* 10 *am-4 pm daily; entry* $2. Here you can see

SASQUATCH

Legendary hairy half-man, whose name comes from the unpronouncable American Indian word *ses'sxac*. This creature is sometimes known as Bigfoot, after the size of the prints he leaves in the mud to encourage local sleuths to follow his elusive trail. The experts, all but a minute fraction of whom have never set eyes on a Sasquatch, maintain that this human animal is closely related to the Himalayan Yeti, popularly known as the Abominable Snowman.

The first man to discover the big-footed footprints of a Sasquatch was the British explorer David Thompson, who in 1811 came across some footprints almost two feet long and eight inches wide. He calculated that the creature which had made these prints was over 12 feet tall.

Since then, many similarly-sized footprints have raised the pulse and the hair of travelers on lonely trails, and there have even been sightings of the Sasquatch. The tales told by those who have actually encountered the Sasquatch tend to concur on several points. The Sasquatch stands on two legs and is *very* big (up to 15 feet tall, and sometimes of enormous girth). He is hairy all over, exudes foul odors, and is likely to give a high-pitched operatic howl.

According to the Russian biologist Boris Porshnev, the Sasquatch is closely related to his equally mythical Siberian counterpart, the Almas. Porshnev is convinced that both of these creatures are in fact the descendants of Neanderthal man.

The first person to have filmed Sasquatch was Roger Patterson. This took place in 1967 at the ominously named Bluff Creek in California. The film shows a shadowy figure blundering about in the distance. He or she bears an uncanny resemblance to the Martian who was filmed emerging from a UFO in the same locality, also during the 1960s.

• *Gator fans at the Florida Field Stadium.*

everything from her typewriter to where she hid her bottle of hooch during Prohibition. The guided tour (on the hour Thursday to Sunday) explains all, giving a useful insight into this remarkable writer.

Rawlings (1896-1953) moved to Cross Creek in 1928 from New England, and lived here for the rest of her life. Her grave is down the road at Island Grove. Rawlings is to rural Florida much what Faulkner was to rural Mississippi.

Be sure to visit the local Yearling Restaurant, whose menu is based on Rawlings' indigenous recipes. See Recommended Restaurants, page 221.

DEVIL'S MILLHOPPER

By Rt 441 5 miles NW of Gainesville, at 4732 North West 53rd Avenue. Florida is pitted with sink-holes. These are usually caused by natural erosion of the limestone strata, followed by geological subsidence. The Devil's Millhopper has a fair claim to being the largest sink-hole in the state. It's almost five acres in area, and according to one source it's over a 1,000 feet deep (others maintain it's only 100 feet deep). Walk down the side of the hole by way of the boardwalk and you can see a wide variety of Alpine plants, ferns and subtropical plants, and a number of waterfalls. *Open 9 am-sunset daily; entry $2 per car.*

FRED BEAR MUSEUM

Off the Interstate Highway (Rt 75), 5 miles SW of Gainesville; open 8 am-6 pm daily; entry $2.50. Despite his name, Fred Bear has killed many large furry animals in his time. He's also shot some smaller ones, and even some with no fur at all – such as elephants and hippos. These victims of Mr Bear's lethal hobby now form an exhibition. Fred has had them stuffed, embalmed, skinned or otherwise preserved. Sometimes he's gone even further, and turned them into imaginative pieces of furniture. How would you like to see a hippo-leg table? Also on display here are a range of arrowheads and the like, made by genuinely pre-historic characters. Fred's other hobby is archery, and nearby you can see his archery factory.

• *Century Tower, Gainesville.*

GAINESVILLE'S SINISTER MYSTERY

In August 1990 Gainesville hit the TV screens nationwide, items even appearing as far afield as Europe and Australia.

The bodies of five hideously mutilated University of Florida students were found. All of them had lived off-campus, but otherwise there appeared to be no common factor linking the killings. After an intense police investigation, a suspect named Danny Rolling was finally arrested. While he was in police custody, in the summer of 1991, two further identical murders took place. Despite this, the police remained convinced that they had the real Gainesville Slasher in Danny Rolling. As far as they were concerned, the two later murders were copycat killings. Danny Rolling was tried for murder, found guilty, and sentenced to the electric chair. He is at present Prisoner Number 109714 on Death Row in the Florida Union Correctional Institution at Starke (see page 223). Is Rolling really the Gainesville Slasher? Either way, there's still a multiple killer at large.

GAINESVILLE 🛏 ✕

Some 60 miles SW of Jacksonville, 90 miles NW of Orlando. A haven of civilization in the midst of rural Florida. Gainesville is the site of the University of Florida, and home to their famous Gators football team.

Three hundred years ago this savannah region was cattle country, and Gainesville languished under the unpromising name of Hogtown. Then in 1854 Florida was granted statehood, and the new state was awarded a federal grant to found two insititutions of higher learning. The East Florida Seminary was established in Gainesville, and in time evolved into the University of Florida. (Its sister, the West Florida Seminary, was established in Tallahasse, and became the Florida State University.)

The University of Florida has played a leading role in the state's commercial success. At the turn of the century, it pioneered experimental citrus farms, which were to be the basis of Florida's economy.

You'll find the large university campus west of downtown, with its main entrance on 13th Street (Rt 441) at University Avenue. The university's older buildings are in the familiar neo-Gothic style so popular a hundred years ago. In the center of the campus is the **Century Tower**, which dates from the centenary of the founding of the institution in 1953. (And should not be mistaken for the Clock Tower in the center of town, another local landmark.) On campus and all over the place, you'll see the celebrated logo of the university's celebrated football team: the Gators. And near the Century Clock Tower you can see where it all happens: the **Florida Field Stadium** which seats more than 70,000 avid Gator fans. The team's performances don't always live up to the unshakeable faith of their followers, but it is unwise to allude to this while you're in town.

There are, however, a few sights on campus which remain consistently up to expectation: **The Harn Museum of Art**, on *Hull Road at South West 34th Street, open 10 am-5 pm, Sun afternoons only, closed Mon.* The museum concentrates mainly on American art – from pre-Columban to contemporary exhibits.

Then there's the **Florida Museum of Natural History,** on *Museum Road, open*

10 am-4 pm Tues-Sat and Sun afternoons; entry free. The most exciting exhibits here are the **models and replicas**, the best of these being the model of a Mayan Palace. The Florida Heritage section gives an easily comprehensible rundown on the state's history.

Outside the university, the district around Main Street has a number of pleasant sidewalk cafes. Gainesville's 50,000-strong student population makes it a pleasant, easygoing and lively place during the school year; at other times it's heat-stunned and empty.

JACKSONVILLE

See Florida Overall: 7, page 121.

GREEN COVE SPRINGS

Ten miles S of Jacksonville on Rt 17. This spot overlooks the St Johns River at one of its wider sections. It used to be part of the St Johns River Riviera, whose resorts attracted rich families from the northeast during winter. Remnants of this former glory remain, and many of the old mansions have been restored.

MCINTOSH

See Micanopy, below.

MICANOPY

W of Rt 441, 12 miles S of Gainesville. In pre-Columbian times this village (pronounced Mick-ah-NO-pee) was a Timucuan Indian

RECOMMENDED HOTELS

GAINESVILLE

Residence Inn by Marriott, $$-$$$; *4001 South West 13th Street, Gainesville 32608 – 2 miles S of downtown off Rt 441; tel. 904 371 2101; all major cards.*

Good pool, free breakfast. Can get packed out on weekends when the Gators are playing at home.

But don't worry, there's a choice of inexpensive accommodations along the same street. Try:

Comfort Inn, $; *2435 South West 13th Street, Gainesville 32608; tel. 904 373 6500; all major cards.*

Basic modern motel.

RECOMMENDED RESTAURANTS

CROSS CREEK

The Yearling Restaurant, $$; *Cross Creek; tel. 904 466 3033; no cards.*

This restaurant is named after Marjorie Kinnan Rawlings' masterpiece *The Yearling*. Its menu features dishes from her *Cross Creek Cookery Book*, which was more than just the indulgence of a famous author. These were the local dishes she made up to give to her needy neighbors. The adventurous will want to try cooter (a soft-shelled aquatic local tortoise), and those who want to turn the tables will be pleased to dig their teeth into alligator tail. See also page 218.

GAINESVILLE

The best cafes and restaurants tend to be around the university campus.

Emiliano's, $-$$; *7 South East 1st Avenue, Gainesville; tel. 904 375 7381; no cards.*

Sidewalk café. Useful for coffee or snacks, especially their *tapas*. Also has a more substantial menu with a Latin-American flavor.

Capriccio, $$; *University Center Hotel, 1535 South West Archer Road, Gainesville; tel. 904 371 3333; all major cards.*

A Mediterranean menu, and a view out over town. Particularly good pasta, and friendly service.

settlement. Then the Spanish arrived and set up a mission to show the locals how much better the Inquisition was than scalping. After the United States bought Florida from the Spanish, white settlers moved in. The Indian settlement has vanished, but many of the houses built by the white pioneers remain. Now these have been transformed into antique and craft shops. On weekends this spot attracts antique lovers and bargain hunters from as far afield as Orlando and Jacksonville.

For somewhere a bit quieter, try **McIntosh,** 10 miles further down Rt 441 by Orange Lake. This village is about 100 years old and on weekends the locals dress up in authentic period costumes and take you on tours of their authentic period houses.

OCALA

See Local Explorations: 3, page 193.

ORLANDO

See Florida Overall: 1, page 33.

PALATKA

On the W bank of the St Johns River 50 miles S of Jacksonville on Rt 17, or 46 miles E of Gainesville on Rt 20. Just over a century ago this was a big tourist center, complete with Mississippi-style paddle steamers. Then came the railway, and everyone headed for warmer territory further south. Now it's a sleepy Central Florida town, with just a few reminders of greater times. One of these is its proud boast of being "The Bass Fishing Capital of the World." See also Ravine State Gardens, this page.

PAYNES PRAIRIE STATE PRESERVE

Off Rt 441 9 miles due S of Gainesville. People have almost certainly been living here for longer than 10,000 years. Recent archaeological digs have unearthed implements dating from 7000 BC. Until late in the 19thC, most of this 1,800-acre site was a large lake. Then one day around a hundred years ago, the lake dried up and disappeared (reversing the more usual Florida phenomenon of sink-holes: see Devil's Millhopper, page 218). The water disppeared so quickly that thousands of fish were found flopping in the mud, and even the local ferry was left high and dry. Now the region is a lake of waving grass, complete with nature trails and swimming spots. Herds of buffalo used to live here, but were wiped out when the white settlers' hunting methods were added to those of the local Indians. But recently a new herd of buffalo has been introduced to the area, and they now roam free without having to worry about being hunted.

RAVINE STATE GARDENS

Just S of Palatka, which is on the St Johns River 50 miles S of Jacksonville on Rt 17, or 46 miles E of Gainesville on Rt 20; open 8 am-dusk; entry $3.50 per car. Florida is so flat that it doesn't have many ravines – but these gardens are more than just a local geological rarity. During the 1930s, the site was chosen for a federal WPA (Workers Project Administration) project to give work to the unemployed, and as a result became transformed into a superb azalea garden. The best time to visit is during February and March, when the flowers are all blooming. But at other times you can still take a pleasant walk through the narrow, sharp-sided ravines, and have a secluded picnic.

ST AUGUSTINE

See Florida Overall: 6, page 110.

ST JOHNS RIVER

It rises in the swampland a few miles inland from Melbourne, midway down Florida's east coast. For almost 300 miles it meanders north through lakes and wide water systems before reaching the sea 15 miles beyond Jacksonville. It is navigable for over 200 miles of its length.

Early Spanish and French explorers soon discovered this navigable route leading into the heart of Florida. Its banks were quickly settled, and in time this became the center of Florida's citrus industry. The region flourished, and in the mid-1800s Florida's first tourists began to arrive here – escaping from the cold winters of the northern United States.

The wide, slow-flowing river was ideal for paddle boats, and these were soon cruising between the hotels and resorts. Towns such as Palatka and Mandarin became the Miami and Palm Beach of their day, and fortunes were made carrying citrus fruits up the river for transshipment to the east coast, and even Europe. For a time, Harriet Beecher Stowe, the author of *Uncle Tom's Cabin,*

• *Herlong Mansion, Micanopy.*

lived in Mandarin. (The house where she lived has now burned down.)

Another distinguished visitor to the St Johns River was the English composer Delius. In 1884 he moved into an orange farm overlooking the river near Jacksonville. (See under Jacksonville, Florida Overall: 7.)

In the 1890s Flagler began building his railway down the east coast. The leisurely steamboats were no match for this modern transportation, and the vacationers soon began traveling further south where it was even warmer during the winter. Then came a series of frosts which killed off the citrus crop, and the citrus industry moved down to the south of the state, which was now linked directly to its markets by Flagler's railway.

The towns which line the St Johns River occupy a comparative backwater, but the river is picturesque, and as popular with fishermen as it ever was.

Recently, the celebrated French oceanographer Jacques Cousteau made a television film here about the rare St Johns manatees, which are in danger of extinction.

At its widest point, just south of Jacksonville, the river is over 8 miles wide, though even further south one of the lakes that it flows through – Lake George – is even wider. Route 17 more or less follows the shores of the St Johns River for most of its length, from Jacksonville in the north almost as far as Orlando in the south.

STARKE

About 25 miles NE of Gainesville. This aptly named spot is the home of Florida's Union Correctional Institution, which houses one of the largest and best-known Death Rows in the United States. The population of this institutional dead end is rapidly being reduced, now that Florida has started reusing the electric chair. (Literally: they never got rid of their old one – keeping it, just in case.) At press time, the three star inmates (in order of demerit) are:

1 Danny Rolling, who shot to international stardom as the The Gainesville Slasher. (see Gainesville's Sinister Mystery, page 220).

2 Paul Hill, a self-effacing and courteous evangelist who gunned down a doctor in cold blood outside a Pensacola abortion clinic.

3 Krishna Maharaj, a British citizen born in Trinidad who was once the second largest racehorse owner in Britain. He was found guilty of shooting a Chinese business rival and his son in a Fort Lauderdale hotel room and has been languishing on Death Row since 1987.

All cells on Death Row have no outside windows, and are expected to be occupied 24 hours a day. Celebrity inmates 1 and 3 both strenuously proclaim their innocence, and they certainly have interesting evidence to support their claims. No. 2 looks forward to becoming a martyr for the Pro-Life cause (though the logical somersault involved in this process will surely exercise theologians for many years to come).

Northern Florida

The Panhandle Inland

180 *miles; map* Hallwag *Florida*

The inland sector of the Panhandle is known as Lower Alabama, and with good reason. This is the true rural Deep South, with isolated farming communities and a timeless economy. It used to be big in the lumber business, but this went into decline around the time Joe Louis last won the world heavyweight boxing title. Since then, not much has happened here. There are not many regions left like this in the United States – or anywhere.

Most people just drive through it on the fast Interstate Rt 10, but if you wish to savor this region of living history, try Rt 90 which meanders through the little towns and rural backwaters. If you've traveled from Tallahassee to Pensacola along the coast (See Florida Overall: 8), exploring the inland Panhandle makes an interesting alternative on the way back.

Despite being in the backwoods, you'll find several particular sights of interest. At Blackwater River, just down the road from Pensacola, you come to "The Canoe Capital of Florida" – quite a boast in a state criss-crossed with hundreds of miles of picturesque canoe trails. Further along the road is De Funiak Springs, where a New York Educational Society once set up its Utopian summer headquarters. Further still there are the famous Florida Caverns, the huge dam at Lake Seminole, and the historic town of Quincy.

You can easily drive it in a day. Allow another day or so if you want to take in the sights.

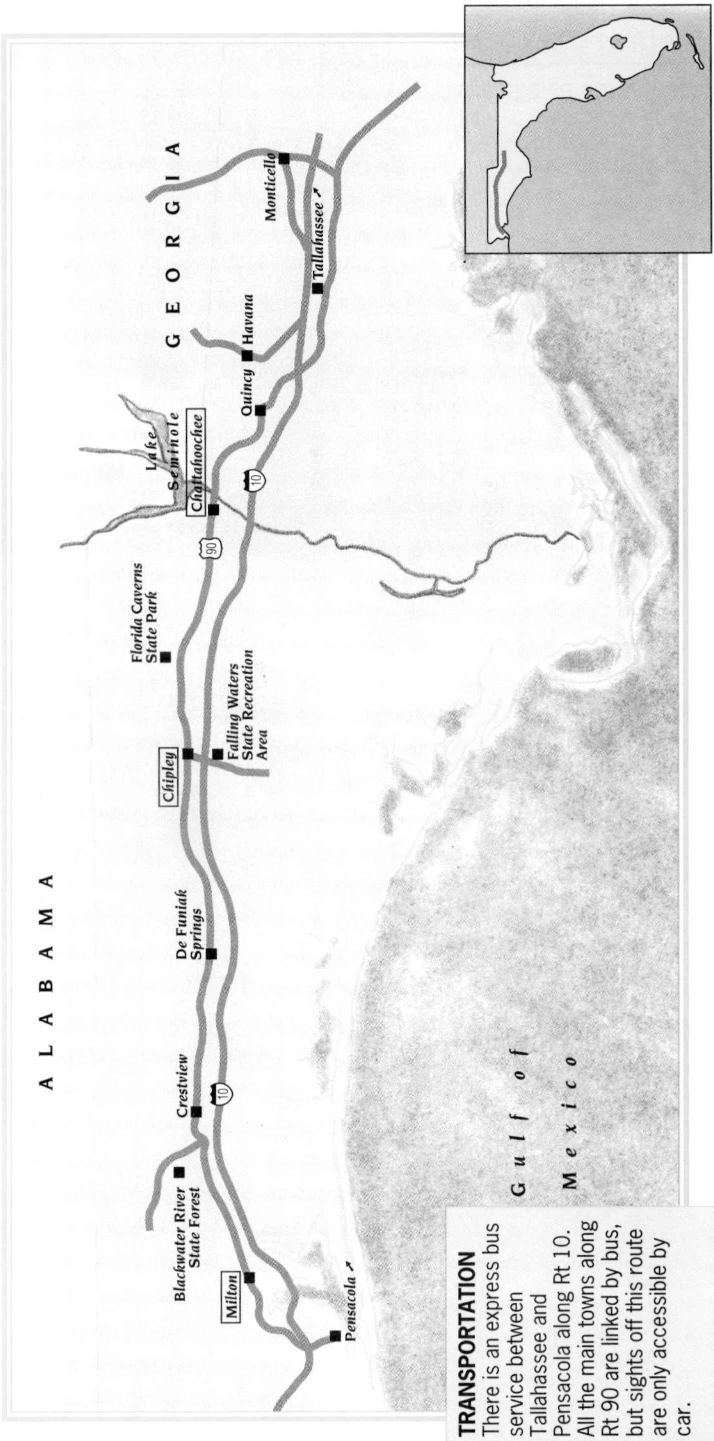

TRANSPORTATION
There is an express bus service between Tallahassee and Pensacola along Rt 10. All the main towns along Rt 90 are linked by bus, but sights off this route are only accessible by car.

SIGHTS & PLACES OF INTEREST

BLACKWATER RIVER STATE FOREST

Stretches E *from* Rt 87, *which leads* N *out of* Milton, *as far as* Rt 4, NE *of* Crestview. Milton *is on* Rt 90 17 *miles* NE *of* Pensacola. These wooded waterlands have earned the accolade of "Canoe capital of Florida." Although the forest attracts hordes in the summer, you can still paddle your own canoe up isolated creeks and picnic in idyllic solitude in the woods.

The main canoeing center is at **Tomahawk Landing** on **Coldwater Creek** on the west side of the park, 11 miles north of Milton on Rt 87. Here you can hire canoes for around $13 a day. If you're an experienced canoeist, they'll rent you one for a three-day trip, and pack you up with gear and provisions so you can get right out into the wilderness.

CRESTVIEW

On Rt 90 45 *miles* E *of* Pensacola.
Way up in the highlands by Florida standards, this 235-foot-high town was given its name in 1882 by the workers from the Louisville and Nashville Railroad Company who built the railway through north-western Florida. (For those who must know these things, the highest point in Florida is 20 miles up the road towards the Georgia border, and rises to all of 345 feet.) The big attraction of Crestview is its utter ordinariness; it's a slice of small-town American life, for those who are so inclined.

CHAUTAUQUA VINEYARDS

The educational society which brought the name Chautauqua all the way from New York to Florida has long since disappeared, much like the Indian language, which gave us this word in the first place.

But the irrepressible word lives on – now in the form of a wine which is produced in some local vineyards. For a tour and a free tasting, turn up at **Chautauqua Winery,** *near the junction of* Rt 331 *with* Rt 10, *open 9 am-5 pm* Mon-Sat, Sun *afternoon only*.
Chautauqua wine has only been going for a few years, but it has already begun picking up prizes.

DE FUNIAK SPRINGS ×

On Rt 90 75 *miles* E *of* Pensacola. A rarity in the backwoods of the Panhandle: an ancient seat of learning. In 1848 the **Knox Hill Academy** was founded here – and until the turn of the century this remained the only institution of higher learning in north-western Florida.

In 1882 the railway arrived, bringing with it an era of prosperity and a name for this hitherto anonymous spot. (Frederick de Funiak was a director of the railroad company.)

Three years later the first tourists arrived – in the form of the New York Chautauqua Educational Society. They were so taken with De Funiak Springs that they decided to establish their winter quarters here. (They were far too serious to call it a vacation home.) In 1909 they built a splendid clapboard auditorium, complete with obligatory dome and columns, which could seat 4,000 people. Later, more grandiose buildings were erected, all of which remain standing. The Chautauqua Educational Society continued to flourish until the Depression, when suddenly there were more important things to think about than education.

Also of interest is the much smaller building at 100 Circle Drive which houses Florida's oldest library, founded 1886. Here you can see an utterly irrelevant but nonetheless fascinating collection of European medieval swords and suits of armor.

The springs themselves comprise a deep, round lake, the enigmatic natural phenomenon which was initially responsible for attracting so much learning to this otherwise unexceptional spot.

FALLING WATERS STATE RECREATION AREA

Head 3 miles S *on* Rt 77 *from* Chipley, *which is on* Rt 90 80 *miles* W *of* Tallahassee. Another Florida first for the Panhandle: this is the only waterfall in the state – apart from those in the lobbies of the stylish hotels in Miami and Palm Beach. The water cascades down an aperture

• *Canoeing through* Blackwater River State Forest.

• *Walton County Chamber of Commerce.*

in the rocks for all of 100 feet (its nearest rival in the Plaza, only manages 50 feet).

Head along the trail and you come to another geological oddity: the only oil well in the region, *open 8 am-sunset; entry* $3.50 *per car.* This is more than 75 years old, and, unlike the waterfall, it never gushed.

FLORIDA CAVERNS STATE PARK

On Rt 167, 2 *miles* NE *of* Mariana. The park itself covers over 1,500 acres, but the main attraction is, of course, the caves; *tours* 9 *am*-4 *pm; cost* $5. These descend to more than 60 feet below the surface and contain the usual unique formations and whimsies of nature – including waterfalls made of stone. The caves were discovered by the Seminole, who used them to hide during the Seminole War in the early 19thC.

The park itself has hiking and canoe trails, places where you can swim, and even an underground river; *open* 8 *am-sunset; entry* $3.50 *per car.*

HAVANA

On Rt 27, 15 *miles* NE *of* Tallahassee. Once upon a time, as its name suggests, this was a center of the tobacco industry. But the Florida version of Havana cigars never quite managed to rival the Cuban version. So around the time Castro boomed, Havana went bust. For a couple of decades or so, everyone just slept it off. Then someone had the bright idea of opening an antique shop. It caught on, and Havana is now the antiques capital of the Panhandle. Around 7th Avenue you'll find restored old brick buildings filled with bric-a-brac, brass lamps and burnished broomsticks. You'll even find some genuine antiques. This is where Tallahassee comes on the weekends to add a bit of class to the home. Keep an eye open for the art galleries, which sometimes have genuine finds.

LAKE SEMINOLE

N *of* Chattahoochee, *which is on* Rt 90 40 *miles* NW *of* Tallahassee. The Jim Woodruff Dam outside Chattahoochee on the Apalachicola River was constructed as part of a large hydroelectric project almost 50 years ago. The dam itself is 6,130 feet wide, and created Lake Seminole, which now spreads into three states (Florida, Georgia and Alabama). The **Three Rivers State Recreation Area** is on the south-west bank of the lake just north of Sneads (which is 6 miles west of Chattahoochee on Rt 90). It offers great fishing, and a nature trail through the woods. You're likely to see all kinds of wildlife – including deer and alligators, and get the occasional glimpse of rare foxes. There's a camping site, and also a lodge where you can stay overnight. (See Recommended Hotels, this page.)

MONTICELLO

On Rt 90 25 miles E of Tallahassee.

This town took its name from Thomas Jefferson's home in Virginia, and they even turned the local courthouse into a replica of it – complete with gleaming silver dome and stopped clock. Time in fact stopped here many, many years ago – when the cotton crop failed.

In the 19thC, Monticello was a thriving cotton center. Dozens of **historic houses** remain from this period. There's even an **Opera House**, which dates from 1890. Napoleon's nephew Prince Achille Murat had a big plantation here, and delighted in serving his chic friends his version of French-American cuisine. Guests endured roast buzzard, hog's trotter and alligator tail. (The latter even caught on, and is now a popular feature on Florida's menus.)

Then the dreaded boll-weevil (*Anthonomus grandis*) arrived from Mexico. Only the beautifully preserved houses dating from this period survive. Sadly, they are almost all privately owned and not open to the public.

PENSACOLA

See Florida Overall: 8, page 134.

QUINCY

On Rt 90 18 miles W of Tallahassee.

Quincy sprang into being with the tobacco boom in the 1820s. Then the tobacco trade hit a bad patch, and things looked very shaky when it was discovered that the local bank had invested most of its capital in a small soft drink company. Fortunately, this company turned out to be Coca Cola.

Quincy has a host of fine old mansions, which are well worth searching out on foot. To help you find your way, ask for a map at the Chamber of Commerce on the corner of Rt 12 (from Havana) at Madison.

TALLAHASSEE

See Florida Overall: 8, page 136.

RECOMMENDED HOTELS

BLACKWATER RIVER STATE FOREST

If you plan to stay up here after a day's canoeing, try:

The Cabins, $-$$; *Tomahawk Landing, Coldwater Creek (on Rt 87 11 miles N of Milton); tel. 904 623 6197; no cards.*

Ranging from basic to a little better than basic. Otherwise there are no accommodations hereabouts – except camping. However, after a day on the water, you'll sleep well, no matter where.

CRESTVIEW

Crestview Holiday Inn, $-$$; *off Interstate Rt 10 at Rt 85, Crestview 32536; tel. 904 682 6111; all major cards.*

In downtown Crestview. Friendly spot, complete with pool and garrulous receptionist. The sort of place, in the sort of town, where Hitchcock used to make you feel at ease – before something nasty happened.

DE FUNIAK SPRINGS

Sunbright Manor, $-$$; *606 Live Oak Avenue, De Funiak Springs 32433; tel. 904 892 0656; no cards.*

Bed-and-breakfast inn at one of the historic homes, run by the helpful and friendly Byrdie Mitchel.

LAKE SEMINOLE

Seminole Lodge, $-$$; *Legion Road, Sneads; tel. 904 593 6886; no cards.*

Has fewer than a dozen rooms, so be sure to make a reservation. Ideal base for fishing or exploring the lake.

RECOMMENDED RESTAURANTS

DE FUNIAK SPRINGS

Mia's Cafe and Gourmet Market, $; *on Baldwin Avenue, De Funiak; tel. 904 892 2647; no cards.*

Great place for a snack, or something more substantial, with a view over the lake.

Western Florida

Tampa Bay Region

60 miles; map Hallwag *Florida*

Tampa Bay is only 75 miles or so down Rt 4 from Orlando, and its vicinity provides an ideal opportunity to sample some of Florida's more traditional delights. The beaches along the Gulf shore barrier islands at St Petersburg and Clearwater are among the finest in Florida. Here you'll find long stretches of pristine white sand, warmed by 360 days of sunshine every year. The technicolor sunsets have to be seen to be believed.

Tampa and St Petersburg are picturesquely situated on either side of the blue waters of Tampa Bay. Tampa was once the "Cigar Capital of the World," and you can still see Ybor City, the old red-brick district where the Cubans set up their thriving cigar factories.

St Petersburg is known for its Dali Museum, which houses the world's greatest collection of this artist's work.

Further up the coast, you can visit Tarpon Springs, with its resident Greek community, which once made this the "World Capital of Sponges." Even if you head as far north as Crystal River, with its mysterious ancient Indian site, you should be able to cover this region in two or three days.

• ***Image in the Dali Museum, St Petersburg.***

TRANSPORTATION
There's an efficient city bus system in Tampa, and frequent buses run across the bridges to St Petersburg and the Gulf beaches. There's also a Greyhound bus service which runs up Rt 19 to Crystal River and beyond (as far as Tallahassee). But the best way to get around this region is by car.

• *A St Petersburg beach – sunny for over 360 days a year.*

SIGHTS & PLACES OF INTEREST

CLEARWATER

On the Gulf shore 12 miles NW of St Petersburg. Clearwater is renowned for its classic palm-fringed beach and its chic hotels. Amongst the latter, the Sheraton Sand Key Resort shot to national prominence in 1987 when kiss-and-tell model Jessica Hahn revealed that she'd enjoyed high jinks here with TV evangelist Jim Bakker. As a result, he lost his sales pitch on the moral high ground and joined the sinners from whom he'd collected millions of dollars in donations.

North of Clearwater Beach, a hurricane gouged an inlet out of the barrier island in 1921, forming two separate islands: Caladesi Island and Honeymoon Island, divided by the aptly named Hurricane Pass. **Caladesi Island** can only be reached by ferry from Dunedin on the mainland, and is now a 600-acre state park. This undeveloped island is great for swimming, and collecting shells on the sandy beaches and has a fine nature trail through the unspoiled hinterland.

Honeymoon Island can be reached by a 3-mile causeway and is justly renowned for its long white sandy beach and spectacular tropical sunsets. This is the last of the main barrier islands before the **Big Bend**, the remote stretch of the Florida coastline which leads in a 150-mile-long arc up to the Panhandle. Unlike the rest of the Florida coastline, the Big Bend has no beaches, and consists mainly of thousands of inhospitable mangrove islands.

CRYSTAL RIVER

67 miles N of St Petersburg on Rt 19. This is as far north as even the most adventurous will want to go along the Big Bend (see end of Clearwater entry, above). Here, at the **Crystal River Wildlife Refuge**, a manatee sanctuary, you get a chance to swim in the glassy water with these rare sea cows. According to the warden here, these all-American manatees are irresistibly attracted if you hum "The Star-Spangled Banner" to them underwater.

Even more interesting is the **Crystal River State Archaeological Park,** *open 8 am-dusk; entry $3.25 per car.* First of all, stop at the visitor center, so you can learn something of the extraordinary history of this ancient native American burial ground.

Almost 500 graves have been excavated at the site, and their contents have revolutionized our knowledge of Florida's earliest settlers. Over one-and-a-half millennia ago, these tribes had a trading network which extended to the Panhandle and beyond. But even more interesting are the links with the ancient Mayans of the Yucatan peninsula. Ceremonial gravestones carved with signs representing the sun god have been found, and these match similar stones found in Mexico. Some archaeologists now believe that this site witnessed lavish sun-worshipping ceremonies, possibly involving gruesome human sacrifices such as those practised in Mexico. You can still see the temple mound, and various burial mounds.

According to a bearded UFO expert I met in town, curious lights are often observed in the night sky above this site. In his view, this was one of the places where alien life first arrived on earth many thousands of years ago – prompting the apes to evolve into human beings of potentially limitless intelligence.

HOMOSASSA SPRINGS

On Rt 19 60 miles N of St Petersburg. The only real point of interest in this somnolent spot is the **Homosassa Springs State Wildlife Park,** *open 9 am-5.30 pm; entry $6.95.* Here you can view the famous **Spring of a Thousand Fish** (and the occasional manatee) from an underwater observatory, take a cruise down the river, and follow trails through the unspoiled countryside.

ORLANDO

See Florida Overall: 1, page 33.

ST PETERSBURG 🛏 ✕

On the Gulf coast across Tampa Bay from Tampa. Tampa and St Petersburg are virtually twin cities now, linked by no fewer than three bridges across the inlet know as Old Tampa Bay. Yet St Pete (as the locals call it) still has its own distinct identity.

St Petersburg occupies the peninsula of Pinellas County. This received its name from the early Spanish explorers, who christened it *Punta Pinal,* meaning Pine Point. The first visitors arrived on Plant's railway, which opened up the region in 1884. Within a year, the distinguished Boston physician Van Bibber was reporting to the American Medical Society that he had found "the healthiest place on earth." He suggested that a community named Health City should be established here. Instead, the place was named St Petersburg by a homesick Russian exile.

From this time onwards, the region became popular with retired folk from the north. Its climate is amongst most pleasant in America. Throughout the year, the average temperature seldom dips below 68 degrees Fahrenheit and seldom rises above 81 degrees Fahrenheit. On average, the city has more than 360 days of sunshine each year – and once made it into the *Guinness Book of Records* for the longest spell of continuously sunny days (768 during the late 1960s).

For years, St Pete had a reputation for being rather a sedate spot. But the retirees who lived here, and made up the majority of the population, didn't mind. They were well looked after: one year the authorities even erected 5,000 new benches along the streets to take the weight off their feet. But things have begun to change in the 1990s, with an influx of younger blood attracted by the superb beaches of the Pinellas "Suncoast" – as the Gulf beaches are known. In recent years the average age of the population has halved, and the St Petersburg beaches have become a major tourist attraction.

The focal point of St Petersburg is the **Pier**, which extends a quarter of a mile into the blue waters of the Tampa Bay at the end of 2nd Avenue North. At the end of the pier you'll find a five-storey upturned pyramid which has restaurants, an aquarium and an observation platform with great views out over the bay.

St Petersburg has several sights, the most exciting of which is undoubtedly:

Dali Museum

1000 South 3rd Street; open 9.30 am-5.30 pm Tues-Sat, Sun and Mon afternoons only; entry $5. This houses the largest collection anywhere of works by the Spanish Surrealist artist Salvador Dali.

This is your chance to decide for yourself: was Dali really one of the 20thC's great artists, or simply a great self-promoting charlatan?

The museum is in a refurbished warehouse overlooking Tampa Bay and contains the collection accumulated by Cleveland magnate A. Reynolds Morse. The main feature of the collection is almost a hundred oil paintings, but there are 1,500 other Dali artifacts (including watercolors, etchings, graphics, sculpture and drawings).

The works of the 1920s and 1930s (such as *The Persistence of Memory*, with its famous melting watches) are probably his finest. But was all the self-publi-

• *Hand rolling cigars in Tampa.*

cizing and charlatanry a necessary part of a great act? Even in the art world, the jury is still out on Salvador Dali. Whatever they say, he's an accessible artist and you won't forget what you see here.

Sunken Gardens

Just N of downtown at 1825 North 4th Street; open 9 am-5.30 pm daily; entry $11. The gardens are laid out in a sink-hole, which dried up. This may not sound very attractive, but the reality is superb. There are more than 5,000 different types of tropical and subtropical plants, trees and flowers on display, most labeled with informative plaques. You can also see monkeys and deer, a rather sad parrot enclosure and other cages of exotic birds. These gardens opened in 1935, making them one of St Pete's oldest attractions. And the comparatively high entry fee means it's seldom crowded.

Museum of Fine Arts

255 Beach Drive North East; open 10 am-5 pm Tues-Sat, Sun afternoons only; entry $5. This museum is in an attractive Mediterranean villa overlooking Tampa

Bay close to the Pier. Inside, you'll find a rather standard city art gallery collection, which contains the usual worthy stuff, a few duds and a few gems. But the fun is working out which is which. As usual, several of the great late 19thC French names (Cézanne, Gauguin, Monet) are represented by more or less interesting works. 20thC artists include Kandinsky and Georgia O'Keefe. If you've previously visited the Dali Museum (this page), it's interesting to speculate on whether Dali deserves a place in such company.

Sunshine Skyway Bridge
See Local Explorations: 9, Page 249.

St Petersburg Historical and Flight One Museum
Right by the Pier, at 335 2nd Avenue North East; open 10 am-5 pm, Mon-Sat, Sun afternoons only; entry $4.50. You mean you didn't know that the world's first scheduled commercial airline flight took off from St Petersburg in 1914? You can even see a model of the Benoist Airboat which made it, hanging in mid-air as if aiming to be the very last commercial airline flight to land.

There are also exhibits outlining the unexciting history of St Petersburg. But it's just these unspectacular shows which sometimes give you the feel of what it was actually like to be around at the time. Try it, and see if it works for you.

TAMPA ×
On the W coast, halfway between the Panhandle and the Keys. Tampa is the commercial center of Florida's west coast. Its picturesque setting on the large natural inlet of Tampa Bay prompts comparison with San Francisco. Most tourists simply pass through Tampa, marveling as they cross one of the bridges over the bay, but not stopping because there's no beach here. The blue waters of Tampa Bay may look beautiful, but they are polluted: Tampa is the seventh busiest port in the U.S. Even so, you're in easy reach of the excellent Gulf shore beaches – and there is enough to see in Tampa to make a stay worthwhile.

When the first Spanish explorers arrived in Tampa Bay in the early 1500s, they found its shores occupied by the Tocobega tribe. The bay featured prominently on early maps of Florida, owing to its perfect anchorage, but surprisingly there was no lasting European settlement here for another two centuries. In 1824 the U.S. Army established an outpost on Tampa Bay called Fort Brooke.

Sixty years later, Henry Plant's west coast railway reached the banks of the Hillsborough River. The first arrivals on the railway found themselves in an unspoiled paradise. The Hillsborough River was dredged, and a regular steamship link was established with Cuba.

Cubans were to play a vital role in the commercial fortunes of Tampa. Yet curiously, the first Cubans to arrive here came from Key West. They brought with them the lucrative cigar industry, and by 1890 Tampa was a thriving community of more than 5,000. Meanwhile, Plant was busy bringing in well-heeled tourists on his railway, and erecting hotels such as the grandiose Tampa Bay Hotel, where they could stay.

In common with the rest of America, Tampa boomed in the 1920s – and then nearly went bust in the 1930s. Nowadays, downtown Tampa is a modernist mega-sculpture of skyscrapers glinting in the sunlight. Yet the old Tampa Bay Hotel still stands (now part of the University of Tampa), and the old red-brick buildings of **Ybor City** where the Cubans first set up their cigar factories over a hundred years ago, are still in evidence (see page 238).

There are a number of sights worth seeing in Tampa:

Busch Gardens
At 3000 East Busch Boulevard, 5 miles NW of downtown; open 9.30 am-6 pm daily; entry $29.95. This is Tampa's answer to Walt Disney World. It's a park on the theme of "The Dark Continent." Here you can visit such African attractions as the Congo, Timbuktu and Dwarf Village. Although colonial-era Africa seems a politically incorrect setting to some, especially to the local African American community, Busch Gardens is a popular spot. It now attracts more tourists than any other attraction in Florida, apart from Walt Disney World.

To give you an idea of what to expect: the Serengeti Plain is a plausi-

• *A male silverback gorilla at Busch Gardens.*

ble reconstruction of the African bush, complete with hippos, zebras, giraffes and ostriches. Timbuktu features Africans crafting their pots, a sandstorm, and a typical amusement arcade such as you would find anywhere in downtown Timbuktu. Nairobi has a petting zoo and a Great Ape Domain. Stanleyville (a colonial name long erased from the map) has a typical African village, and the geographically curious Tanganyika Tidal Wave Ride. The Congo section has Bengal tigers and "The greatest roller coaster in the southeastern United States." Finally, The Crown Colony has the Anheuser-Busch hospitality tent, where you can sample the beer that was responsible for all this.

• *Right: Busch Gardens roller coaster.*

Hillsborough River State Park

On Rt 301, 15 miles NE of town; open 8 am -sunset daily; entry $3.25 per vehicle.

This large woodland preserve stretches over 3,000 acres. You can follow nature trails through the woods, go canoeing on the river and have an interesting double-sided history lesson. **Fort Foster** is a reconstructed army outpost, just as it would have been in 1836 during the Seminole Indian War. Inside, there are a few costumed soldiers who'll tell you a few surprising tales about what it was really like in those days. (Apparently more died of dysentery than from arrows.) After this you can cross the river and visit the Seminole Indian camp, and get their side of the story.

Henry B. Plant Museum

401 West Kennedy Boulevard; open 10 am-4 pm Tues-Sat, Sun afternoons only; entry $3. This occupies the left wing of the old Tampa Bay Hotel, which Plant put up in 1891 to house the tourists who came in on his railway. When Plant built this 500-room domed and minareted hotel, it had more guest rooms than Tampa had inhabitants. But Plant promised the astonished locals that he would "turn this sandheap into the Champs Elysées." Unfortunately, his $3-million Tampa Bay Hotel soon ended up with as many overnight guests as

• *Canoeing on Hillsborough River.*

• *Henry* B. *Plant museum.*

the Arc de Triomphe. It was only occupied for a few months during the winter season, then left deserted to rot during the long hot summer. Now it's been refurbished, and is part of the University of Tampa.

The museum contains a collection of Victorian furniture, Venetian mirrors, candelabras and expensive nick-nacks such as would have graced the hotel in the old days. Mrs Plant was determined that the interior of her husband's hotel should epitomize the standards of her day (as well as living up to the exterior).

Tampa Museum of Art

601 *Doyle Carlton Drive; open* 10 *am*-5 *pm* Tues-Sat, *Sun afternoons only; entry* $3.50. There are two entirely different collections on display, spread through seven galleries. The first includes Ancient Egyptian artifacts and classical antiquities from Ancient Greece and Rome. The other collection specializes in 20thC American art. The gallery also hosts major traveling exhibitions. For details of these, phone 813 223 8128.

Museum of Science and Industry

N *of Busch Gardens at* 4810 East Fowler Avenue; *open* 9 *am*-4.30 *pm* Sun-Thurs, *and* 9 *am*-9 *pm* Fri *and* Sat; *entry* $5.50. This is the top attraction of its kind in Florida, and even holds its own against the more presentation-conscious Walt Disney World. Star features include a hurricane simulator and simulated space flights at the **Challenger Learning Center.** (Advance booking for the latter is *essential*: 1 800 400 MOSI.) This is very much a hands-on interactive museum which combines fun with genuine opportunities to learn.

Ybor City

Last but not least is the entire district known as Ybor City, and pronounced E-bor. This is the old Cuban section, and is just north of downtown around 7th Avenue (known locally as La Setima). In the 1880s this was just a wilderness outside the tiny settlement of Tampa. Then 15,000 Cubans moved here from Key West to set up a local cigar industry. The new steamship service to Cuba ensured that there was a regular supply of the finest Havana leaf, and for almost half a century Tampa became "Cigar Capital of the World." The cigar trade was badly hit by the Depression. At the same time, smokers began switching to cigarettes. The final blow came with automation, which put thousands of skilled Cuban cigar rollers out of work.

You can still see cigars being manufactured (on machines) in the **Villazon and Co.** factory at 3104 Armenia Street; but nowadays, as you wander the quaint old red-brick streets, you're more likely to smell Cuban coffee from one of the cafes than the rich, evocative cigar odors. **Ybor Square,** at 1901 13th Street, used to be an old cigar factory, but now it's a pleasant mall of shops and restaurants. Here you can still see cigars being hand rolled in the old way, and buy one to take home. This was where the Cuban poet Jose Marti exhorted his fellow Cubans to accompany him back to Cuba and fight for independence from the Spanish, and you can see his statue in the park opposite.

If you want to learn more about early life in Ybor City, head for the **Ybor City State Museum** at 1818 *9th Avenue, open* 9 *am*-12 *noon and* 1 *pm*-5*pm* Tues-Sat; *entry* $1. The huge wall photos will give you a picture of what conditions were like in the factories, and just along 9th Avenue you can see half a dozen restored cigar workers' homes. These are *open* 9 *am*-4 *pm daily; entry* $4.50.

TARPON SPRINGS

On Rt 19, 25 miles N of St Petersburg.

This is Greek Florida, and will be instantly recognizable to anyone who has visited the Aegean. The cafes serve Greek coffee and ouzo, and there's bouzouki music in the restaurants, which feature moussaka and baklava on their menus. Greek is spoken on the streets and in the shops.

The Greeks arrived here in 1900 to set about harvesting the plentiful sponge beds of the Gulf. Business was soon thriving, but unfortunately some of the beds were in deeper water than those in Greece. So the harvesters began using ancient diving suits, often with disastrous results.

Despite the Depression, by the 1930s Tarpon Springs was the "World Capital of Sponges," with a fleet of more than 200 Greek skiffs putting out to harvest beds all the way along the Gulf shore of Florida and beyond. This $4-million business continued to thrive during the Second World War, when Tarpon sponges were much in demand for military field hospitals. Then disaster struck when Red Tide Disease (bacterial blight) wiped out many of the beds. By the time they had recovered, synthetic sponges had begun to flood the market. The boom days were over, but the Greeks remained. Florida bears many similarities to their native land (blue skies, blue seas, and long hot summer days), and they felt at home here. Today there are still a few sponge fishermen, but most of the 20,000 Greek community make their living ashore.

• *Tiles showing sponge fishing in Tarpon Springs.*

• *A sponge fisherman cleans his catch, Tarpon Springs.*

The main thing about Tarpon Springs is its Greek atmosphere. If you want to learn more about the history of the local sponge business, visit **Spongerama**, *open 10 am-6 pm daily; entry free.* This is housed in a former sponge factory and has some fascinating old photos. You'll see sponges on sale all over the place, and if you want to see a sponge diver at work, there's a boat trip from the harbor ($4).

Also of interest is **St Nicholas Orthodox Cathedral** on Pinellas Avenue at Orange Street. This was financed by a 0.5 percent contribution from the yearly sponge sales during the boom era, and completed in 1943. Its interior is typically neo-Byzantine, complete with icons and ornate incense burners. The marble slabs which decorate its interior came from the Greek Pavilion at the 1939 New York World's Fair, and the statue of St Nicholas occasionally sheds miraculous tears.

Those with an interest in miracles will also want to visit the **Shrine of St Michael Taxiarchis**, which is northwest of downtown on Hope Street. This simple shrine was erected by a local mother in 1939 when her son had a miraculous deathbed recovery after she called on St Michael. Since then, various visitors to this shrine have miraculously risen from their beds, been cured of blindness, discovered they could hear again, or regained the use of crippled limbs. It's all there in the free booklet, One of the icons here is also apparently given to weeping – which is said to be a bad omen. I was reliably informed by a local miracle expert that this phenomenon last took place in July 1992, just before Hurricane Andrew struck Florida. Fortunately, St Michael interceded, and Hurricane Andrew miraculously bypassed Tarpon Springs.

WEEKI WACHEE

On Rt 19, 45 miles N of St Petersburg. Whichever way you pronounce it, there's little here to interest tourists. The high point is the "pre-historic" **Harold's Auto Center**. It is shaped like a dinosaur, and if Harold is not busy, he'll pose for a photo in front of his concrete monster.

The low point is reached by the **Weeki Wachee** mermaids, who perform underwater for tourists.

RECOMMENDED HOTELS

CLEARWATER

Palm Pavilion Inn, $$; *18 Bay Esplanade, CLearwater Beach 34630; tel. 813 446 6777; cards AE, MC, V.*

Superb Art Deco hotel, right on the beach. Rooms look out over the Gulf for superb sunsets, or over Clearwater Harbor at the back for dawn-watchers.

ST PETERSBURG

This is your best base for exploring the entire Tampa Bay area, and the good news is that there is a wide range of inexpensive accommodations. Naturally, the places out by the beach tend to be more expensive, but only a little. In town, try:

Landmark, $; *1930 4th Street, St Petersburg 33701; tel. 813 895 1629; no cards.*

Basic urban accommodations in motel-style rooms. Helpful reception. If this is full, there are plenty more similar spots along 4th Avenue.

Out at the beach, try:

Captain's Quarters Inn, $$; *10035 Gulf Boulevard, Treasure Island, St Petersburg 33706; tel. 813 360 1659; cards MC, V.*

Right by the Gulf, on Treasure Island (the next one north from St Petersburg Beach). Standard decor with a naval flavor – as good a beach spot as you'll find, for the price.

TAMPA

Hotels in Tampa tend to be expensive. The best range of inexpensive accommodations is a few miles northeast of downtown near Busch Gardens.

Comfort Inn, $-$$; *2106 East Busch Boulevard, Tampa 33612; tel. 813 931 3313; all major cards.*

Standard motel rooms, just west of Busch Gardens.

For something a little more upscale, try:

Holiday Inn Busch Gardens, $$; 2701 *East Fowler Avenue, Tampa* 33612; *tel.* 813 971 4710; *all major cards.*

All the usual Holiday Inn facilities, including a pleasant pool. Just west of Busch gardens.

RECOMMENDED RESTAURANTS

ST PETERSBURG

For the best view in the area, try:

Cha Cha Coconuts, $-$$; 800 *2nd Avenue North East, St Petersburg; tel.* 813 822 6655; *all major cards.*

This is the one at the top of the inverted pyramid at the end of the pier. Views out over Tampa Bay. Basic menu of burgers and inexpensive seafood.

(If you prefer something fancier, you can always try the fourth-floor **Columbia ($$;** *tel.* 813 822 8000), branch of a celebrated Ybor City restaurant, which serves excellent Spanish cuisine).

Out at the beach, try:

Hurricane Seafood Restaurant, $-$$; 807 *Gulf Way, St Petersburg Beach; tel.* 813 360 9558; *cards* MC, V.

Here's where it all happens on the beach. After your hard day of surf and sand, this is where you unwind over that much-anticipated sundowner. The sun deck overlooking the Gulf is the place to contemplate that long moment between the flushed golden light of sunset and the first lilac of evening. Next you can nourish the inner self on something a little more solid in the restaurant – which is justly renowned for its seafood. And after that you can bop the night away at Stormy's, the disco next door.

Expect a happy crowd in the season.

TAMPA

The liveliest place to eat at in Ybor City is:

Cafe Creole and Oyster Bar, $-$$; 1330 *9th Avenue, Ybor City, Tampa; tel.* 813 247 6283; *all major cards.*

Back in the 1890s this was the casino club where the Cuban factory owners and their cronies used to meet and gamble. After falling into disrepair, it's now been restored as a local landmark with much of its former atmosphere. The cuisine is largely creole, with many excellent gumbo dishes and some imaginative seafood.

For something extra special, try:

Bern's Steakhouse, $$$; 1208 *South Howard Avenue, Tampa; tel.* 813 251 2421; *cards* CB, DC, MC, V.

Some claim that this is the finest steakhouse in America. Forget the decor: the red flock wallpaper is hardly inspired, but the steaks are. The owner Bern Laxer even raises the beef on his own ranch. The chief steak-chef has been here more than 20 years; and just to tickle your palate, they also serve two dozen different types of caviar. The Steakhouse also boasts one of the largest (and finest) wine cellars outside France. Non-red-meat-eaters will also be impressed with their superb fresh fish.

They come from far and wide for this one, so reservations are essential.

TARPON SPRINGS

There's only one way to eat in Tarpon Springs, and that's Greek. There are several good inexpensive spots, but the best cuisine in town is at:

Pappas, $$; 10 *West Dodecanese Boulevard, Tarpon Springs; tel.* 813 937 5101; *all major cards.*

Popular with locals and tourists alike, the Greek food here is utterly authentic and served with true Greek panache.

Western Florida

South of Tampa

60 miles; map Hallwag Florida

This section covers the beginning (or northern section) of Florida's southwest, a stretch of coastline justly renowned for its beaches. They are found mainly along the barrier islands, which can easily be reached from the mainland at regular intervals. Bradenton is a business and commercial center which has little to offer the passing visitor, but its beaches out at Anna Maria Island are another matter.

From here you can drive along Rt 789 through the barrier islands down to Sarasota, which does have plenty to offer. It claims to be the "Culture Capital" of Florida, and with justice. Here you can visit one of the finest art galleries in America, watch drama at any one of the two performing arts centers, or take in the local symphony orchestra. Sarasota is also the city made famous by the Ringling Brothers Circus ("the Greatest Show on Earth"), which established its winter quarters here 70 years ago.

The circus has now moved its winter quarters 20 miles down the coast to Venice, another pleasant seaside resort with superb beaches.

You could easily drive through this entire region in a morning, but if you want to explore the beaches of the barrier islands, and maybe take in a few of the sights, you should allow a couple of days.

TRANSPORTATION
There's an infrequent train service between Tampa and Sarasota, via Bradenton. There are also regular buses which run down Rt 41, linking all the main towns. But if you want to explore, the best way is by car.

• *Ca'd'Zan, Sarasota.*

SIGHTS & PLACES OF INTEREST

ANNA MARIA ISLAND

See Recommended Restaurants, page 251.

BRADENTON 🛏 ✕

On Rt 41 S of the S end of Sunshine Skyway Bridge. A very quiet spot, which has done its best to attract tourists by creating a number of historical sights. Aficionados of recreated history will relish the **De Soto National Memorial Park.** Nothing about this site is authentic. The Spanish explorer Hernando de Soto landed in Florida in 1539. But he didn't land here: no one knows the exact spot of his landfall. Regardless, de Soto's "original campsite" has been faithfully restored. During the winter season (December-April) locals dress up in meticulously recreated 20thC versions of 16thC period costumes. They then attempt to show visitors what it was like to live in the good old days of homeopathic medicine and the Spanish Inquisition, plagued by mosquitoes and irate Indians.

Those whose thirst for de Sotiana remains unslaked should be sure to visit the **South Florida History Museum** at *201 10th Street in the heart of downtown Bradenton; open 10 am-5 pm Tues-Sat, Sun afternoons only; entry* $5. Here they even have a reconstruction of de Soto's home.

On the weekends the entire population of Bradenton decamps to the **beaches.** You'll find these 8 miles west of town at the end of Rt 64.

From here you can drive 15 miles south along Rt 789 across the barrier islands, all the way down to Sarasota. On the way you take in 20-mile **Longboat Key** with its exclusive millionaire villas shielded by fringes of trees. The beaches are all but inaccessible. Then you come to a livelier spot – Lido Key – see Sarasota, page 246.

ELLENTON

On Rt 75 25 miles S of Tampa on the N shore of the wide Manatee River estuary. The major tourist sight here is the

DE SOTO'S EXPEDITION

In the early 16thC, rumors began to reach Spain of vast amounts of gold to be found at a place called Apalachee in northern Florida. An expedition was dispatched, but it found that landing at Apalachee was impossible, the local Indians were extremely unfriendly and anyway it didn't look as if there was any gold at all. Another expedition was immediately dispatched, and the few survivors returned with similar tales.

Third time round, the Spaniards decided to do things properly. The celebrated commander Hernando de Soto was put in charge of an expedition of a 1,000 warriors and 350 horses. On his own, he augmented this with dozens of hunting greyhounds (just the thing for the swamps), and packs of bloodhounds (for hunting the Indians).

De Soto reached the New World in 1539. In order to avoid the fate of his unfortunate predecessors, he wisely chose to land further south, somewhere near Tampa Bay.

He then struck north, encountering mosquitoes and Indians. The expedition made it to somewhere near modern Tallahassee, where they paused to make sure of their entry in the *Guinness Book of Records* by enjoying the first Christmas ever celebrated on American soil. They then continued west in search of gold. In the course of their travels, they accidentally discovered the Mississippi River. More mangrove swamps, mosquitoes and Indians were discovered on the other side – but there was still no sign of gold.

The expedition lasted three years, lost many Spanish lives (including that of de Soto), and succeeded in establishing the Mississippi River as the western border of Florida (a mistake which was eventually remedied). The expedition reports are among the earliest written descriptions of life in the interior of America, but as those involved weren't interested in the interior of America, the accounts are mainly about the awfulness of their own lives.

• *Longboat Key.*

• *Richard Gamble's mansion,* Ellenton.

Gamble Plantation.

Richard Gamble started out as a cotton planter in Tallahassee. After failing at his chosen trade, he moved south to this spot, where he went into the sugar business. In 1850 he built the first mansion on the west coast, and set up the first slave plantation in Florida. (This was, and remained, the most southerly slave plantation in the United States.)

There were no bricks here when Gamble arrived, so he had his house built out of blocks made from crushed seashells, molasses and sand. In hot weather, the unbearable stickiness thus took on an added dimension. Later, in the Civil War, Gamble became a major in the Confederate army. At the end of the war the Confederate Secretary of State fled here, and hid in Gamble's mansion while they both pondered their next career move.

The house remains just as it looked in the old days. There is an amiable guide who will take you on a tour of the pre-Civil War furnishings.

LIDO AND SIESTA KEYS

See Sarasota, page 246.

LONGBOAT KEY

See Bradenton, *page* 246.

MYAKKA RIVER STATE PARK

About 6 miles S *of Sarasota, turn inland* E *on* Rt 72 *for* 12 *miles.* This park claims that it's "a wildlife area larger than Walt Disney World." You can see alligators, wild turkeys, deer and all kinds of other wildlife; hire canoes for expeditions across the lakes or set off along miles and miles of hiking trails. This is just how the region looked more than 500 years ago, and makes a pleasant change from the much-vaunted "natural paradise" of the beaches.

• *Myakka River State Park.*

ST PETERSBURG

See Local Explorations: 8, page 232.

SARASOTA

On the coast 50 miles S of Tampa on Rt 41. Known both as the "Culture Capital" of Florida, and "the City the Circus Built." According to legend, this region was first explored by de Soto, though the historical evidence points to his having landed at Tampa Bay and heading north. Despite such quibblings, Sarasota is almost certainly named after de Soto's daughter Sara. Over the years, the final *o* of Sara-Soto became transformed into a more acceptably feminine *a* – but apart from this linguistic feat, nothing much happened here for the next 300 years. Then at the turn of the century, the circus came to town.

John Ringling, moving spirit of the great Ringling Brothers Circus, decided this was just the place for his winter quarters. Each year the circus would

• *Sarasota Opera House.*

• *Ca'd'Zan, John Ringling's house in Sarasota.*

move in during the late fall, at the end of yet another summer-long tour of the United States. The circus made John Ringling a vast fortune, and part of this he lavished on the little backwater of Sarasota – as well as on the palatial mansion he built for himself here. This residence was soon stuffed with extravagant European masterpieces (he seems to have had a particular taste for the Rococo.) Ringling gave Sarasota its taste for culture, a taste which it

SARASOTA FESTIVALS
Sarasota has a succession of cultural festivals throughout the year, which cater to all tastes. The best are in April (jazz), June (classical music) and November (French films).

• *Van Wezel Performing Arts Center, Sarasota.*

has not lost to this day. If you're lucky, the only Rococo you'll encounter in town nowadays will be in the form of a Mozart overture played by the **Florida West Coast Symphony Orchestra**. Drama is represented by the **Asolo and Van Wezel Performing Arts Centers**. The circus has long since left town (departing down the coast to Venice in 1957) but its legacy survives in the form of Ringling's lavish estate and the city's flourishing cultural tradition.

This reputation for culture has attracted artists, sculptors and writers from all over the United States. The writer John D. McDonald made his home here and wrote his celebrated Travis McGee novels, which sold more than 25 milion copies worldwide. However, McDonald never claimed that it was the cultural atmosphere which attracted him to Sarasota. He, like perhaps a few other of those artistic souls, was most attracted by the 360 sunny days a year.

There are several things to be seen in Sarasota:

JOHN RINGLING

John Ringling was an archetypical U.S. legend. He co-founded the Ringling Brothers Circus in 1884 during the years of heavy immigration and before the era of the silent movies. It was also the time when railways were opening up the entire United States. The universal appeal of the traveling circus, which went beyond language and drew on older European traditions, filled a huge gap in the market. Hard-working immigrant Americans were sorely in need of cheap entertainment outside the saloons and burlesque shows. The circus provided a spectacular show for the whole family, and was continually on the move finding new audiences. It traveled all over the United States, billed as "the Greatest Show on Earth." (Later, others' shows were also to use this title, which Ringling was irritated to discover he couldn't copyright. However, Ringling claimed that he was the first to lay claim to it.)

The Ringling Brothers Circus was soon making a fortune, and by the turn of the century John Ringling was worth almost a quarter of a *billion* dollars. In present-day terms this would have put him in the same class as the King of Saudi Arabia and the Queen of England.

John Ringling looked the part, and lived it. Well over 6 feet tall and weighing 280 pounds, he had "the chest of a sea elephant, the chin of a prizefighter." With his new fortune, he proceeded to buy up everything in sight. Land, art, oil wells, stocks and shares – you name it. Then one year he came down to Sarasota, fell in love with the place, and virtually bought that too.

Next year, instead of wintering in Bridgeport, Connecticut, the Ringling Brothers Circus moved into sunny Sarasota, thus saving on heating costs to keep the tropical animals warm. The move was accompanied by vast publicity. Everyone soon got the message: sunny Florida was the place to go. The surrounding land (which Ringling had already bought) shot up in price. After investing in barren, worthless land on the barrier islands, he proceeded to build a causeway out to them, linking them to the mainland and his self-created local real-estate boom. At the same time he built a vast Venetian mansion as a winter residence for himself and his wife Mable. On the same estate he also built a museum, which he filled with historic art treasures from Europe – see entries, page 249.

Then tragedy struck. In 1927 his beloved Mable died. Hardly had John Ringling got over this than he was hit by the Wall Street Crash. Within the space of a few days millions of dollars were wiped off his fortune. Then his debts were called in, and finally the tax man began making the usual unreasonable demands for back taxes. The Crash was followed by the Depression, which hit the circus revenues badly. Seven years later the great John Ringling died, a broken man, with just $300 in his bank account.

• *Sunshine Skyway Bridge.*

The Ringling Estate

N of town on Rt 41 at 5401 Bayshore Road (call 351 1660 for current details); open 10 am-5.30 pm daily; entry $8. Down by the seashore you'll find **Ca'd'Zan**, the residence which Ringling built for himself in 1925. This was based on Mable Ringling's two favorite buildings: the Doge's Palace in Venice and the tower of Madison Square Gardens in New York City. Ca'd'Zan cost $1.5 million and its name is taken from Venetian dialect, meaning the House of John. Inside, Mable installed her very own $50,000 organ, on which she entertained her guests, and a huge Italian marble fireplace in case they got cold. To decorate the ballroom, she brought in the stage designer of the Ziegfield Follies, and a marble terrace was extended to the water's edge so she could berth her gondola. As you might expect, the result, both internally and externally, is part hodgepodge and part delight.

Alas, the same cannot be said for the other two attractions here. The **John and Mable Ringling Museum of Art** is housed in a pleasant neo-Renaissance Italian *palazzo*. Inside, it contains the works of European masters which Ringling himself collected when he went on tours of Europe looking to sign up new performers for his circus. The collection very much reflects Ringling's personal taste, which may or may not match yours. It includes works by Rubens and a bronze copy of Michelangelo's *David*.

In the garages, you'll find the **Circus Museum** containing a number of old wagons, sequinned outfits, circus posters and other memorabilia. You may find all this extremely boring or heart-rendingly poignant – except for the superb human cannon, which remains a masterwork in its own right.

Bellm's Cars and Music of Yesterday

By the Ringling Estate on Rt 41 at 550 North Miami Trail; open 9.30 am-6 pm daily; entry $7.50. There are more than 100 classic cars in this collection, including the usual Rolls Royces and such, but by far the most interesting is the 1920s Pierce Arrow once owned by John Ringling. They also have almost 2,000 old music-making machines on display. Some of these live up to their name, others just make a pseudo-melodic noise. Almost all are colorful, in one way or another. Most intriguing of all is the jumbo Belgian organ.

Beaches

The best beaches in Sarasota are across the causeways on the barrier islands – either at **Lido Key**, or further south at **Siesta Key**.

SUNSHINE SKYWAY BRIDGE

Carries Rt 275 across the mouth of Tampa Bay. One of America's most exciting bridges. It begins at sea level, soars up on pillars 250 feet above the blue waters of Tampa Bay, crosses between two Aeolian harp-shaped pinnacles, and then glides symmetrically down again to the other side of the bay. It's well over 10 miles long, and looks as exciting as it sounds. You'll see large ocean-going vessels passing far below as you cross the central span, and the view out over the bay is exhilarating.

The bridge has a history. In the midst of a spring storm in 1980, a huge bulk carrier trying to make it to port crashed into one of the bridge's central pillars.

• *Formal gardens of the John and Mable Ringling Museum of Art.*

The central span of the southbound carriageway crashed down into the bay. The rain was lashing so hard across the roadway that the first drivers on the scene were unable to see what had happened. They glided into the abyss, followed by a Greyhound bus. In all, 35 people died that day. The spectacular bridge you see today is just *half* of the original twin-span edifice.

Naturally after such an event, the bridge began to assume its own mythology. On the anniversary of that stormy day in 1980, drivers have reported hearing fading screams as they cross the central span of the bridge. A ghostly hitch-hiker is also apparently a regular feature. But how can you tell he's a ghost? You pick him up as you ascend towards the central span, and when you arrive on the far shore you discover he's gone.

All this is yours for just the $1 toll.

TAMPA

See Local Explorations: 8, page 235.

VENICE 🛏

On the coast 22 miles S of Sarasota on Rt 41. There are canals all over the place here, and much of the architecture has an Italian flavor. This makes Venice, Florida look nothing like Venice, Italy – despite local claims to the contrary. In fact, it's much pleasanter in certain ways. The canals don't smell, and the beaches here are far better than the Venice Lido's. The best beaches are at the **Venice Inlet**, to the east of the main road (Rt 41).

In 1959 the Ringling Circus (by now combined with Barnum and Bailey) moved its winter quarters from Sarasota down the coast to the sleepy seaside resort of Venice. The circus base is just south of town at 1401 South Ringling Drive. During December and January they try out the new season's shows tel. 813 484 9511 for details. See also page 248.

Also here is the famous **Ringling Clown College**, generally considered the best of its kind outside Eastern Europe. There are often as many as 100 applicants for each of its 60 places. The course is exceptionally demanding. Only half the class graduate as fully fledged clowns and are taken on by professional circuses. I was reliably informed by a member of Ringling's staff: "That college produces the best clowns outside Congress."

VENICE INLET

See Venice, above.

RECOMMENDED HOTELS

BRADENTON
The best places to stay are west of town out by the beaches. Try:

Catalina Beach resort, $$; *1325 Gulf Drive North, Bradenton Beach 34217; tel. 813 778 6616; all major cards.*
Right across from the beach, also has its own pool. You can sometimes rent windsurfers here.

SARASOTA
You can't miss the motels in Sarasota. They're lined up all the way along the North Tamiami Trail (Rt 41), whichever way you come into town. Try:

Econo Lodge, $; *5340 North Tamiami Trail, Sarasota 34234; tel. 813 355 8867; all major cards.*
Basic motel accommodation, with a friendly welcome at the desk.

If you want to stay by the beach you usually have to pay a bit more. An exception is:

Lido Apartment Motel, $-$$; *528 South Polk Drive; Lido Key, Sarasota 34236; tel. 813 388 9830; all major cards.*
Rooms vary in price, but you can sometimes pick up a real bargain here, even in the season.

For somewhere more stylish which won't cost you an arm and a leg, try:

Holiday Inn, $$-$$$; *233 Ben Franklin Drive, Lido Key, Sarasota 34236; tel. 813 388 2914; all major cards.*
Right on the beach (with its own covered access). Also has its own pool. Most rooms have a balcony overlooking the Gulf. Complimentary sublime sunsets.

VENICE
Can be expensive during the winter season (December to April).

• A *typical Florida motel.*

Day Inn, $$-$$$; *1710 South Miami Trail, Venice 34293; tel. 813 493 1593; cards AE, MC, V.*
Largish motel on the main road (Rt 41), complete with pool and restaurant.

RECOMMENDED RESTAURANTS

BRADENTON
Sandbar, $$; *100 Spring Avenue, Anna Maria Island; tel. 813 778 0444; cards DC, MC, V.*
They boast "We are seafood." The fish is great, and so is the view out over the sea from the outside deck.

SARASOTA
For something special, try:

Cafe l'Europe, $$-$$$; *431 St Armand's Circle, St Armand's Key, Sarasota; tel. 813 388 4415; all major cards.*
In the fashionable heart of town. And some of their prices are certainly in keeping with those in the sophisticated local boutiques. However, the quality of their French cuisine justifies the damage to your bank balance. The lamb in mustard sauce is justly famous, as is the wine list.

INDEX

A
Amelia Island 120
  hotels 128
  restaurants 129
American Police Hall of Fame and Museum 156
Anheuser-Busch Brewery 123
Apalachicola 132
  hotels 139
  restaurants 140
Apalachicola National Forest 132
Appleton Museum of Art 194
Atlantic Center for the Arts 109

B
Babcock Wilderness Adventures 208
Bacardi Art Gallery 156
Bahia Honda Key 88
  hotels 102
Bardin 218
Bartow 168
Bass Museum of Art 156
Belle Glade 57
Bellm's Cars and Music of Yesterday 249
Big Cypress Swamp National Preserve 200
Big Pine Key 88
  hotels 102
  restaurants 104
Biltmore Hotel 66, 72
Biscayne National Park 64
Blackwater River State Forest 226, 227
  hotels 229
Blizzard Beach 42
Blue Spring State Park 192
  hotels 197
Boca Raton 176-8
  hotels 188
  restaurants 189
Bok Tower Gardens 171-2
Bonita Springs 208
Bonnet House 180-1
Bradenton 244
  hotels 251
  restaurants 251
Brighton Seminole Indian Reservation 57
Busch Gardens 235-6

C
Cabbage Key 208
  hotels 212
Canaveral National Seashore 56
canoe trails 68, 69, 70, 132, 182, 194, 226
"canopy roads" 138
Cape Canaveral Air Force Base 55
Cape Florida Lighthouse 155
Cap's Place, Lighthouse Point 182, 184
Captain Tony's 105
Captiva Island 214-5
  hotels 212
Cassadaga 192
Castillo de San Marcos 111, 114
catfish, The walking 49
Cedar Key 192-3
celebrations
  Conch Republic 95
  Sunset 98
Chalet Suzanne 172
Chautauqua Vineyards 226
Chokoloskee Island 201
churches 114, 115, 240
Circus Museum 249
Civil War Soldiers Museum 135
Clearwater 232
  hotels 240
Cocoa 48
Cocoa Beach 48-9
  hotels 59
  restaurants 60
Coconut Grove 151
  map of 161
  a stroll through 160
Collier Automotive Museum 204
Conch Republic 94-5
Coral Castle 64
Coral Gables 64-5
  hotels 72
  restaurants 73
coral reefs 64, 77, 81-2, 101, 178, 187
Corkscrew Swamp Sanctuary 208
Crestview 226
  hotels 229
Cross Creek 218-19
  restaurants 221
Crystal River 232-3
Cummer Gallery of Art 121-2
Curry Mansion 100
cycling
  in Miami 146
  Palm Beach Cycle Trail 187
Cypress Gardens 168

D
Dali Museum 233-4
Davie 178
Daytona Beach 108-9
  hotels 117
  restaurants 117
De Funiak Springs 226
  hotels 229
  restaurants 229
De Land 193
  hotels 197
  restaurants 197
De Soto National Memorial Park 244
Deerfield Beach 178-9
Delius's Cottage 123
Delray Beach 179
  hotels 188
Destin 132
  hotels 139
  restaurants 140
Devil's Millhopper 219
Disney, Walt 43
Disney-MGM Studios 40
diving *see sub-aqua*
dolphins 80
Downtown, Miami 151-52
Dreher Park Zoo 60
Driftwood Inn 58, 59

E
Edison, Thomas 209-11
Edison Winter Home 210-11
Ellenton 244-5
Elliott Key 64
Elliott Museum 50-1
Ernest Hemingway House and Museum 95

Everglades, The 66-70
Everglades City 200-1
hotels 205
restaurants 205

F

Fairchild Tropical Garden 71
Falling Waters State Recreation Area 226, 228
Famu 138
Fernandina Beach 120
festivals 108, 127, 151, 155, 178, 192-3, 247
fishing, main areas 49, 57, 80, 125, 196
Flagler, Henry 27, 76, 96, 112, 116, 184, 186
Flamingo 69-70
hotels 72
restaurants 73
Florida Caverns State Park 228
Florida City
restaurants 73
Florida Folk Festival 127
Florida Keys, background 76-7
Florida Museum of Natural History 220-1
Fort Caroline National Memorial 110, 123-4
Fort Foster 236
Fort Jefferson 88-90
Fort Lauderdale 179-82
hotels 188
restaurants 189
Fort Myers 208-12
hotels 212
restaurants 213
Fort Myers Beach 213
hotels 212
restaurants 213
Fort Pierce 49-52
hotels 59
restaurants 60-1
Fort Walton Beach 132
restaurants 140
Fred Bear Museum 219
Fruit and Spice Park 71

G

Gainesville 220-1
hotels 221
restaurants 221
Gamble Plantation 245
Gatorama, Palmdale 172
Gatorland Zoo 32
Gillespie Museum of Minerals 193
Gold Coast 174-89
Gold Coast Railway Museum 71
golf, Palm Beach 60-1
Goombay Festival 151
Green Cove Spring 221
Gulf Islands National Seashore 135

H

Haines City 168
Harbor Branch Oceanography Institution 49-50
Harn Museum of Art 220
Haulover Beach Park 156
Havana 228
Henry B. Plant Museum 236, 238
Henry Ford Winter Home 211-2
hiking *see walking trails*
Hillsborough River State Park 236
HMS Bounty 156-7
Hobie Beach 156
Hollywood 182
Homestead
hotels 72
restaurants 73
Homosassa Springs 233
Hoover Dike 57, 68
Hugh Taylor Birch State Recreation Area 181
Hurricane Andrew 65
Hurricane Memorial 77

I

Ichetucknee Springs 121
India Key 77-8
International Swimming Hall of Fame 181
Islamorada 76-80
hotels 82-3
restaurants 84

J

Jacksonville 121-4
hotels 128
restaurants 129
Jacksonville Beach
hotels 128
Jacksonville Beaches 124
restaurants 129
John and Mabel Ringling Museum of Art 249
John Pennekamp Coral Reef State Park 81-2
Julee Cottage, Pensacola 134
Jungle Larry's Zoo Park 204-5
Juniper Springs 194, 196
Juno Beach 52
Jupiter 52
restaurants 61
Jupiter Island 52

K

Kennedy Compound, Palm Beach 187
Kennedy Space Center 52-5
Key Biscayne 152-3
Key Largo 80-4
hotels 83
restaurants 84-5
Key West 90, 94-101
history of 92-3
hotels 102-3
restaurants 104
Kissimmee 32
hotels 44
restaurants 45
Knott House 137
Koreshan State Historic Site 213-4

L

Lake Alfred 168
Lake City 124-5
Lake Jackson 138
Lake Kissimmee State Park 172
Lake Okeechobee 57, 68
Lake Seminole 228-9
hotels 229
Lake Wales 170-2
hotels 173
restaurants 173
Lakeland 168, 170
hotels 173
Lantana 182
Lighthouse Museum,

Key West 96
Lighthouse Point, 182, 184
lighthouses 52, 96, 120, 153, 155, 215
Lightner Museum 115-16
Lignumvitae Key 80
Lion Safari Country, West Palm Beach 60
Little Haiti 153
Little Havana 153-5
Little Torch Key
hotels 103
Little White House 98-9
loggerhead turtles, Melbourne 56
Longboat Key 244
Looe Key 101
hotels 103
Loxahatchee Historical Museum 52
Loxahatchee National Wildlife Refuge 182

M

manatees 56,192, 232
mangrove swamps 50, 192, 201
Marathon 85
hotels 83
restaurants 85
Marco Island 201-2
Maritime Museum of the Florida Keys 82, 84
Matheson Hammock Park 71
McLarty Treasure Museum 58
Mel Fisher Maritime Heritage Society Museum 97
Melbourne 56
Merritt Island National Wildlife Refuge 56
Meto-Dade Cultural Center 156
Metrorail 144
Metrozoo 71
Miami 142-65
Cubans 154
hotels 162-3
restaurants 164-5
Micanopy 221-2
Miccosukee Indian Village 200
restaurants 205
Mizner, Addison 176, 177, 184-5
Mizner Park 177
Monkey Jungle 72
Monticello 229
Morikami Museum and Japanese Garden 179
Mosquito Lagoon 56
Mount Dora 193
museums
American Police Hall of Fame and Museum 156
Belle Glade 57
Bellm's Cars and Music of Yesterday 249
Birthplace of Speed Museum 108
Circus Museum 249
Civil War Soldiers Museum 135
Collier Automotive Museum 204
Daytona Museum of Arts and Sciences 108
Don Garlits Museum of Drag Racing 194
Ernest Hemingway House and Museum 95
Florida Museum of Natural History 220-1
Fort Lauderdale Museum of Discovery and Science 181
Fred Bear Museum 219
Gallery of Crime and Punishment 133
Gillespie Museum of Minerals 193
Gold Coast Railway Museum 71
Henry B. Plant Museum 236, 238
Historical Museum of Southern Florida 156
Jacksonville Art Museum 121
Lake Wales Depot Museum 170
Lighthouse Museum 96
Lightner Museum 115-6
Maritime Museum of the Florida Keys 82, 84
McLarty Treasure Museum 58
Mel Fisher Maritime Heritage Society Museum 97
Morikami Museum and Japanese Garden 179
Museum of Florida History 138
Museum of Science and Space Transit Planetarium 157
Museum of Weapons and Early American History 116
National Baseball Hall of Fame 168
National Museum of Naval Aviation 135
Pioneer Museum 73
Ripley's Believe it or Not 34, 112
Seminole County Historical Museum 196
Singing Pines Children's Museum 177
South Florida History Museum 244
South Florida Science Museum 61
Spanish Quarter Living Museum 115
St. Petersburg Historical and Flight One Museum 235
Tampa Museum of Science and Industry 238
Teddy Bear Museum 204
Weeks Air Museum 73
Wolfsonian Museum 160
World Museum of Cartoon Art 177
Wrecker's Museum 97
Ybor City State Museum 238

Myakka River State
Park 245

N
Naples 202, 204
hotels 205
restaurants 205
National Baseball
Hall of Fame 168
National Greek
Orthodox Shrine 114
National Key Deer
Refuge 88
National Museum of
Naval Aviation 135
New Smyrna Beach 109
Niceville 132-3
nightlife
Miami 157
Pleasure Island 42
No Name Key 88
Norton Art Gallery 58

O
Ocala 193-4
hotels 197
restaurants 197
Ocala National
Forest 194, 196
Okeechobee
hotels 59
Oklawaha 196
Old Bainbridge Road
138
Old Floresta 177-8
O'Leno 121
Olustee Battlefield
Site 125, 126
Orchid Jungle 72
Orlando 33
hotels 44
restaurant 45
Ormond Beach 108
Osceola National
Forest 125

P
Palatka 222
Palm Beach 184-7
hotels 188
restaurants 189
Palm Beach Polo and
Country Club 60
Palmdale 172
Panama City 134
Panama City Beach
133-4
hotels 139
restaurants 140-1
Parrot Jungle 72-3
Paynes Prairie State
Preserve 222
Pensacola 134-5
hotels 139
restaurants 141
Pensacola Beach 135
hotels 139
Perdido Key 135
Pigeon Key 101
Pioneer Museum 73
Plantation Key 85
Pleasure Island 42
polo 60, 177
Pompano Beach 187
Port St. Joe 135-6

Q
Quincy 229

R
racehorses 193
Ravine State Gardens
222
Reynolds, Burt 52
Ringling Brothers
Circus 246-8, 249,
250
Ringling Clown College
250
Ripley's Believe It
Or Not 34, 112
River Country 41
Royal Palm Polo
Sports Club 177

S
Salt Springs 196
Sanford 196
Sanibel Island 214-5
hotels 212
restaurants 213
Sarasota 246-9
hotels 251
restaurants 251
Sasquatch 218
Sea World, Olando
34-5
Sebastian Inlet
mystery 56
Sebring 172
Seminole County
Historical Museum
196
Seven Mile Bridge
101
Shark Valley 200
Shell Coast 206-15
Shell Factory, The
212
shell hunting,
Sanibel 214
Shelton Sanford
Museum 196
shopping
Coconut Grove
160
Downtown 151
Grifs Western
178
Jacksonville 124
Lake Alfred 168
Little Haiti 153
Miami 165
Mizner Park 177
Mount Dora 193
Palm Beach
186-7
Silver Springs 196-7
Singing Pines
Children's Museum
177
Sloppy Joe's, Key
West 95, 105
Society of the Four
Arts 186
South Beach 155-7
map 159
South Florida
History Museum 244
South Florida
Science Museum 61
Southernmost Point,
U.S.A. 97-8
Spanish Quarter
Living Museum 115
Spongerama, Tarpon
Springs 240
Spook Hill 170
St. Augustine 110-6
hotels 117
restaurants 117
St. George Island 136
hotels 139
St. Johns River 222-3
St. Michael
Taxiarchis, Shrine
of 240
St. Nicholas
Orthodox Cathedral
240
St. Petersburg 233-5
hotels 240
restaurants 241
St. Vincent Island 136
Stranahan House,
Fort Lauderdale 181
Starke 223
Stephen Foster Folk
Culture Center
125, 127

Stiltsville 153
subaqua diving 80, 81, 101, 196
sugar plantations 57
Sugarloaf Key
  hotels 103
  restaurants 104-5
Summerland Key
  restaurants 105
Sunken Gardens, St. Petersburg 234
Sunset Celebrations, Key West 98
Sunshine Skyway Bridge 249-50
surfing
  Cocoa Beach 48-9
  Fort Pierce Inlet 50
Suwannee River 125, 127

T

Tallahassee 136-8
  hotels 139-40
  restaurants 141
Tamiami Trail 200
Tampa 235-8
  hotels 240-1
  restaurants 241
Tampa Bay 230-41
Tarpon Springs 239-40
  restaurants 241
Tate's Hell Swamp 138
Tavernier 84
Ted Smallwood's Store 201
Teddy Bear Museum, Naples 204
Ten Thousand Islands 201
time zones, in Florida 133
Titusville 57
Torrey Island 57
Tupperware World Headquarters, Kissimmee 32
Typhoon Lagoon 41

U

UDT-Seal Museum 52
Universal Studios, Orlando 36-7

V

Venetian Pool, Coral Gables 65-6
Venice 250
  hotels 251
Vero Beach 58
  hotels 59
Villa Viscaya 157-8

W

Wakulla Springs 138
walking trails (main)
  Boca Raton 178
  Everglades 68-9
  Haulover Beach Park 156
  Highlands Hammock State Park 172
  Loxahatchee National Wildlife Refuge 182
  Ocala National Forest 194
  Salt Springs 196
Walt Disney World 38-41
Weeki Wachee 240
Weeks Air Museum 73
West Palm Beach 58-61
  hotels 59
  restaurants 61
Wet 'n' Wild, Orlando 33
White Springs 125, 127
Whitehall 186
wildlife reserves
  Babcock Wilderness Adventures 208
  Big Pine Key 88
  Blue Spring State Park 199
  Crandon Park Beach 152
  Deerfield Beach 178-9
  Everglades 66-9
  Hugh Taylor Birch State Recreation Area 181
  Jackson Island Wildlife Refuge 50
  Loxahatchee National Wildlife Refuge 182
  Merritt Island National Wildlife Refuge 56
  Shark Valley 200
  St. Vincent Island 136
windsurfing 156, 201-2
Winter Haven
  hotels 173
  restaurants 173
World Speed records 108
Worth Avenue, shopping 186-7
Wrecker's Museum 97
Wright, Frank Lloyd 169, 170

Y

Ybor City 238

Z

zoos
  Busch Gardens 235-6
  Dreher Park 60
  Gatorland 32
  Jacksonville Zoo 123
  Jungle Larry's Zoo Park 204-5
  Lion Safari Country 60
  Metrozoo 71
  Monkey Jungle 72
Zoroyda Castle 116